Modern Studies in Philosophy

KIERKEGAARD

Modern Studies in Philosophy is a series of anthologies presenting contemporary interpretations and evaluations of the works of major philosophers. The editors have selected articles designed to show the systematic structure of the thought of these philosophers, and to reveal the relevance of their views to the problems of current interest. These volumes are intended to be contributions to contemporary debates as well as to the history of philosophy; they not only trace the origins of many problems important to modern philosophy, but also introduce major philosophers as interlocutors in current discussions.

Modern Studies in Philosophy is prepared under the general editorship of Amelie Oksenberg Rorty, Livingston College, Rutgers University.

JOSIAH THOMPSON is Associate Professor of Philosophy at Haverford College. He previously taught at Yale University where he received his Ph.D. in 1964. He is the author of *Six Seconds in Dallas* (1967), a study of the Kennedy assassination, and of two books on Kierkegaard: *The Lonely Labyrinth* (1967) and *Kierkegaard: A Biographical Essay* (1973).

Modern Studies in Philosophy

Amelie Oksenberg Rorty, General Editor

KIERKEGAARD

A Collection of Critical Essays

EDITED BY

JOSIAH THOMPSON

1972

ANCHOR BOOKS

Doubleday & Company, Inc.

Garden City, New York

This anthology has been especially prepared for Anchor Books
and has never before appeared in book form.

Anchor Books edition: 1972

ISBN: 0-385-01978-5
Library of Congress Catalog Card Number 78–175420

PREFACE

In 1944, eighty-nine years after Kierkegaard's death and nearly one hundred years after the publication of his most important works, the University of Copenhagen sponsored a prize competition on the topic "The History of Kierkegaard Studies in the Scandinavian Countries." Aage Henriksen won the competition with an incisive account of Scandinavian criticism up to that time. "A point of view," he concluded, "which neither violates the totality nor the separate parts [of Kierkegaard's authorship] does not seem to have been attained by anybody. The core of the authorship has not been penetrated."

Much the same thing could be said of Kierkegaardian criticism outside Scandinavia. There are a wealth of popularized introductions to him as the "father of existentialism," enough abstruse readings of his alleged conflict with Hegel to fill many a philosophical journal, and a surfeit of clerical attempts to pitch his tent within one or another religious camp. But the number of books or essays in any language that show a sensitivity to the enormous range and complexity of his work can be counted on the fingers of one hand. Henriksen's conclusion easily can be generalized to encompass the totality of Kierkegaardian criticism—"The core of the authorship has not been penetrated."

Why is this the case?

The problem of translation may play a minor role here. Although many of Kierkegaard's works were translated into German during the nineteenth century, it was 1940 before any sizable number had been translated into French and English; he has been accorded critical attention in the French- and English-speaking worlds for only thirty years. But surely this must be only an incidental factor, since it fails to explain the paucity of successful criticism in German and in the Scandinavian languages. The source of the difficulty must lie deeper—most likely in the strange and complex character of the works themselves.

In an essay included in this volume John Updike points out that "duplicity was the very engine of Kierkegaard's thought," that he was a "man in love with duplicity and irony and all double-edged things." Updike's judgment is most emphatically confirmed in that series of pseudonymous works that flowed from Kierkegaard's pen during the years 1842–46. Although often the last to be translated, these mercurial and puzzling works have become the basis of Kierkegaard's modern reputation. Yet it is precisely here that the critics have so often been frustrated by Kierkegaard's unwillingness to speak directly. The world of the pseudonyms is a world of stratagem and illusion, a world of trap doors and hidden panels, where one is never quite sure where one is or to whom one is listening. In this questionable territory the critic must proceed with great caution, for the persona he at one moment identifies with Kierkegaard may in the next turn out to be only the author's foil. Even worse, a false step or wrong turn may expose the critic himself to the author's derision. The very *duplicity* of this literature, then, is both its essential quality and also its surest defense against critical penetration.

But these works are not duplicitous and difficult simply because Kierkegaard was a "man in love with duplicity and irony and all double-edged things." To Kierkegaard's mind, their content dictated their form. Their terrain is the terrain of individual human consciousness, and their single theme is the impossibility of locating any firm reference points in the quicksand of that terrain. On occasion after occasion he tells us what a desperately difficult thing it is to be a human being—*difficult* because we seem to secrete illusion from our very pores; *desperate* because we cannot stop yearning for the replacement of illusion by a reality so unknown it can only be called divine. For Kierkegaard, human consciousness *is* duplicitous; "double-mindedness" (*tvesyndethed*) is both its essential character and most private cross. Since illusion and pretense, image and ambiguity, are for Kierkegaard the very ambience of consciousness, he quite naturally turns to duplicity as a means of communication. Direct communication, he believes, is suited only for unimportant matters—grocery bills, logical truths, taxonomies. To talk about ourselves and what makes our lives ebb and flow (what Kierkegaard called "the ethico-religious"), we must use language in a different way, letting metaphor replace literal sense, and ambiguity fertilize the private spaces of our imagination. Hence the inordinate difficulty of Kierkegaard's works. He uses pseudonyms so as *not* to speak directly, convinced that the formal indirection of his style is dictated by the content of his utterance.

One final point. There may be no "core" of Kierkegaard's authorship to be "penetrated." Henriksen's metaphor suggests that the essential meaning of Kierkegaard's work still lies hidden, to be revealed by an as yet unidentified critical approach. But if the earlier discussion of duplicity and indirect communication is to be taken seriously, we may have to construct a new metaphor for talking about Kierkegaard. Instead of thinking of his authorship as having a *single* core of meaning, we might think of it as having (like a multi-faceted jewel) many *different* meanings depending on the angle from which it is illuminated.

Viewing his work in this way, I have tried to choose essays for this volume that light up Kierkegaard's work from many different directions. The selections offered here are in no way definitive. They are intended only to give the reader some sense of the shape and direction of recent Kierkegaardian criticism. They are arranged in order of their generality, moving from fairly long accounts of Kierkegaard's thought as a whole to shorter essays on specific topics. A bibliographical supplement brings the international bibliography (published in 1962) up to date for the English language, and an Index Locorum provides the references needed to use this collection as a rough commentary to many of Kierkegaard's works.

I am particularly grateful to Louis Mackey and Stephen Crites for providing unpublished essays. Amelie Rorty, the general editor of this series, was extremely generous with suggestions and encouragement. Paul Drymalski and Ronnie Shushan of Doubleday were patient and ever helpful during the three long years this book has been in preparation.

May 1972   Josiah Thompson
                            Haverford, Pennsylvania

CONTENTS

SØREN AABYE KIERKEGAARD

A Chronology

1756	SK's father, Michael Pedersen Kierkegaard, born in Sæding, West Jutland.
1768	MPK goes to live with his uncle, a hosier, in Copenhagen.
1777	Sæding village priest releases MPK from serfdom.
1788	MPK receives royal patent "to deal in East Indian and Chinese wares, as well as goods coming from our West Indian islands . . . and to sell the same at wholesale and retail to all and sundry."
1794	MPK marries Kirstine Røyen.
1796	Kirstine Røyen Kierkegaard dies childless; MPK inherits his uncle's fortune.
1797	MPK retires from business in February. In April he marries Kirstine's maid, Ane Lund. A daughter, Maren Kirstine, is born in September.
1799	Nicoline Kirstine born on October 25.
1801	Petrea Severine born on September 7.
1805	A first son, Peter Christian, born on July 6.
1807	Søren Michael born on March 23.
1809	Niels Andreas born on April 30.
1813	The year of the "crazy money"; financial crisis in Denmark. A last child, Søren Aabye, born on May 5.
1821	SK enrolls in Copenhagen's *Borgerdydskole*.

1828   SK confirmed by Pastor (later Bishop)
        J. P. Mynster.

1830   SK graduates from the *Borgerdydskole* and
        enters the University.

1834   SK makes his journalistic debut, publishing a
        piece in *Flyvendepost* entitled "Also a
        Defense of Woman's Superior Capacity."

1835   SK spends a summer holiday at Gilleleje in
        northern Sjælland. Writes down his resolve
        "to find the truth which is true for me."

1836   SK publishes two additional articles in
        Flyvendepost.

1837   SK meets Regine Olsen for the first time while
        visiting the Rørdams in Frederiksberg. In
        September he begins teaching Latin at the
        Borgerdydskole and moves to his own
        apartment on Løvstræde.

1838   MPK dies on August 9. SK inherits over
        30,000 rigsdaler. His first book, *From the
        Papers of One Still Living,* is published in
        September.

1840   SK completes his examination for the
        theological degree, visits his ancestral home in
        Jutland, and on September 10 becomes
        engaged to Regine Olsen. In November he
        enters the Pastoral Seminary for practical
        training in the ministry. In April he moves
        from his flat on Kultorvet to Nørregade
        230 A.

1841   In January SK preaches a sermon in Holmen's
        Kirke. In the summer he defends and
        publishes his dissertation for the MA degree,
        The Concept of Irony. In October he breaks
        his engagement to Regine and flees to Berlin.

1842   SK attends Schelling's lectures in Berlin, but returns to Copenhagen in March. Writes *Either/Or*. Begins, but does not complete or publish, *De Omnibus Dubitandum Est*.

1843   *Either/Or* published in February. SK makes a short visit to Berlin in May. *Two Edifying Discourses* is published in May and *Four Edifying Discourses* in December. In October *Fear and Trembling, Repetition,* and *Three Edifying Discourses* are published.

1844   *Three Edifying Discourses, Philosophical Fragments, The Concept of Dread,* and *Prefaces* are all published in June. *Two Edifying Discourses* is published in March and *Four Edifying Discourses* in August. In October SK moves from Nørregade 230 A back to the family town house at Nytorv 2.

1845   *Three Discourses on Imagined Occasions* and *Stages on Life's Way* are both published in April. SK spends two weeks in Berlin during May.

1846   *Corsaren* attacks SK in January. *Concluding Unscientific Postscript* is published in February, followed by *A Literary Review* in March. In May SK once again makes a two-week visit to Berlin. In October Meyer Goldschmidt resigns as editor of *Corsaren* and leaves Denmark.

1847   *Edifying Discourses in Various Spirits* is published in March and *Works of Love* in September. In November Regine marries Friedrich Schlegel. In December SK sells the family home at Nytorv 2.

1848   In early spring SK leases an apartment at the corner of Rosenborggade and Tornebuskgade.

Christian Discourses is published in April, and in July the two-part article "The Crisis and a Crisis in an Actress's Life." By November he has finished *The Point of View for My Work as an Author* but this book will not be published until after his death.

1849   *The Lilies of the Field and the Birds of the Air* and *Two Minor Ethical-Religious Treatises* are both published in May. *The Sickness unto Death* is published in July and *Three Discourses at Communion on Fridays* in November.

1850   In April SK moves to another apartment at Nørregade 43. *Training in Christianity* is published in September and *An Edifying Discourse* in December.

1851   In January SK publishes in *Fædrelandet* "An Open Letter . . . Dr. Rudelbach." In April he moves outside the city's walls to Østerbro 108 A. In August *Two Discourses at Communion on Fridays* and *On My Work as an Author* are published. In September *For Self-Examination* is published.

1852   In April or October SK moves back inside the walls to a cramped, two-room flat let out of a larger apartment at Klædeboderne 5–6. He continues writing in his journal and completes *Judge for Yourself* (published in 1876).

1853   On Easter Monday SK writes in his journal: "The Christian thing is not to produce but to exist." Six months later his journal falls silent.

1854   Bishop Mynster dies in January. Hans Martensen is named bishop in April. In February SK writes an article attacking the established Church, but does not publish it until December.

1855   *This Must Be Said; So Let It Now Be Said,*
Christ's Judgment on Official Christianity,
and *The Unchangeableness of God* are
published in May, June, and September
respectively. From January through May SK
attacks the Church in various articles
published in *Fædrelandet.* In May he begins
publishing his own broadside, *The Instant,*
which goes through nine issues before he falls
ill in September. On October 2 he enters
Frederiks Hospital, and dies there on
November 11, most likely of a staphylococcus
infection of the lungs. His funeral a week
later ends in a near-riot at graveside.

THE POETRY OF INWARDNESS

Louis Mackey

The Man Without a Present

Infandum me jubes, Regina, renovare dolorem:[1] these words, which Kierkegaard set as an epigram over the account of his unhappy betrothal to Regina Olsen,[2] might stand for an epitaph over the man and his work.[2] The biography of Kierkegaard has been written so often that it would be tiresome even to recapitulate it here.[3] But it is worth recalling that his entire life was a retelling—to his journals, to himself, to God, and to posterity—of a grief inexpressibly out of proportion to the events that occasioned it. The public circumstances of Kierkegaard's life were inconsiderable: a troubled devotion to his father, a broken engagement, a squabble with a tabloid paper, and a flurry of pamphlets

From *Existential Philosophers,* edited by George A. Schrader, Jr. (New York: McGraw-Hill, 1967). Reprinted by permission of the author and McGraw-Hill Book Company.

[1] "Thou biddest me, O Queen, renew an unspeakable grief." Kierkegaard is slightly misquoting *Aeneid* II, 3: *Infandum, regina, jubes renovare dolorem.*

[2] Alexander Dru, ed. and tr., *The Journals of Søren Kierkegaard,* Oxford University Press, London, 1938, no. 367. In another entry (ibid., no. 717) Kierkegaard writes: "By a strange freemasonry I can make these words of the poet a motto for part of my life's suffering: *Infandum me jubes Regina renovare dolorem.*"

[3] The fullest accounts of Kierkegaard's life in English are Johannes Hohlenberg's *Sören Kierkegaard,* Pantheon, New York, 1954, Walter Lowrie's *Kierkegaard,* Oxford University Press, London, 1938, and Harper Torchbooks, New York, 1962, and the same author's *A Short Life of Kierkegaard,* Princeton University Press, Princeton, N.J., 1942.

flung at a Church so secure in its Establishment that it scarcely stirred itself to reprove him. Yet at the bidding of these—an old man confused by guilt, a guileless girl half in love and half mesmerized, a brightly irresponsible journalist, and a pair of comfortable bishops—he renewed daily the anguished self-examination that was his real life. This self-scrutiny appears poetically transformed in the fourteen volumes of his published writings, and lies pathetically naked before the reader of the eighteen volumes of his journals.[4]

Kierkegaard's life was spent "in the service of the Idea."[5] Whatever befell him was reflected and doubly reflected, translated almost before it happened from experience into idea. His every overt action—and they are few—had been so prepared and doubly prepared in advance that the actual performance was but a tired epilogue to the exhausting ideational drama. In his youth he was told by one of his professors that he was "too polemical"; in the year before his death he was still shining this remark into the dark corners of his personality, looking for the goblins.[6] His assault on the Danish Church had deployed inwardly through persecution and martyrdom before he ever uttered a critical word; when he did finally "speak out," the proper episcopal indignation he aroused could not begin to measure up to the epic crucifixion projected in his journals.[7]

He was, as he himself might have said, infinitely dialectical. Things that move ordinary men to a simple

[4] The standard Danish editions of Kierkegaard's published and unpublished writings are listed in the bibliography at the end of this essay.

[5] Cf. Dru, op. cit., nos. 22, 70. Cf. also Søren Kierkegaard, *Repetition*, Princeton University Press, Princeton, N.J. 1946, pp. 145–46.

[6] Dru, op. cit., nos. 626, 1191, 1252, 1333, 1334.

[7] The journals for the last few years of Kierkegaard's life are filled with this preoccupation. Cf. in particular ibid., nos. 1260 and 1275, as well as numerous notes from the year 1852

readjustment of their circumstances necessitated in Kierkegaard a total upheaval of the personality. Every event, every action or passion, every concern, required a recasting *de novo* of his image of himself. The result was that these same events, actions, passions, and concerns, given absolute significance as ideal possibilities, lost all meaning as realities.

For this reason, the substance of his life was a pervasive melancholy formed in the crucible in which he transmuted all experience into reflection.[8] Living as he did in possibility, out beyond the real, there was no one to whom he could express that unutterable grief, the being of which nonetheless was its own everlasting reiteration. He could find no contemporaries, because he was in truth a man without a present. His life was essentially over and done with before it had begun: in the midst of life he was as one already dead. *"Periissem nisi periissem,"* he wrote, "is and always will be the motto of my life. Therefore I have been able to endure what would long ago have killed another who was not already dead."[9]

It is understandable that this motif should thread through his writings. Kierkegaard's melancholy produced and reproduced itself by a kind of superfetation of the spirit; by its own dialectic it destroyed the innocence it mourned and made impossible the "repetition" it yearned for. Virginity, of the spirit as of the flesh, is never loved until it is lost, and by then it cannot—short of a miracle—be restored. So Kierkegaard's "spheres of existence"—the aesthetic, ethical, and religious ways of life which the first part of this chapter will examine—are determined by the round of recol-

---

on. Cf. also Kierkegaard, *The Point of View*, Oxford University Press, London, 1939, and Harper Torchbooks, New York, 1962, pp. 100–2.

[8] Cf. Dru, op. cit., index references to "melancholy," but especially nos. 641, 921, 952, 1299.

[9] Ibid., no. 767. The Latin means, "I had perished, had I not perished."

lections, pains, and longings that articulate his inner
life.

Periissem nisi periissem is the motto affixed to
Quidam's diary ("Guilty?/Not Guilty?") in *Stages on
Life's Way*.[10] The anonymous author of "The Unhappiest Man" and other essays in the first volume of
Either/Or belongs to a nocturnal society lugubriously
and synthetically named *Symparanekromenoi,* "the fellowship of the deceased."[11] All of Kierkegaard's
writings lament an immediacy hopelessly lost in reflection, a youth-that-never-was recollected in the im-
puissance of eternal old age. His vision of Christian
consummation is a miraculous and elusive *redintegratio
in statum pristinum,* a new immediacy, a contemporaneity with oneself possible only by virtue of the
absurd. Between paradise lost and paradise regained
he pitches an ethical struggle to fuse the actual and
the ideal, a struggle whose desperate issue is the everlasting recollection of guilt.

Immediacy—never possessed but always forfeit,
vainly sought and paradoxically bestowed—is the
cantus firmus about which the polyphonic Kierkegaardian literature shapes its varied and often dissonant
counterpoint. In order to hear the strange music ringing from this Phalarian bull,[12] it is necessary to attune
oneself first of all to Kierkegaard's understanding of
immediacy.

[10] Kierkegaard, *Stages on Life's Way,* Princeton University
Press, Princeton, N.J., 1945, p. 187.

[11] Kierkegaard, *Either/Or,* Princeton University Press,
Princeton, N.J., 1944, and Doubleday Anchor Books, Garden
City, N.Y., 1959, vol. I, pp. 135, 163, 215. I refer here and
throughout to the paperback reprint, which is a revised translation.

[12] Cf. ibid., vol. I, p. 19.

1

Such Stuff as Dreams Are Made On

The word "immediacy" is a bit of jargon that Kierkegaard picked up from Hegel and the Hegelians. There
is no point in pursuing the technical meaning of this
term in Hegel's system, but it is important to get the
general sense of the word as a way into Kierkegaard's
mind. It is common to equate *immediate* experience
with *direct* experience, experience *simply given* and
simply had before the onset of reflection. Life as it is
before it doubles back on itself in the "mediation" of
self-consciousness is "immediate existence." If nature
be opposed to the reflexive operations of freedom, then
a man's immediacy is what he is "by nature."

Traditionally "aesthetic" has come to mean "pertaining to beauty and the fine arts," but in Kierkegaard
it retains its etymological sense of *aisthesis,* "sense
perception." He defines what he calls the "aesthetic,"
as a dimension of existence and as an overall design
for living, by means of the immediate. "The aesthetic
in a man is that by which he immediately is what he
is."[13] If we could discover what human nature is, then
we could catch ourselves in our immediacy, and we
would understand what Kierkegaard means by the aesthetic.

But the difficulty with immediacy is that it never *is*
where it is asked about. Asking about immediacy is
already an act of reflection once removed from the
immediate. Just as a man cannot look himself straight
in the eye, so immediacy cannot be got at directly; it
can only be divined as the prelapsarian origin mirrored
but never substantially present in every condition of
self-awareness. This alienation of the self from its immediacy infects the philosophical attempt to comprehend human nature categorially, but it is more arresting

13 Ibid., vol. II, p. 182.

in the case of the man who tries to *be* his immediacy.

Kierkegaard's *"A"* is such a man. The anonymous dilettante whose dilations fill *Either/Or* I is a representative aesthetic personality. In view of the identity of the aesthetic with the immediate, one might expect him to be a man whose overriding aim is the direct satisfaction of his wants. It is true that he lives for pleasure. Yet he is disenchanted enough to know that no life is lived on the strength of impulse alone. True to the paradox of immediacy, desire and gratification are presented not as *A*'s life but as the chief *preoccupation* of his life.

A is a perfervid admirer of Mozart's *Don Juan*. In his essay "The Immediate Stages of the Erotic or the Musical Erotic" he praises Mozart's opera as a perfect work of art, "classic and immortal," on the grounds that it realizes a total fusion of form and content.[14] In *Don Juan,* as *A* hears it, the musical form is so happily wedded to the passional content that together they body forth sexual desire in its immediacy. Don Juan's sensuality is pure undifferentiated desire. He craves *woman,* wholesale and without discrimination of age or beauty: *pur chè porti la gonella, voi sapete quel chè fà.*[15] His passion is a force of nature, unriven by reflection and undisturbed by moral misgivings. Mozart's music is the artistic analogue of this passion, an aural energy not yet articulated into the intelligible forms of speech. There are words, of course, but their very absurdity ("one thousand and three in Spain . . .") negates their significance as language and hurls them back into the floodtide of sound. In Mozart's opera *A* finds immediacy immediately presented, the content of immediacy interfusing and interfused by immediate form.

[14] Ibid., vol. I, pp. 45–134, especially p. 47. In *A*'s interpretation of *Don Giovanni,* the Commendatore is not part of the unity of the opera, but a voice of divine judgment morally shattering this unity *ab extra.*

[15] From the libretto of Mozart's *Don Giovanni.* "If only she wears a petticoat, you know what he does."

In this exquisite alchemy art (reflection) *is* nature (the immediate).

Yet there is ambiguity in this achievement. *Don Juan* is after all *art*. It is to art that one must go if he wants to find the immediate given in its immediacy. *Don Juan* could never happen in real life: one thousand and three in Spain! Global sexuality is a fictive biology of the heroes of imagination. Pure immediacy cannot be experienced as the content of an actual life; it can only be savored as fantasy.

This contradiction is implicitly recognized in *A*'s analysis of *Don Juan*. He is fascinated by the Don because he is a pure type, and by the opera because it is the pure presentation of a pure type. Mozart's masterpiece is the embodiment of the most abstract idea (sensuality) in the most abstract medium (music). Sensuality is "abstraction" because, as immediate, it is not yet parceled out into specific preferences for discrete objects (*pur chè porti la gonella . . .*), and not yet constrained by moral necessity to accept the discipline of a part within an ordered whole. Sensuality *simpliciter* is only the abstract dynamic, the "exuberant joy," of life. Music is similarly abstract. Language—naming, defining, judging, and discoursing—is the spirit's vehicle for the tenor of the concrete. Music with its moving and interacting tonal patterns mimics the syntactic form of language but altogether lacks its semantic commitment: it is the abstract dynamic of spirit without the content of spirit.[16] By *A*'s logic of inversion, that which appears to be most concrete evaporates into the airiest of abstractions.

It is this logic that prompts *A*'s genuflection in the presence of pure types purely enshrined in a pure medium. Too sophisticated to be a sensualist himself, he is reconciled to *admiring,* in its artful and only possible realization, that perfection which he cannot

[16] Kierkegaard, op. cit., vol. I, pp. 52–55, 63–72, 100.

be. The man who wishes to be only what he immediately is, will, if he is honest, be driven by the logic of immediacy to the antithesis of immediacy: enthusiasm for a beautiful but impossible ideal. The internal nexus joining "aesthetic" in its etymological sense to "aesthetic" in its traditional connotation is hereby exposed: Art is the transfiguration of nature by self-consciousness.

But *A* is too thorough a dialectician and too determined an aesthete to *repose* in admiration at the expense of enjoyment. If he cannot make immediacy his life, he will make life itself an art. This reversal takes place already in the essay on *Don Juan*. No sooner has *A* declared the essential abstractness of the opera and its theme than he turns around to deliver an encomium of the infinite richness of every work of art. In passages reminiscent of Kant's doctrine of Aesthetical Ideas, he speculates: Because the unity of form and content in a consummate work of art precludes any *definitive* critical analysis, no understanding of the work is ever final; but for that very reason the possibilities for understanding it are infinite. His rationale is quasi-Hegelian: That which lacks all determinacy is receptive to any and every determination. If the most concrete, by reason of its density, is the most abstract, then the most abstract, by reason of its emptiness, is potentially the most concrete.

This turn in his theory of art offers *A* a way out of his personal impasse. The aesthete, knowing that he cannot have his pleasures by instinct, seeks to contrive them by craft. He cannot attain to the condition of nature; he will therefore aspire to the condition of art. *A*'s *diapsalmata* or "refrains," and his paper on "The Rotation Method" are ventures in the art of living.[17] The aphorisms, directed *ad se ipsum*, are the fruits in his own person of the counsel advanced in his "essay in the theory of social prudence."

[17] Ibid., vol. I, pp. 17–42, 279–96.

The burden of *A*'s moods is clearly heard in these
typical *diapsalmata:*

> *I do not care for anything. I do not care to ride,*
> *for the exercise is too violent. I do not care to walk,*
> *walking is too strenuous. I do not care to lie down,*
> *for I should either have to remain lying, and I do not*
> *care to do that, or I should have to get up again, and*
> *I do not care to do that either.* Summa summarum:
> *I do not care at all.*[18]

> *Let others complain that the age is wicked: my*
> *complaint is that it is paltry; for it lacks passion.*
> *Men's thoughts are thin and flimsy like lace, they are*
> *themselves pitiable like the lacemakers. The thoughts*
> *of their hearts are too paltry to be sinful. . . . They*
> *do their duty, these shopkeeping souls, but they clip*
> *the coin a trifle, like the Jews; they think that even if*
> *the Lord keeps ever so careful a set of books, they*
> *may still cheat Him a little. Out upon them! . . .*[19]

> *The essence of pleasure does not lie in the thing*
> *enjoyed, but in the accompanying consciousness. If*
> *I had a humble spirit in my service who, when I*
> *asked for a glass of water, brought me the world's*
> *costliest wines blended in a chalice, I should dismiss*
> *him, in order to teach him that pleasure consists not*
> *in what I enjoy, but in having my own way.*[20]

The last of these is the root and reconciliation of
the first two. What the aesthete is after—the condition
of all subsequent pleasure—is "having his own way."
On the one hand he does not care to do anything; for
anything he does puts him under the compulsion to do
something else. At the same time he despises the paltry
caution that shortchanges its vices for the sake of hig-
gled virtues; to balk at *les grandes passions* is to stop
short of a full realization of one's possibilities. It is

[18] Ibid., vol. I, pp. 19–20.
[19] Ibid., vol. I, p. 27.
[20] Ibid., vol. I, p. 30.

necessary to enjoy everything and to care about nothing.

In an "ecstatic lecture" *A* defines the "sum and substance of all philosophy" in a series of monotonous dilemmas: If you marry, you will regret it, and if you do not marry, you will regret that; if you trust a woman, you will regret it, and if you do not trust a woman, you will regret that; hang yourself and you will regret it, don't hang yourself and you will likewise regret that, *ad infinitum*. Either/or: for any *x*, either you do *x* or you do not do *x*, and in any case you will be sorry. Every decision and every action entail regret for the alternate possibility concurrently and irrevocably renounced. Therefore, one should so live *aeterno modo* that he abrogates the law of contradiction in advance by—doing nothing. No decisions, no regrets; no actions, no consequences. The path to free enjoyment is the way of *dolce far niente*.[21]

But the sweet life of indolence calls for delicate management. One cannot, for example, *resolutely* do nothing and survive the resolution unscathed. To do nothing in an affirmative way is just as constraining as doing something: If you do something, you will regret it, and if you do nothing, you will regret that. Strictly speaking, one should not even do nothing. But this is also, strictly speaking, impossible: like it or not, one will either lie down or stand up. Some practical expedients are required.

One course that recommends itself is romantic frenzy: Let yourself go. Since it is a matter of indifference what a man does, then anything he goes at is fine and beautiful if he does it with total abandon. But the romantic is a very poor counselor. Wiser by an eternity, *A* knows that if he lets himself go, he will *certainly* regret that. The secret of enjoyment is neither to do nothing nor to do anything with all one's might. The secret is to do *everything* in such a way that one rigor-

[21] Ibid., vol. I, pp. 37–39.

ously *avoids all commitments.* The art of living is neither an impossible self-denial nor a prodigal self-squandering, but the most fastidious self-discipline.

Self-discipline, as a technique for maximizing pleasure and minimizing boredom, is the prescription of *A*'s disquisition on the rotation method. The artful hedonist rotates his pleasures as the farmer rotates his crops. To this end he must be prepared to allow any or all of his desires to lie fallow at any time. The first precept of this *ascesis* is the counsel of despair: *nil admirari.* "It is impossible to live artistically before one has made up one's mind to abandon hope; for hope precludes self-limitation."[22] Hope exposes the hopeful to the possibility of frustration; therefore walk circumspectly that you may forget the unsettling at will and redeem the tedious with recollection. The art of recollection—the imaginative revision of a delightful past—and the art of forgetting—the sidestep by which one diverts himself from the path of a disgruntling present—together compose the dear desperation that can shield the aesthete forever (*aeterno modo*) from the threat of the future, "insure" him "against sticking fast in some relationship of life, and make possible the realization of a complete freedom."[23]

From this synderesis follow the particular maxims of aesthetic praxis: Take fullest advantage of people, but beware the obligations of friendship; enjoy love, but shun marriage; cultivate the arts, but see that you reap no profit therefrom. Whatever the situation, stay in control. Now there is only one way a man can stay in control of every situation, and that is by first assuming complete control of himself. He cannot produce at will the events and environs of his life; he cannot even create his own moods. But he can determine the *meaning* these circumstances will have for him by the practice of systematic *arbitrariness.*[24] Suppose, for ex-

[22] Ibid., vol. I, p. 288.
[23] Ibid., vol. I, p. 291.
[24] Ibid., vol. I, pp. 295–96.

ample, he goes to church (no experienced aesthete
would neglect the charming possibilities offered by the
practice of religion): he will so attend to the sermon
that he refuses the pastoral edification in order to
beatify himself with observations of the pastoral
Adam's apple. In an erotic *pas de deux* he will be the
curious voyeur of his own athletic lovemaking. By seizing the occasion and turning it to capricious ends, he
makes and unmakes his situation as it pleases him.
By his hopeless withdrawal from immediacy he perfects
his freedom; by his arbitrary return to immediacy he
keeps his independence and simultaneously gives his
life content. The varied round of pleasures is enabled
by the larger "rotation method," the dialectical circle
of withdrawal and return.

So the pattern of *A*'s life duplicates the structure of
Don Juan. As in the aesthetic unity of the opera the
most vacuous abstraction is by implication the most
teeming concretion, so in the aesthetic unity of *A*'s
existence the kenosis implied in his *nil admirari* is the
emancipation by which he releases himself for the arbitrary pursuit of every pleasure. The practical dilemma
of the hedonist is resolved in the light of the art theorist's analysis of immediacy. However circuitous the
route, *A* comes at last to the land of heart's desire.

Yet the solution is suspect, because it does not match
A's character as this is delineated in *Either/Or* I. The
discussion so far, intent on the rationale by which *A*
orders his life, has overlooked several aspects of the
life itself. It has ignored the heavy sadness that palls
the *diapsalmata,* and the fascination with death and
dereliction in essays like "Shadowgraphs,"[25] "The Ancient Tragical Motif as Reflected in the Modern,"[26]
and "The Unhappiest Man."[27] In particular it has said
nothing of *A*'s membership in the *Symparanekromenoi.*
These are strange themes and strange predilections for

[25] Ibid., vol. I, pp. 163–213.
[26] Ibid., vol. I, pp. 135–62.
[27] Ibid., vol. I, pp. 215–28.

a hedonist, and yet they follow irresistibly from the
aesthetic presupposition that life consists in enjoyment:
"There are well-known insects which die in the moment
of fecundation. So it is with all joy; life's supreme and
richest moment of pleasure is coupled with death."[28]
The familiar connection between sexual consummation and death is the consequence of a less obvious
but more intimate and fundamental conjunction of
death and delight.

"Death," says *A,* addressing the *Symparanekromenoi,* "is for us the greatest happiness."[29] In his lecture on "The Ancient Tragical Motif," subtitled "an
essay in the fragmentary," he outlines the metaphysical
and artistic tenets held by the brotherhood of defunct
men. Reality, in their view, is a show of accidental
events, of which the only thing one can confidently say
is: It passes. Reality is essentially *pastness.* But it is
a pastness without finality or fulfillment: reality is as
desultory as it is fleeting. That which is past without
being perfected is dead. Reality aesthetically conceived
is death.

Theory of art follows ontology. The literati of the
Symparanekromenoi are dedicated to the production
of works marked by a "gleaming transitoriness." Their
essays are "anacoluthic," "fragmentary pursuits"; or
as *A* finally sums it up: "Let us then describe our
purpose as an attempt . . . in the art of writing posthumous papers."[30] Since for these aesthetes art is not
distinct from life, their art of living is an imaginative
dying before their death. The fellowship of the deceased are those who have chosen death as a way of
life. "The unhappiest man" in the world is the man who
absents himself from experience, whose hope and
whose memory are equally vain, because his future is
already past in anticipation and his past forever imminent in recollection. A man without a present, his

28 Ibid., vol. I, p. 20.
29 Ibid., vol. I, p. 165.
30 Ibid., vol. I, pp. 149–51, especially p. 150.

14   Louis Mackey

life a possibility never tried and never to be overtaken, but ever cherished, he is embalmed before his birth. "But what do I say: the unhappiest, the happiest I ought to say, for this is indeed a gift of the gods which no one can give himself."[31] The unhappiest man, and paradoxically the happiest, the man whose life is death, is the aesthete himself.

The paradox is illumined by a recapitulation of the aesthetic project and its execution. The aesthete wants enjoyment, but enjoyment cannot simply be had, it must be arranged. Life must be made an art, but the art of living requires a total detachment from everything merely given and possibly unpleasant, as well as a disinterested arbitrariness in the concoction of actual pleasures. The perennial threat to this insouciance is misfortune, and the supreme misfortune is death. Fate, in its double role of chance and necessity, and especially death, inevitable in its outcome but inconstant in its choice of time and place and manner, seem to constitute the absolute frustration of aesthetic freedom. The one gift that cannot be refused is death. Suicide will not work: the aesthete could not consistently kill himself unless he could survive to enjoy the event.

Two consequences follow: First, the aesthete worships fate. In the *ultimatum* of death it sets the outer limit to his *nil admirari* and his caprice; it is the one power he cannot transcend or overwhelm. *A*'s devotion to tragic literature is the offering he lays on the altar of his god. But (and this is the second consequence) the tragic corpus itself is the divine liturgy in which death is transubstantiated to art. In the celebration of this liturgy the aesthete receives the bread and wine of his own communion with life. The holy mystery of aestheticism is that everything—even misfortune and death—can be enjoyed. In possibility, Kierkegaard liked to say, everything is possible. In the grace of this possibility the aesthete consumes his god and enters into his beatitude.

[31] Ibid., vol. I, p. 228.

But it must not be forgotten that this is a Black Mass. The aesthete's communion is a foretaste of death. His beatitude—prefigured already in his initial retreat from life and now perfected in his tragic necrolatry—is *melancholy*. Melancholy is the ultimate and only consistent form of aesthetic enjoyment. Over the entrance to the aesthetic life burn the prophetic words: *lasciate ogni speranza, voi ch'entrate.*[32] The art of living is the art of enjoying despair.

> I say of my sorrow what the Englishman says of his house: my sorrow is my castle.[33]
>
> My life is like an eternal night; when at last I die, then I can say with Achilles:
>
> Du bist vollbracht, Nachtwache meines Daseyns.[34]

But if the prospect is dreary, the achievement is magnificent. *A* is unequivocally intent on living aesthetically, and he accepts the consequences of his project with matchless consistency. To say that he is effete is no refutation: he embraces his vanity with the enthusiasm of despair. To complain that he is gloomy is beside the point: he savors the wormwood and the gall with bittersweet relish. Seen from inside his skin, any protest against his way of life—in the interests of sanity, sound sense, morals, or piety—is bound to seem philistine. He is, to give him his proper name, the *poet* par excellence. His medium is not words, but himself: he is the living *poiesis,* the root and branch of which all merely verbal making is but the flower.

Unlike Don Juan, who must vanish when the house lights go up, *A* might really exist, does indeed exist as the father of us all. Like most men most of the time and all men some of the time, he seeks (but with exemplary single-mindedness) the richest satisfaction

---

[32] From Dante's *Inferno*, III, 9. "All hope abandon, ye who enter here."

[33] Kierkegaard, op. cit., vol. I, p. 21.

[34] Ibid., vol. I, p. 35.

of desire compatible with the widest exercise of freedom. That this involves him in paradox is a fact he
sees and welcomes, because he is more honest and
more thorough than the rest of us. His life is the in-
defatigable process of reconciling its own contradictions. Each stage of the Hegelian dialectic is driven by
its inner contradictions into a higher stage. In the Kierkegaardian dialectic, each of the "stages on life's way"
contains its contradictions—is, in fact, the *project* of so
containing them. While the typical Hegelian protago-
nist is the abstraction of an abstraction (*Herrschaft* and
Knechtschaft), the Kierkegaardian "existence-spheres"
come to focus in *dramatis personae* who struggle to
assimilate their problems into the integrity of their individual personalities.

A then is a real man, or, as he is ensconced in his
literary productions, an "existential possibility." The
excellence of his poetic achievement is validated by
the cogency of his *modus vivendi:* he exists his poetry
and poetizes his existence. To call him "aesthete" is to
acknowledge the hypostatic union of immediacy and
freedom where art is incarnate in life and life is re-
deemed in art.

At the end of the first volume of *Either/Or,* hard
on the heels of "The Rotation Method" and balancing
in bulk the long essay on *Don Juan* with which the
book opens, stands the "Diary of the Seducer."[35] Apparently alien to the rest of the book—allegedly found
among the papers of *A,* who in turn claims to have
copied it out on the sly, it purports to be the private
journals of the one Johannes nicknamed "the Seducer"
—the Diary is also somewhat deceptive. It is indeed the
record of a seduction, but any salacious expectations
raised by the title are laid in the perusal. The carnal
climax occurs in the interval between the ultimate and
penultimate entries, while the remaining 140-odd pages

[35] Ibid., vol. I, pp. 297–440.

detail the intricate procedure by which the seduction is accomplished. Having sighted and fancied Cordelia Wahl, Johannes determines upon her undoing, lays his snares, and takes his prey. Once he has her he immediately releases her (having introduced her, as he puts it, into a "higher sphere" of consciousness),[36] for her interest is gone with her maidenhood.

More interesting than the story itself is Johannes' theory of seduction and the techniques by which the theory is implemented. Seduction, as Johannes understands it, is not the act of defloration, nor does it presuppose an excessive concern with sex. To seduce a woman means: with no force but with much art to secure the free capitulation of her mind to yours. That sexuality will be the normal context for such an enterprise is obvious; but it is strictly incidental to the real objective, which is the conquest of the spirit and not the congress of the flesh. It is difficult but not impossible to imagine Johannes a eunuch. When a woman has acknowledged herself captivated, be her body never so intact, she is possessed more effectively than if she were captured by rape.

The character and the escapades of Johannes the Seducer suggest a comparison with Don Juan. The Don is sensuality pure and simple, to the exclusion of intellect. He is no more a seducer than is the force that through the green fuse drives the flower. Johannes is an intellect that can become sensual at will: "He lived far too intellectually to be a seducer in the common understanding of the word. Sometimes, however, he assumed a parastatic body, and was then sheer sensuality."[37] *Pur chè porti la gonella, voi sapete quel chè fà* describes the amorphous longings of Don Juan; the Seducer's more discriminating desire is presaged in the motto of his Diary, *Sua passion' predomi-*

[36] Ibid., vol. I, p. 432.
[37] Ibid., vol. I, pp. 303–4.

nante è la giovin principiante.[38] The texts are from
the same libretto, and it is not surprising to find *A,*
in his commentary on *Don Juan,* imagining another
kind of seducer, a seducer who will enjoy not the satisfaction of desire, but the "deception," the "cunning,"
the "how, the method"[39] of seduction. Johannes is
this "reflective Don Juan,"[40] whose pleasure is the
seducing and not the rewards of seduction. Don Juan
wants women, and for his purposes they are all sisters.
His Teutonic namesake wants the excitement of a contest of minds, and for this end he needs a very particular woman: *la giovin principiante,* old enough to have
a mind of her own, woman enough to want to give it
away, and young enough to be unscarred by previous
combats.

Johannes is after Cordelia's mind and the thrill of
beguiling it. As he is scrupulous in his choice of victims, so he is ingenious in the selection and use of his
weapons. He brings to his task resources of cunning,
psychological insight, and patience—especially patience;
Cordelia is five months in the making—that would tax
and tire the ordinary sensualist. He shifts his moods
in Cordelia's presence with calculated randomness: be-
wilderment begets attraction. He drones for hours with
her old aunt about the high price of butter: boredom
gives franchise to erotic fancy. He arranges to have
her courted by an obliging boor: contempt of Edward
becomes a bond that ties Cordelia to Johannes. He is
betrothed to Cordelia, and promptly breaks the engagement: transferred from public trust to clandestine
adventure, her desire burns sweeter and stronger.
Johannes never makes a move to seduce, and by that
fact is made more seductive. His strategy, consistent
with his theory of seduction, is to make himself an object at once terrifying and fascinating, *mysterium tre-*

[38] Again from *Don Giovanni.* "His ruling passion is the
fresh young girl." Cf. Kierkegaard, op. cit., vol. I, p. 298.

[39] Ibid., vol. I, pp. 107, 98.

[40] Ibid., vol. I, p. 107.

mendum et fascinans. He makes himself—to adduce what Kierkegaard sometimes calls *the* aesthetic category—"interesting." Bewitched at last, Cordelia throws herself into his arms, unable any longer to deny him the love he has evoked but never demanded. When she finally succumbs, it is not clear to her just who has done what and to whom. It is almost, in retrospect, as if she had seduced him. This, of course, is exactly the effect Johannes has wanted and so faultlessly prepared: that his desire should become hers, that she should freely but helplessly surrender herself to her destroyer.

His journal gives us primarily Johannes' view of Johannes, and from within he looks very much like *A*. He is, by his own admission, a poet. Seduction is a kind of *poiesis* worked in the medium of woman's sexuality. If Johannes is careless of Cordelia and her feelings, it is only because he is so painstakingly careful of his artistry. He is faithless with Cordelia the girl, but only because of a higher fidelity to Cordelia "the Idea," who is privileged to be immortalized in his art. His pact is with the aesthetic, and that involves, as the case of *A* has already shown, detachment and arbitrariness in relation to actual persons and events. All love—poetically viewed—is essentially faithless.[41]

Johannes could if he wished offer justification for his practice, though he is far too pure an aesthete to defend himself morally. The qualities by which he seduces girls are just those qualities of tact, diplomacy, and skill in the handling of people which are universally honored among men of affairs. If from a certain perspective he seems cold, cruel, inhumane, it is only because he does successfully what most men mostly bungle: he uses people exclusively for his own ends. If it be objected that he has deceived Cordelia, he can reply: Yes, but for her own good; I found her a girl, I left her a woman. She is not ruined by her seduction, but made; she has become for the first time free, self-

[41] Ibid., vol. I, p. 432.

conscious, and mature. Her husband—if she finds one—will be indebted to Johannes for his services. The seducer, by norms and devices commonly approved, but with much greater expertness in the application, is the benefactor of mankind.

Cordelia, however, is differently impressed. Her letters (four of them are incorporated in Johannes' Diary)[42] speak alternately confusion, outraged innocence, pathos, self-pity, and—preeminently—horror. She shudders at the awareness that she has been possessed by a demon, she has made love to a "parastatic" body! Her lover dwells in splendid and terrible isolation in a phantom realm behind the real world. In the whimsicality of his moods he appears suddenly out of nowhere and as quickly vanishes again, so that Cordelia has often found herself "embracing a cloud."[43] Because he willed to be her god, Johannes has become her devil. The aesthetic integrity of his personality is, from Cordelia's point of view, the dreadful vacuity of one who does not *practice* deception but *is* deceit itself. Johannes' fidelity in the "service of the Idea" necessitates in principle a betrayal of every real relationship. He declares to the world—and to Cordelia in the very act of making love to her—"What have I to do with thee?"[44]

That Cordelia should feel this way is hardly astounding. More important is the fact that *A* himself is aghast at Johannes. The account of his transcription of the Diary begins in Gothic mystery ("I cannot conceal from myself, scarcely can I master the anxiety which grips me at this moment . . ."),[45] moves to the realization that Johannes is a "depraved personality,"[46] and concludes to a prediction of derangement. *A,* who

[42] Ibid., vol. I, pp. 305–6, 308–9.
[43] Ibid., vol. I, p. 305.
[44] Cf. Matt. 8:28ff.
[45] Kierkegaard, *Either/Or,* vol. I, p. 299.
[46] Ibid., vol. I, p. 299.

is a confidant of Cordelia's and sees the desolation of her virginity, prophesies that Johannes will eventually outsmart himself:

> *As he has led others astray, so he ends, I think, by going astray himself. . . . He who goes astray inwardly . . . soon discovers that he is going about in a circle from which he cannot escape. I think it will be this way with him later, to a still more terrible extent. I can imagine nothing more excruciating than an intriguing mind, which has lost the thread of its continuity and now turns its whole acumen against itself, when conscience awakens and compels the schemer to extricate himself from this confusion.*[47]

Strange to hear *A* speaking of conscience, and ominous that he does so only in the presence of Johannes the Seducer. He confesses that he is

> *never quite able to control the anxiety that grips me every time I think about the case. I, too, am carried away into that nebulous realm, that dream world, where every moment one is afraid of his own shadow. Often I seek in vain to tear myself away; I follow along like a menacing shadow, an accuser who is mute. How strange! He has spread the deepest secrecy over everything, and yet there is an even deeper secret, and that is the fact that I am privy to it. . . . There is really nothing else which involves so much seduction and so great a curse as a secret.*[48]

A man who wills mystification as an end may wind up caught in the springs and elastics and false bottoms of his own legerdemain; the secrecy that is a condition of seduction may become a solitary confinement in which the seducer goes mad for want of another against whom he can rectify his wild imaginings.

[47] Ibid., vol. I, p. 304.
[48] Ibid., vol. I, p. 306.

Yet it is not Johannes who is on the brink of madness, but *A;* it is not Johannes in whom conscience starts, but *A.* Of Johannes, *A* says:

> *Conscience exists for him only as a higher degree of consciousness, which expresses itself in a disquietude that does not, in a more profound sense, accuse him, but which keeps him awake, and gives him no rest in his barren activity. Nor is he mad; for the multitude of finite thoughts are not petrified in the eternity of madness.*[49]

Not Johannes' secret life, but *A*'s privy involvement in *l'affaire* Cordelia—as an observer tranced in fascinated terror—is the beginning of insanity. *Johannes is the omen of madness and the awakening of conscience in* A.

Johannes sees himself as an artist, a poetizer of girls. To Cordelia he is an incubus with whom she has lain to her soul's damnation. For *A* Johannes is just *himself looked at from without.* The demonia of the seducer is the melancholy innocence of the aesthete seen from the other side, the side of his relations to other people with whom, willy-nilly, he is involved, and whom, willy-nilly, he draws into the vortex of his own confusion. *A,* who knows both Johannes and Cordelia, is granted this double recognition of himself and the awful wisdom it brings: the wisdom of fear and of a conscience born in fear.

But the intimacy between *A* and Johannes goes even deeper. In the general preface to *Either/Or,* Victor Eremita, the pseudonymous editor, argues his conviction that *A* is the author, and not as he claims the pilferer, of the "Diary of the Seducer." For

> *the dominant mood in* A's *preface in a manner betrays the poet. It seems as if* A *had actually become*

[49] Ibid., vol. I, pp. 304–5.

afraid of his poem, as if it continued to terrify him, like a troubled dream when it is told. If it were an actual occurrence which he had become privy to, then it seems strange that the preface shows no trace of A's joy in seeing the realization of the idea which had so often floated before his mind. . . . [The reference is to the reflective seducer imagined in the essay on Don Juan.] *I find no trace of such joy in the preface, but rather, as was said, a certain horror and trembling, which might well have its cause in his poetical relationship to this idea.*[50]

The suggestion that Johannes is a possibility projected by *A* is confirmed by the latter's remark that the Diary is a "poetic reproduction" of experience, and "therefore neither historically exact nor simply fiction, not indicative but subjunctive."[51] It is written in the mood of "as if"; Johannes looks so much like *A* because he is a poetic elongation of *A*'s personality. The madness and the moral upheaval on which he is verging are the unfolding of possibilities already latent in *A* himself. In the "Diary of the Seducer" *A* has imaginatively pushed his way of life beyond its extreme limit, and he is appalled when he sees where it is leading him.

But Johannes *is* a possibility, not a person. Just as pure sensuality (Don Juan) is possible only in art, so also is pure reflection (Johannes the Seducer). In *Don Juan* the unity of form and content is perfect because the distinction between them has not yet been drawn. In the journals of Johannes the separation between nature and freedom is so complete that it can never be healed. It is no accident that Don Juan and the Seducer have names—indeed the same name—univocal names appropriate to pure types, whereas *A* is as anonymous and equivocal as immediacy itself. For neither Don Juan nor Johannes is a possibility that can

[50] Ibid., vol. I, p. 9.
[51] Ibid., vol. I, p. 300.

be actualized. They are, rather, the ideal *terminus a quo* and the equally ideal *terminus ad quem* of the aesthetic life, which *A* alone and ambiguously *lives*. In Don Juan art is impossibly submerged in life; in Johannes life is impossibly lost for the sake of art. Inspired to enthusiasm by the one, recoiling in dread from the other, the aesthete strikes between them the precarious unhappy equilibrium of his own life in art. His existence is such stuff as dreams—bad dreams—are made on, and his little life is rounded with the sleep of unconscious nature. But that is merely to say that he is man—man as he immediately, aesthetically *is,* haunted by memories of bestial innocence and nightmares of demonic experience, melancholy in the assumption of his uncertain destiny.

It is therefore to *A* the man, not to Don Juan the myth or Johannes the menace, that Kierkegaard's champion of the ethical life addresses his solemn admonitions.

2

World Enough and Time

Volume II of *Either/Or* consists of a brace of very long letters and a sermon. The sermon (of which more later) is by an unnamed priest. The author of the letters is called *B,* to distinguish him from *A,* the author of volume I; but his letters tell us that his name is Wilhelm, that he is married and a father, and that he is an Assessor, or judge in the lower courts. The letters are addressed to *A,* who is a friend of Judge Wilhelm and a frequent visitor in the older man's home. The first letter defends "The Aesthetic Validity of Marriage" against the casual eroticism of the aesthete.[52] The second, to be considered here, bears the formidable title "The Equilibrium between the Aesthetical and the Ethical in the Composition of Per-

[52] Ibid., vol. II, pp. 5–157.

sonality."[53] Under this head the Judge mounts an attack on *A*'s way of life and constructs a rationale for his own ethical mode of existence.

His approach is in keeping with his status in society and his epistolary form. He writes loosely and at his ease, from the security of an official position and the warmth of an idyllic marriage. His attitude is never argumentative and his concern never theoretical. Though his form permits him occasional digressions into philosophy, he is at bottom always the judge and paterfamilias, and his letter is appropriately compounded of advice and counsel, fireside wisdom, friendly exhortation, and occasionally sharp accusation. His purpose is exclusively practical: to get *A* to change his way of life.

The whole point of his critique of aestheticism is just that: it is not *practical*. Seizing on the catchword "either/or," which *A* had used as a pretext for idleness, the Assessor throws it back in his face. For an ethical man this motto epitomizes the utter seriousness with which he confronts a choice between two exclusive alternatives. For *A* it is a retreat into that eternity of imagination where all contraries are reconciled in a harmony of indifference. For the speculative fancy the opposition of good and evil has no force. The idea of one is no better and no worse than the idea of the other, and there is no choice to be made between them. The aesthete, insofar as he lives *aeterno modo*, makes no choices; and since a man's character is constituted by the choices he makes, the aesthete has no self. But such a stasis cannot be sustained. *A* recognizes that he must do something; and so he acts, but he acts arbitrarily and without commitments. Ideally he is detached from life; actually he samples everything life has to offer—with the proviso that he is not buying. This means, in ethical terms: ideally his self is a vain imagination, actually it is dissolute in the

[53] Ibid., vol. II, pp. 161–338.

etymological sense of "dissolved." His virtuosity, his
ability to acquit himself in any situation and to play at
everything, means that he is nothing but a *poseur*. His
life is an endless series of masks in an endless masquerade, dissipated in its own external relations. The
aesthete—this is the Assessor's charge—is trying to com-
bine Don Juan (pure immediacy) with Johannes the
Seducer (pure reflection), but the project is impossible, and he constantly comes apart at the seams. On
the one hand he withdraws to demonic vacuity, on the
other he returns in a plenitude of chaos; but never
shall the two meet in the identity of a single personality
informed by a fixed and steady character. You are im-
practical, the Judge tells *A,* in the radical sense that
you cannot even be a self on your own terms.[54]

The same futility can be observed in the aesthete's
attempts to deal with time. The connection between
time and personal identity is clear from a consideration
of the nature of choice. *A*'s "choices" do not commit
him to anything, which is to say that they are all for the
moment. Decisive choosing binds the chooser to the
consequences of his choice, either permanently or for
a specified period of time. Ethical choice takes the form
of vow or public contract; it decides a man's character
for the future, it defines him in advance. Only that
man has a self whose personality is continuous through
time, and this requires that he be willing to put his
future in trust by means of his choices. So it is that
the Assessor takes marriage (the vow) and vocation
(involving contractual obligation) as paradigm cases
of ethical choice.

Moreover, it is natural that Judge Wilhelm should
adduce the problem of time. As a judge he is daily
encountering the necessity of decision. Making a decision requires preliminary deliberation, and in the
course of this deliberation there is a moment of indifference, in which several alternatives are present and

[54] Ibid., vol. II, pp. 161–64.

the will can incline any way. But whereas the aesthete wants to remain poised in this indifference—lest some pleasure elude him—the ethical man knows that the moment of indifference is also the instant of resolution, which must be seized or lost forever. Life moves forward, and this movement prohibits everlasting deliberation about alternatives. At some point one alternative must be chosen to the exclusion of its opposite—Guilty? Not guilty?—else both of them are irrecoverably gone. For the aesthete, a possibility is an everpresent opportunity for enjoyment; for the ethical man, it is the now-or-never demand for decision. Therefore the Judge can say: I am fighting for possibility, for freedom, and for the future.[55]

The aesthete has no future; his existence is a recollection of eternity, never a resolution in time. He loses his possibilities in the attempt to preserve them inviolate, for he never actualizes them, and a possibility unactualized is as profitable as miser's gold. His ideal of noninvolvement is a freedom suspended from decision, not a freedom engaged to decide, and it is therefore barren. Yet—the other side of the paradox returns —the aesthete does face a future, he does actualize his possibilities, he does choose. But he does it *malgré lui*. Lost to the world in deliberation, he acts on impulse, he vacillates, he chooses by default or by accident. But the possibilities he actualizes in this way are not his own, they are things that happen to him. And the actions he arbitrarily elects to perform show by their arbitrariness that they are actions to negate action, chosen for the purpose of avoiding the consequences of choice. By his way of life he assumes an irresponsibility for his actions, which prevents him from choosing in an ethical sense. Judge Wilhelm believes that *A* is torn in contradiction between the rich but abstract ideality of his imagination and the pointless hither-and-thither of his actual life. From an ethi-

---

[55] Ibid., vol. II, p. 180.

cal point of view his anonymity signifies not concreteness, but the extremes of emptiness and formlessness
to which his way of life alternately compels him. His
either/or is at the level of theory an indifferent both/
and, and at the level of action an equally indifferent
neither/nor. The ethical either/or—a resolute choice
shaping the personality through time by reference to
an ideal apprehended in the instant of reflection—exceeds the compass of his aestheticism.

The Judge's accusation can be further generalized:
The aesthete confuses the theoretical and the practical
domains. He takes for the whole of life what is at best
a part of it, the idealizing activity of imagination and
intellect. There is no doubt, Judge Wilhelm tells him,
that "if to deliberate were the proper task for a human
life, you would be pretty close to perfection."[56] The
Judge acknowledges *A*'s superiority as a dialectician
and for that reason does not question the logic of his
position. What he questions is the propriety of logic
as a way of life. If a man makes a career of theorizing,
he identifies his existence with the "instant of deliberation," which, however, "like the Platonic instant, has
no existence, least of all in the abstract sense in which
you [*A*] would hold it fast."[57] The instant of deliberation is the momentary withdrawal from existence in
which the ethical man surveys his possibilities and
gathers his forces for a return via decisive choice and
action. But the aesthete, striving to hold the moment
fast in contemplation, makes his whole life a withdrawal from the arena of decision and action.

The man who confuses theory and practice can go
mad in his theoretical isolation, as the case of the Seducer has shown. But he can also be tripped up in
practice. Suppose, says the Judge, a charming and
gifted young man, for whom you feel a genuine affection, should come to you for advice on how to conduct

[56] Ibid., vol. II, p. 169.
[57] Ibid., vol. II, p. 167.

his life. You initiate him into the mysteries of your aestheticism, he disappears from your society for a time, and then reappears older and wiser. Wiser, however, with your own wisdom—cynicism, hatred of life, and melancholy. Is it not conceivable that you might be taken aback? Might you not deplore your own personality reflected in another whom you love? If you are able to be affected in this way by another human being, then your aestheticism is not consistent. A perfectly consistent aestheticism would amount to the demonia of the seducer; this is a possibility *A* has shrunk from in horror. Judge Wilhelm asks him to imagine, not a fanciful extension of his personality, but an actual *alter ego* who might show him what sort of man he really is. And this, the Judge adds, is a consummation devoutly to be wished. The only hope for the aesthete is that he may be caught off guard and moved to acknowledge the extremity of his condition.[58]

The Assessor knows that it will take more than a disturbing personal experience to dislodge *A* from his aestheticism. But the example of the young friend clears the way for a devastating conclusion. The art of living requires that the aesthete stay in control of himself and his situation. However, the case of the young man suggests that he is not in control at all. His aim is enjoyment. *"But,"* Judge Wilhelm counters, *"he who says that he wants to enjoy life always posits a condition which either lies outside the individual or is in the individual in such a way that it is not posited by the individual himself."*[59] That this is the case with health, beauty, love, wealth, fame, status, talent, pleasure, and the like is obvious.[60] But it is also the case with that view of life which Judge Wilhelm describes as "the

[58] Ibid., vol. II, pp. 163–67.
[59] Ibid., vol. II, p. 184.
[60] Ibid., vol. II, pp. 185–95.

most refined and superior"[61] of all aesthetic views,
the view of *A* himself:

> *Your thought has hurried on ahead, you have seen
> through the vanity of all things, but you have got no
> further. Occasionally you plunge into pleasure, and
> every instant you are devoting yourself to it you make
> the discovery in your consciousness that it is vanity.
> So you are constantly beyond yourself, that is, in
> despair. . . . You are like a dying man, you die daily,
> not in the serious significance usually attached to this
> word, but life has lost its reality, and, as you say,
> you always count your days by the number of times
> notice is served on you to quit your lodging.*[62]

The Assessor perceives that *A*'s melancholy is the
most sophisticated form of aestheticism. But it is nevertheless desperate, and it betokens the loss of a world.
However consistent it may be in itself, it cannot be
made consistent with reality. The aesthete, who thinks
to conquer fate by anticipating and transforming in
tragedy the worst it can bring, may still be shattered
by the best. It does no good to proclaim oneself the
unhappiest man:

> *He who says that sorrow is the meaning of life has
> joy outside him in the same way that he who would be
> joyful has sorrow outside him. Joy may take him by
> surprise in exactly the same way that sorrow may take
> the other by surprise. His life view thus hinges upon
> a condition which is not in his power, for it is really
> just as little in a man's power to give up being joyful
> as to give up being sorrowful. But every life view
> which hinges upon a condition outside itself is de-
> spair.*[63]

[61] Ibid., vol. II, p. 198.
[62] Ibid., vol. II, pp. 199, 200.
[63] Ibid., vol. II, p. 240.

If he is surprised by joy, the aesthete has lost the mastery of life on which the success of his aestheticism depends. That he can be so surprised is clear. Though he is prepared to transport everything that happens to him into the never-never land of reflection, he must nevertheless wait for it to happen. However effete, he is always liable to be taken unawares by some happenstance that he could not neutralize *a priori* and in the concrete—and that on the terms of his own metaphysic. He may make a garden of his melancholy and water it with poetic tears, but the flowers and the weeds still grow where they list. That his life, even in its most tragic and poignant moments, is only a pose is made evident by the fact—surely disconcerting to a member of the *Symparanekromenoi*—that there are days when he is happy in spite of himself.

In his very joy the aesthete is in despair, a despair quite different from the hopelessness which he recommends as a condition of freedom. The despair of which Judge Wilhelm speaks is a consequence of unfreedom, of the aesthete's unconditional dependence upon conditions beyond his control.

> So it appears that every aesthetic view of life is despair, and that everyone who lives aesthetically is in despair, whether he knows it or not. But when one knows it (*and you indeed know it*), a higher form of existence is an imperative requirement.[64]

The words in parentheses are important, for they mark the possibility of a transition to a "higher form of existence." The aesthete knows that he is sick unto death, and still persists in his aestheticism. His choice —the one real choice that he makes—is the election of a way of life whose inevitable end is despair. That is why Judge Wilhelm reminds *A* of the teaching of the Church that melancholy (*acedia*) is a sin, and adds

[64] Ibid., vol. II, p. 197.

that "a man may have sorrow and distress, yea, it may
be so great that it pursues him throughout his whole
life, and this may even be beautiful and true, but a man
becomes melancholy only by his own fault."[65] Stifling
though it be, *the aesthete's unfreedom is an unfreedom
that he has freely undertaken* by choosing to live aesthetically. It is an unfreedom, therefore, from which
he can by another free choice emancipate himself. The
way of emancipation is the passage from an aesthetic
to an ethical mode of existence.

To characterize the ethical life is to move from the
Assessor's accusation of *A* to the advice which he,
still judge and husband, has ready to hand. His first
admonition, and the first step toward a higher "stage"
on life's way, is: Despair! The initial movement toward
the ethical is the same as the terminal moment of the
aesthetic. The same and yet different; for the despair
which Judge Wilhelm recommends is not the despair
which the aesthete nurtures as the last end of a life
of enjoyment. It is a *despair of the life of enjoyment
as such,* and thus *the gateway into a new kind of life.*
You can see, says the Judge to *A,* that your life is
desperate. Accept this fact and break with aestheticism
altogether, give up without reservation your impossible
attempt to achieve freedom and selfhood at the level
of immediacy. You will *ipso facto* have elevated yourself to the true freedom and the concrete selfhood of
the ethical man. "The aesthetical in a man is that by
which he is immediately what he is; the ethical is that
whereby he becomes what he becomes."[66] By giving
up the vain endeavor to *be* himself (aesthetic), a man
is first enabled to *become* himself (ethical).

This election of despair is the critical breach with
immediacy that distinguishes the aesthetic from the
ethical. The aesthete, in spite of all his reflection, remains "in his immediacy." His art of living is an at-

[65] Ibid., vol. II, p. 190.
[66] Ibid., vol. II, p. 182.

tempt so to arrange the given that it can be (reflectively, to be sure) enjoyed as it is. The ethical man undertakes the wholesale reconstruction of his nature in the light of his duty and in the power of his freedom, to the end that he may thereby make himself what he is obligated to become. "So then," the Judge repeats,

> *choose despair, for despair is a choice; . . . one cannot despair without choosing. And when a man despairs he chooses again—and what is it he chooses? He chooses himself, not in his immediacy, not as this fortuitous individual, but he chooses himself in his eternal validity.*[67]

What the aesthete must do is to abandon his whole way of life. And then he will be in a position to become himself. In fact, by this first authentic act of freedom, he will already have become a real person. By despairing of himself qua aesthetic he will at once have chosen himself qua ethical in his eternal validity. For his eternal validity as a self is nothing other than the freedom by which he chooses himself. The "absolute" self of which Judge Wilhelm speaks, the self which a man becomes by decisively resolving against a life of enjoyment, is just freedom.[68]

The self so chosen both comes into existence with the choice and exists prior to the choice as something to be chosen. What exists before the choice is the self as immediately given. The self that comes to be by the choice is the same self lifted from nature to self-consciousness by means of freedom.

> *In this case choice performs at one and the same time the two dialectical movements: that which is chosen does not exist and comes into existence with the choice; that which is chosen exists, otherwise*

[67] Ibid., vol. II, p. 215.
[68] Ibid., vol. II, pp. 217–18.

> *there would not be a choice. For in case what I chose did not exist but absolutely came into existence with the choice, I would not be choosing, I would be creating; but I do not create myself, I choose myself. Therefore, while nature is created out of nothing, while I myself as an immediate personality am created out of nothing, as a free spirit I am born of the principle of contradiction [either/or], or born by the fact that I choose myself.*[69]

The freedom by which a man chooses himself in his eternal validity is not abstract, like that of the aesthete, but concrete; for the self which is chosen is the self that is given in the whole of its natural and historical determinations. Likewise the choice itself is not a once-for-all bit of derring-do (the sort of thing an aesthete might try off and on), but a daily reengagement of the whole personality in the terms and consequences of the original decision. Self-choice is not only the entrance to the ethical life; it is also the constitutive principle by which that life is structured. As such it is compounded of the two essential moments of *repentance* and *duty*. In the *present* resolution of self-choice a man takes all of his *past* into his freedom (repentance) and freely programs his entire *future* (duty).

The necessity and the significance of *repentance* in an ethical mode of existence are obvious if it is noted that a man who chooses himself ethically chooses to be absolutely responsible for whatever he is and becomes. But the self for which he assumes responsibility has a spatial and temporal spread; in particular it has a past. This past becomes his when he accepts the liability for it, and he cannot reject it without going back on his self-choice. Yet there is much in any man's past that cannot be affirmed as good. It must therefore be affirmed as guilty. The affirmation of oneself as guilty is repentance. Repentance is the movement of freedom

[69] Ibid., vol. II, pp. 219–20.

by which a man gets under the whole weight of his past and shoulders it for the future.[70] For "my life does not begin in time with nothing, and if I cannot repent the past, freedom is a dream."[71]

Free self-choice is the choice of oneself as guilty. Any other understanding of freedom is either paltry or abstract, the paltriness which the aesthete despises or the abstraction that he is condemned to remain. Judge Wilhelm wants to make clear to *A* that any qualifications introduced at this point would be no more than a craven effort to get an easy acquittal for aestheticism. It is easy to see why Kierkegaard entrusts the commendation of the ethical life into the hands of Judge Wilhelm; for to live ethically is to sit in judgment on oneself and hand down the bitter verdict: Guilty.[72]

Repentance, however, is but one moment of the ethical choice; the correlative movement in the opposite direction is *duty*. The aesthetic life was structured by a dialectic of withdrawal and return. The same dialectic repeats itself in the ethical life, but in radically altered form, now concretely temporal rather than abstractly eternal. Having attained the level of freedom by despairing of aestheticism, the ethical man concurrently chooses himself in his eternal validity. The movement of repentance is the element of withdrawal in this self-choice; by repentance he gets all the way outside himself, behind his own past. In the life of duty he returns to himself and advances into his future.

The self that is repented is the past actuality of the individual who chooses; but insofar as he chooses it, it becomes his future possibility. Nature overtaken by freedom and considered in relation to the future becomes task. The task of the ethical man is to take his given nature in hand and make it his responsibility. And to accept oneself as one's own responsibility is

[70] Ibid., vol. II, pp. 220–23, 229, 236, 252–53.
[71] Ibid., vol. II, p. 244.
[72] Ibid., vol. II, pp. 221–22.

to acknowledge the claim of duty. "For as soon as in despair a person has found himself, has absolutely chosen himself, has repented himself, he has himself as a task under an eternal responsibility, and thus duty is posited in its absoluteness."[73]

Duty conceived is abstract. But duty acted on is as concrete as the individual himself. The principle of duty can be stated in a form applicable to every man without exception: Thou shalt become thyself. But particular duties (what a modern moralist might call values) cannot be defined in theory, they can only be discovered in situation. Particular duties arise, for each person, out of the exigencies of his particular nature and the particular circumstances in which he finds himself. Judge Wilhelm, as a married man, a father, and a civil servant, has no difficulty descrying the duties that are appropriate to his station in life. And neither, he suggests, will anyone who is seriously committed to the principle of duty, who has not kept back some little aesthetic reservation by which he hopes to get himself an occasional moral holiday.[74] That is why the Assessor does not represent the primary ethical choice as a choice *between* good and evil, but as a choice *of* good and evil as the constitutive categories for one's life. The distinction between good and evil does not exist for the aesthete; morality is not an immediate qualification of human nature. To choose to lead one's life in terms of the opposition of good and evil is to take the ethical as against the aesthetic mode of self-understanding.[75] But for that reason the choice of the ethical *is* the choice of the good; for the good in an abstract sense is just the free resolution to become oneself by the way of repentance and duty. "As soon as one can get a man to stand at the crossways in such a position that there is no recourse but to choose, he

[73] Ibid., vol. II, p. 275.
[74] Ibid., vol. II, pp. 258–75.
[75] Ibid., vol. II, pp. 171–73, especially p. 173.

will choose the right."[76] Not that the ethical man does
what is right in every case; but even when he does
wrong in some particular, his commitment to the principle of good is still primary. The fundamental orientation of his will, which shows itself in his repentance
and his recognition of the principle of duty, is right.
In this respect he is opposed to the demoniac like
Johannes the Seducer, who is imprisoned in evil even
though he may incidentally do good.

Ethics, for Judge Wilhelm, is not a matter of values
but of being. It is not in the first place a question of
following a certain set of moral rules; it is the determination to become a certain kind of person. As over
against the aesthete, who drifts through life neutrally
occupied with imaginative possibilities and therefore
never becomes a self, the ethical man sustains in day-
to-day exercise of will the resolution by which he ever
consolidates his personality around the either/or:
good/evil. If by repenting the past a man can assume
the burden of responsibility for himself, and if by daily
facing the future in dutiful resolve he can build the
integrity of this self, then it may be added that his

> *eternal dignity consists in the fact that he can have a
> history, the divine element in him consists in the fact
> that he himself, if he will, can impart to this history
> continuity, for this it acquires only when it is not the
> sum of all that has happened to me or befallen me
> but is my own work, in such a way that even what
> has befallen me is by me transformed and translated
> from necessity to freedom.*[77]

Now, however, although the choice of the ethical
way of life entails the rejection of the aesthete's way
of life, the aesthetic element in existence remains. A
man does not eliminate his immediacy by choosing

[76] Ibid., vol. II, p. 172; cf. p. 171.
[77] Ibid., vol. II, p. 255.

to live his life in other than immediate categories. Therefore it is incumbent on Judge Wilhelm to show that the ethical life does justice to this aesthetic component. And he does so at great length. The ethical choice is so far from negating the aesthetic element of life that it is the necessary condition of genuine aesthetic enjoyment. For example, suppose a man possesses great wealth. So long as he continues to live aesthetically his wealth is his fate. He is dependent upon it for his enjoyment; his wealth owns him, he does not own it. If he then makes the ethical choice of himself, he becomes free with respect to his wealth. His life no longer depends upon it or upon any gift of fortune; good fortune or bad, he is master of himself. He can enjoy his wealth and enjoy it freely— because it has become a matter of indifference to him. This indifference may sound like the aesthete's hopelessness, but there is a new twist. In his hopelessness the aesthete remains enslaved to the fate he flees. In ethical self-choice a man buys his immediacy back out of slavery to nature and fate, and makes it his own. The ethical choice does not destroy the aesthetic, but redeems it.[78]

The transfiguration of the aesthetic by the ethical is the theme of much of Judge Wilhelm's letter, and works itself out in a series of contrasts between the aesthetic and the ethical ways of life. The ethical, he says, is the *universal,* as opposed to the aesthetic, which is *differential.* While the aesthete's personality is always built on his possession of some talent that differentiates him from the mass of men, the ethical man refuses to take any advantage from such gifts. The fact that one is a genius or "the unhappiest man" in the world is ethically irrelevant, and no man devoted to duty would claim any virtue either from his excellence or his wretchedness. The ethical choice equalizes men in a way that most men, their lives aesthetically

[78] Ibid., vol. II, pp. 257–58.

determined, find it hard to tolerate. It is difficult to resist the temptation to hold back from the universal some little difference, be it only one's misery, that sets one apart from the herd. Yet it is ethically intolerable that a man's character should depend on luck, or that men should be distinguished from each other *as men* by aesthetic accidents. Of course all the aesthetic differences remain within the context of the ethical choice; but there they exist as freely appropriated and ethically neutral.[79]

The ethical universal (duty) is a *concrete* universal as opposed to the *abstract* or poetic universal. Duty works intimately into and through the finite world, while poetry can only retreat from it. The poet may be the child of eternity, but he has not the seriousness of eternity, which is its ability to incarnate itself in time. Mysticism, asceticism, monasticism the Assessor regards as a kind of aesthetic *contemptus mundi* masquerading as religious; intrusive in their relation to God, they take the ethical decision in vain and deceive themselves out of a world. The ethical man takes his place in the world in the midst of the community of men; he knows that it is his duty to reveal himself to others, while the aesthete—whether poet, demon, or mystic—always remains in the concealment of his aesthetic differentia. Though he can conceive of a man who, because of some unique vocation, finds it impossible to "realize the universal," the Judge can see nothing in the life of such an "exception" but unrelieved misery. If such a man is "reconciled to the universal" at all, it will only be by remorse over his inability to actualize the universal directly.[80]

In the light of these observations it is easy to see why the Judge exults in the view that every man has a calling and is obliged to work in order to live—whereas the aesthete, for whom the necessity of work-

79 Ibid., vol. II, pp. 259–66.
80 Ibid., vol. II, pp. 245–59.

ing would be burdensome, requires (the accident of)
opulence in order to carry out his project of enjoyment. The contractual obligation involved in work
points up the ethical conviction that there is an order
of things in which every man can find a place, a place
where he can accomplish the universal (by earning . . .) in his own individuality (. . . his living).
Such a man is his own providence, and that is no more
than to say that he lives ethically.[81]

Finally, Judge Wilhelm's ardent advocacy of marriage, as against romantic love and seduction, expresses
the way in which the ethical self-choice works itself
out in time and transfigures a man's immediacy. Bio-
logically bound to the bearing and rearing of children,
the life of woman is limited and defined by the cycle
of conception, gestation, parturition, and maturation.
She therefore understands time more intimately than
any masculine philosopher; she and not man deserves
to be called the lord and master of nature. Her ethical
role, consequently, is to be man's finitude, and this
she achieves only in her capacity as wife and mother.
To treat her as an ideal (seduction), or as an occasion
(romance), is to defraud her and oneself of destiny.
It is only in marriage—where it becomes duty via the
solemn vow—that love achieves actuality in time. Any
other view of love treats it as an abstraction or as an
accident, betrays it or loses it by default. The freedom
that is vainly sought in seduction, and the pleasure
that is vainly demanded of romance, first become realities in the ethical context of marriage, where immediacy ("falling in love") is taken up in freedom (the
vow) and made concrete in the public trust and private
devotion of family life.[82]

So Judge Wilhelm concludes—or rather does not
conclude, for he is as garrulous as time itself. The

[81] Ibid., vol. II, pp. 281–302, especially pp. 287, 297.
[82] Ibid., vol. II, pp. 302–21.

length of his letters suggests that his wife's expert management of his finitude leaves him infinite leisure for distributing extra-professional counsel. But that in a way is his point: Only by advancing to an ethical understanding of himself does a man find world enough and time to achieve a stable equilibrium of the aesthetical and the ethical in the constitution of his personality. "What I wanted to do," he writes by way of rounding off *A*'s lesson in morals,

> was to show how the ethical, in the regions which border on the aesthetical, is so far from depriving life of its beauty that it bestows beauty upon it. It affords peace, assurance, and security, for it calls to us constantly: Quod petis, hic est.[83]

Judge Wilhelm can address *A* as he does because they are struck by a common perplexity: the contradiction between nature and freedom in the human self. And they are engaged by a common problem: how to work these conflicting elements into a single personality. *A,* as aesthete, wants simply to be himself as he is. And the Assessor's reply is that this cannot be done, for what a man is immediately is just this contradiction of immediacy and reflection. The equilibrium which *A* tries to maintain is worse than precarious, it is impossible. Forever vacillating, losing nature for the sake of freedom, and losing freedom for the sake of nature, he ends by losing himself as the particular worldly and temporal person he is bound to become. The "composition" (*Udarbejdelse*) of personality which the Assessor presses upon him is etymologically a "working-out" or "elaboration" of the self in the temporal order of the world. The victory that Judge Wilhelm wins in the arena of the finite is more than an equilibrium: it is the concrete oppor-

[83] Ibid., vol. II, p. 328.

tunity—world enough and time—to reconcile what he
is and what he can be in the integrity of what he
becomes.

3

All in All

Judge Wilhelm means to be a practical man. Consideration of his theories is fittingly supplemented by a
scrutiny of his practice. His extravagant praise of connubial love suggests in particular a closer look at his
marriage. That marriage, he boasts, is as nearly perfect
as an earthly union can be. "I have never," he says,
"experienced any conflict between love and duty, nor
for that matter any serious marital conflicts at all."[84]
One need not be a cynic (though perhaps one needs
to be married) to remark that such an idyllic relationship could only be imagined by a bachelor like Kierkegaard. Even if we allow for nineteenth-century conventions about the place of woman in home and
society, Judge Wilhelm's marriage is prima facie
suspect.

It is suspect because of its tidiness and its facility.
The Assessor's wife has presumably "chosen herself
in her eternal validity"; otherwise she would not have
been capable of the marriage vow. And yet, by her
husband's theory, her reality consists in being his "finitude." She organizes the Judge's finitude in a way that
is perfectly consonant with his will. Her "absolute"
self is identical with her relationship to her man. She
is all freedom qua human, and all nature qua woman
and wife.

It appears that the Judge has protested too much.
At one and the same time he affirms his wife's freedom
and the nice compliance of her freedom with his. Is
this not, in a very subtle way, just what Johannes did
with Cordelia? Judge Wilhelm says that sentimentality,

because it is unrealistic, is the same as heartlessness.[85]
Is it not sentimental of him to base "the aesthetic validity of marriage" on his wife's docility? Hasn't he
handled her rather heartlessly by presuming that her
freedom is his nature? To the extent that he makes
of his wife's humanity a willing plasticity to his own
prerogative the Judge, like the Seducer, is sentimen-
tally calloused. "I cannot blame the Judge," says the
voice of another pseudonym,

> *for his enthusiastic zeal in behalf of marriage; but
> nevertheless I think that the Judge, supposing I could
> get hold of him and whisper a little secret in his ear,
> will concede that there are difficulties he did not take
> into account.*[86]

The suspicion that there is a dishonesty lurking in
the upright heart of Judge Wilhelm is borne out by
the "Ultimatum" that concludes *Either/Or* II.[87] As
the "Diary of the Seducer" draws the ultimate consequences of aestheticism, so this ultimatum exposes the
presuppositions of the ethical life. In form it is a sermon, composed by an old classmate of the Assessor,
now priest of a lonely parish on the northern moors
of Jutland. The sermon has been sent by its author
to Judge Wilhelm, who in turn passes it along to *A*.
The priest in his religious solitude reminds the Judge
of his young friend's aesthetic isolation.[88] The sermon
says briefly all that Judge Wilhelm said at length in
his letters; indeed it says more and says it more felici-
tously. In the note which accompanies the sermon,
the Judge advises *A* to read it and think of himself,
for, he adds, "I have read it and thought of myself."[89]

[85] Cf. ibid., vol. II, p. 183.

[86] Kierkegaard, *Concluding Unscientific Postscript*, Princeton University Press, Princeton, N.J., 1944, p. 161.

[87] Kierkegaard, *Either/Or,* vol. II, pp. 339–56.

[88] Ibid., vol. II, p. 341.

[89] Ibid., vol. II, p. 342.

Just as *A* was unsettled by the vision of his extremity in the Seducer's Diary, so Judge Wilhelm is disturbed by this sermon, which is no more than the last word on his own life. It is an ultimatum issued to the ethicist by a representative of the religious.

The title of the sermon is "The Edification Implied in the Thought that as against God We Are Always in the Wrong." Its text (Luke 19:41–48) describes the prophetic lamentations of Jesus over Jerusalem. From the inclusion of the innocent with the guilty in the sack of Jerusalem, the priest infers: Are we not all guilty as over against God? And is this not the most edifying (*opbyggelige,* literally "upbuilding" or "constructive") thought a man can have? Trying to calculate one's moral worth by reference to human standards leads to disquietude and doubt of self, never to certainty and self-assurance. But before God we are always in the wrong, and in this knowledge we find rest and peace.

The words of Jesus to the doomed city of Jerusalem may be an oblique complaint of the fluency of Judge Wilhelm's self-understanding:[90] "If thou hadst known in this thy day, even thou, the things which belong unto thy peace! but now they are hid from thine eyes. . . . Thou knewest not the time of thy visitation." The Judge confidently builds his peace on the conviction of the essential rightness of his life: When a man lives ethically he is always good in principle even though he occasionally does wrong. The Jutland priest counters: Whatever the relative rights and wrongs of a man's conduct, he can find repose only in the understanding that he is always guilty as against the Absolute.

Kierkegaard's priest is suggesting that dogged persistence in an ethical way of life will bring a man to the

---

[90] Cf. ibid., vol. II, pp. 243–44, for Judge Wilhelm's use of this same text against the aesthete. It is standard practice for Kierkegaard's pseudonyms to comment on each other, often with the effect of reciprocal or transitive irony. See the last section of this chapter.

point where he must either choose to acknowledge
himself absolutely in the wrong or lose himself in a
maze of casuistries. If he does not reach this point he
deceives himself and shortchanges his principles. The
sermon strikes at the assumptions that underlie Judge
Wilhelm's views, especially his assumption of an easy
harmony of freedom and nature in human action. To
make his point, the priest examines the case of a relationship between two lovers. Love is the Judge's spe-
cialty, but the priest considers a possibility that never
arises in the Assessor's life or thought. Suppose, he
says, there is a radical conflict between lover and beloved. How can such a conflict be reconciled? Will the
lover spend himself computing the rights and wrongs
of each party to the relationship? Even if that were not
an impossible task, such pettiness would hardly be-
speak a deep and sincere love. Will he assert his own
rightness as against the beloved? If he does, then it is
not the beloved but his rightness that he loves. The
true lover will neither defend himself nor bargain for
advantages; the true lover will without reservation
choose to be in the wrong that his beloved may be
right and their love secured. Only the thought that he
is in the wrong will quiet his anxiety, heal the breach,
and preserve their love.[91]

It may be objected that a human relationship is a
thing compounded of relativities and appropriately judged by less than absolute standards. No man
is absolutely right or absolutely wrong over against
another man. There will be a comparative right and a
comparative wrong, but no total guilt. This objection
would be valid were it not that Judge Wilhelm's ethics
makes an absolute claim; he must either make good
the claim or relapse into the "paltriness" which both
he and the aesthete disdain.

According to Judge Wilhelm a man *chooses himself
absolutely* when in repentance he takes his whole past

[91] Ibid., vol. II, pp. 349–50.

and in duty his whole future under the lordship of his freedom. It is his freedom assuming responsibility for his nature that constitutes his absolute worth as a human being. The priest does not contest the notion that a human being has absolute worth or that it is by his freedom that he has it. His doubts, reflected in the story of the unhappy lovers, concern man's ability to master his own life as completely as the Judge's theory requires. If the Judge supposes that such conflicts are impossible in his own marriage, that marriage is built on an illusion. And when such conflicts occur, they cannot be resolved by moral computation in a way that meets the Judge's ethical demand. No man acquires his "eternal validity" by coming off better in a quarrel with his wife. If the ethical man is in earnest about choosing himself in his eternal validity, he will have to choose himself as he is in relation to the Absolute. And if the true lover would not wish to be right as against his beloved, what man could will to be anything but absolutely in the wrong before God?[92] If Judge Wilhelm means what he says, he will make the leap from an ethical to a religious mode of existence.

Judge Wilhelm thinks that a man can get behind his whole history and push. He claims to do by means of repentance what he finds the aesthete unable to do by means of imagination: to overtake himself and take himself over completely. But he cannot get himself in hand, as the case of his marriage shows. He may try to persuade himself of the malleability of his own—and his wife's!—immediacy. But the slightest discord in their marital harmony will reveal obscurities of nature not illumined by freedom. The attempt to explore these recesses will issue either in the degradation of marriage into moral horse trading, or in the hardening of sentimentality into self-deception. The act of repentance does not solve all the concrete problems to which a man may be exposed in daily life. Nor does devotion to

duty guarantee a man against the contingency of future
moral impasse: the Judge may yet encounter actual
duties he cannot perform and particular obligations
he cannot fulfill. He may, for example, find himself
presented by his children, for whom he has assumed responsibility by begetting them, with unsurmountable
barriers to his own rectitude. If the aesthete can be
surprised by unquenchable joy, Judge Wilhelm may
be brought up short by unredeemable guilt. He is not
his own captain after all. Aesthetic freedom flees from
life; ethical freedom takes life as a task. But ethical
freedom can no more empower a man to control his
destiny than aesthetic freedom can shield him from
it.

Of course the Judge is no stranger to guilt. But
whereas he takes his guilt as a moral challenge, he
would be better advised to see it as moral defeat. The
affirmation of guilt does nothing to get rid of it, and
herein lies the tragedy of the ethical life. If a man is
to achieve selfhood by freedom, he must shoulder
responsibility for the past, even for "the sins of the
fathers."[93] But he is incapable of eliminating or re-
forming that past and therefore barred from meeting the
absolute demand of duty. The ethical battle is lost
before it begins. A man may recognize this and console
himself with that "worldly wisdom" which the priest
caricatures in the words: One does what one can.[94]
But who knows what he can do? He may either assume that he can do all that he should, which is presuming too much; or he may conclude that he only
can do what in fact he does, and by this he gets rid
of repentance, duty, and his title to absolute worth
at one stroke. In any case freedom, which is potent
to make a man guilty, is impotent to remove guilt.
The evil that a man does is his own doing, and he is
answerable for it. But since it has become an ineradi-

[93] Cf. ibid., vol. II, p. 222.
[94] Ibid., vol. II, pp. 346–48, 353–54.

cable part of his past, he cannot answer to one in a thousand. A man can no more consolidate his self ethically than he can compose it poetically, for immediacy conspires to righteousness as little as it does to beauty. The ethical man is involved in a complicity with evil and a duplicity in himself from which he can find release nowhere but in religion. When he admits defeat, a man's personality is constituted absolutely (. . . as against God) in the only way it can be (always in the wrong . . .).

So long as he continues to be satisfied with what he ekes out by his own freedom, Judge Wilhelm knows not the things that belong to his peace. In the despair which he commends to *A* and enacts as the prelude to his own life he is close to apprehending his predicament. But he identifies despair with self-choice, and so reveals that the despair was incomplete. A thoroughgoing despair would exhaust the self and leave it no strength with which to make reprise of itself. Speaking *in persona* Johannes Climacus, Kierkegaard says:

> The difficulty is, that the ethical self is supposed to be found immanently in the despair, so that the individual by persisting in his despair at last wins himself. . . . But this avails nothing. When I despair, I use myself to despair, and therefore I can indeed by myself despair of everything; but when I do this, I cannot by myself come back. In this moment of decision it is that the individual needs divine assistance. . . .[95]

But Judge Wilhelm does not discern the time of his visitation and misses the *divinum auxilium* to sink back into the comfortable fiction of his own competence.

To be fair to him, Judge Wilhelm is a pious man. The name of God occurs frequently in his letters; he even speaks of learning about God through pain and

[95] Kierkegaard, *Concluding Unscientific Postscript*, pp. 230–31.

distress.[96] But where his piety is not a vague surcharge of feeling, it tends to be a vague support for his self-confidence. He writes, for instance, of his delight that he "can come to the aid of the Deity" by freely appropriating everything that happens to him, the joyful as well as the sorrowful.[97] Yet it is a long way from religion as ethical prop and ethical decor to the knowledge of God of which the Jutland priest is speaking. The God of the religious way of life appears not in ethical victory, but only in the shipwreck of freedom on the shoals of guilt. Judge Wilhelm's religion is as sentimental as his marriage. It too easily becomes a caviling with God, a will to be always in the right and to have the world on his own terms. His distrust of the people he calls "exceptions," those unfortunate people who cannot put body and soul together in the ethically approved fashion, his satisfaction with his own familial and social life, and his ever-sanguine conscience show that he has not chosen himself with utter honesty. His ethics succeeds aesthetically as well as it does because he cheats a little here and there—which is to say, he cheats absolutely. A serious choice of himself would not automatically bring him to a lovely concord of freedom and nature, man and wife, individual and society. A serious self-choice would isolate him before God in the awareness of his inadequacy to render account of himself. It would leave him no alternatives but God or nothing.

Therefore, the priest tells his hearers, choose yourself. But choose yourself as you are: in the wrong against God. You lose yourself eternally as long as you continue to absolutize your freedom. You gain yourself eternally as soon as you recognize your nothingness. The decision for absolute guilt—and it is a decision, not reached by calculation but taken in freedom—is the only edifying (constructive) decision available. This is the act of freedom by which a man's self

96 Kierkegaard, *Either/Or*, vol. II, pp. 241–43.
97 Ibid., vol. II, p. 255; cf. also p. 125.

acquires absolute worth: the choice of his self as worthless in relation to God. If a man would not deceive himself with a tender notion of himself, let him abandon the hope that he can justify his life, and prefer the sober consolation of guilt. If he would not stultify himself with the thought that he can always do well by doing good, let him inspire himself to action by the thought of guilt, unencumbered by the necessity to be right or to become ever and ever righter. If he would not be reduced to the jejune expedient of making himself up as he goes along ("One does what one can"), let him take the painful but redeeming option of religion.

Summarizing the "stages on life's way," Kierkegaard wrote, "While aesthetic existence is essentially enjoyment, and ethical existence, essentially struggle and victory, religious existence is essentially suffering. . . ."[98] An aesthete's life is organized around pleasure, an ethical life around the opposition of good and evil. The religious life is a life in which *God* is acknowledged as the sole sufficient point of reference for human existence. Reflection on the nature of God shows that such a life is necessarily a life of suffering.

God may be called Absolute Reality, Absolute Power, *id quo majus cogitari non potest, ipsum esse, Qui est*—or any of an indefinite number of comparable names. And they are all correct. But none of them really defines or describes God. For if God is the *Absolute,* then He is transcendent of everything that can be known by men, all of which is but relative. God is altogether *other* than man and man's world. His existence, therefore, cannot be proven nor His nature conceived. To demonstrate or delineate God would be to bring Him within the ambit of finite reason and so to demean His absoluteness. Anything said about God discredits Him, except this confession itself.[99]

[98] Kierkegaard, *Concluding Unscientific Postscript*, p. 256.

[99] This theme runs throughout all of Kierkegaard's writings. For a concise statement of it, cf. Kierkegaard, *Philosophical*

Nevertheless God can be experienced. Because He is wholly other than man, He can be encountered as the negation of everything human. This is what happens in the experience of guilt; when a man admits the impossibility of legislating, enacting, and warranting his own conduct, he is exposed to God. God is the infinite nothingness that appears in the failure of the finite. Whenever some finite hope or finite assurance breaks down, there is an access to God. Whenever all human possibilities—aesthetic, intellectual, moral—are exhausted, there God is present. This is true especially of man's religiousness; human attempts to make contact with God must be frustrated before God Himself can break through. For if God is God, then every endeavor to build one's life (edify oneself) on anything less than the recognition of God—be it so crass as pleasure, so respectable as duty, or so sublime as piety—is an idol interposed between man and God. It is only when his idols crumble that a man can know God.

This knowledge of God, attained in the disaster of everything taken for God, but not God, is *identical with* the experience of the nothingness of man. Though He is in Himself the fullness of reality (*ens realissimum*) as the classical theologians said, God is only known to man as man's emptiness. Where there is uncertainty, despair, the consciousness of guilt, suffering without relief—there also is the experience of God. There *is* God, for the meaning of God in human experience is just the suffering of guilt implicit in the renunciation of every idol. God is, from a human point of view, urgently and manifestly at hand only in the dissolution of man and man's idolatry.[100]

Judge Wilhelm's idol is his freedom and his sup-

Fragments, Princeton University Press, Princeton, N.J., 1962, chap. III, "The Absolute Paradox: A Metaphysical Crotchet."

[100] Another persistent Kierkegaardian theme. Cf. Kierkegaard, *Edifying Discourses,* Augsburg, Minneapolis, 1943–46, vol. IV, pp. 7–47; Kierkegaard, *Thoughts on Crucial Situations in Human Life,* Augsburg, Minneapolis, 1941, pp. 1–41.

posed self-mastery. Yet that idol is his way to God. It is an idol because he makes an absolute claim for it; it can lead him to God because it fails to support the weight laid upon it, and in crashing down brings his life to the ground with it. There, his half-gods destroyed, the ethical man is before God. His guilt is the time of his visitation. For any man who entrusts his life to his own or any finite power, it is a terrible thing to fall into the hands of the living God. For such a man God is wrath; as the only Absolute, He is the enemy of man's attempt to be his own destiny. Man is always "against" God insofar as he understands himself in aesthetic or ethical terms, and therefore always guilty.

But God, whom no man can see and live, is also the source of all being, the creator and revivifier of men. The thought of guilt is the edifying thought, because it provides the solid ground on which life can be built without fear of ruin. There is, as Kierkegaard says, a necessary misunderstanding between man and God, since they are opposites. But there is also the possibility for man of an enthusiastic endurance of this misunderstanding.[101] This endurance, which Kierkegaard calls "worship," is the other side of the encounter with God.

"Worship," in Kierkegaard's language, means the recognition in practice of the "infinite qualitative difference" between man and God, the everlasting remembering of guilt.[102] Such a worship is entirely private, since God and His relation to man exceed all liturgical representation and devotional expression. Nevertheless it is the reservoir from which the religious man draws the waters of life. When he owns himself guilty, he is not confessing that he broke some of God's rules; the consciousness of inevitable and total guilt could not be arrived at by drawing up a balance

[101] Kierkegaard, *Concluding Unscientific Postscript*, pp. 239–40.
[102] Ibid., p. 369.

sheet. Kierkegaard's word for guilt (*Skyld*) means originally "debt." To know oneself guilty in a religious sense is to know oneself *in debt to* God. The religious man *owes himself* completely to God.[103] He is aware that the self which is reduced to impotence in the presence of God is also upheld by the divine power. In his weakness he is sustained by a power not his own, for he has dried up his sources in despair. Unlike the aesthete, who poetizes himself, and the ethical man, who sits in judgment on himself, the religious man *receives* himself as a gift from God. Outwardly he does not differ from other men: he enjoys life like the aesthete, and he works at his responsibilities like the ethical man. Yet he is inwardly supported neither by fate nor by freedom, but by the consciousness that all he is or does is a divine gratuity.

The difference between the religious man and the ordinary man, Kierkegaard often describes in language like this: The ordinary man gets up in the morning, shaves, dresses, eats breakfast, kisses his wife good-bye, and goes to work; the religious man gets up in the morning, shaves, dresses, eats breakfast, kisses his wife good-bye, and goes to work. The difference, in other words, is invisible. For the ordinary man these things are his life, and if they are taken away his life is over. For the religious man God is his life; wife, work, and the like are concessions with which he is indulged, though he has no stake in them nor they in him. If God were to withdraw them all—well and good. He is prepared to give them up, in fact has already given them up in the suffering with which he detaches his self from the world and commits it to God. And when he finds (unlike the aesthete and the ethical man he is ever mindful of his weakness) that he has not the strength to perfect this resignation, when he clings to that which he should let go of—especially then in the depths of guilt he is restored to himself. He is both

103 Kierkegaard, *Edifying Discourses*, vol. II, p. 77.

given and forgiven his self. God's annihilation is a
creation, and the suffering of guilt by man is one with
the sufferance of guilt by God.[104] This is the unique
"withdrawal and return" of the religious life, parallel-
ing but transcending like movements in the aesthetic
and ethical spheres.

Kierkegaard's edifying discourses, which he published under his own name and in which he speaks
directly from the religious point of view, portray this
dialectic of annihilation and restoration over and over
again from many approaches. One of the simplest is a
discourse on the text of St. James, "Every Good and
Every Perfect Gift is from Above."[105] The believer
acknowledges, he says, that everything comes ultimately
from God. Man's opportunity and his task is to receive
what God gives. Whatever happens is a good and perfect gift if it is received with the recollection of guilt
(total indebtedness) and with thanksgiving to God.
Prosperity may tempt a man to the impudence of complacency; adversity can tempt him to the despair of
self-rejection. The religious man must remember God
and his own guilt and give thanks, in prosperity or
adversity, for whatever happens. The aesthete thinks
that life owes him a living; the ethical man is proud to
earn his own living. The religious man renounces every
attempt to get a purchase on life and makes himself
nothing before God but a grateful and humble recipient. This is no more than an alternate way of saying
that "we are always in the wrong" against God. The
religious man has learned the lesson of Job: We "have
no rights" (*have altid Uret*) to maintain against God.
His claim on us is absolute—He is God—but we have
no claim on Him nor on the world nor on ourselves.
Our selves and our world, like every good and every
perfect gift, come from above.

[104] Kierkegaard, *Concluding Unscientific Postscript*, pp.
347–493 passim.
[105] Jas. 1:17ff. Kierkegaard, *Edifying Discourses*, vol. I, pp.
34–55.

This discourse, along with many others, makes evident that the religious life is a repetition, but at a higher level, of the aesthetic life. Like the aesthete, the religious man receives rather than makes himself; but whereas the aesthete is at the mercy of a fate which he frantically tries to elude, the religious man is at the mercy of God, which he embraces with enthusiasm. Like the aesthete, the religious man is a spiritual hermit (compare Victor Eremita, editor of *Either/Or,* with the lonely Jutland priest); but whereas the aesthete is demonically shut up in himself, the religious man is alone with God, the giver of all good. Like the aesthete, the religious man suffers; but whereas the aesthete suffers his own vanity, the religious man is oppressed by the excess of divine bounty. The difference and the similarity are due to the fact that the religious man has passed through the crisis of ethical freedom and its demise in guilt. He is able and willing to receive himself because he knows the futility of trying to create himself. He can repose in solitude because he has been disabused of the idea that he can effect a neat consonance of freedom and nature. He can sorrow joyfully, because he knows that his abasement is God's glory.

Yet what Judge Wilhelm said of immediacy—that it is given its rightful place by ethics—can be said of both the aesthetic and the ethical by the religious man. The life that is received from God includes moral striving as well as enjoyment; from his private understanding with God the religious man is enabled to return to the life of community. The pleasures of love and the daily responsibilities of marriage—which in his heart he sacrifices to God—are given back to him with the cup of his religious suffering. He knows that he has them as moratoria from God. They are not his fate, but neither must he accrue them out of his own resources. That he is in debt to God means that he is released by God to the possession of his life without concern lest he lose it and without the anxiety of failure; for he has

already failed and he has already given up succeeding.
Woe to the man, Kierkegaard says, who succeeds
against God! Blessed the man who is strong enough to
be weak and poor in spirit before God![106]

"A man has only one God," Kierkegaard wrote,
"and if he cannot reach an understanding with Him,
to whom, then, shall he go?"[107] That he himself is
nothing means to the religious man that God is all in all.
This is the unfailing certainty that emancipates him
from slavery to nature and himself, and delivers him
to his beatitude. The self which he could not find in
nature or in flight from nature, the self that he could
not earn for himself, he first receives—in its eternal and
absolute validity—when he abandons it to God. By the
decision to be in the wrong as against God he is armed
against despair and inspired to action. No longer tormented by the bad dreams of the aesthete nor defeated
by the illusions of the ethicist, he knows in his day the
things that belong to his peace. In the confidence that
God is all and in all he has found the rock on which to
edify his life.

4

Naked and Alone We Came into Exile

On his own allegation Kierkegaard's writing was
coerced from him by the press of two urgent questions:
What is it to be a man? and What is it to be a Christian?
Not that there was in his day a shortage of answers
to these questions; he felt there were too many and too
facile answers, and not enough understanding of the
questions. The voracious Hegelian philosophy had dialectically devoured human existence and Christian

---

[106] Cf. Kierkegaard, *Repetition*, p. 133; Kierkegaard, *Fear
and Trembling* and *The Sickness unto Death*, Doubleday Anchor Books, Garden City, N.Y., 1954, p. 31.

[107] Kierkegaard, *Thoughts on Crucial Situations in Human
Life*, p. 33.

faith, and was regurgitating their speculative meaning in compendia predigested for popular consumption. Kierkegaard distrusted the agility with which speculation explained everything, and set himself to make things hard that everyone else was making easy.[108] His program in books like the *Philosophical Fragments* and the *Concluding Unscientific Postscript* was to rehearse the difficulty of the questions by means of a polemic against the ready speculative answers.

Kierkegaard was convinced that the questions—What does it mean to exist? What does it mean to believe?— were so ordered that the latter could not be discussed until the sense of the former had been clarified. It is after all a *man* who *believes*. Moreover, the question of the meaning of human existence had to be raised existentially before the attack on speculation could have its effect.[109] In the stages on life's way Kierkegaard prepares an existential setting for philosophical consideration of this question. The stages, not described by a disinterested observer but dramatized by representative *personae,* suggest that human existence is amenable to a diversity of living interpretations, each consistent in itself, each provident of a unique perspective on the others, and each irreducibly distinct from the others. For in spite of the ascending scale in which he presents them (aesthetic, ethical, religious), and in spite of his own commitment to the religious, Kierkegaard never lost sight of the fact that each existence-sphere is a way of life eligible and enactable by a human being, and that the only passage from one stage to another is a radically free choice entailing a wholesale revision of the personality and its world.

To the question: What is man? there are as many existing answers as there are existing men. The stages on life's way are the larger categories into which the answers fall, but each man by living his own individual

108 Kierkegaard, *Concluding Unscientific Postscript*, pp. 164–67.

109 Ibid., pp. 223–24.

life works out his own unique solution to the problem of the meaning of human existence. This fact supplies a motif for Kierkegaard's critique of speculative philosophy. If life has an indefinite plurality of meanings in the concrete, then it has no one definitive meaning in the abstract, and it is perverse of the theorist to "discover" such a meaning and package it for retail distribution.

With this consideration and the previous discussion in mind it is possible to unravel passages like this:

> Man *is* spirit. But what is spirit? Spirit is the self. But what is the self? The self is a relation which relates itself to its own self, or it is that in the relation, that the relation relates itself to its own self; the self is not the relation, but that the relation relates itself to its own self. Man is a synthesis of infinity and finitude, the temporal and the eternal, freedom and necessity, in short a synthesis. A synthesis is a relation between two. So regarded man is not yet a self.
>
> In the relation between two the relation is the third term as a negative unity, and the two relate themselves to the relation, and in the relation to the relation; such a relation is that between body and soul, when man is regarded as soul. If on the contrary the relation relates itself to its own self, then this relation is the positive third term, and this is the self.[110]

This is not the gobbledygook it seems to be, though there is good reason why it must seem so.

By classical philosophers the human self was interpreted as a psychophysical duality. Plato takes man to be a synthesis of reason and appetite. What he calls "spirit" is merely the togetherness that unites the other two. It is "the third term as a negative unity" of *eros* and *nous,* in and to which they are bound. Allied in the good man with reason and in the bad man with de-

---

[110] Kierkegaard, *Fear and Trembling* and *The Sickness unto Death,* p. 146.

sire, "spirit" is *nothing but* the ascendancy of one over the other in a given personality.[111] The pagan, Kierkegaard says, always conceives the self as *nature*. For Plato the soul, like any other object or event, is a point of engagement for the cosmic forces of form and dynamic. For Aristotle the human self, like any other entity, is a substantial juncture of form (soul) with matter (body).[112] It is in either case the nature of the universe, writ small in human nature, that determines man to be what he is.

Suppose now the self is understood as *spirit*. According to Kierkegaard, this is the view of Christianity, though its vision has often been skewed by the Greek spectacles through which it has looked at its own revelation. In this version the union of psychic and somatic elements in the self is effected not by the nature of things, but by some "positive third term." This third term that positively joins body and soul ("that in the relation, that the relation relates itself to its own self") is the *self-consciousness* by which the psychophysical synthesis transcends itself as nature and asserts itself as spirit. The self as spirit is the natural synthesis of body and soul become *conscious* of itself and *free* with respect to itself.

Freedom (or self-consciousness: the terms are finally synonymous in Kierkegaard) does not fit the naturalistic understanding of man at all. It is not the substantial essence of man (as such it would be determined), nor an accidental attribute or operation of man (it is the *sine qua non* of selfhood), nor an essential property or power of man (as such it would be causally implicated in his essence and so determined). It cannot be defined, derived, or demonstrated by a study of human nature, for definition, derivation, and demonstration are equivalent to determination, and a freedom determined by nature is a contradic-

---

[111] *Republic*, 434D–441C; *Phaedrus*, 246Aff.

[112] *De Anima*, II, 1, 2.

tion in terms. Presupposed in every human act, self-consciousness is necessarily inscrutable; it is always behind the thinker and within him, never wholly outside him or before him. Freedom can only be conceived *via remotionis* as the original undemonstrable source, the undefinable insubstantial essence, and the continuing self-initiating act of spirit.[113]

This is the "relation which relates itself to its own self": freedom, self-consciousness, or (which is the same thing) the self understood as spirit. Its reality is indicated by men's moments of ultimate self-surpassing —e.g., suicidal despair and self-sacrificing love—and by the ostensible difference between man and beast—such as the ubiquity of culture among men and its total absence among animals; the fact that the beast never gives himself an image of himself, whereas man is always trying to live up to the self he thinks he is or wants to be; the circumstance that man the adverbial creature lusts shamefully, loves beautifully, and kills cruelly, while the beast can only mate, tend its young, and prey. But though it is everywhere hinted at, the self remains a mystery that eludes the understanding. That is why Kierkegaard "defines" it in impossibly tortured paradoxes. He is holding the jargon of his contemporaries against them, to show that when one tries to grasp human nature categorically, he comes up with nonsense.

Yet the irony is soberly drawn, and the paradoxes mean just what they say. Human existence is not a unity of form and matter embedded in nature. Existence as spirit is the collision in man of nature (the psychophysical synthesis) and freedom (the self-consciousness of this synthesis which robs it of substantiality and negates it as nature).[114] "The self is not the relation, but that the relation relates itself to its own self."

---

[113] Kierkegaard, *The Concept of Dread*, Princeton University Press, Princeton, N.J., 1957, pp. 20, 96–97, 99–101.
[114] Kierkegaard, *Concluding Unscientific Postscript*, pp. 74–86.

Kierkegaard often describes human existence as a passion (*Lidenskab, passio*) inflicted by the straits in which the self is placed: Man must forge his self by freedom, but the very capacity of transcendence that makes him a man upsets the stability of any self so achieved. To be spirit is to forfeit the security of nature; to be free is to lack the solace of natural determination.[115] Unlike the animal who simply *is* what he *is,* man suffers as spirit the need and the contradiction of *becoming* what he *can be.*

The rationale for the "gobbledygook" is now clear enough: If we try to understand man as he is, we fail; for by nature man is not. "So regarded man is not yet a self." The theoretical discussion of immediacy reinforces the conclusion at which the aesthete arrived existentially: Immediately man is nothing but a lack (of a given self), a prospect (of acquiring himself as spirit), and a friction (between nature and freedom as the conditions of spiritual selfhood). The aesthete is described as "an existential possibility that cannot win through to existence."[116] Answering to the chaotic poetry of the aesthetic life, the aesthetic element in man ("that by which he immediately is what he is") is limned in contradictions. The force of Kierkegaard's paradoxes is to define human nature by pointing up the impossibility of defining it. His existential philosophy —which could not be written until the inhabitants of the existence-spheres had exfoliated imaginatively the richness and the poverty, the glory and the horror of human life—is a ponderous ironic epitaph over every philosophy of existence.

It is therefore important, when reading Kierkegaard's "philosophical" works, to respect their avowed fragmentary and unscientific character. Above all it is necessary to take him at his word when he says he has

115 Ibid., pp. 177–78, 276–78, 313–14.
116 Ibid., p. 226; cf. pp. 262–64.

no opinions and proposes no doctrines.[117] For the
matter under discussion is human existence, concerning which the point to be made is that opinions and
doctrines are beside the point.

In 1842 and 1843 Kierkegaard made sketches for a
book to be called *Johannes Climacus,* or *De Omnibus
Dubitandum Est: A Story.*[118] *De omnibus dubitandum
est* had been the motto of Descartes, but the Hegelians
had interpreted methodological doubt to mean: Philosophy cannot begin by assuming anything; the philosopher must isolate and think through all of his presuppositions so as to get behind them to an absolute
starting-point for constructive speculation. The formula
of Cartesian doubt became for the Hegelians the charter
of philosophical absolutism.

Kierkegaard knew that the program of universal
doubt could not be carried through. The philosopher
can no more get behind all his presuppositions than
Judge Wilhelm could get behind his whole history; to
do so he would have to step outside space and time
and his own intellectual skin. Reflective thought, gen-
erating as many problems as it solves, is potentially
infinite. Its momentum is never halted by itself, but by
an act of will incalculably arbitrary in relation to the
possibilities yet to be considered. The simplest question
becomes a hydra of prosyllogisms if one attempts to
evoke a completely rational answer: Which girl shall I
marry? becomes Shall I marry? What is marriage? What
is man? *ad infinitum.* In the end one marries—or does
not marry—without sufficient reason. Human deliber-
ations are never final, and there is no absolute beginning for philosophy.[119] If a philosopher says he has

[117] Ibid., pp. 545–50; Kierkegaard, *Philosophical Fragments,*
pp. 5–7.

[118] Stanford University Press, Stanford, Calif., 1958.

[119] The whole of *Johannes Climacus* pokes fun at the attempt to find an absolute starting point for philosophy; cf. especially pp. 130–42. Cf. also Kierkegaard, *Concluding Unscientific Postscript,* pp. 101–6.

doubted everything he is lying, and in fact the wind-bagging arrogance of the Hegelians proved them charlatans who never meant to practice what they preached. *Johannes Climacus* was to be the story of a young man ingenuously in love with thought, who took the philosophers literally and *did* doubt everything, beginning with common sense and science, moving through history, ethics, and religion, and ending with himself. He doubted himself or rather, despaired of himself—for he was not a philosopher writing about doubt but a man actually doubting—so thoroughly that he lost himself beyond hope of recovery. The thread of his personality was snapped, a victim of the irresponsible gabble of the philosophers.[120]

But the book was never finished. Kierkegaard soon perceived that it was not an excess of doubt, but an excess of certainty that was the real peril. Not skeptical modesty but the grandiloquent self-assurance of speculative thought prevented men from apprehending the paradox of existence and the prerequisites of faith. *Philosophical Fragments* and *Concluding Unscientific Postscript* are devoted to undermining this assurance by exposing the weakness of its foundations.

Philosophical Fragments (ascribed to Johannes Climacus as author) poses the question:

> *Is an historical point of departure possible for an eternal consciousness; how can such a point of departure have any other than a merely historical interest; is it possible to base an eternal happiness upon historical knowledge?*[121]

In effect this is the question: Is Christianity true? though the problem is not dressed in its "historical costume."[122] More significant is the fact that the ques-

---

120 Kierkegaard, *Johannes Climacus*, pp. 101–2.
121 Kierkegaard, *Philosophical Fragments*, title page.
122 Ibid., p. 137.

tion is not answered. In his Preface Johannes Climacus warns the reader that he cherishes no opinion in the matter, but only executes a kind of nimble dance with death in the service of thought, to the honor of God, and for his own satisfaction.[123] The question is proposed "in ignorance, by one who does not even know what can have led him to ask it."[124]

What is given in lieu of an answer is two hypotheses: (1) that the temporal moment in which a man glimpses eternal truth is but an insignificant episode in the career of his immortal soul; (2) that the "historical point of departure for an eternal consciousness" is a crucial instant in which the truth first comes to exist for him who learns it. These are the hypotheses, respectively, of Socrates, for whom learning is a recollection, occasionable at any time by any teacher, of truths already latent in the mind of the learner; and of Christ, for whom learning is a conversion of the soul from the willful error of Sin, by a unique Teacher who, in an instant that is the Fullness of Time, imparts both the Truth and the Faith to acknowledge it, a Teacher who is therefore Judge, Saviour, Redeemer, Atoner, God-in-Time.[125]

The opposition of Socrates the midwife to Christ the Mediator is not the opposition of human reason to the irrational, Greek philosophy versus the scandal of the Cross. The Socratic ignorance testifies that human reason is invested with the potency to transcend itself in that which is other than itself. In its passion to think a reality distinct from itself, to immolate itself in sheer transparency to its object, reason is unwittingly at one with the eternal purposes of God in the Paradox of the God-Man. Man's offense at the unreasonableness of Christianity is the self-assertion of reason by which it defrauds itself of its beatitude, while faith is the happy self-surrender of reason to the Mystery of Reve-

123 Ibid., pp. 5–7.
124 Ibid., p. 9.
125 Ibid., pp. 11–27.

lation by which it is fulfilled. Christianity is not the frustration but the paradoxical satisfaction of human reason.[126]

What Climacus is getting at in the *Fragments*—hypothetically in chapter I, poetically in chapter II, metaphysically in chapter III and the Interlude, and epistemologically in chapters IV and V—is that the historicity of human life screws every truth, Greek or Christian, into a paradox, since truth is timeless and the truthseeker temporal.[127] For Socratic recollection the love of wisdom (philosophy) issues in the paradox: One must learn how to die. Rooted in the Miracle of Incarnation, Christian faith incurs a dialectical complication of Socratic recollection by taking the historicity of man to be his reality and not an accident of his eternal essence.

Climacus forces his reader into a corner where he must admit, not that the Christian hypothesis is true, for that "is an entirely different question, which cannot be decided in the same breath,"[128] but that there is no honest way of understanding human existence that can avoid contradiction. The enemy of human integrity is not doubt, as Kierkegaard had thought when he began *Johannes Climacus*. Socratic recollection respects the uncertainty of human knowledge by telling likely stories and ironically postponing all conclusions until the life hereafter; faith, which accepts uncertainty and transcends it in an act of assent, comprehends doubt within itself as a threat that is constantly being overcome.[129] The antagonist is not the man who denies the reality of eternity (the skeptic Sextus Empiricus or the sophist Protagoras), but the man who mitigates the reality of time in the interest of a simplistic doctrine of

[126] Ibid., pp. 46–67.
[127] Cf. Kierkegaard, *Concluding Unscientific Postscript*, pp. 169–210.
[128] Kierkegaard, *Philosophical Fragments*, p. 139.
[129] Ibid., pp. 97–106.

man. The final battle is pitched between the essentialist
philosopher who views life under the aspect of eternity
and the existential thinker who grapples daily with the
paradoxes of his life and surmounts them in recollection or in faith.[130]

But even this puts the matter much too abstractly
and neatly. The character of the *Philosophical Fragments* may suggest a metaphysical reading. But
Johannes Climacus—in his Preface, by his hypothetical
method, and in the whimsical conversations with an
imaginary interlocutor that follow each chapter—has
taken pains to disarm such an interpretation in advance.
By making light of everything he says, by accusing himself of plagiarizing God,[131] he reneges the conclusions
he implies and comes up with no results after all. The
book is literally fragmentary, "scrapings and parings of
systematic thought."[132] To the philosophical reader
who begs his theoretical opinion, Climacus' reply is
firm: No, thank you, I will not have this dance.

The motto of the book—a German rendition of
Shakespeare's "Many a good hanging has prevented a
bad marriage"—is "Better well hung than ill wed."[133]
Climacus' intent is to hang his reader on the contradiction—that there is no certainty in human knowledge
and that every moment is nevertheless a *kairos* that
demands decisive thought—rather than marry him
to a systematic "higher synthesis" that is eternally
finished with life before life is through with the thinker.
At the same time, inasmuch as it formally negates its
results and imposes on its reader the necessity of decision, the book is inversely self-justifying. Otherwise,
Climacus concludes: "How will we ever come to be-

[130] Ibid., pp. 47–48; Kierkegaard, *Concluding Unscientific
Postscript*, pp. 267–322.

[131] Kierkegaard, *Philosophical Fragments*, pp. 26–27, 43–45,
57–60, 66–67, 81–88, 132–38.

[132] Kierkegaard, *Concluding Unscientific Postscript*, p. 2.

[133] Kierkegaard, *Philosophical Fragments*, p. 2.

gin?" Just as the monks never finished telling the history of the world because they started anew each time with Creation, so we shall never get to live if we wait for the philosophers to explain life first.[134] To be hanged on the necessity of decision is the good hanging that prevents a bad marriage.

The details of the argument in the *Fragments,* as Climacus' interlocutor points out, can all be traced back to standard philosophical and theological sources.[135] The book is not designed to make a contribution to philosophy or theology—something that "every divinity student would be able to furnish"[136]— but to get the reader to risk his life in the service of understanding, to the glory of God, and for his own good. Insofar as it necessitates an intensified self-knowledge, it is a book in existential philosophy. And in view of the total incommensurability between essentialist speculation and Christian belief, the *Fragments* performs the only service any apologetic can render: It nails you to the incommensurability and leaves you hanging.

The *Fragments* approaches the problem of man by contrasting Socrates and Christ with each other and with the philosopher who "goes beyond" both by understanding neither. The philosopher of course is no "honest" Greek, but a "mendacious" Hegelian who makes bold to domicile human existence in the paragraphs of that "System" of "absolute knowledge" which in its completeness and finality claims to reflect unambiguously the workings of Absolute Mind. The *Concluding Unscientific Postscript* to the *Philosophical Fragments* (also by Johannes Climacus) affronts the deiform thinker outright by informing him that human life and its problems are nowhere contained in his philosophy.

134 Ibid., p. 138.
135 Ibid., pp. 26–27, 43–45, 66–67, 132–38.
136 Cf. Kierkegaard, *Concluding Unscientific Postscript,* p. 14.

Climacus remarks in the *Postscript* that Hegel had absentmindedly neglected to include an ethics in his philosophical system.[137] By this he does not mean that Hegel had forgotten to discuss matters ethical. Hegel's absentmindedness was of a less obvious sort. In his zeal to exhibit the rationality of history, *der Gang Gottes in der Welt,* he had failed to make provision for the *subject* of ethical concerns, the existing human being. If we sit in the Hegelian grandstand and look at the human individual, regarding him simply in his particularity, he becomes a perishing irrationality, the litter cast by the Absolute along the freeways of world history. To be sure he furthers the aims of God, but he does so chiefly in his capacity as cannon fodder. On the other hand, if we consider him in his "essential reality" and "universal truth," he is at once rapt into dialectical union with God. The soldier of the *Grande Armée,* who is (personally) splattered by a cannon ball, is (essentially) privileged to suffer the Golgotha of Absolute Spirit.

What Climacus calls "objective thought"—thinking that reifies whatever it thinks about—understands any individual, human or otherwise, only by regarding it as an instance of a universal. Underscoring *instance,* the individual is as nugatory as the dissected frogs discarded by a college zoology class. With the accent on *universal,* the individual takes on the dignity of an exemplar Idea in the mind of God. This kind of analysis may be appropriate for garlic and sapphires, mud and axletrees. It is inevitable that scientific thought should aspire to the condition of logic and conceive its objects as universals or cases of universals. But the human person is neither a category nor a statistic. Both dimensions are present in each man—he is at once eternal verity and vanishing trifle—but present as unsettled potentialities which he is obliged to arbitrate in a lifelong process of self-becoming. Because

137 Ibid., pp. 108, 110.

human existence is caught in the toils of time, particularity, and finitude, this process is a perpetual striving, spasmodically illuminated by intelligence and fancy, but uncheered by any promise of millennial reconciliation, either in a life after death or in the depths of present existence. No man can give himself apocalyptic surety of immortality, though he may *believe* in it ardently enough to die for it. And no man is helped by the idealist eschatology that asks him to sacrifice his self for a meaning so deeply rooted in being that it is unavailable for his personal comfort. Selfhood is neither given as an antecedent nor guaranteed as a consequent; it is a possibility which may be won or lost, but never enjoyed.[138]

In short, speculative philosophy is of no use if a man wants wisdom to live by. If it does not misconceive human existence naturalistically in the manner of pagan realism, it seeks prematurely to quiet the raging of spirit by recourse to the "fantastic shadow play"[139] of idealism. The philosopher who confuses life with intellection and scribbles paper answers to flesh-and-blood questions is like the poet insofar as he flees to an abstract eternity from the turmoils of time. But he lacks the poet's imaginative virtuosity, the endlessly resourceful ingenuity by which the aesthete lives his withdrawal from life. The philosopher therefore has not the poetic melancholy, and his life is not, like the poet's, tragic. He is a comic or at best a pathetic figure: the self-deceived *Privatdozent* who really believes that he breaks wind *sub specie aeternitatis,* or the drab old professor whose self is but the cast-off walking stick of his system.

For the existing individual there is neither a home in nature nor a place of rest beyond it. Man is "an infinite existing spirit."[140] And there is, as Kierkegaard said, "no such thing as immediate health of the

138 Ibid., pp. 97–113, 115–47, 267–322.
139 Ibid., p. 292.
140 Ibid., p. 75.

spirit."[141] Immediately man is but the possibility of
spirit, a bare "to be able"[142] anxiously placed between ideality (the domain of intellect and imagination) and reality (the spatiotemporal stretch of becoming). As spirit he is neither Platonic Idea nor
positivistic fact nor the perfect splice that classical
naturalism envisaged. His existence—the subjectivity
that Climacus says is truth and reality[143]—is his concern to catch an evanescent possibility in the mesh of
fact, and to regiment a scattered actuality under the
hegemony of ideal meanings. His "ethical [here =
"existential"] reality" is neither inner intent (intentions
are as cheap as the aesthete's daydreams) nor outer
act (the case of Judge Wilhelm shows the recalcitrance
of nature to man's resolutions), but the tension of his
will to move creatively from project to performance.[144]
In this tension and its pathos he has his life.

The freedom that is essential to selfhood and the
skein of contradiction from which this selfhood must
be woven proliferate problems that cannot even be
programmed by philosophic thought; nor do they admit the kind of solutions that can be appended as a
footnote to section 14 of the System, or filed for ready
reference on grave occasions. They can only be apprehended by a "subjective thinking"—thinking born in
passion rather than in disinterested curiosity, concerned
not with the contemplation of life in general but with
the conduct of this life in particular—that continually
experiences the anguish of the human estate and holds
out in its presence by continual resolve. The subjective
thinker is like the ethical man in that he is free (the
possibility of spirit) and therefore must himself integrate the given elements of personality into the unity
of a person (the obligation to become oneself). But

[141] Kierkegaard, *Fear and Trembling* and *The Sickness unto
Death*, p. 158.
[142] Kierkegaard, *The Concept of Dread*, pp. 40, 44.
[143] Kierkegaard, *Concluding Unscientific Postscript*, p. 306.
[144] Ibid., pp. 267–307.

he is more dreadfully on his own than Judge Wilhelm ever dreamed of. What he is by nature (say a male American twenty-one years old) is but a cluster of ambiguous possibilities whose eventuality (husband or hermit, patriot or expatriate, believer or blasphemer, success or suicide) is determined by the man himself. In this determination he is guided by no eternal truths (the temporality of his life stains their white radiance with uncertainty and change) and by no hard facts (his self-transcendence dissolves the brutality and dense reality of fact and brings it into the whirl of possibility). Knowledge is either (like logic and metaphysics) true in the abstract but doubtful in its application to existence; or empirically problematic (like natural science and history), its truth a desideratum ever out of reach.[145] "Subjective thinking" must be a "double reflection" that simultaneously sees the insufficiency of knowledge and tenaciously holds to the norm of its decisions.

To be man is to be, without security of nature or knowledge, compelled to make a security, a truth, for oneself. "Only the truth which edifies"—that is, builds up your self—"is truth for you." A human being is a freedom caught in the intersection of time and eternity, there constrained to mold in decision and action the integrity, the existing truth at once actual and ideal, that he does not have by nature and cannot find by taking thought.[146] Human existence is an *interest* (*inter-esse*), a being-between the terms of a contradiction that cannot be resolved but must be resolutely endured, an unrelieved and unceasing concern with the passion, the possibility, and the predicament of becoming oneself.[147]

Neither is the individual supported, in his quest for

145 Ibid., pp. 169–71.
146 Ibid., pp. 84–85.
147 Ibid., p. 279.

selfhood, by the solidarity of human society.[148] The
freedom which is the franchise of spirit disintegrates
every natural community, splintering family, state, and
race into a multitude of single human beings, each
isolated with the problems, pains, and prospects of his
own person. The existence of other men presents him
not with a public in which he is firmly set as a part
sustained by an organic whole, but only with further
possibilities—beckoning, tempting, or threatening—that
he must take into the gamut of his inner life.[149] His
own inwardness is the only reality to which he has entrance without trespass, and the only reality with which
he is properly occupied. The reality of others he can
only know, and by knowing, distance.[150] Whatever
community of spirit is established among men is strung
precariously across the chasm of freedom and made
fast at the ends only in the solitude of the self-concern
of each person. Sprung from nature but cut loose from
her umbilical, capable of knowledge but deprived of a
certainty equal to the demands of action, the existing
individual also stands, in the midst of his fellowmen,
essentially alone.

But this, as Climacus says whenever the philosophical rhetoric threatens to run away from him and tear
through the streets like a town crier of inwardness,
sounds a little too much like seriousness.[151] The *Postscript* is a humorous book. Its technique is not solemnly
to define man (not even with the bizarre solemnities of
existentialism), but to destroy by irony and indirection,
by lyric and by lampoon, the self-confidence of those
thinkers who are so thoughtless as to suppose that
man can be solemnly defined. When Climacus "defines"

---

[148] Cf. Kierkegaard, *The Present Age*, Oxford University
Press, London, 1940; also " 'The Individual': Two 'Notes' con-
cerning My Work as an Author" in Kierkegaard, *The Point of
View*.

[149] Kierkegaard, *Concluding Unscientific Postscript*, pp. 67–
74, 320–22.

[150] Ibid., pp. 282–92, 305.

[151] Ibid., pp. 163, 210; cf. also p. 71.

truth as "subjectivity," "an objective uncertainty held
fast in an appropriation process of the most passionate
inwardness,"[152] he is writing a satire on definition to
recall his reader from the illusory certainties of knowledge to the awareness that every belief and every truth
claim has no surer warrant than the freedom and the
fervor of him who asserts it. When he says that every
individual is isolated in his inwardness, he is not proposing a theory of human community, but reminding
those men who put their trust in the ways of culture and
the verdict of history that this commitment is an expression of their personal choice of themselves and not
a child of the *Zeitgeist* or a mass product of institutions and conventions.[153] The *Concluding Unscientific
Postscript*, faithful to the paradox of existence and the
"dialectics of communication," is a whimsical book
with a frighteningly sober purpose: to lead its reader
down a path of merriment to the brink of the bottom-
less pit of freedom and to surprise him with the awful
responsibility he bears for his own life. Read as a philosophical treatise it is nonsense; but the sense of the
nonsense is to strip away every veil that covers the
gravity of the human condition and thereby to force
the reader back on his own resources. To read the book
as Kierkegaard wrote it is to experience that dreadful
rebirth by which each of us comes naked and alone
into the exile of this extremity of spirit.

5

The Way of the Cross

The *Concluding Unscientific Postscript* opens with the
question: How can I, Johannes Climacus, become a
Christian? How can I or any man avail himself of the
eternal blessedness Christianity offers its adherents?[154]

152 Ibid., p. 182.
153 Ibid., pp. 115–67.
154 Ibid., p. 19.

Its conclusion is apparently irrelevant, largely negative, and certainly unscientific: Man exists in alienation from the world, without the consolations of objective certainty, without the uplifting arm of human community, without the vision of historical destiny, in a chaos of maybes. For such a being the quasi-aesthetic makeshifts of the philosopher have no valence, the poet's life is but the sigh of a shadow, and the brave self-confidence of the ethical man a whistling among the tombstones.

Yet the result is not negligible, for the man who has come up against his self in the emptiness of its need and the weight of its responsibility has also stood in the terrible presence of God. The situation of the existing individual which Kierkegaard's philosophical works depict by the tongue in cheek of theoretical indirection is the same as the situation of man presupposed in the edifying discourses: before God. God is at hand, Climacus writes, whenever the uncertainty of all things is thought without limit.[155] The uncertainty of all things is the fruition of freedom, which transforms all realities into possibilities. But he who rubs the wonderful lamp of freedom and invokes the geni of possibility has called up the Spirit that is his Lord.[156] For

> God is *that all things are possible, and that all things are possible is God; and only the man whose being has been so shaken that he became spirit by understanding that all things are possible, only he has had dealings with God.*[157]

To live in the anxiety of freedom, without finite support or encouragement, is to live by the power of God.

[155] Ibid., p. 80.
[156] Ibid., p. 124.
[157] Kierkegaard, *Fear and Trembling* and *The Sickness unto Death,* pp. 173–74.

When he describes the human predicament in terms of paradox and insists that human freedom is absolute, Kierkegaard is not recommending an heroic defiance of the absurdity of existence without God. The bravado of some of his epigoni would strike him as vainglorious rhetoric decorating an aesthetic refusal to face the real absurdity: that in the weakness of the finite the strength of the Infinite is given to man. His polemic against the philosophers recapitulates the wisdom of the stages: The exploitation of human freedom is the exhaustion of human potency in renunciation (of finite security), suffering (the pain of the excision of finite hope), and guilt (the total indebtedness of the finite to the Infinite).[158] The *Postscript* is Kierkegaard's "speeches on religion to its cultured despisers," but in a spirit quite unlike that of Schleiermacher the sentimental theologian, the voluble humorist Climacus wants to call the distracted attention of the philosophers to the terse piety of the Jutland priest: There is no greater edification than that implied in the thought that as against God we are always in the wrong. Its dark humor is comprehended in the realization that the *Concluding Unscientific Postscript* is a systematic destruction of all the idols of System that come between man's want and God's abundance.

How, then, does a man become a Christian? Johannes Climacus—"John the Climber"—cannot vouch for the reality. His name and his testimony reveal that he himself is only on the way up, not yet arrived. But the condition—the possibility—of becoming a Christian is well within his bailiwick: First become a man, and when you are driven by this exertion into the narrows of despair, when you have become spirit by the recognition that absolute freedom is identical with absolute dependence, when you are alone in fear and trembling,

---

[158] Cf. Kierkegaard, *Concluding Unscientific Postscript*, pp. 347–493, for an elaborate analysis of these moments of the religious consciousness.

without sustenance of nature, knowledge, or community, with no recourse but God—then and only then may the threat and the promise of Christianity surge redemptively from the abyss.

The actuality of Christianity, its annihilating word of condemnation and its comfortable word of reconciliation, is the theme of Climacus' opposite number, the "ideal Christian" Anti-Climacus. In the first part of *Training in Christianity,* Anti-Climacus, following the *Fragments,* defines Christian faith as contemporaneity with Christ. He develops this definition in a rhapsody on the text, "Come hither to me, all ye that labor and are heavy laden, I will give you rest."[159] He who issues this invitation is Christ, and in order to appreciate the invitation it is necessary to know more about the identity of the inviter.

The Christian Church has enshrined its dogmatic understanding of Christ in the Nicene Creed:

> one Lord Jesus Christ, the only-begotten Son of God;
> Born of the Father before all ages, God from God,
> Light from Light, Very God from Very God; Begotten not made; Consubstantial with the Father;
> Through whom all things were made: Who for us men and for our salvation came down from heaven,
> And was incarnate by the Holy Ghost of the Virgin Mary, And was made man. . . .

But the symbolic formula sets its object at the distance of cognition. It is in the New Testament that Jesus of Nazareth, His appearance as a man to men, may be more readily approached. The contending attractions and repulsions of His personality compel that "infinite interest" in His *reality* that is forbidden to the "possibility-relations" of ordinary human intercourse.[160]

[159] Matt. 11:28. Kierkegaard, *Training in Christianity,* Princeton University Press, Princeton, N.J., 1947, pp. 5–72.

[160] Kierkegaard, *Concluding Unscientific Postscript,* pp. 289–91.

Anti-Climacus is sensitive to the attractions of Jesus' person. In contrast to human charity, which must insist upon its due if it is not to become condescension, He offers His aid gratuitously to all who labor and are laden. Unlike human sympathy, which must retain its superiority to evil lest it become impotent, His compassion is a self-emptying by which He undertakes the sufferings of the wretched of the earth. Ignoring the distinctions which human affection must make if it is not to become effete, His invitation is extended to all who travail. No man can be the bond of another's peace, but here the Helper is the Help, He is Himself the rest He offers: "Abide with me, for in abiding with me there is rest."

The mercy of God poured out through the Christ, transcending the inevitable and legitimate limitations of human solicitude, proffers healing and refuge to all men. Wherefore Anti-Climacus' repeated exclamation: Wonderful! That repose of the spirit always longed for and never attained, that ideal of love which in human relations is but a deceitful romance, is here truth and reality. Wonderful![161]

But this very "wonderful!" sows the seed of offense. Approached by another human being with the words: "Come to me, and I will be everything to you, your joy, peace, light, health, and comfort!" who would not draw back in suspicion? What man, disillusioned by his trial of human love, would not smell fraud? All experience warns against the allurement here offered; all experience testifies that the promise cannot be kept. What man, presented with this invitation, would not, sadly no doubt, but wisely and firmly, send his regrets?

This is what men have done.[162] But they have done it dishonestly. The comfortable promise of Christianity is contained in the invitation: "Come hither to me, all ye that labor and are heavy laden, and I will give you rest." The offense of Christianity is that the invi-

---

[161] Kierkegaard, *Training in Christianity,* pp. 10–15.
[162] Ibid., p. 25.

tation—which only God has the right and the might to
make—was given by one whom his biographers describe
as an itinerant teacher of dubious origin and ignomini-
ous end. This is the Absolute Paradox of which the
Fragments speak: that God assumed the unlovely
form of a servant, made Himself intimate with every
grief and shame that break the human heart, and won
beatitude for men by assuming the penalty of their
guilt. The comfort of Christianity is promised only to
those who can surmount their offense at the Absurdity
of Christianity: that the historical son of Mary is the
eternal Son of God.

Naturally men wanted the blessedness and the consolation of Christianity, but they wanted it without the
offense. Instead of rejecting outright the unpleasant
Galilean and His invitation, they pretended to accept
Him, but in fact put in His place a set of convenient
illusions. The name of this pretense and these illusions
is Christendom.

One of the pleasantest of Christendom's self-deceits
is the fantasy that Anti-Climacus calls the illusion of
"Christ in glory." According to orthodox Christian
belief the crucified, risen, and ascended Christ now sits
in majesty *ad dexteram patris.* So be it. But it was not
the glorified Christ who issued the invitation, "Come
hither to me. . . ." Christianity did not enter the world
as an authoritatively magnificent communication wafted
to earth from realms of heavenly splendor, and to this
day Christ has uttered not a word from his celestial
throne. The Christ who speaks in the Gospels—the only
Christ who has ever spoken to men—is the man of
sorrows, mocked, scourged, spit upon, and slaughtered,
the repellent Nazarene with no form nor comeliness
that men should desire Him.

"Christ in glory" is only a promise and an expectation. He is not and never has been a reality present
among men. To ascribe the gospel to the glorified
Christ is a revision of Christianity that misrepresents it
as a divinely beautiful poem. It is natural that a militant

Church should anticipate its own triumph, natural even that it should be sometimes deceived by its longings. The picture of Christ in glory is theologically correct and aesthetically proper, as an expression of the believer's hope and the groaning of the creation for redemption. But it is a deceit if it puts a fairy-tale prince in place of the sign of offense as the object of faith. Christianity demands no less than a "contemporaneous" meeting of human pride with Christ in His humiliation. It does not flatter men with the lie that they can transcend their terrestrial limitations and aspire to God, but offends them with the good news ("Come hither to me. . . .") that God has condescended to the littleness of their finitude and the pinch of their predicament.[163]

Equally illusive and equally common is the notion that the consequences of the life of Jesus, especially the centuries-long continuity of the Church, demonstrate the truth of the claim that He is divine. But even if perfect knowledge of the "historical Jesus" were not impossible, it would still not amount to a knowledge of the Christ, the subject of Peter's confession and the object of the Christian's trust. Historical research necessarily remains within the framework of the presupposition that men are only men. One may prove—or try to, since historical evidence is never more than approximation to proof—that Caesar was a hero or scoundrel. But no historian would argue that he was a ghost or an angel or an avatar of the Buddha, or even for that matter a man. Reincarnations and free-floating spirits are outside the historian's domain. His province, marked out in advance and so conditioning but never established by the historical method, is human action. Assuming that his subjects are men, he endeavors to show from the consequences of their lives their relative significance within the bounds of that assumption.

[163] Ibid., pp. 26–28.

By no means then could one demonstrate historically that Caesar (or Jesus) was (or was not) *God*. Because of the absolute difference between God and man, the project would be, from the historian's point of view, vain, and from the believer's perspective, blasphemous. The belief that Jesus of Nazareth is God will not be made less paradoxical by centuries upon centuries of ecclesiastical success. Until the beatific vision it will remain an article of faith to which no historical evidence is even remotely relevant.[164]

When the inherent repugnance of the Christian claim and the limitations of historical knowledge are not respected, men are hoodwinked by the illusion of familiarity, which Anti-Climacus calls the "misfortune of Christendom." The sign of offense (Christ in His humiliation) is replaced by the standard of victory (Christ in triumph) and whittled to the dimensions of human ingenuity (the proof of the centuries). Christianity becomes a culture phenomenon, a folk religion, and a second nature for all who are born in Christendom. The advent of "Christian civilization"—Christendom—is the end of Christianity. Where He is not eclipsed by Santa Claus and the Easter bunny, the man who was numbered among the malefactors has become, for a bourgeois society, the symbol of the *status quo* of those who profess the faith out of the depths of the insecurity of their own privilege, and for the disinherited *illuminati* of that society, the rallying point of social change. Once His cause is espoused by human intelligence and imagination, Christ becomes whatever men want Him to be by dint of ceasing to be the one thing He is: a scandal and a stone of stumbling.[165]

The contemporaries of Jesus were more consistent: they were offended and they put Him to death, out of human honesty and godly fear. They could not gloss

164 Ibid., pp. 28–34.
165 Ibid., pp. 37–39.

the absurdity that so plainly declared itself: the son of the carpenter and the maiden, conceived out of wedlock, familiar of whores and tax collectors, says that He is the Son of God. It was not the riffraff of Judaea, but the pillars of state and church, that crucified Jesus, thinking they did God service. Humanity essentially and at its best rebels against His person and His profession. The contradictions may be softened for us by our historical and spiritual distance from A.D.30, but to the men of Jesus' time they were sharp enough. He promises eternal life (wonderful!), but He cannot keep His own skin. "Cast not your pearls before swine," He warns His disciples, but what are these followers of His if not the most swinish of the vulgar herd? He preaches in the synogogue—in order to damn the Establishment. This undistinguished man, who says that God does not dwell in the temple at Jerusalem, accepts divine honors from the crowd. He grandly forgives the sins of slatterns and denounces the Pharisees, who of all men honor the law with meticulous observance. He is immoral (Except a man hate father and mother . . .), imprudent (Take no thought for the morrow . . .), and silly (The meek shall inherit the earth!).

So He came to a bad end, just as anyone with a scrap of sense might have predicted: This is madness and will come to a bad end. Losing the patronage of the mob, running afoul the authorities, getting Himself executed, He vindicates every negative judgment ever laid against Him, including the consummate accusation: pity. If He really were the Son of God, He would surely come down from the cross, but He doesn't. He saved others, Himself He cannot save. Therefore He was wrong, and now He is lost. Poor man.[166]

This is the logic of offense. Once a man is disabused of the trumperies of theological fantasy and the ir-

[166] Ibid., pp. 40–60.

relevancies of historical criticism, once he makes himself contemporaneous with Jesus, then offense is his
only natural and reasonable response. Anti-Climacus
takes the polemic between man and the God of Christianity to be absolute. There is no passage from the
human to the divine, and the divine itself appearing in
the human milieu can only fester opposition to itself.
It was no accident that Jesus was crucified; crucifixion
would be at any time and in any place the consistent
—and from a purely human point of view justifiable—
rejoinder of men to the claim made by and about the
Christ. Man crucifies God: this is the truth about man
and about his relationship to Christianity.

But if the logic of offense is unexceptionable, how
is *faith* possible? If Golgotha is a necessary truth, what
is the sense of Christianity? Let Anti-Climacus reply:

> *Christianity did not come into the world . . . as an*
> *admirable example of the gentle art of consolation—*
> *but as the absolute. It is out of love God wills it so,*
> *but also it is God who wills it, and He wills what He*
> *will. . . . But what, then, is the use of Christianity?*
> *It is, then, merely a plague to us! Ah, yes, that too*
> *can be said: relatively understood, the absolute is the*
> *greatest plague. . . . Christianity seems madness,*
> *since it is incommensurable with any finite where-*
> *fore. What is the use of it, then? The answer is: Hold*
> *thy peace! It is the absolute!*[167]

To become a Christian demands, in view of the absolute difference between God and man and the absolute impossibility of assimilating the divine to the
human, that one "be transformed into likeness with
God."[168] But this can happen only if a man has first
become contemporary with Christ, the Absolute invad-

167 Ibid., p. 66.
168 Ibid., p. 67.

ing the realm of the relative. "For in relation to the absolute there is only one tense: the present."

> *Christ is . . . not at all a merely historical person,*
> *since as the Paradox [the Eternal-in-time] He is an*
> *extremely unhistorical person. . . . What really oc-*
> *curred (the past) is not . . . the real. It lacks the*
> *determinant of truth (as inwardness) and of all re-*
> *ligiousness, the* for thee. *The past is not reality—for*
> *me: only the contemporary is reality for me. What*
> *thou dost live contemporaneous with is reality—for*
> *thee.*[169]

As "the historical event which on principle could not happen,"[170] Christ is not Himself a homogeneous part of human history. He is the irruption of the Absolute into history, and for that reason the "sign of contradiction"[171] and the signal for offense. But He is also and for the same reason a possible object of faith. Reality is *that which is present for you.* Christ as the Absolute is never past, but perpetually present, so that any man at any time can become His contemporary.

A man becomes the contemporary of Christ and is transformed into the likeness of God only if he participates in the life of Christ. And this he does if, like the God-man Himself, he suffers the offense and the contradiction of God and man in his own person.

> *If thou canst not endure contemporaneousness,*
> *canst not endure the sight in reality, if thou art un-*
> *able to go out in the street and perceive that it is God*
> *in this horrible procession, and that this is thy case*

---

[169] Ibid., pp. 67–68.

[170] Cf. Kierkegaard, *Philosophical Fragments*, pp. 107–10, 124–26; also Kierkegaard, *Concluding Unscientific Postscript*, pp. 512–13.

[171] Kierkegaard, *Training in Christianity*, pp. 124–27.

> *wert thou to fall down and worship Him—then thou
> art not* essentially *a Christian.*[172]

To have faith is like Simon to bend publicly under
the cross of Christ in the dead march down the street
of sorrows and out to the place of skulls. *Via crucis:*
that is the true contemporaneity with Christ, the true
participation in his abjection, transformation into the
only likeness of God that God has ever vouchsafed us.
This is the embarrassment of faith.

And if a man has not faith, then

> *What thou hast to do . . . is unconditionally to
> admit this to thyself, so that above all thou mayest
> preserve humility and fear and trembling with rela-
> tion to what it means in truth to be a Christian. For
> that is the way thou must take to learn and to get
> training in fleeing to grace in such a wise that thou
> dost not take it in vain.*[173]

The "training in Christianity" which Anti-Climacus
recommends is simply honesty before God and with
oneself about one's inability to be a Christian. The
condition for becoming a Christian, said Climacus, is
that one first become a man. The practice of Christianity, says Anti-Climacus, begins with the candid
confession of offense:

> *In how far a man may succeed essentially in be-
> coming a Christian, no one can tell him. But dread
> and fear and despair are of no avail. Candor before
> God is the first and last. Candidly to admit to oneself
> where one is, with candor before God holding the
> task in view—however slowly it goes, though one
> only creeps forward: yet one thing a man has, he is
> in the right position. . . .*[174]

[172] Ibid., p. 69.
[173] Ibid., p. 69.
[174] Ibid., pp. 69–70.

Offense is the natural human reaction to Christ; the honest avowal that one is offended is the only contribution a man can make toward his own participation in the promises of Christ. Strictly speaking it is not within a man's power to believe; faith is a divine visitation for which the only preparation he can make is the admission of his own unworthiness. The prevenience and the prerogative belong to God.[175] Let a man recognize the absolute claim that God has made in the person of Jesus, and then let him acknowledge without evasion that he cannot meet this claim.

> *And then no further; then for the rest let him attend to his work, be glad in it, love his wife, be glad in her, bring up his children with joyfulness, love his fellowmen, rejoice in life.*[176]

The only power a man has before God is the capacity to admit his impotence; this is what Christianity calls the *consciousness of sin*. The power of God to make good man's failure is *grace*.[177] "Only the consciousness of sin is the expression of absolute respect" for God (worship), and

> *only consciousness of sin is the way of entrance, is the vision, which, by being absolute respect, can see the gentleness, lovingkindness, and compassion of Christianity.*[178]

The religion of the edifying discourses Kierkegaard labels "Religion A." Its worship is man's enthusiastic endurance of his alienation from God, renouncing the world, suffering the pain of this severance, and ending in the everlasting recollection of guilt (total indebted-

[175] Kierkegaard, *Philosophical Fragments*, pp. 17–22, 68–88, 111–32.
[176] Kierkegaard, *Training in Christianity*, p. 71.
[177] Ibid., p. 71.
[178] Ibid., p. 72.

ness) against God. The religion of the discourses is the immanent expression of the discrepancy between the finite and the infinite. Christianity ("Religion B") transforms this "religion of immanence" dialectically with its claim that God has entered time in order to reconcile the world to Himself.[179] God gives Himself to men, and men refuse Him; therefore Christianity proclaims that men's alienation from God is self-incurred. Sin is the paradoxical Christian inversion of guilt. In the wake of the originality of sin, the suffering of Religion A is grotesquely malapropos: "dread and fear and despair are of no avail." Not spiritual debauch, but straight-faced confession of sin, is the entry into grace. Nor is the renunciation of the world demanded; the salvation of the Christian (the forgiveness of sin) is God's permission to be—not in "hidden inwardness," but in the publicity of the marketplace—the man he is: to attend to his work, be glad in his wife, bring up his children, love his fellowmen, and enjoy life. Here is the relevance of the Christian Absurdity: that which a man's burning wish and his determined resolution cannot effect, the pearl of price without which all else is vanity, is here granted. His self—the self that is dissipated in aesthetics, dissembled in ethics, and suffered in religion—is restored *in statum pristinum* in the life of faith. To the man racked on the contradictions of existence and worn out in the struggle to become himself, Christianity offers in this world the "new immediacy" of life by grace, and the hope of Paradise in the world beyond.

In his determination not to sell the consolations of Christianity too cheap, Kierkegaard more often dwells on the consciousness of sin than on the emoluments of grace. In his resolution to respect the boundaries of thought, he never allows himself to fancy the wonders

[179] Kierkegaard, *Concluding Unscientific Postscript*, pp. 493–519.

of Heaven. But in "three godly discourses" on the
lilies of the field and the birds of the air he counters
the resignation, suffering, and guilt of Religion A with
a meditation on the silence, obedience, and joy in
which the Christian relinquishes the project of becoming himself and receives his being from the hand of
God. No longer the "unhappiest man" lost in recollection and anticipation, nor the ethical man straining
to pull past and future together in resolution, nor the
religious man with his Now drained into eternity, the
contemporary of Christ who seeks not himself but
"God's kingdom and his righteousness" dwells in the
power and the glory of the presence of that kingdom,
its everlasting Today.[180] Another trio of discourses
on the same text celebrates the contentment, the
splendor, and the happiness of "common humanity"
created and recreated by the grace that is given with
faith on the other side of offense through the consciousness of sin.[181]

But it is the consciousness of sin and that alone
through which a man may enter into Christianity. The
Paradox of Christ—that tormented manhood that nevertheless enjoyed the consubstantial presence of the
Father—is the Pattern for the life of the believer, and
that life is, for all its joy, a *Via crucis*. *Imitatio Christi*
is a Way of the Cross that extends until the *eschaton*,
in the hope of a blessedness beyond time and existence and man's ability to conceive, a Resurrection
whose reality rests inscrutably in the depths of the
divine power and love, a depth which not even faith
can fathom, and about which therefore both Kierkegaard and his pseudonyms are silent.

[180] "The Lilies of the Field and the Birds of the Air: Three
Godly Discourses" in Kierkegaard, *Christian Discourses,* Oxford University Press, London, 1940, pp. 311–56.
[181] "What We Learn from the Lilies of the Field and the
Birds of the Air: Three Discourses" in Kierkegaard, *The Gospel
of Suffering,* Augsburg, Minneapolis, 1948, pp. 165–236.

The Poetry of Inwardness

"Every divinity student" would presumably be able to
furnish the information that the Christianity of Anti-
Climacus is incomplete and distorted. Its substitution
of absurdity for mystery draws a Nestorian cloud over
the Incarnation and darkens even a Lutheran understanding of Sacrament. Anti-Climacus' compulsion for
a contemporaneity that leaps the centuries all but
pushes the history out of sacred history; not the historical Jesus but the historicity of Jesus becomes the
sting of the Christian Paradox. The eternal presence
of Christ, which makes contemporaneity possible, not
unnaturally renders the Church of Christ and all
but the barest bones of Scripture embarrassingly
superfluous.[182]

To all such proper protest Kierkegaard would reply
that *Training in Christianity* was only a "corrective"[183]
recommended to the complacent debility of the "present age." The works of Anti-Climacus are a volley of
thoughts that wound from behind,[184] aimed at "revival
and increase of inwardness"[185] among Christians, not
at a theological synthesis for the benefit of the professors of Christianity. Theologians may doubt the
apologetic wisdom of mounting Calvary in Tivoli Gar-
dens to shock the merrymakers, but Anti-Climacus
will excuse his loud insistence on the Crucifixion and
his casual suppression of the Resurrection by reference
to his incendiary purpose.

In other words, Anti-Climacus is a pseudonym. He
is that "ideal Christian" that never was and never will
be. From the aerie of his faith he perceives that what
he administers is not the Christianity of the New Testa-

---

[182] Cf. Kierkegaard, *Philosophical Fragments*, pp. 130–31.

[183] Dru, op. cit., no. 1141; Kierkegaard, *The Point of View*,
p. 156.

[184] Kierkegaard, *Christian Discourses*, pp. 167ff.

[185] Kierkegaard, *Training in Christianity*, p. 5.

ment *toute entière,* but an attack on a Christendom grown prosperously fat and philosophically flatulent. Kierkegaard was not always able to make the distinction; to his own discredit and derangement he often forgot it in the broadsides that he nailed to the doors of the Establishment in his last days.[186] But Anti-Climacus is clear: this is not the New Reformation, it is an outrageous exaggeration "for edification and awakening."[187]

The pseudonymous extravagance of Anti-Climacus forces into the foreground the problem of hermeneutics. Every reader of Kierkegaard's works knows that he declares them to be "indirect communications"; yet it is by no means patent what the indirectness consists in and what it communicates. It is easy to see what a direct communication is. A man with knowledge of certain realities forms concepts that are the mental symbols of those realities, and expresses what he thinks by means of words which are the spoken or written signs of his concepts. When a hearer or reader apprehends the verbal symbols, translates them into the concepts they stand for, and these in turn into the realities signified, the process is complete. The communication is direct because both communicator and recipient are capable of the same knowledge of the same realities, and in order to share that knowledge need avail themselves only of symbolic vehicles the being of which is exclusively their translucence to the tenor of the knowledge in question. The direct route from mind to mind is a segment of that larger communion in which minds are bound to the intelligible totality of being.

The centrality of freedom in "human nature" and in Kierkegaard's "message"—the freedom that sets both these classical entities in quotes—riddles the totality

---

[186] Cf. Kierkegaard, *Attack upon "Christendom,"* Princeton University Press, Princeton, N.J., 1946, passim.

[187] Kierkegaard, *Fear and Trembling* and *The Sickness unto Death,* p. 141.

and intelligibility of being, dismembers the community of men with each other and the cosmos, and deflects all existential discourse into the detour of indirection. Pseudonymity is the most striking of the devices by which this diaspora is acknowledged in Kierkegaard's writings.

Kierkegaard's misbegotten attempt to deceive Regina about his real character should not be confused with his literary employment of pseudonyms. When he signed his books with impossible names like *Johannes de Silentio* (John of Silence) and *Vigilius Haufniensis* (Watchman of Copenhagen), no one in the gossipy little world of Danish letters had any doubt about their origin. Nor did he mean they should; his purpose was not mystification but distance. By refusing to answer for his writings he detached them from his personality so as to let their scheme reinforce the freedom that was their theme.

The effects of this pseudonymity are many and subtle. At the first level of analysis the attribution of the works to representative characters permits these spokesmen of the existence-spheres a liberty they would not have as expressions of the opinions of Kierkegaard. The difference between *personae* and persons is crucial: the pseudonyms are not mouthpieces through which Kierkegaard hopes to get a hearing for his views, but fictive personalities whose lives are poetically observed and reported. As the poet is silent in his poem, so Kierkegaard is silent in his books. This is the second level of pseudonymity: the disappearance of the poet behind the *persona*. By contemplating his *persona* in the fulguration of imaginative possibility—infinitely ambiguous and dialectical—and creating him in that illustrious shifting light of fancy, the poet guarantees the *persona* objectivity and himself the silence that seals that objectivity.[188]

[188] For an excellent treatment of the relation of poet to *persona* in Kierkegaard's pseudonymous writings, cf. Aage Henriksen, *Kierkegaards Romaner,* Glydendalske Boghandel Nor-

Because the imagination is dialectically agile to traverse possibilities without end, a third level of pseudonymity discovers itself: the distinction of poet and *persona* not only qualifies the relation of Kierkegaard to his books, but is repeated and complicated within the books themselves. In *Either/Or* Victor Eremita edits the papers of *A* and Judge Wilhelm; the Judge holds a mirror up to *A* at the same time that he transcribes and is transfixed by the sermon of the Jutland priest; *A* examines the complex entanglements of (among many others) Mozart, Don Juan, Leporello, and the Don's victims, while simultaneously he authors his own undoing in the diary of Johannes the Seducer. The writers are interlocked with each other like the pieces in a Chinese puzzle, and the reader is never certain who is being seen through whose eyes—who is poet and who *persona*—at any moment. More intricate because more compressed is the network of *personae* in *Repetition*. Ostensibly the work is a casebook novel in which Constantin Constantius, the experimental psychologist and dilettante author, reports the history of a Kierkegaardian young man who falls in love, realizes that he cannot marry the girl, nearly achieves a religious reconciliation to his sorrow by reading *Job,* but is at last made a poet by the girl's magnanimity in marrying someone else. "Really" the book investigates the possibility of "repetition"—of restoring a personality to integrity after it has been broken by grief and guilt. With an irony appropriate to the investigation the two pseudonyms are diffracted into a series of masks that satirize themselves and each other (several times over) and finally the reader, who is presented at the end with a calling card, bearing a blank space for his name, and an admonition to be reconciled to the flippancy and

disk Forlag, København, 1954; cf. also the same author's "Kierkegaard's Reviews of Literature" in *Symposion Kierkegaardianum,* Orbis Litterarum, tome X, fasc. 1–2, Munksgaard, København, 1955, pp. 75–83.

incoherence of the book.[189] The reader who recovers *himself* from the farcical shadow play of the novel will have achieved repetition, and the heretics eager to ascertain the author's position will get nothing to run with.

The use of pseudonyms first severs Kierkegaard's *personae* from Kierkegaard. At the second level pseudonymity obliterates Kierkegaard the poet. Finally the identities of the pseudonyms themselves are so scrambled that they become masks without faces, and their works self-standing objects unbuttressed by human subjects. The blank calling card inserted in *Repetition,* and the concluding exordium of *Either/Or* ("Only the truth which edifies is truth for you"),[190] along with like hints in the other books, direct the reader to supply the necessary personal identity: his own. So the form of Kierkegaard's writings insinuates their content: subjectivity, inwardness, the passionate appropriation of objective uncertainty, is the only truth possible for an existing individual.[191]

Pseudonymity as such is only a gambit, a powerful but not isolated tactic in the overall strategy of indirect communication. Its import is expanded by a consideration of Kierkegaard's discussions of irony and humor.

---

[189] Kierkegaard, *Repetition,* p. 147, 158–59. For my awareness of the formal complexity of *Repetition* I am indebted to an unpublished study by a former student, Kathryn Pulley Respess. Her evaluation of the techniques of indirect communication differs from that here proposed; she concludes that Kierkegaard rather than diverting attention from himself only focuses the reader's interest more sharply on his own personality. In her estimation the technique is a failure, and must fail insofar as every communication, however indirect, presupposes an act of direct communication as its basis.

[190] Kierkegaard, *Either/Or,* vol. II, p. 356.

[191] The fact that the edifying discourses **are** not pseudonymous is significant. They give direct expression to a point of view that is religious, but not distinctively Christian. This is the only point of view for which Kierkegaard felt he could assume personal responsibility.

These modes of obliquity are said to be *confinia* bound-
ing the stages on life's way, irony separating the aesthetic from the ethical, humor dividing the ethical from
the religious. As such they open halfway houses to
people in progress: the aesthete who is disenchanted
with aestheticism but not yet gathered for ethical choice
will look with ironic duplicity on his own life; the ethicist who is disabused of his moral self-confidence but
not yet ready for religion will smile good-humoredly at
his eagerness in well-doing. After their respective leaps
have been made, the aesthete-turned-ethicist and the
ethicist-become-religious will continue to wear irony
and humor as incognitos in which to go among their
erstwhile peers. Knowing the gulf that parts him from
his former friends, the newly arrived ethicist will hide
his eternal validity under a bushel of irony when he
addresses them. The religious man's converse with his
ethical associates will take the form of a jest the humor
of which dissembles his own suffering.[192]

Irony and humor are modes of communication se-
cretively arch rather than conventionally sincere. As
the ethicist thinks to master existence by resolve, so his
irony scrutinizes the contradictions of life through the
stern jaundice of the ideal; the religious man, resigned
to suffer what he cannot subdue, wrings his humor
out of a sympathy with those contradictions. In either
case irony and humor disengage the communication
from the communicator so as to signalize and to charge
the gap between communicator and recipient. Between
two freedoms they insert a "doubly-reflected" work of
artfulness condensing the inwardness of the communicator into an explosive shock of recognition for the
recipient.[193]

---

[192] Kierkegaard, *Concluding Unscientific Postscript*, pp.
400–4, 446–68, 489–93; cf. Frithiof Brandt, *Søren Kierkegaard*,
Det Danske Selskab in cooperation with the Press and Information Department of the Danish Foreign Office, Copenhagen,
1963, pp. 29–30.

[193] Ibid., pp. 73, 320–22.

The meaning of indirect communication emerges as the pattern of existential distance, personal detachment, and artistic mediation woven into the motley of Kierkegaard's works and exemplified by such instances as pseudonymity, irony, and humor. The same pattern is visible in the superficially argumentative but fundamentally satiric texture of *Philosophical Fragments* and *Concluding Unscientific Postscript;* it could also be traced in such diverse fabrics as the "dialectical lyric" of *Fear and Trembling,* the psychological microscopy of *The Sickness unto Death,* and the pedantic posturing of *The Concept of Dread.* Its genres are as illimitable as possibility and as devious as imagination. But the routine is the same throughout all its expressions: to interpose between author and reader an anonymous object so articulated by the author that it deploys upon contact into a phalanx of possibilities for the reader. Such communication is indirect because it turns author and reader away from each other toward "some third thing, something more abstract, which neither of them is."[194] Such indirection is a communication of subjective truth because the impersonality of the object returns the reader to the arena where the possibilities it displays must be acted on: his inwardness.[195]

The method of indirection is prefigured in the peirastics, anatreptics, and maieutics of the Socratic dialogues. Kierkegaard discovered it there and in what he took to be the compassionate cunning of the Incarnation.[196] More immediately he was impelled to wield the Romantic irony as a weapon against the pretensions of the Romantic philosophers and their theological imitators. His own practice of indirect communication,

[194] Ibid., p. 455.

[195] Ibid., p. 320.

[196] Cf. Dru, op. cit., nos. 427, 1122; Kierkegaard, *Philosophical Fragments,* pp. 68–88, and *Training in Christianity,* pp. 124–44. Cf. also Kierkegaard, *The Concept of Irony with Constant Reference to Socrates,* Harper & Row, N.Y., 1966.

which he describes as "elusive and artistic,"[197] is not unlike the techniques evolved by modern poets and familiar to contemporary literary critics. It is a commonplace of twentieth-century criticism to distinguish sharply between poetic language and prosaic discourse. The terms of the distinction are differently defined by different critics, but the theme is not lost amid their partisan variations on it. In "direct" or prosaic language, words are straightforward expressions of the writer's meaning; his language is a symbolic extension of his mind, as unambiguous as he can keep it. The speech of a poet does not utter his inner states, but rather builds meanings into a freestanding structure of language. Paradox, self-concealment, plural connotations, distentions of metaphor and the like are shears by which he clips the umbilical of his fancy's child and sends it out on its own. His art is not the externalizing of himself, but the objectifying of a work of words: *poiesis*.

What the poet produces is a verbal object (*poiema*) in which meanings, released from any personal interest he may vest in them, are neither affirmed nor denied, but simply placed. A poem in this sense does not *mean* —it does not urge the feelings and opinions of the poet on the reader; it *is*—as a thing made it is self-sufficient (*perfectum*) and bears no message not indigenous to its perfection.

But the poetic object, however much it dispatches the poet's words from the poet, is nevertheless an object and as such commands a response. A direct communication (indicative prose utterance) is a request for assent, and the proper response is some degree of belief or disbelief: one swears by a religious dogma, abandons a moral conviction, gives moderate credence to a scientific hypothesis, denies a factual allegation, etc. But it would be out of place to believe in, to doubt, or to disavow a poem, since the poet makes no claim to

[197] Kierkegaard, *Concluding Unscientific Postscript*, p. 73.

which such attitudes would be relevant. At the same time a poem is not a bit of mute decor that is adequately appreciated when it is savored. Its locutions embody meanings, and its sensuousness addresses the intelligence. Kierkegaard would say that a poetic object, like any object, but with the preternatural vivacity induced by art, functions as a *possibility* when it is apprehended by a subject. And that in two distinct but related ways: as a term of knowing and as a challenge to action.[198]

A poem calls not for belief but for knowledge, not for admiration but for personal appropriation. A theory, a doctrine, a statement of fact purport to say something about realities, and for that reason must be believed or doubted or rejected. A poem gives insight into possibilities by fashioning them in words; as a symbol that incarnates what it symbolizes such a verbal structure is the avenue and the object of an act of gnosis.

Kierkegaard's correlation of reality with belief and of possibility with knowledge[199] instructs the interpretation of his own poetry of indirect communication. His books, *poiemata* and not statements of his views on human life, are out of the reach of the ordinary distinction of truth and falsity, which strictly applies only to the yeas and nays of the intellect compounding and dividing. Yet they open ways—if *A*'s analysis of *Don Juan* is correct, infinite ways—for understanding; they are seeds of possibility fecund with meanings, buds that flower perennially for the reflective imagination. Because they are works of irony and humor, they deftly evade the kind of evaluation that suits the generalizations of scientists and the theories of theorizing philosophers. Poems like jokes may be refused; they are never refuted. They may be rich or sparse, superficial or penetrating, estimable in a variety of ways, but they are never propositionally right or wrong. As po-

198 Ibid., pp. 67–74, 320–22.
199 Ibid., pp. 282–307.

etry Kierkegaard's works fertilize the seeing intellect and bring to birth the offspring of the visionary fancy; as poetic irony and poetic humor they survive the misplaced and ineffectual assaults of a literal-minded and prosaic critique.

Not to mention the misplaced and impotent embrace of a literal-minded and prosaic espousal. The heresy of paraphrase and the intentional fallacy tempt the reader of Kierkegaard as they tempt readers of poetry generally. The pitfalls of the latter trap those earnest endeavors to determine what Kierkegaard "really means"—which, if they do not conveniently leave out everything that conflicts with what the scholar thinks Kierkegaard ought to mean, conclude either that Kierkegaard is a fool deaf to the most resounding self-contradictions or that he is saying something so precious and so deep that it cannot help sounding silly. Taken as instruments of his intent, his works add up to magnificent nonsense. But the truth is that Kierkegaard the poet of inwardness did not "really mean" anything. His "intent" is to exfoliate existential possibilities, not to offer a systematic appraisal of reality as seen from his point of view; like all poets he is concerned not with mentioning but with making.

That it is heretical to paraphrase Kierkegaard is equally noteworthy. The "arguments" of his pseudonyms on behalf of religion and Christianity, as these are paraphrased in this chapter, make abundantly clear by their unpersuasive formality just how important is the contextual setting of the originals. Any paraphrase of Kierkegaard must carry a disclaimer and an injunction to return to the source. It is for this reason that the influence of Kierkegaard on contemporary existential philosophy and theology is so questionable in spite of its vast publicity value for the Dane. Existential theologians tend to offer in place of the historic faith of the historical Church in the historical Incarnation an abstract of the dialectic of Climacus—an ersatz congenial to a disinherited generation oppressed by life

and incapable of supernatural faith.[200] But it was
manifestly not part of Kierkegaard's program to found
a school of theology on the barren crisis of despair,
only to recall men to the divine imperative and to the
conditions of faith in their own sufferings and their
own freedom.

By the philosophers who follow in his train Kierkegaard has been prolifically pilfered from,[201] his paradoxes have been twisted into doctrinal parodies of
themselves, his mischievous recalcitrance to system has
been chastised and solemnly invested with systematic
dignity. There is no private property in the realm of
the spirit, and there is no reason why everyone should
not take from Kierkegaard what serves his turn. But
it is impossible not to imagine Kierkegaard sharpening
his wit and going to hilarious work on those contemporary ontologies of freedom that are determined to
make inwardness academically respectable. The mysteries of the epoché and the disdain of the *existentiale*
thinker for his *existentielle* gaucheries would impress
Kierkegaard as so many new attempts—only slightly
less honest than Hegel's—to give human existence the
dubious prestige of professorial sanction. He would
insist—and the form of his insistence would reduplicate
the content—that system enslaves and that only poetry
can adequately communicate inwardness in such a way
as to emancipate the recipient.[202] Only *poiesis,* which
cuts the tie that binds words and men and things, joints
a verbal framework tough enough to contain the negativity of freedom without breaking; only poetry can
crystallize limitless possibilities in an object capable

[200] Paul Tillich is a particularly striking case in point. See
his *Systematic Theology,* vol. II, The University of Chicago
Press, Chicago, 1957, and *The Courage to Be,* Yale University
Press, New Haven, Conn., 1952.

[201] The largest borrowings are by Martin Heidegger. He has
acknowledged the importance for his own work of *The Concept
of Dread,* and, in a grudging way, of the edifying discourses.

[202] Kierkegaard, *Concluding Unscientific Postscript,* p. 69.

of engaging the understanding and enticing the imagination ("making aware") without seducing or prostituting the spirit.

The theories of the systematic thinker—it was Hegel's genius that he saw this fact and his perversity that he exploited it—inevitably tend to be set up as ends and to usurp the place of the realities they should serve. The poetic object, however, not only rejoices the mind with its objectivity; it also, by its repellent aloofness, challenges its reader to his own activity of actualization. This is the second sense in which it functions as possibility. The success of an indirect communication depends upon its capacity to awaken in the recipient an awareness that the possibilities it objectifies—alluring, exciting, or frightening—are his own. He has not received the communication until he has read the concluding *de te fabula narratur* that can turn him from the wonder of the object to an engagement with the urgency and the unfinality of his own existence.

Kierkegaard's poetic is a rhetoric designed to coerce its reader to freedom. By the impassioned detachment with which it marshals the resources of spirit, it lays on him the necessity to act and deprives him of any warrant for action except his own freedom. The Kierkegaardian corpus can neither be "believed" nor "followed": it is and was meant to be—poetically—the impetus, the occasion, and the demand for the reader's own advance to selfhood and to a solitary meeting with the divine. Not by exhorting him to this or that line of conduct, not by offering him the chance to let knowledge or admiration go proxy for decision, but by vividly summoning before him the richness and the risk ingredient in his freedom, Kierkegaard's works impart to "that individual" who is their true reader the opportunity and the need of achieving himself in the sight of God.[203]

Kierkegaard's writings are public domain, and as

[203] Ibid., pp. 320–22.

such they may and will be made to serve a variety of purposes. But they are most consistently and most rewardingly understood as the poetry of inwardness their author fashioned them to be. Their *poetry* opens to the inquiring intellect and the restless imagination the infinite wealth of possibility that is the material of human selfhood. As the poetry of *inwardness* they drive their reader through the calm of contemplation into the passion of personal appropriation.

BIBLIOGRAPHY

Kierkegaard in Danish

1. *Samlede Vaerker,* Ud. af A. B. Drachman, J. L. Heiberg, H. O. Lange, Anden Udgave, Bind I–XV, Gyldendalske Boghandel Nordisk Forlag, København, 1920–31. (A new printing of this edition is available from the same publisher, 1962–64. The new printing is in 20 volumes, and is supervised by Peter P. Rohde.)
2. *Søren Kierkegaards Papirer,* Ud. af P. A. Heiberg, V. Kuhr, E. Torsting, Bind I–XI i 18 afdelinger, Gyldendalske Boghandel Nordisk Forlag, København, 1909–48.
3. *Breve og Aktstykker vedrørende Søren Kierkegaard,* Ud. ved Niels Thulstrup, Bind I–II, Ejnar Munksgaard, København, 1953.

Kierkegaard in English

(In the following list only the most recent editions are given. When a paperback reprint incorporates important revisions in the translation, that edition alone is listed.)

1. *Kierkegaard's Attack Upon Christendom,* Princeton University Press, Princeton, N.J., 1946.
2. *Christian Discourses,* Oxford University Press, London, 1940.
3. *The Concept of Dread,* 2d ed., Princeton University Press, Princeton, N.J., 1957.

4. *The Concept of Irony with Constant Reference to Socrates,* Harper & Row, New York, 1966.

5. *Concluding Unscientific Postscript,* Princeton University Press, Princeton, N.J., 1944.

6. *Crisis in the Life of an Actress and Other Essays on Drama,* Harper Torchbooks, Harper & Row, New York, 1967.

7. *Edifying Discourses,* vols. I–IV, Augsburg, Minneapolis, 1943–46.

8. *Either/Or,* vols. I–II, Anchor Books, Doubleday & Company, Inc., Garden City, N.Y., 1959.

9. *Fear and Trembling* and *The Sickness Unto Death,* Anchor Books, Doubleday & Company, Inc., Garden City, N.Y., 1954.

10. *For Self-Examination* and *Judge for Yourselves!* Princeton University Press, Princeton, N.J., 1944.

11. *For Self-Examination,* another translation, Augsburg, Minneapolis, 1940.

12. *The Gospel of Suffering,* Augsburg, Minneapolis, 1948.

13. *Johannes Climacus: or De Omnibus Dubitandum Est,* Stanford University Press, Stanford, Calif., 1958.

14. *Judge for Yourselves!* (See above, *For Self-Examination,* etc.)

15. *On Authority and Revelation,* Princeton University Press, Princeton, N.J., 1955.

16. *Philosophical Fragments,* Princeton University Press, Princeton, N.J., 2d ed., 1962.

17. *The Point of View for My Work as an Author,* Harper Torchbooks, Harper & Row, New York, 1962.

18. *The Present Age,* Oxford University Press, London, 1940.

19. *Purity of Heart,* Harper & Row, New York, 1948.

20. *Repetition,* Princeton University Press, Princeton, N.J., 1946.

21. *The Sickness Unto Death,* (see above, *Fear and Trembling,* etc.)

22. *Stages on Life's Way,* Princeton University Press, Princeton, N.J., 1945.

23. *Thoughts on Crucial Situations in Human Life,* Augsburg, Minneapolis, 1941.

24. *Training in Christianity,* Princeton University Press, Princeton, N.J., 1947.

25. *Works of Love,* Harper & Row, New York, 1962.

26. *The Journals of Søren Kierkegaard,* edited and translated by Alexander Dru, Oxford University Press, London, 1938.

27. *Søren Kierkegaard's Journals and Papers, Volume 1, A–E,*
    edited and translated by Howard V. and Edna H. Hong,
    Indiana University Press, Bloomington, Indiana, 1967.

28. *Søren Kierkegaard's Journals and Papers, Volume 2, F–K,*
    edited and translated by Howard V. and Edna H. Hong,
    Indiana University Press, Bloomington, Indiana, 1970.

29. *The Last Years: Journals 1853–1855,* edited and translated
    by Ronald Gregor Smith, Harper & Row, New York, 1965.

THE MASTER OF IRONY

Josiah Thompson

1

On the next to last day of December 1845 the manuscript of Kierkegaard's final pseudonymous work, *Concluding Unscientific Postscript,* was delivered to Bianco Luno's print shop.[1] Three sheets, however, were kept back—"in order," so Kierkegaard indicated, "not to be left lying around the print shop"[2]—and were only delivered later when the printing was nearly complete. Along with these three sheets came instructions in Israel Levin's handwriting to bind them (unpaginated) into the end of the book like a dust cover. This odd document, slipped furtively into the *Postscript* at the last moment, was entitled "A First and Last Declaration." It began with the admission that Kierkegaard was "the author, as people would call it"[3] of the long series of pseudonymous works published over the pre-

This essay was written especially for this volume. A revised version may be found in Chapter 12 of the author's book *Kierkegaard: A Biographical Essay* (New York: Alfred A. Knopf, Inc., 1973).

[1] *Af Søren Kierkegaards Efterladte Papirer, Bd. II.,* edited by H. P. Barfod (Copenhagen: C. A. Reitzels Forlag, 1872), p. 269 note.

[2] *Søren Kierkegaards Papirer,* edited by P. A. Heiberg, V. Kuhr, and E. Torsting. Volumes I–XI, in 18 parts (Copenhagen: Gyldendalske Boghandel Nordisk Forlag, 1909–48). Volume VII[1], Part B, Entry 81.4. In the future all references to this, the standard edition of Kierkegaard's *Papirer,* will be indicated by volume number (in Roman numerals), part, and entry number. Under this system, the present reference becomes simply VII[1] A 81.4.

[3] *Concluding Unscientific Postscript* (Princeton: Princeton University Press, 1941), p. 551 unpaginated. *Søren Kierke-*

ceding three years. As the "Declaration" quickly made clear, however, it was not simply an admission that Kierkegaard wanted to make. Rather, it was a plea he meant to urge, a plea for the independence of the pseudonyms from his own person:

> What is written is indeed my own, but only insofar as I put into the mouth of the poetically actual individual whom I *produced*, his life-view expressed in audible lines. . . . So in the pseudonymous works there is not a single word which is mine, I have no opinion about them except as a third person, no knowledge of their meaning except as a reader, not the remotest private relation to them. . . . My wish, my prayer, is that if it might occur to anyone to cite a particular saying from the books, he would do me the favor to cite the name of the respective pseudonym. . . .[4]

Historically speaking, this advice has proven difficult to follow. For in the century since Kierkegaard's death there has hardly been an essay written on the pseudonymous series that has failed to contain some reference to their real author and his twisted life. When we our-

------

gaards Samlede Vaerker, edited by A. B. Drachmann, J. L. Heiberg, and H. O. Lange, First Edition (1901–6) (Copenhagen: Gyldendalske Boghandels Forlag, 1902), Volume VII, p. 545 unpaginated. All the translations have been checked against the original Danish, and, in almost every case, revised somewhat to assure accuracy and consistency. All future references to Kierkegaard's published works will involve an abbreviated reference to the English translation and to the Danish edition given above. In future references the *Concluding Unscientific Postscript* will be abbreviated to *CUP*, while Volume VII (and other volumes) of the *Samlede Vaerker* will be abbreviated to *SV*, VII. Using the abbreviated reference system, the reference above becomes: *CUP*, 551 unpaginated; *SV*, VII, 545 unpaginated.

[4] *CUP*, 551–52 unpaginated; *SV*, VII, 545–46 unpaginated.

selves try to follow his advice, we recognize immediately why it has been so often ignored. With his words ringing in our ears ("in the pseudonymous works there is not a single word which is mine . . .") we pick up the first pseudonymous work, *Either/Or,* and dutifully note his absence from the title page. We go on to note the complicated web of multiple pseudonyms in which the secret of its authorship is wrapped, and agree not to identify Kierkegaard with any of his creations. Yet, as Stephen Crites has pointed out, this really does us no good: "For there he is on every page, the spindly figure with the umbrella, the hypochondriacal young man born old, with his eccentricities, his love affair that we are sick of hearing about, his abysmal melancholia."[5] No matter how ardently we would like to follow Kierkegaard's advice, we discover that we cannot leave his life behind. He implores that we forget about him and pay attention to his characters. But he *is* his characters in so many ways. His ironic glance is theirs. His rasping voice, his isolation in the midst of bustle, his hyperconsciousness—all are theirs. It is almost as if his own life had been refracted by a powerful prism into a multitude of different images. But with each image there was some mark of the original, some spoor of "the spindly figure with the umbrella." This, we may suspect, was what he himself had in mind when he remarked to his friend, Emil Boesen, how each of his works bore the "birthmark" of his personality.[6]

Just what is this characteristic Kierkegaardian "birthmark"? What is it that in spite of Kierkegaard's claim to the contrary makes the paternity of each of the pseudonymous works so clear?

It is true, of course, that Kierkegaard used some

[5] Stephen Crites, "The Author and the Authorship: Recent Kierkegaard Literature," *Journal of the American Academy of Religion,* Volume XXXVIII (March 1970), p. 38.

[6] Letter from SK to Emil Boesen, May 25, 1843. Printed in Niels Thulstrup (ed.), *Breve og Akstykker vedrørende Søren Kierkegaard, I* (Copenhagen: Munksgaard, 1953), p. 121.

material from his own journal in the writings of his pseudonyms. Twenty-seven of the first twenty-eight "Diapsalmata" (or refrains) in *Either/Or* were lifted verbatim from his journal,[7] and later on, the young man in *Stages on Life's Way* used word for word Kierkegaard's own letter to Regine in returning his fiancée's ring.[8] But these are only isolated cases and together with the borrowing of an idea here, a simile there, cannot account for the Kierkegaardian flavor of these books. To find the origins of this identifying "signature" we must look elsewhere—to the style of the works, to the character of the pseudonyms, and to the predicament they severally share.

Today most Danes make their first acquaintance with Kierkegaard in the Gymnasium, where he is studied as a master stylist of the language. The remarkable lightness and flexibility he brought to Danish, his ear for the music of words, his eye for the limpid image, the sure metaphor, his ability to dress the most abstract idea in the garments of concreteness, to unravel complexity into simplicity—all these characteristics of his extraordinary style are duly noted and admired by successive generations of seventeen-year-olds. It surely cannot be denied that Kierkegaard is a clever, even brilliant, writer and that his works are lit up at points with stylistic fireworks. But what is most Kierkegaardian is not the fireworks but the background against which they explode. For Kierkegaard is first and foremost an enormously diffuse writer.

There are individual parts of books—the "Unhappiest Man" essay in *Either/Or,* parts of *Fear and Trembling* and the *Postscript*—and at least one complete work (*Philosophical Fragments*) that are masterpieces of concision. But Kierkegaard's basic style is just the opposite. Not concise, but prolix, he seems to

[7] These are listed in *Papirer*, Volume III, pp. 321–23.

[8] See X[5] A 149.8 and *Stages on Life's Way* (Princeton: Princeton University Press, 1945), p. 304 (afterward cited as *Stages*).

drown the reader in a flood of words. Loosely moving
from one theme to another, he sometimes finishes the
first train of thought before moving on, and sometimes
does not. What he called "the vegetative luxuriance of
my style"[9] cannot be ascribed to any particular pseudonym. For it also characterizes the "edifying discourses"
he was simultaneously publishing under his own name
and qualifies a variety of pseudonyms. The fact is that
Kierkegaard was simply a very long-winded writer.

Part of this general looseness undoubtedly springs
from the particular conditions under which these books
were published. Kierkegaard had no editor, and all
his books through August 1847 were published on a
commission basis[10]—he paid the printer himself and
then gave the bookseller a percentage of the list price
to sell them. Since his funds during these years were
quite ample, there was no external check on the bulk
of his production. Publishing a book of three hundred
pages instead of one of two hundred pages simply
meant that both the copyist and the printer had to be
paid more for their labors. The result was that, with
the possible exception of *Philosophical Fragments,*
there is not one of Kierkegaard's pseudonymous works
that would not have benefited from some judicious
pruning.

But Kierkegaard's prolixity is not to be confused
with mere loquacity. Rather there is a compulsive
quality to his *longueur.* His writing, he told us, "was
the prompting of an irresistible inward impulse";[11] it
was a "necessary emptying-out [*Udtømmelse*]."[12]
During the years of his pseudonymous production the

[9] VIII[1] A 120.

[10] See Frithiof Brandt and Else Rammel, *Søren Kierkegaard
og Pengene* (Copenhagen: Levin & Munksgaard, 1935), pp.
11–34.

[11] *The Point of View for My Work as an Author* (New
York: Harper Torchbooks, 1962), p. 7 (afterward cited as
Point of View); SV, XIII, 519.

[12] *Point of View*, 73; SV, XIII, 562.

bulk of his journal remained small; in all of 1843,
1844, and 1845 it amounted to only 145 pages, while
in 1848 it grew to 349 pages, and two years later, in
1850, it had swollen to 671 pages. Without friends,
family, or confidantes Kierkegaard was emptying out
his thoughts and feelings through his pseudonyms. His
pen danced across the page without pause, not because
he enjoyed the diversion, but because he felt he *must*
write, must drain the watershed of ideas and fancies
that had built up over the years. And so the shower
bath descended, a steady flow of arguments, images,
stories, and characters: in February 1843, *Either/Or,*
a massive two-volume work of 838 pages; eight months
later, two shorter works, *Repetition* and *Fear and
Trembling;* eight months later, three more, *Philosophical Fragments, Prefaces,* and *The Concept of Dread;*
ten months later, in April 1845, the large (383 pages)
Stages on Life's Way; and finally, in February 1846,
the even larger (480 pages) *Concluding Unscientific
Postscript.* And all the while, we should not forget,
he was publishing no less than twenty-one religious
discourses under his own name. No wonder then that
this enormous productive outpouring sometimes seems
to run out of control, cascading over the reader like a
torrent. In much of this production one feels the
author's intoxication with language, and one also feels
a certain chill in remembering his remark that "to produce was my life."[13] For these works were his life.
Instead of pursuing a profession, or marrying, or even
enjoying himself, he *wrote*—and wrote furiously, concentrating all his energy and will in an orgy of creation.
Thus the general looseness of these works, products
not of a craftsman's leisure, but of a solitary's "irresistible impulse."

Kierkegaard's prolixity of style, of course, cannot be
disentangled from our impressions of the pseudonyms
he created. For what we are given in these books are

[13] X² A 442.

not the activities of a group of characters, but rather the essays, diaries, letters, commentaries, and lyrical outbursts of the pseudonymous authors. And they are a talkative lot: Judge William rambling through 70,000-word "letters" to his young friend; the aesthete *A* running on through page after page of pseudo-Hegelian criticism; Frater Taciturnus' long-winded commentary in *Stages on Life's Way;* Johannes Climacus' *tour de force* of humorous philosophizing in the *Postscript*. But this general garrulity is not their most outstanding characteristic nor is it what gives to them (and to their works) a Kierkegaardian signature.

Georg Brandes has remarked on the "hothouse" quality of Kierkegaard's imagination, how his pseudonyms are "bloodless" and "brain-figment like."[14] But Brandes at least partially misses the point. For it is not that Kierkegaard's craft has failed in producing characters that are "bloodless," but rather that his craft has succeeded in producing characters whose very essence is to lack flesh. When the aesthete of *Either/Or* observes that his imaginary creation, Johannes the Seducer, seemed to live in "a world of gauze, lighter, more ethereal, qualitatively different from the actual world,"[15] he offers a description that might with equal justice be applied to any of Kierkegaard's pseudonyms. Like their author they all seem inordinately "ghostly," moving in an ambience of mentality, never rooted in the world through their bodies, never richly desiring, nor painfully suffering. Disembodied to a marked degree, they are all hermits in life, without parents or home, wife or job, appetite or fear. In a single case (Judge William) we encounter a pseudonym with a family, but, as we shall see, his wife and child function more as poetic reference points than as flesh-and-blood

[14] Georg Brandes, *Søren Kierkegaard: En kritisk Fremstilling i Grundrids* (Copenhagen: Gyldendals Uglebøger, 1967), p. 17.

[15] *Either/Or*, I (Garden City, N.Y.: Anchor Books, 1959), p. 302 (afterward cited as *E/O*, I); *SV*, I, 278.

relations. Lonely, intelligent, sometimes wittily humorous, these pseudonyms appear most often as "strangers and aliens in the world,"[16] happy (when they are happy) only in their thoughts and reveries.

Their "ghostly" character is suggested by their names. There is first of all Victor Eremita, whose last name, Kierkegaard himself tells us, locates him "in the cloister."[17] Next is Constantine Constantius, who, mired in his "constant constancy," cannot receive the thunderstorm of "repetition" that revives his young friend and restores him to life. Then there is Johannes de Silentio, that "knight of infinite resignation," who can only stand astonished before the imagined faith of Abraham. Next is Vigilius Haufniensis, the pedantic psychologist, whose name is a Latin transcription for "the watchman of Copenhagen." There is William Afham, who describes himself as "'pure being' and therefore less than nothing,"[18] and in the same volume, Frater Taciturnus, the taciturn priest of the final stage anterior to faith. Finally, there is Johannes Climacus, who, although unable to make the movements of faith, nevertheless can lay out the ladder leading to it. From their names can be read their characters—hermetic, constant, silent, taciturn, and watchful. Never participants in life, they are its critics and spectators.

Their actions are perhaps as revealing as their names. For the odd thing about all these Kierkegaardian characters is that their primary activity seems to be imagining still other characters, thinking of the thoughts they might think and of the arguments they might profess. Victor Eremita imagines an aesthete, and then

[16] This is a phrase commonly applied to the pseudonyms. See, for example, *Fear and Trembling* (Princeton: Princeton University Press, 1968), p. 61; *Either/Or*, II (Garden City, N.Y.: Anchor Books, 1959), pp. 85–86 (afterward cited as *E/O*, II).

[17] *Point of View*, 18; *SV*, XIII, 526.

[18] *Stages*, 93; *SV*, VI, 83.

provides a series of essays as they might be written by him. Not to be outdone, the aesthete mimics his creator by imagining still another character, Johannes the Seducer, going so far as to write his 150-page diary. Johannes de Silentio embroiders various themes on the biblical story of Abraham, and completes his reflections by imagining a modern hero—the knight of faith as tax collector. Constantine Constantius finally admits that the "young man" whose letters he has presented is really a figment of his imagination. Frater Taciturnus likewise reveals that the "Quidam" whose diary the reader has just read is really not an actual person but a "thought experiment." The remaining pseudonyms content themselves not with inventing fictional characters, but with producing arguments concerning the nature of original sin, the difference between the Socratic and the Christian standpoints, the distinction between "objective" and "subjective" truth. Like their author, all these pseudonyms are "cloistered" from the world, and in their respective monastic cells, they all mimic his singular life-activity—thinking and imagining. Removed thus from the world, they are alive without feeling alive, they are human but only abstractly so. And it is this abstraction of their lives that haunts them. Each, troubled by his ineradicable "thinness," keeps returning to the image of a life that has been made lively, a humanity richly and passionately fulfilled. And here their thoughts are drawn into a fatal dialectic. For, like insomniacs proposing sleep, they imaginatively propose to themselves an actuality of selfhood which is flawed by the very fact that it is imaginary. Like the insomniac, they remain ever wakeful, ever conscious of the ideality of their dream, and thus end where they began—in the cloister. More than anything else it is this refusal of the pseudonym to be taken in by his dream, his steadfast irony, that gives these works their Kierkegaardian signature.

2

To point out the Kierkegaardian signature of these works is not finally to refuse Kierkegaard's advice. On the contrary, it is only by scrupulously following that advice that we can be led to their central meaning. There is an all-important correlation, a kind of doubling, that characterizes Kierkegaard's relation to his pseudonyms. For precisely in the same way that the pseudonyms maintain their distance from their imaginative creations, precisely in this way does Kierkegaard maintain his distance from the pseudonyms. Kierkegaard tells us he is absent from the pseudonyms, affirms that in these works his own voice is silent. What he tells us is the truth, and nothing said above about their Kierkegaardian signature should distract us from this truth. For the views of the pseudonyms are not Kierkegaard's. If anything, they are the views he has outlived or outthought. As certain well-to-do matrons hand on their old clothes to their maids, so Kierkegaard has handed on his old, outworn visions to his pseudonyms. Thus it requires no special prescience to recognize in the portrait of the aesthetic life painted in *Either/Or* only an extrapolation of the life Kierkegaard tried to live in the late 1830s, or to understand that, later on in the same work, when Judge William sings the praises of marriage, he is only dressing up the hopes Kierkegaard earlier entertained for himself and Regine. In 1848 he characterized his pseudonyms in this way:

> One will perceive the significance of the pseudonyms and why I must be pseudonymous in relation to all aesthetic production, because I led my own life in entirely different categories and understood from the beginning that this productivity was something interim, a deceit, a necessary emptying-out.[19]

[19] *Point of View*, 85–86 note; *SV*, XIII, 570 note.

In *The Point of View*—the posthumously published piece from which this citation is drawn—Kierkegaard never made clear just what these "entirely different categories" were, but in a journal entry from the same year he was more explicit. Looking back over the work of the last seven years he wrote: "As poet and thinker I have represented all things in the medium of imagination, myself living in resignation."[20]

Thus the distance that Kierkegaard maintains between himself and his pseudonyms is meant to indicate (at least in part) his own incapacity to believe the content of their visions. Just as the pseudonyms remain ever wakeful in their irony, so Kierkegaard's silence—his absence from these works—indicates a similar wakefulness. The central focus of the pseudonymous works is neither ethics nor religion nor aesthetics, but rather the dialectic of the life of imagination. Their achievement, as we shall see, lies in the construction of a literature of self-reference, a series of works that comment repeatedly on the imaginative act involved in their own creation. They are a "deceit," then, only to the extent that they are not about what they appear to be about. To take them "seriously" is not to take them seriously. To paraphrase them, earnestly to elucidate the "philosophy" expounded or the metaphysics presupposed in this or that work, is to miss the point that ultimately they seek to show the vanity of all philosophy and metaphysics. To grasp the core of Kierkegaard's pseudonymous authorship is first to grasp its essential *duplicity*.

With these works in mind, John Updike has remarked that "duplicity was the very engine of Kierkegaard's thought," that he was a "man in love with duplicity and irony and all double-edged things."[21] In the pseudonyms this duplicity is all-pervasive. For here we find pseudonyms curled within pseudonyms

[20] VIII[1] A 650.

[21] John Updike, "The Fork," see below in this volume pp. 175, 182.

like "Chinese puzzle boxes."[22] Here we find elaborate
hoaxes that disappear in an eyeblink as the pseudonym
admits his ploy. Here we have Kierkegaard going to
extreme lengths to conceal his authorship, while at the
same time writing a tongue-in-cheek letter to *Fædrelandet* asking, "Who is the author of *Either/Or?*"[23]
The world of the pseudonyms is a world of stratagem
and pretense, of "acoustic illusion"[24] and "thought
experiment."[25] It is a world of artifice and subterfuge,
a world of trap doors and hidden panels, of sudden
surprises and shapes only half-recognized in a mirror.
Thus we have pseudonyms pretending *not* to be other
pseudonyms—Constantine Constantius pretending not
to be "the young man" (and then admitting it), Frater
Taciturnus pretending not to be Quidam (and then
admitting it), the aesthete *A* pretending not to be
Johannes the Seducer (and then implying the two are
self-identical). More importantly, through the device
of parody, we have books pretending to be books they
are not. *Either/Or,* to choose a notable example, appears dressed in the familiar trappings of the Romantic
Novel—the letter, the aphorism, the essay are all very
much in evidence. For all the world it would seem
to have been staged on the same platform as *Wilhelm
Meister.* But as Louis Mackey has pointed out, it is in
reality a parody of Goethe's great universal novel—
"a *Bildungsroman* but without *Bildung.*"[26] Or take the

[22] Victor Eremita describes the structure of *Either/Or* in
these words at *E/O,* I, 9; *SV,* I, x.

[23] This published letter may be found at *SV,* XIII, 407–10.

[24] This is the subtitle of an appendix to Chapter III of *Philosophical Fragments.* See *Philosophical Fragments* (Princeton:
Princeton University Press, 1962), pp. 61–67 (afterward cited
as *PF*); *SV,* IV, 215–19.

[25] The pseudonym Frater Taciturnus describes Quidam's
diary in these words in his closing "Epistle to the Reader."
See *Stages,* 363–436; *SV,* VI, 371–450.

[26] Louis Mackey, *Kierkegaard: A Kind of Poet* (Philadelphia: University of Pennsylvania Press, 1971), p. 274.

Concluding Unscientific Postscript, that massive work of 480 large pages which is entitled a "postscript" to a tiny work of 164 small pages. A glance at its complicated table of contents would lead the casual reader to suspect that here the philosophical urge to system building has run amok. Yet the target of the book is really systematic philosophy, and in the pseudonym's absurd conclusion that the difficulty of belief can itself become a criterion of true belief, we recognize that the attempt to save philosophy from the philosophers has itself become a target of satire. Finally, in the comic profusion of pseudonyms and the transparency of their stratagems in *Stages on Life's Way,* the device of pseudonymity itself is parodied. The ambience of all these works is the ambience of duplicity, and their essential theme is the inherent volatility of human consciousness. In their elaborate hoaxes and sudden surprises, in their trickery and satire, there is an underlying black humor. For finally the joke is on the reader, and the smarter the reader, the sooner he is able to grasp the joke. But to see through all the pseudonyms, to recognize that the vision of any one is not to be preferred to that of any other, is finally to join Kierkegaard in his cloister. It is to share with him that peculiarly modern laceration—"I must believe, but I can't believe"—which since his time has become ever more painful. The essentially duplicitous character of the pseudonyms is then essential to their meaning, and this duplicity is founded on the simple yet all-important fact that in the pseudonyms Kierkegaard is *absent.*

But how can a man be absent from his words?

Years before, in the master's thesis that won him the whimsical sobriquet "Master of Irony," Kierkegaard answered this question. Even more importantly, in the latter stages of this work, written in 1841 as he slowly, painfully disengaged himself from Regine, he laid out the problematic that was to order the pseudonymous series. As Georg Brandes pointed out a

century ago, *The Concept of Irony* is "the true point
of departure for Kierkegaard's authorship."[27]

The ironist, of course, is the man who is absent from
his words. In ordinary speech, writes Kierkegaard, a
person can be pinned down in what he says. The ordinary speaker means what he says and hence is bound
to that meaning. But "the ironic figure of speech can-
cels itself"[28] since the ironic speaker's meaning is not
in what is said: "If . . . what is said is not my meaning,
or the opposite of my meaning, then I am free both in
relation to others and in relation to myself."[29] The
ironist, absent from his words, is epitomized by Socrates, whose ironic turn of speech was not just a conversational gambit but rather expressed a life-view
culminating in "infinite negativity."[30]

In the last third of the book Kierkegaard turns from
a consideration of Socratic irony to the concept of irony
itself. It is here, in his portrait of the ironist's ultimate
refusal of the world, that we can discern the outlines
of the problematic that will later guide the pseudonymous series.

Praising Hegel's characterization of irony as "infinite absolute negativity,"[31] he goes on to point out
how the ironist must live among his contemporaries
as "a stranger and an alien."[32] "The whole of existence has become alien to the ironic subject," he points
out. "He in turn has become estranged from existence
and that because actuality has lost its validity for him,

---

[27] Cited by Lee Capel in the Historical Introduction to his
translation of *The Concept of Irony* (New York: Harper &
Row, 1966), pp. 7–8. This work will be afterward cited as
Irony. Capel's reference is to the 1877 edition of the work by
Brandes mentioned above, *Søren Kierkegaard: En kritisk Frem-
stilling i Grundrids*, p. 187.

[28] *Irony*, 265; *SV*, XIII, 323.

[29] *Irony*, 265; *SV*, XIII, 322.

[30] *Irony*, 240; *SV*, XIII, 297.

[31] *Irony*, 271; *SV*, XIII, 329.

[32] *Irony*, 263; *SV*, XIII, 321.

as he, too, to a certain extent, has become unreal."[33]
This theme of the hostility of the ironist to actuality,
his attempt poetically to derealize it (and the consequent derealization of self this entails), becomes the
guiding idea of the final section of the book. "Irony is
free," we are told, "free from all the cares of actuality.
. . . When one is free in this way, only then does one
live poetically, and it is well-known that irony's great
demand was that one should *live poetically*."[34] But
what does it mean to live poetically? Choosing a Hegelian terminology (perhaps not without a trace of
irony) Kierkegaard suggests that the project of "living
poetically" is really the attempt to translate the *an sich*
(in-itself) character of the world and the self into *für
sich* (for-itself): "But really to live poetically, to be
able poetically to create himself, the ironist must have
no *an sich*."[35] The ironist's project is then one of perpetually remaking himself and his world. Repeatedly
he seeks to extirpate the otherness of the world so that,
like Narcissus, he can stand unencumbered in the presence of his own image:

> As he is not inclined to fit himself to his surround-
> ings, so his surroundings must be shaped to fit him,
> that is, he poeticizes not only himself but his surround-
> ings as well. . . . When the given actuality loses its
> validity for the ironist, this is not because it is an
> outlived actuality which shall be replaced by a truer,
> but because the ironist is the eternal ego for whom
> no actuality is adequate.[36]

This "eternal ego for whom no actuality is adequate" is, of course, no one else but that solitary individual we have come to know in the journal entries
of the 1830s and 40s. As the outlines of Kierkegaard's

[33] *Irony,* 276; *SV,* XIII, 333.
[34] *Irony,* 296–97; *SV,* XIII, 351.
[35] *Irony,* 298; *SV,* XIII, 352–53.
[36] *Irony,* 300; *SV,* XIII, 354–55.

sketch of the ironist are filled in, it comes more and
more to resemble a self-portrait:

> The ironist stands proudly withdrawn into himself;
> he lets mankind pass before him, as did Adam the
> animals, and finds no companionship for himself. By
> this he constantly comes into conflict with the ac-
> tuality to which he belongs. . . . For him life is a
> drama, and what engrosses him is the ingenious
> unfolding of that drama. He is himself a spectator
> even when performing some act. . . . He is inspired
> by the virtues of self-sacrifice as a spectator is in-
> spired by them in a theater; he is a severe critic who
> well knows when such virtues become insipid and
> false. He even feels remorse, but aesthetically not
> morally. In the moment of remorse he is aesthetically
> above his remorse examining whether it be poetically
> correct, whether it might be a suitable reply in the
> mouth of some poetic character.
>
> Because the ironist poeticizes both himself and his
> surroundings with the greatest possible license, be-
> cause he lives completely hypothetically and subjunc-
> tively, his life finally loses all continuity. With this he
> sinks completely into mood. His life becomes *sheer
> mood*. . . . The ironist is a poet. . . . He poeticizes
> everything, especially his feelings. . . . He imagines
> that it is he who evokes the feeling, and he keeps on
> imagining until he becomes so spiritually exhausted
> that he must cease. Feeling has therefore no reality
> for the ironist, and he seldom gives expression to
> his feelings except in the form of an opposition. His
> grief hides itself in the incognito of the jest, his joy
> is wrapped in lament.[37]

The term "ironist" may appear somewhat strange
for describing this figure who tries, despairingly, to
poeticize all of existence. Even in this passage, Kierke-

[37] *Irony*, 300–2; *SV*, XIII, 354–56.

gaard at one point calls him a "poet" and at another notes that he lives "metaphysically" and "aesthetically."[38] Later in the same chapter he remarks that "throughout the discussion I use the expressions: *irony* and the *ironist,* but I could as easily say: *romanticism* and the *romanticist*. Both expressions designate the same thing."[39] Again in offering a commentary on Friedrich Schlegel's novel, *Lucinde,* he indicates that the subject of his portrait is really the man who "allows imagination alone to rule":

> When the imagination is allowed to rule in this way it prostrates and anaesthetizes the soul, robs it of all moral tension, and makes of life a dream.[40]

But the point of this long discussion has not been to demonstrate that Kierkegaard painted the portrait of the ironist-poet-aesthete-romanticist in traits drawn from his own person. The great importance of Kierkegaard's dissertation on irony lies rather in the clarity with which it shows Kierkegaard's grasp of his own standpoint. The standpoint of irony (inferentially his own) is not a point of destination but of departure; in the closing pages of *Irony* it is revealed as a stage to be overcome.

Significantly, Kierkegaard closes his discussion of romantic irony with a treatment of the work of K. W. F. Solger and Solger's contention that man is really *der Nichtige*—the being who is not. He rejects Solger's standpoint ("Solger has run wild in the negative"[41]), but not before hinting that in his concept of *der Nichtige* Solger had offered a category which exactly fits the ironist. For the ironist is really the naysayer, the man who negates in its very foundations the

---

[38] These words occur in the parts of the passage not excerpted above.

[39] *Irony,* 292; *SV,* XIII, 347–48.

[40] *Irony,* 308; *SV,* XIII, 362.

[41] *Irony,* 323; *SV,* XIII, 376.

actuality of the world. Not only absent from his words, he is also absent from himself: He does not "possess himself in infinite clarity" but has "his infinity outside himself."[42] He has become "intoxicated by the infinity of possibles."[43] The task of the ironist, Kierkegaard suggests, is to master irony, indeed to overcome it. And this stage of mastered irony is described in the final section of the dissertation as a stage where actuality is again actualized. "Actuality will therefore not be rejected," Kierkegaard writes, "and longing shall be a healthy love, not a kittenish ruse for sneaking out of the world."[44]

It was not insignificant that Poul Møller charged Kierkegaard with being "so polemical through and through that it's just terrible," nor was it insignificant that Kierkegaard's mind kept drifting back to this remark nearly twenty years after it was made.[45] For in some primordial sense, Kierkegaard was a man absent from himself. "Each time I wish to say something," he complained in 1837, "there is another who says it at the very same moment. It is as if I were always thinking double, as if my other self were always somehow ahead of me."[46]

The dissertation on irony ended with the demand that irony be overcome so that actuality might be realized. This, in essence, was both Kierkegaard's desire and his problem. Experience had become for him a kind of sieve through which actuality seeped. Like the ironist, his mind had become "intoxicated" by possibilities, escaping, like a leak of gas, into the imaginary. His problem—and ultimately the problem of the pseudonyms—was how to stop that leak, how to prevent consciousness from "sneaking out of the world." In *Either/Or* (parts of which were written simultaneously

[42] *Irony*, 313; *SV*, XIII, 367.
[43] *Irony*, 335; *SV*, XIII, 279.
[44] *Irony*, 341; *SV*, XIII, 392.
[45] See XI¹ A 275, 276.
[46] I A 333.

with *Irony*) this problem was given flesh and substance. Since in large measure the other pseudonymous works only explore the consequences of this problem, *Either/Or* will repay our very close attention.

3

There is first of all the ambiguity of authorship. Kierkegaard was, of course, the actual author of *Either/Or,* but his name appears nowhere on the title page, and in the months following its publication on February 20, 1843, there were few in Copenhagen who knew the real author's identity.[47] Its pseudonymous "editor," Victor Eremita, complicates the question by likewise disclaiming responsibility for its authorship, claiming that he found the manuscript in the secret drawer of a desk. By comparing the handwriting he was able to conclude that the manuscript was the work of two persons: a civil magistrate named William (whom Victor designates *B*) and a nameless "young friend" of the magistrate (whom Victor designates *A*). The papers of Judge William consist first of two long letters (really treatises) on the subject of marriage and ethics. These two letters are in turn followed by a sermon written (so Judge William tells us) by an obscure Jutland priest. Together, the sermon and the two letters make up the second volume of *Either/Or,* leaving the first volume to be made up of the scattered papers of *A*. These cover a wide range. There are a number of aphorisms and lyrical outbursts grouped under the rubric "Diapsalmata"—a Greek word meaning "refrain." There are several essays in literary criticism as well as speeches written for a private club of aesthetes. Finally, there is the famous "Diary of the

---

[47] Cf. the following contemporary reviews of *Either/Or:* Meyer Goldschmidt, *Corsaren,* No. 129 (March 10, 1843), pp. 1–3; Anonymous, *For Lit. og Kritik,* I (1843), pp. 377–405; Anonymous, *Fædrelandet,* February 20, 1843; J. L. Heiberg, *Intelligensblade,* II (1843), p. 289.

Seducer." Here once again the putative author, *A*, disclaims authorship, claiming in his preface to the diary that he stole it from a friend named "Johannes." But *A*'s disclaimer is itself denied by Victor Eremita, who, in his preface to the whole work, tells us that Johannes the Seducer is most likely a creature of *A*'s imagination and that *A*'s attempt to pass himself off as only the editor of Johannes' diary is "an old trick of the novelist."[48] To wrap the enigma of authorship in still further mystery, Victor hints that his own "editorship" may again be a novelistic ruse and that he himself may very well be the true author of the whole work.[49]

Why all this deception and masquerade? Why pseudonym wrapped in pseudonym "like parts in a Chinese puzzle box"?[50] If we ask for the real author of *Either/Or* Søren Kierkegaard presents himself. But his figure soon merges with his pseudonym, the hermetic Victor. And Victor is so volatile as to become quickly two other characters—the Judge and the aesthete—whose volatility propels them into still further pseudonyms. When we ask for a person we are given a *persona*, and when we enter the interior world of this *persona*, we find it in motion, spinning off through fantasy into yet another *persona*. We search in vain for actuality, for substance. All we find is human consciousness in its intrinsic volatility, its perpetual "elsewhere." It is precisely this volatility that is the central focus of the book.

Like both Kierkegaard and the ironist before him, the aesthete is presented to us as living *beyond himself*, a characteristic made ironically clear in his preface to the "Diary of the Seducer." The Seducer's life, the aesthete points out, has "been an attempt to realize the task of living poetically."[51] The diary reflects this fundamental project in its odd use of the present tense, a use which "is neither historically exact nor simply

[48] *E/O*, I, 9; *SV*, I, x.
[49] *E/O*, I, 13; *SV*, I, xv.
[50] *E/O*, I, 9; *SV*, I, x.
[51] *E/O*, I, 300; *SV*, I, 276.

fiction, not indicative but subjunctive."[52] Again and again the Seducer describes incidents in the present tense as if they were occurring before his very eyes. But as the aesthete remarks in his preface to the diary, this is impossible, since everything in the diary "is recorded, naturally, after it has happened."[53] This deliberate mixing of present with past, however, has a point; it is, in fact, the very essence of the aesthetic project whose final goal is not just a new or more intense experience, but (as the aesthete makes clear) the reproduction of "experience more or less poetically."[54] "How can we account for the fact that the Diary has acquired such a poetic coloration?" he asks. "It is explained by . . . [the Seducer's] poetic nature, which, we might say, is not rich enough, or, perhaps, not poor enough, to distinguish poetry and reality from one another."[55] The Seducer's act in writing the diary hence exemplifies that deliberate mixing of immediate experience with imaginative reconstruction which is the core of the aesthetic project.

But now the irony inherent in the "Chinese puzzle box" structure of the book makes itself felt. For the aesthete ends his preface to the diary by concluding that the Seducer's project ends in failure:

> Many people who appear bodily in the actual world do not belong in it. . . . But the fact that a man can thus dwindle away, almost vanish from reality, may be a symptom of health or of sickness. . . . He did not belong to reality, and yet he had much to do with it. . . . He was not unequal to the weight of reality; he was not too weak to bear it, not at all, he was too strong; but this strength was really a sickness.[56]

[52] *E/O*, I, 300; *SV*, I, 276.
[53] *E/O*, I, 300; *SV*, I, 276.
[54] *E/O*, I, 300; *SV*, I, 276.
[55] *E/O*, I, 301; *SV*, I, 277.
[56] *E/O*, I, 302; *SV*, I, 278.

As readers of Victor Eremita's original preface, we know that the diary is not the product of the Seducer's recollection, but that both Seducer and diary are products of the aesthete's imagination. We know that in describing the Seducer, the aesthete is really describing himself, and that in pointing out the necessary failure of the Seducer's project, he is also remarking the necessary failure of his own life. Fundamentally, then, the aesthete is presented to us as *beyond himself*. "Your thought was hurried on ahead," the Judge admonishes him in *Either/Or*, II, "you have seen through the vanity of everything, but you have got no further. . . . So you are constantly beyond yourself, that is, in despair [*i fortvivlelsen*]."[57] Here the Danish term, *fortvivlelse*, carries more significance than its English counterpart, since it bears within it a morpheme signaling the doubling of consciousness (*tvivl* in Danish means "doubt"; *tvivlesyg* "skepticism"; *tvetydighed* "ambiguity").[58] Thus to speak of the aesthete as "in despair" is to ascribe to him a doubled consciousness; he perseveres in his project, but at every moment he is beyond it, recognizing its nullity. It is this recognition that is communicated ironically through his preface to the Seducer's diary, and it is this recognition that makes of him (like the ironist before him) a man *absent* from himself.

A portrait of the man who "is always absent, never present to himself"[59] is sketched with almost algebraic brevity in a little essay entitled "The Unhappiest Man." Originally intended by the aesthete *A* as an address to be delivered to the *Symparenekromenoi* (a Greek coinage meaning "society of co-deceased ones"), it catalogues the ways in which one can be absent from one-

[57] *E/O*, II, 199; *SV*, II, 175.

[58] See *Purity of Heart* (New York: Harper & Brothers, 1948), pp. 59ff. and *SV*, VIII, 164ff. where Kierkegaard makes precisely this etymological point about the "double-mindedness" [*tvesyndethed*] of "despair" [*fortvivlelse*].

[59] *E/O*, I, 96; *SV*, I, 96.

self either in the future or in the past, either in hope or in recollection. But the uniquely unhappy man is he whose faulted presence in both past and future prevents his real presence in either: "When the hoping individual would have a future which can have no reality for him, or when the man of memory would remember a time which has had no reality, then we have the essentially unhappy individuals."[60] For the truly unhappy man "it is memory which prevents him from being present in hope, and hope which prevents him from being present in memory."[61] The consequence of this distancing of self into two mutually repellent temporal modes is the loss of temporality itself:

> His life is restless and without content. He is not present to himself in the moment. He is not present to himself in the future, for the future has already been experienced. He is not present to himself in the past, for the past has not yet come. . . . Alone, he has the whole world over against him as the alter with which he finds himself in conflict. . . . In one sense he cannot die, for he has not really lived; in another sense he cannot live, for he is already dead. . . . He has no time for anything, not because his time is taken up with something else, but because he has no time at all.[62]

Although it may not be apparent from the brief description offered above, the "unhappiest man" is really the aesthete. For it is the aesthete who above all wants to recapture the past. "The first kiss," he remarks at one point, "is qualitatively different from all others."[63] On page after page of *Either/Or* we see him in search of those inimitable "firsts"—not only the first kiss, but also the first love, the first dance, the first sensation of

[60] *E/O*, I, 221–22; *SV*, I, 198.
[61] *E/O*, I, 223; *SV*, I, 198.
[62] *E/O*, I, 224; *SV*, I, 199–200.
[63] *E/O*, I, 412; *SV*, I, 384.

falling in love.[64] "Like the Spanish knight of the doleful countenance," the Judge cautions him, "you are
fighting for a vanished time."[65] Vainly trying to recapture in the future the "firstness" of things that now
lie buried in the past, he is a creature of nostalgia. The
desperation of his search, moreover, soon becomes
apparent in his removal from time itself. "I feel the
way a chessman must," he complains, "when the op-
ponent says of it: that piece cannot be moved."[66]
At another point: "Time flows, life is a stream, people
say, and so on. I do not notice it. Time stands still,
and I with it."[67] His world has become a "still life"
where time, change, and growth are hauntingly absent. In place of vitality and movement we encounter
only a paralysis of emotion and purpose, an all-
embracing indolence: "How terrible tedium is—terribly
tedious. . . . I lie stretched out inactive; the only
thing I see is emptiness. The only thing I feed on is
emptiness. I do not even suffer pain."[68] Immersed in
this great emptiness which muffles the sounds of the
outside world, he is left alone with a consciousness that
never changes. Through all the essays of *Either/Or,* I,
runs the common complaint of the aesthete: life is
trivial and empty; he has seen through it; boredom is
everywhere.

This is a complaint familiar not only from Kierkegaard's journal, but also from the pages of *The Concept of Irony.* The true novelty of *Either/Or* lies not
in painting this familiar portrait in even deeper tones,
but in plotting the development that culminates in the
aesthetic life. Oddly enough, the absence from self
which so torments the aesthete turns out also to be the
motivating force behind his development. Or to put it
another way: if it is important to recognize that the

[64] See *E/O,* I, 317, 400, 412.

[65] *E/O,* II, 127; *SV,* II, 143.

[66] *E/O,* I, 24; *SV,* I, 6. Cf. II A 435.

[67] *E/O,* I, 25; *SV,* I, 10.

[68] *E/O,* I, 36; *SV,* I, 21.

aesthetic life ends in "despair" (*fortvivlelse*), it is equally important to acknowledge that it begins in "dread" (*angest*).

The first essay in *Either/Or,* entitled "The Immediate Stages of the Erotic," offers a description of the stages which culminate in the full-blown aesthetic life. Briefly, they might be indicated by the terms "dreaming," "seeking," and "desiring." The first stage is exemplified operatically by the Page in Mozart's *Figaro.* Desire is here not yet qualified as desire; it is "present only as a presentiment about itself, is without movement, without disquiet, only gently rocked by an unclarified inner emotion."[69] The first stage evolves into a more qualified one midway between dreaming and explicit desiring. This second stage—also exemplified by a Mozart character (Papageno in *The Magic Flute*)—manifests itself in a yearning after a yet unspecified object. The two earlier stages culminate finally in explicit desiring, symbolized by Mozart's Don Juan. Finding its object, desire now becomes determinate. It is this stage of outright desiring which exemplifies the aesthetic life.

These various stages quite clearly plot an ascent through varying levels of consciousness. What is being offered in this essay is really a developmental account of how Romantic Man—Solger's *der Nichtige*—comes to self-consciousness. The signal characteristic of this movement up the scale of consciousness is its inspiration by what Kierkegaard calls "dread" (*angest*).

Little over a year later Kierkegaard will devote a whole volume to the description of "dread." "Dread," we will be told, "is a qualification of the dreaming spirit. . . . When awake the difference between my self and my other is posited; sleeping it is suspended; dreaming it is a nothing vaguely hinted at."[70] In dread, consciousness is dreaming in man and this dreaming

[69] *E/O,* I, 75; *SV,* I, 58.
[70] *The Concept of Dread* (Princeton: Princeton University Press, 1946), p. 38 (afterward cited as *Dread*); *SV,* IV, 313.

state (parallel to its description in *Either/Or*) is both painful and sweet. "Dread," Kierkegaard continues, "is a sympathetic antipathy, an antipathetic sympathy. . . . If we observe children we find this dread more definitely indicated as a seeking after adventure, a thirst for the prodigious, the mysterious."[71] And finally (again as suggested in *Either/Or*), in this state one dreams, but one dreams of nothing:

> In this state there is peace and rest, but at the same time there is something else, which is not dissension and strife, for there is nothing to strive with. What is it then? Nothing. But what effect does nothing have? It feeds dread.[72]

The vague apprehension of dread rests in the very bosom of the dawning consciousness. It is this apprehension which provides the energy for the ascent to consciousness. In the dreaming state man is aware of a vague lack, an emptiness. He feels as if the tiniest of cracks has opened in the pure substance of his being; a nothingness has intruded and with its entrance there has arisen the possibility of movement. With the first vague hints of a "homesickness for himself"[73] he turns outward to the world to recover the closure which was his, and now is lost. The vague yearning of the dream becomes a thirst for adventure, a quest of discovery:

> The longing breaks away from the earth and starts out wandering; the flower gets wings and flits inconstant and unwearied here and there. . . . Swiftly the

[71] *Dread*, 38; *SV*, IV, 313–14.

[72] *Dread*, 38; *SV*, IV, 313.

[73] Kierkegaard applies this phrase to the fictitious Quidam in *Stages on Life's Way*, p. 303 (*SV*, VI, 307). It would appear to characterize vividly at least one aspect of dread. See also II A 127 and II A 191. At X² A 384 Kierkegaard remarks that "dread is really nothing but impatience."

objects vanish and reappear; but still before every disappearance is a present enjoyment, a moment of contact, short but sweet, evanescent as the gleam of a glowworm, inconstant and fleeting as the touch of a butterfly. . . . Only momentarily is a deeper desire suspected, but this suspicion is forgotten. In Papageno desire aims at discoveries.[74]

In each isolated moment of discovery the dreamer-become-seeker experiences a moment of contact—a brief, poignant taste of the original unity that was his. For a moment he savors it; but then in a flash it is gone. Yet no matter, he can find another object, another scintillation of enjoyment to replace the present one. And so he skips from moment to moment, from sparkle to sparkle, with hardly a glance toward the deeper desire which lingers in the background.

In the next stage—the stage of outright desiring exemplified by Don Juan—this deeper desire becomes more pressing. For Don Juan is inspired by dread:

There is a dread in him, but this dread is his energy. In him it is not a subjectively reflected dread, but a substantial dread. Don Juan's life is not despair; but it is the whole power of sensuousness which is born in dread, and Don Juan himself is this dread.[75]

What should be clear from this developmental account is that the aesthete is fundamentally a narcissist. Like the young Camus, he can "never forget that part of the self that lies sleeping in the world."[76] From the very beginning it has been the vague awareness of absence—of his self as somehow lost "out there" in the world—that has informed the whole movement from dreaming to desiring, and ultimately, to despairing.

[74] *E/O*, I, 79; *SV*, I, 62.

[75] *E/O*, I, 128; *SV*, I, 108.

[76] Albert Camus, *Carnets: Mai 1935–Février 1942* (Paris: Gallimard, 1962), p. 38.

Tormented by the memory of a primordial unity that once was his and now is lost forever, he tries to recover it in the world. But the world is other than the self, opposed to it, unutterably alien. Still, the aesthete perseveres, seeking (in his words) to reduce all experience "to a sounding board for the soul's own music."[77] Yet here his project enters a fatal dialectic. For he both requires otherness, and seeks its destruction. The Seducer requires his young fiancée's freedom (otherwise there could be no seduction), but his aim is to subjugate it. More generally, the aesthete seeks not actual experience, but actual experience lit up with ideality, the world made image. Ultimately what he seeks is a kind of unconsciousness, the absorption into "a single mood, a single color,"[78] yet he seeks it deliberately, consciously. The wound he has tried to close is therefore exacerbated; consciousness grows; he becomes not less but *more* wakeful. Finding the world recalcitrant, he slips deeper and deeper into a dream world where immediate sensations are muted, and where he is stimulated only by the fantastic shapes of his imagination. To use the words *A* applies to the Seducer: "He comes to dwindle away, aye, almost vanish from reality. . . . He soon discovers that he is going about in a circle from which he cannot escape. . . . Like a startled deer, pursued by despair, he constantly seeks a way out, and finds only a way in, through which he goes back into himself."[79]

The way out of this labyrinth of self is proposed by Judge William in the second volume of *Either/Or*. In an analysis prefigured in the closing paragraphs of *The Concept of Irony,* he sees *A*'s problem to be a lack of actuality. In refusing the actuality of the world (its resistance and alterity) *A* has drained actuality from his own person, has permitted it to bubble off into the imaginary. Faced with this problem, the Judge's ad-

[77] *E/O,* I, 290; *SV,* I, 266.

[78] *E/O,* I, 23; *SV,* I, 9.

[79] *E/O,* I, 302, 304; *SV,* I, 278, 280.

vice to *A* is deceptively simple. How is *A* to achieve actuality and reverse the diaspora of his life? By *choosing* himself, says the Judge:

> He who chooses himself ethically chooses himself as this definite individual. . . . The individual thus becomes conscious of himself as this definite individual with these talents, these dispositions, these instincts, these passions, influenced by these definite surroundings, as this definite environment. But being conscious of himself in this way he assumes responsibility for all this. He does not hesitate as to whether he shall include this particular trait or the other. . . . He has his place in the world, and with freedom he chooses his place, that is, he chooses this very place. He is a definite individual, in the choice he makes himself a definite individual, for he chooses himself.[80]

In choosing himself, according to the Judge, the ethical man affirms his identity in all its concreteness. He is *this* person, born in *this* town, of *these* parents, at *this* time; *this* is his situation, and in choosing himself he accepts it unconditionally. Yet curiously, this very choice of the situation allegedly transforms it. For by freely taking it on, it is, according to the Judge, transferred from the realm of necessity to the realm of freedom: "All that has happened to me or befallen me is by me transformed and translated from necessity to freedom."[81] What previously was alien and unwanted, the ineluctable evidence of one's facticity, is now penetrated with freedom. "He who lives ethically," the Judge remarks, "has seen himself, knows himself, penetrates with his consciousness his whole concretion."[82]

This choice of oneself *in situ* has yet another di-

[80] *E/O,* II, 255–56; *SV,* II, 225.
[81] *E/O,* II, 255; *SV,* II, 224.
[82] *E/O,* II, 263; *SV,* II, 231.

mension. For the fact that the ethical man chooses himself concretely involves a necessary transformation of his relation to the future—of his possibilities.

> He who chooses himself ethically has himself as his task, and not as a possibility, not as a toy to be played with arbitrarily. He can choose himself ethically only when he chooses himself in continuity, and so he has himself as a manifestly defined task.[83]

For the aesthete, the future and possibility are blank and open. They are, *A* admits in one of his diapsalmata, like the empty space into which a spider hurls itself.[84] But in the Judge's portrait of the ethical man this empty space has been transformed into the firm outlines of a life-task. It is as if in discovering his identity in the act of ethical choice, the ethical man also discovered how this identity should be realized. While on the one hand the self he chooses is factual and past, on the other hand it is potential and future.

> Although he himself is his aim, this aim is nevertheless another, for the self which is the aim is not an abstract self which fits anywhere and hence nowhere, but a concrete self which stands in reciprocal relations with these surroundings, these conditions of life, this natural order.[85]

The self he chooses is of course himself. But this self includes vectors toward the future—gifts, talents, potentialities—and these also are included in the choice. By choosing the past in such a way that the future becomes definite the ethical man knits up the fracture in the tenses made evident in his despair. Future flows out of past naturally and confidently; the personality is consolidated; the individual attains mastery over

[83] *E/O*, II, 262; *SV*, II, 231.
[84] *E/O*, I, 24; *SV*, I, 8.
[85] *E/O*, II, 267; *SV*, II, 235.

himself: "The fact that the individual sees his possibility as his task expresses precisely his sovereignty over himself."[86]

Now it is just this aim of gaining "sovereignty over himself" which summarizes the ethical man's project as it is pictured by Judge William. He *wills* now to penetrate his whole being with the consciousness of his choice. "Only when in his choice a man has assumed himself," the Judge continues, "is clad in himself, has so totally penetrated himself that every movement is attended by the consciousness of a responsibility for himself, only then has he chosen himself ethically."[87]

We can think of the ethical man's choice of himself as a curious kind of marriage vow—a vow which marries him not to another person but to life itself. The Judge speaks of "the consolidation, the penetrating shudder through all thoughts and joints which is marriage,"[88] and this description might just as aptly be applied to the ethical man's choice of himself. For above all it is a "deed," an *act* which only the individual can perform for himself, an *act* by virtue of which *uno tenore* he can break free of the chrysalis which the Judge calls "despair" (*fortvivlelse*): "Behold, my young friend, this life of yours is despair. It is as though you were caught and ensnared and could nevermore either in time or eternity slip free."[89] There is despair and there is life; between the two (alleges the Judge) stretches the healing act of choice whereby the individual once and for all becomes concrete by "marrying" himself to life.

If only the young man will choose, then, according to the Judge, "the world will become beautiful to you and joyful, although you can see it with different eyes than before, and your liberated spirit will soar up into

[86] *E/O*, II, 256; *SV*, II, 226.
[87] *E/O*, II, 252; *SV*, II, 222.
[88] *E/O*, II, 67; *SV*, II, 61.
[89] *E/O*, II, 209–10; *SV*, II, 185.

the world of freedom."[90] This idyll the far side of
despair is described by the Judge in the closing pages
of *Either/Or,* where he claims to offer glimpses of his
own existence as husband, father, and man of affairs.
He admits that he too now and then comes to "sub-
side into himself," permitting a "melancholy" to gain
ascendancy over him.[91] But swiftly the presence of
his wife resuscitates him.

> When I am sitting thus lost and abandoned and
> then look at my wife walking about the room lightly
> and youthfully, always occupied, always with some-
> thing to attend to, my eye involuntarily follows her
> movement, I take part in everything she undertakes,
> and it ends with my being again reconciled with time,
> finding that time acquires significance for me, that the
> instant moves swiftly.[92]

Here are the rich tones, the luminous atmosphere,
the romance for the commonplace so characteristic of
a Vermeer interior. The Judge tells how he returns
from work to the beautiful tones of his wife's lullaby,
how he enters to "hear the cry of the little one," which
to his ear "is not inharmonious."[93] There is a peace
here, a feeling of time passing happily, of a harmony
of individual and world that is quite touching. Here
is the ideal of the ethical life, the husband, father, and
man of affairs who has become fully actual through
contracting a binding commitment to life:

> So our hero lives by his work, his work is at the
> same time his calling, hence he works with pleasure.
> The fact that it is his calling brings him into asso-
> ciation with other men, and in performing his job
> he accomplishes what he could wish to accomplish

[90] *E/O,* II, 223; *SV,* II, 196.
[91] *E/O,* II, 312; *SV,* II, 275.
[92] *E/O,* II, 312; *SV,* II, 275.
[93] *E/O,* II, 329; *SV,* II, 290.

> in the world. He is married, contented with his home, and time passes swiftly for him, he cannot comprehend how time might be a burden to a man or an enemy of his happiness; on the contrary, time appears to him a true blessing.[94]

This is indeed a touching picture—and also, when we stop to think of it, a picture that rings false to the core. For this is not Judge William's own existence, but an image of the bourgeois life as idyll that he is imagining. And even in his supposed "descriptions" of his wife there is more than a soupçon of the poetic. For we never meet her directly but only through his refraction of her into the ideal wife, the eternal feminine with her exemplary "comprehension of finiteness."[95] As we consider the Judge's letters as a whole, we come to recognize his own fundamental volatility. For these letters do not bear witness to a character firmly anchored in the concrete through action, but to an extravagant bourgeois who has substituted a romance of the commonplace for the aesthete's diary of seduction. His mind is filled with visions—visions of a life that has become lively through self-choice, of a wife whose sole function is to cure his melancholy with her cheerful innocence, finally, of a lonely religiosity that takes determinate form in the sermon of a nameless Jutland priest. Much as the "Diary of the Seducer" closes *Either/Or*, Volume I by pointing beyond the aesthete's standpoint, so this sermon ends Volume II by pointing beyond the Judge's standpoint.

The title of the sermon is "The Edification Implied in the Thought that as Against God We Are Always in the Wrong" and it takes its departure from Luke XIX, 41: Christ's prophecy of the sack of Jerusalem and the consequent suffering of guilty and innocent alike. The lesson of the sermon is the disastrous result of trying to calculate one's own moral worth, an at-

[94] *E/O*, II, 310; *SV*, II, 273–74.
[95] *E/O*, II, 316; *SV*, II, 279.

tempt that leads inevitably to self-doubt and, ultimately, to despair. "One does what one can?" the
Jutland priest asks (using one of the Judge's favorite
expressions). "Was not this precisely the reason for
your disquietude? Was it not for this reason your
dread was so painful . . . , that the more earnestly
you desired to act, so much the more dreadful became
the duplicity in which you found yourself involved,
wondering whether you had done what you could."[96]
But the Judge's project was meant to vanquish "dread"
and "duplicity" by unifying the personality once and
for all. In a preface to this sermon—allegedly a gift
the Judge is sending along to his "young friend"—he
gives a hint that in sending the sermon he means to
acknowledge the failure of the ethical life. "Take it,"
he implores his young friend, "I have read it and
thought of myself—read it then and think of yourself"
(emphasis added).[97]

If the Judge had thought of himself while reading
(or even writing) the sermon, he could have seen
clearly why his notion of ethical choice must turn out
to be a chimera. For how can it be brought about that
"all that has happened to me or befallen me is by me
transformed and translated from necessity to freedom?" How can the accidents of my birth, the fact
that I was born in 1935 and not 1835, that my parents
were white and not black, that my body is ugly or
beautiful, my mind quick or slow . . . how can these
given facts be "translated from necessity to freedom"?
For I did not cause my givenness, it stands outside
me, supporting the only freedom I can attain to—the
possibility of determining its meaning. We can vaguely
understand what it might be like to achieve such a
translation; the resistance of the world, its "otherness,"
would have been banished. But in understanding this
we also understand that such a proposal is only an

[96] *E/O*, II, 347; *SV*, II, 310–11.
[97] *E/O*, II, 342; *SV*, II, 304.

imaginative fancy, the wish of a mind that still desperately wants to escape its worldly condition.

Then too there is the Judge's supposition that the self, so to speak, can pull itself up by its own bootstraps, banishing despair and becoming actual through one mighty act of will. His dream is of an act of will that suddenly, and paradoxically, annihilates the distinction in the self between will and anything else. But I must use my will to will the concentration into will, and at just this point does the project become contradictory. For when nothing is left to confront the self as alien or other, at just this point does will itself become impossible. Judge William's dream of a self become actual as pure will is revealed as just that—a dream, a romantic fancy. His dream is only to be distinguished from the aesthete's project by its content, not by its form. Both remain essentially *dissipated* individuals, their minds ablaze with visions they cannot fulfill, their lives volatilized into plans, justifications, theories, arguments, fancies.

It becomes possible now to understand more clearly the charade of pseudonymity in which the book is wrapped. The point is that Victor Eremita is lucid. He is no more taken in by the aesthete's paean to enjoyment than he is by the Judge's vision of marriage. "Strictly speaking," Kierkegaard later confided, "*Either/Or* was written in a cloister, which thought is hidden in the pseudonym: *Victor Eremita*."[98] Smiling ironically, Victor stands apart from the visions of both Judge and aesthete. Both, assuredly, are products of his imagination, and he recognizes this—they are his creatures; they are *only* imaginary. Yet here lies the secret of the "Chinese puzzle boxes." For Victor has labeled them "imaginary," and thus distanced himself from them, precisely by suggesting that they are real persons whose papers he found in a desk. For both Victor and Kierkegaard the device of pseudonymity

[98] *Point of View*, 18; *SV*, XIII, 526.

is a tool for distancing. Each distances himself from
his creation by disclaiming paternity, and in so doing
each means to teach an important lesson: "These are
only ideas and images, *personae* not persons," they
seem to be saying; "do not confuse them with the real.
They are my own. I gave them birth, and I know all
too well that the pen impregnates only possibility."
At the end of the book we are left only with questions
and phantoms. Is the Seducer real or imaginary? And
the Jutland priest? The Judge himself? The aesthete?
The curtain falls on this book to the accompaniment
of unknown laughter from the wings. To use the aesthete's own words: "The curtain falls, the play is over;
only the situation's fantastic shadow-play which irony
directs, remains for contemplation. The immediately
real situation is the unreal situation; behind this there
appears a new situation which is no less false, and
so forth."[99]

4

Inevitably, our lives slip away from us. We try to grasp
actuality, but it seeps away. Tantalized by possibilities
we become, in part, fantastic even to ourselves, our
minds teeming with endless theories we can never vali-
date, plans we can never realize, doubts we can never
assuage. The wound of consciousness remains.

In brief, this is the outlook presented by *Either/Or*.
Both aesthete and Judge are presented as existing *beyond* their own standpoints. Each exemplifies a definite
life-view, but both have transcended the views they
represent. Both remain in "despair" since neither has
been able to extirpate his own essential volatility. The
failure of the aesthete's and the Judge's projects, however, should come as no surprise, since as early as *The
Concept of Irony* Kierkegaard had suggested that only
religiosity offered an antidote to despair. "The true
happiness," he wrote, "wherein the subject no longer

[99] *E/O*, I, 275; *SV*, I, 249.

dreams but in infinite clarity possesses himself . . . is only possible for the religious individual. . . . Only the religious is capable of effecting this true reconciliation [between self and actuality] for it renders actuality infinite for me."[100] In the works which followed *Either/Or* Kierkegaard explored with ever deepening intensity the notion of a religious cure for the sickness of despair. Man is divided against himself, a split creature whose life boils off endlessly into the imaginary. Experiencing his consciousness as a wound that begs for closure yet resists it, he seeks a reintegration of self that lies always beyond his grasp. This is the picture that emerges from the remaining books of Kierkegaard's pseudonymous authorship, a picture etched with special vividness in the work of two pseudonyms—Johannes de Silentio, author of *Fear and Trembling,* and Johannes Climacus, author of *Philosophical Fragments* and the *Concluding Unscientific Postscript.*

"Not merely in the realm of commerce but in the world of ideas as well our age is organizing a regular clearance sale."[101] With this nod toward the world of commerce *Fear and Trembling* begins. One hundred or so pages later it ends on a similarly commercial note: "One time in Holland when the market was rather dull for spices the merchants had several cargoes dumped into the sea to peg up prices. . . ."[102] This framing of the book between two commercial metaphors is not accidental, but suggests an essential polarity. On the one side is the world of commerce and sanity, the commercial men with their dollar calculi, the docents who, according to Johannes de Silentio, "live secure in existence . . . [with] a *solid* position and *sure* prospects in a well-ordered state, they

[100] *Irony,* 313; *SV,* XIII, 367.
[101] *Fear and Trembling* (Princeton: Princeton University Press, 1968), p. 22 (afterward cited as *FT*); *SV,* III, 57.
[102] *FT,* 129; *SV,* III, 166.

have centuries and even millenniums between them
and the concussions of existence."[103] On the other
side are those singular individuals—Mary, mother of
Jesus; the Apostles; above all, Abraham—who in their
own lives have suffered such "concussions." These
special individuals, their psyches stretched on the rack
of ambiguity, have become febrile. Minds inflamed
with absurdity, their lives burn with an unearthly glow.

In all of Kierkegaard's authorship there is nothing
so powerful and also so typical as the opening Prelude
to *Fear and Trembling*. Here Johannes de Silentio pursues the story of Abraham through a series of variations, each one attempting (yet failing) to make clear
the ambiguity of Abraham's position. In each version
Abraham arises early, saddles the donkeys, and, accompanied by Isaac, makes his way to Mt. Moriah.
In the first version Abraham turns away from his son:

> . . . and when Isaac saw Abraham's face it was
> changed, his glance was wild, his form was horror.
> He seized Isaac by the throat, threw him to the
> ground, and said, "Stupid boy, dost thou then suppose
> that this is God's bidding? No it is my desire." Then
> Abraham in a low voice said to himself, "O Lord in
> heaven, I thank Thee. Above all it is better for him
> to believe that I am inhuman, rather than that he
> should lose faith in Thee."[104]

In all versions Isaac's life is saved by the appearance
of the ram, but the effects on father and son are various.
In the second version, Abraham's "eyes were darkened
. . . because he could not forget that God had required this of him."[105] In the third version, Abraham
could never forget that it was a sin to be willing to
sacrifice Isaac. In the fourth version, Isaac saw that
Abraham's left hand "was clenched in despair, that a

[103] *FT*, 73; *SV*, III, 112.
[104] *FT*, 27; *SV*, III, 64.
[105] *FT*, 28; *SV*, III, 65.

tremor passed through his body,"[106] and this was sufficient for Isaac to lose his faith. None of these versions, Johannes de Silentio suggests, adequately characterizes the ambiguity of Abraham's position. "The ethical expression for what Abraham did," Johannes points out, "is that he would murder Isaac; the religious expression is that he would sacrifice Isaac; but precisely in this contradiction consists the dread which can well make a man sleepless, and yet Abraham is not what he is without this dread."[107] Yet perhaps the most dreadful consequence of this contradiction is the radical solitude it enforces on Abraham. For strictly speaking, "Abraham cannot talk."[108] That is, he cannot talk about the one thing that most concerns him, his faith: "The dread and distress in this paradox is that, humanly speaking, he can in no way make himself understandable."[109]

Another way of expressing the central polarity of the book is to see it tensed between sanity and madness. On the one hand we have the world of society, language, and justification. This ultimately is the home of the ethical man who "translates himself into the universal, who edits as it were a pure and elegant edition of himself, as free from errors as possible, and readable by everyone."[110] The ethical man has language at his disposal, and can justify himself in terms of allegedly universal norms. Therein lies his security. But the man who has stepped beyond good and evil has no such comfortable resting place. "He knows," writes Johannes de Silentio, "that it is beautiful to be born as the individual who has the universal as his home, his friendly resting place. . . . But he knows also that higher than this there winds a lonely path, narrow and steep; he knows that it is terrible to be

[106] *FT*, 29; *SV*, III, 67.
[107] *FT*, 41; *SV*, III, 82.
[108] *FT*, 70; *SV*, III, 110.
[109] *FT*, 84; *SV*, III, 122–23.
[110] *FT*, 86; *SV*, III, 124.

born outside the universal. . . . Humanly speaking he
is mad and cannot make himself intelligible to anyone.
And yet it is the mildest expression to say that he is
mad."[111] Beyond language, beyond justification, beyond understanding, the religious man makes his solitary way. He lacks even the security of the true madman who (*ex hypothesi*) is wholly and irrevocably
mad, whereas the man of faith is a failed madman
who never puts behind him the temptation of sanity.
He "is kept sleepless," remarks Johannes, "for he is
constantly tried, and every instant there is the possibility of being able to return repentently to the universal."[112] Tempted by this possibility, the religious
man "is kept in constant tension."[113]

It is just this tension which is the central focus of
the book. Johannes de Silentio admits that he has never
met in person what he calls "a knight of faith." Johannes is, by his own admission, "a shrewd pate, and
every such person always has great difficulty in making
the movements of faith."[114] Unable to understand the
faith of an Abraham, he must rest content to stand
"astonished . . . paralyzed . . . blind"[115] before him.
Yet if Johannes cannot understand Abraham, he can
at least understand what it is that he cannot understand. And here we are returned to the concepts of
ambiguity and tension. For what both attracts Johannes
to Abraham and also appalls him is the way Abraham's
life seems to have been both intensified and unified
by *tension*. This applies to other exemplars of the religious life. Many people, suggests Johannes, might
read the New Testament with a kind of romantic longing, but "what they leave out is the distress, the dread,
the paradox."[116] To be Mary, mother of Jesus, or to

111 *FT*, 86; *SV*, III, 124.
112 *FT*, 88; *SV*, III, 126.
113 *FT*, 89; *SV*, III, 127.
114 *FT*, 43; *SV*, III, 84.
115 *FT*, 36; *SV*, III, 74.
116 *FT*, 75; *SV*, III, 114.

be one of the twelve Apostles, is to participate in the mutilation of one's sanity. Religiosity is to be defined by that unique heightening of consciousness—"the holy, pure and humble expression of the divine madness which the pagans admired"[117]—where the individual dwells in ambiguity as his element. Abraham, Mary, the Apostles, all seem to glow with an unearthly light. Under the impress of Johannes' coloration, these exemplars of the religious life appear to have pushed ambiguity to its limit; they have inflamed their consciousnesses, and made of their lives something fiery and wondrous. If consciousness be a wound, then the religious man is he who has deliberately exacerbated it, salted it with paradox. Yet in his very pain, his "fear and trembling" so to speak, he may discover an ambiguous sign of his election. "The knight of faith," writes Johannes, "feels the pain of not being able to make himself intelligible. . . . The pain is his assurance that he is on the right way."[118]

Kant once suggested that it was his intention "to deny knowledge in order to make room for faith."[119] In much fuller measure this slogan may be applied to the efforts of Kierkegaard's pseudonym, Johannes Climacus. For if faith points toward the trammeled madness of an Abraham, then it is sanity and sanity's world (noon in bourgeois Copenhagen) that is faith's enemy. The task of a true defender of the faith will then be the undermining of sanity, and sanity's stepchild, language. This task Johannes Climacus undertakes. Equipped with a dialectical wit and a wry sense of humor, he sets out to show that both the commonsense hovel of the man in the street and the wondrous palace of the speculative philosopher are both built

[117] *FT*, 37; *SV*, III, 75.

[118] *FT*, 90; *SV*, III, 128.

[119] Immanuel Kant, *Critique of Pure Reason*, translated by Norman Kemp Smith (New York: St. Martin's Press, Inc., 1961), p. 29.

in the sand. As principal weapon, he chooses a traditional scepticism.

"The Greek sceptic," Johannes Climacus reminds
us in *Philosophical Fragments,* "did not deny the validity of sensation or immediate cognition; error, he
says, has an entirely different ground, for it comes
from the conclusions I draw. If only I can refrain from
drawing conclusions, I will never be deceived. If my
senses, for example, show me an object that seems
round at a distance but square near at hand, or a stick
bent in the water which is straight when taken out,
the senses have not deceived me. But I run the risk
of being deceived when I draw a conclusion about the
stick or the object."[120] The most obvious and least
justified conclusion I am inclined to draw, according
to Climacus, is that something *exists.* I peer through
a telescope at a distant star. The pinprick of light recorded on my retina is indisputable, but "the star becomes involved in doubt the moment . . . [I seek] to
become aware of its having come into existence. It is
as if reflection took the star away from the senses."[121]
But this is a necessary consequence, since existence
is always a postulate and never a conclusion:

> Thus I always reason from existence, not towards
> existence. . . . I do not for example prove that a
> stone exists, but that some existing thing is a stone.
> The procedure in a court of justice does not prove
> that a criminal exists, but that the accused, whose
> existence is given, is a criminal. Whether we call
> existence an *accessorium* or the eternal *prius,* it is
> never subject to demonstration.[122]

If I can never demonstrate the existence of anything,
how then can I know anything exists? You cannot
know it, argues Climacus, you must *believe* it.

[120] *Philosophical Fragments* (Princeton: Princeton University Press, 1962), p. 102 (afterward cited as *PF*); *SV,* IV, 246.
[121] *PF,* 100; *SV,* IV, 245.
[122] *PF,* 50; *SV,* IV, 207.

In the uncompleted draft for a book by Johannes Climacus entitled *De Omnibus Dubitandum Est,* Kierkegaard gave a fuller account of his understanding of doubt. Doubt comes in with reflection, suggests Climacus, with speech:

> Cannot consciousness then remain in immediacy? If man could not speak, then he would remain in immediacy. . . . Immediacy is actuality. Speech is ideality. Consciousness is opposition or contradiction. The moment I express reality the opposition is there.
>
> The possibility of doubt then lies in consciousness, whose very essence is to be a kind of contradiction or opposition. It is produced by, and itself produces, duplicity [*dupplicitet*].[123]

Climacus goes on to make the point that "the word 'doubt' [*tvivl*] stands connected etymologically with the word 'two,' "[124] and suggests that this duality springs from the opposition within consciousness between actuality and ideality. Not just to sense the world, but to think it (i.e., be conscious of it) means to suffer this opposition, and with it, doubt. Doubt, then, is an essential attribute of consciousness since it makes evident nothing less than the fundamental opposition which *is* consciousness. "If ideality and actuality," Climacus points out, "could enter into partnership with each other in all innocence and without opposition and friction, then there never would be any such thing as consciousness. For consciousness only appears when they collide."[125] If doubt be defined in this way, then it is clear that it can never be overcome, since to overcome doubt would be to overcome consciousness itself. The opposite of doubt must then be an act of the mind that lets the opposition of consciousness abide, but

[123] *Johannes Climacus or, De Omnibus Dubitandum Est* (Stanford: Stanford University Press, 1958), p. 148 (afterward cited as *JC*); IV B 1, p. 146.
[124] *JC*, 151; IV B 1, p. 148.
[125] *JC*, 153; IV B 1, p. 149.

somehow robs it of its bite. This act Johannes
Climacus calls "belief" [*tro*].

In *Fragments* Climacus makes clear that he means
to give the Danish term *tro* a double sense. "In the
eminential sense" it will refer to the Christian's *faith*,
his capacity to believe against reason the awful paradox of God's entry into time through Christ.[126] As
the mental act that somehow holds together oppositions of incalculable severity, *tro* in this sense is "the
category of despair" [*fortvivlelsens categori*].[127] But
there is another "direct and ordinary sense" of *tro* that
refers not to the relationship of the mind to the Christian paradox, but to "the relationship of the mind to
the historical."[128] Although Climacus does not point
this out, we might complete the schematism by saying
that *tro* in this second sense meaning *belief* is "the category of doubt." In both senses *tro* is founded on opposition, ultimately on the opposition which is consciousness itself. Also in both senses, *tro* is seen as a mental
act that both respects yet defeats the opposition which
founds it. "Defeat" may be too strong a word, for uncertainty (just another name for the opposition) is
never really defeated by *tro,* but only ignored, un-
coupled, put out of circuit. Thus Climacus argues that
"in the certainty of belief [*tro*] there is always present
a negated uncertainty, in every way corresponding to
the becoming of existence. Belief believes what it does
not see; it does not believe that the star is there, for
that it sees, but it believes that the star has come into
existence."[129]

The essential claim, then, is that the existence of anything cannot be known, but must be believed. Surely,
there must be a part of us that resists this claim, since
in our own lives we constantly and easily distinguish
between existent and non-existent entities. Would we,

126 *PF*, 108; *SV*, IV, 250.
127 *CUP*, 179 note; *SV*, VII, 167 note.
128 *PF*, 108; *SV*, VII, 250.
129 *PF*, 101; *SV*, IV, 245.

for example, be inclined to believe in the existence of something which could not be apprehended publicly, in different circumstances, by different observers? Is not "publicity" itself a criterion of existence? Climacus never directly takes up the question of existence criteria, but his answer is not difficult to frame. He would point out simply that whatever criteria we choose, we must still *believe* their legitimacy. And if we choose to say that legitimacy itself has criteria, we have only moved our belief to a second level. This is precisely the thrust of his long discussion of the uncertainty of all historical knowledge.[130] Certain knowledge, he avers, can only be found within the structures of logic and mathematics; but outside their precincts, in the coming-into-being and passing-away of life in the world, we must be satisfied with *belief*.[131]

Earlier, in *Fear and Trembling,* Johannes de Silentio observed that reason was the "broker" of the "whole of finiteness."[132] This finite whole has now been brought into question. For it is reason which has populated this whole with supposed real, existent entities—reason is constantly making inferences about rocks and criminals and philosophers—and now the reality of all these entities has been questioned. Suddenly, the daylight world of Copenhagen, the world of commerce and sanity, has been revealed in its insubstantiality, hanging as it does from the thread of belief.

In his sequel to *Fragments, Concluding Unscientific Postscript,* Climacus explores some of the consequences of this argument. "The apparent trustworthiness of sense," he reiterates, "is an illusion. . . . The trustworthiness claimed by a knowledge of the historical is also a deception."[133] But if this be true, then the

---

[130] See the discussion of this in the "Interlude" section of *Philosophical Fragments,* pp. 89–110.

[131] See Chapter II of the *Postscript,* "The Subjective Truth, Inwardness; Truth is Subjectivity," pp. 169–224.

[132] *FT,* 46; *SV,* III, 87.

[133] *CUP,* 280; *SV,* VII, 271.

comfortable life of a Copenhagen burgher can only be
seen as a kind of comprehensive forgetfulness. Immersed in his habitual round of activities, perpetually
justifying himself in terms of rights and duties, the
bourgeois turns out not to be living at all, but rather
to be fleeing life, trying desperately to shield himself
from its ambiguity and terror. If the very being of consciousness is to be divided against itself, if simply to
think the world means to grasp it duplicitously, then a
full human life must witness this duplicity. Hence
Climacus urges not that the hypertension of consciousness be relaxed, but that it be tightened to ever greater
levels of intensity. In a metaphor resonant with significance, he says of his hero, the "existential" or "subjective" thinker:

> He is conscious of the negativity of the infinite in
> existence, and he constantly keeps the wound of the
> negative open, which medically is sometimes the con-
> dition for a cure. The others let the wound heal over
> and become positive; that is, they are deceived.[134]

The essential polarity of the *Postscript* is between
the deceived and the undeceived. But now the deceived
are no longer (as in *Fear and Trembling*) those who
"live secure in existence [with] a *solid* position and
sure prospects in a well-ordered state," but are rather
the speculative philosophers, who, infatuated with their
orotund visions, have simply rushed headlong out of
existence. "Philosophy and the philosophers simply de-
sert existence," Climacus writes, "leaving the rest of
us to face the worst."[135] Their desertion is carried out
by means of a sleight-of-hand trick that substitutes ideal
being [*vaesen*] for factual being [*vaeren*]. Climacus
has already pointed out in *Fragments* how this thread-
bare magic made possible the ontological argument—
obviously the more perfect a thing is, the more it is,

---

[134] *CUP*, 78; *SV*, VII, 66.
[135] *CUP*, 267; *SV*, VII, 258.

but the "isness" here is not factual but ideal, the being of essence.[136] In the *Postscript* he pushes this distinction further, arguing that the principles of speculative philosophy ultimately reduce to tautologies. The speculative philosopher, according to Climacus, pretends to a finality and certainty of judgment which is misplaced, since his utterances, if properly understood, turn out to be either empirical generalizations (hence uncertain) or logical truths (hence necessarily irrelevant to existence).[137]

In his drive toward a systematic understanding of the world, the philosopher "fantastically dissipates the concept *existence*."[138] Even more importantly, by imagining that he grasps everything *sub specie aeternitatis* he dissipates his own existence and becomes "merely fantastic."[139] According to Climacus, he is "a sort of phantom,"[140] "a fantastic entity rather than a human being,"[141] who has introduced "a fictitious decisiveness" into philosophy.[142] His "so-called pure thought is in general a psychological curiosity, a remarkable species of combining and construing in a fantastic medium, the medium of pure being."[143] Unfortunately for him, he cannot live in that medium, but once a month must pick up his paycheck. He remains, then, a kind of duplex being, "a fantastic creature who moves in the pure being of abstract thought, and on the other hand, a sometimes pitiful professorial figure which the former deposits, about as when one puts down a walking stick."[144]

On the one hand the speculative philosopher is a

[136] *PF*, 51–52 note; *SV*, IV, 208–9 note.
[137] See *CUP*, Chapter II.
[138] *CUP*, 111; *SV*, VII, 100.
[139] *CUP*, 172; *SV*, VII, 160.
[140] *CUP*, 169; *SV*, VII, 157.
[141] *CUP*, 178; *SV*, VII, 166.
[142] *CUP*, 203; *SV*, VII, 190.
[143] *CUP*, 269; *SV*, VII, 260.
[144] *CUP*, 268; *SV*, VII, 259.

comic figure who has simply forgotten what it means to exist. On the other hand he manifests a pronounced morbidity in attempting to reduce being to thought, actual life to a kind of "shadow existence":

> The politicians have pointed out that wars will ultimately cease, everything being decided in the cabinets of the diplomats. . . . If only the same sort of thing does not happen also in daily life, so that we cease to live, while professors and *privatdocents* speculatively determine the relationship of the different factors to man in general. It seems to me that there is something human in the horrors of even the bloodiest war in comparison with this diplomatic stillness; and likewise there seems to me something horrible, something bewitched, in the dead insensibility by which actual life is reduced to a shadow existence.[145]

Like Johannes the Seducer, this "comic unreality,"[146] who has "either been terrified or tricked into becoming a phantom,"[147] comes to "dwindle away, aye, almost vanish from reality."[148]

On the other hand, the subjective thinker accepts existence in all its pain and ambiguity. "[His] scene is not the fairyland of the imagination," Climacus cautions. "His scene is inwardness in existing as a human being."[149] The first step toward nurturing this inwardness lies in recognizing what Climacus calls the "doubleness [*dobbelthed*] characteristic of existence."[150] This doubleness consists in the fact that one must both think and exist, although thinking directs itself toward the common and the universal, while

[145] *CUP*, 308; *SV*, VII, 298.
[146] *CUP*, 284; *SV*, VII, 275.
[147] *CUP*, 274; *SV*, VII, 265.
[148] *E/O*, I, 302; *SV*, I, 278.
[149] *CUP*, 320; *SV*, VII, 310.
[150] *CUP*, 69; *SV*, VII, 57.

existing is particular. "The subjective thinker," writes Climacus, "is an existing individual and a thinker at one and the same time; he does not abstract from the contradiction and from existence, but lives in it while at the same time thinking."[151] But what does the subjective thinker think about? He thinks about himself; he tries "to understand himself in existence."[152] It is for this reason that the content of the subjective thinker's thought lies within the boundaries of what we might call "the ethico-religious." Only those ideas that can be expressed by living them can have relevance to the subjective thinker. "All essential knowledge," writes Climacus, "relates to existence . . . [and] only ethical and ethico-religious knowledge has an essential relation to existence."[153] The subjective thinker is not the moralist or the preacher whose speech is filled with "edification" for others. Rather he is the solitary individual who tries to express in his own life the content of an ethical or religious norm. "To abstract from existence," cautions Climacus, "is to remove the difficulty. To remain in existence so as to understand one thing in one moment and another thing in another moment, is not to understand oneself. But to understand the greatest oppositions together, and to understand oneself existing in them is very difficult."[154] The subjective thinker chooses to live the dissonance of these oppositions. Knowing that he can never justify or found the ideality he lives, he nevertheless perseveres. The ethical life "consists in that true hypertension of the infinite in the spirit of man,"[155] and it is this hypertension that the subjective thinker accepts. His activity "consists precisely in his active interpenetration of himself by re-

151 *CUP,* 314; *SV,* VII, 304.

152 *CUP,* 316; *SV,* VII, 306.

153 *CUP,* 176–77; *SV,* VII, 165. The term translated as "knowledge" is *erkjenden.*

154 *CUP,* 316; *SV,* VII, 307.

155 *CUP,* 123; *SV,* VII, 112.

flection concerning his own existence, so that he really thinks what he thinks by making a reality of it."[156]

Climacus uses various terms to describe his hero. Sometimes he is the "subjective thinker," at other times the "existential thinker," at still other times the "concrete thinker."[157] But the basic identity is clear. In contradistinction to the ghostlike presence of the speculative philosopher, the subjective thinker is a fully actual, richly alive human being. Opposed to the dissipation of the philosopher, his life has become progressively concentrated and dense. His subjectivity has suffered an "infinite concentration in itself"[158] relative to his *telos*. "Purity of heart," Kierkegaard will later write, "is to will one thing,"[159] and it is this purity and concentration of self that the subjective thinker gradually realizes. But since his activity is directly proportional to the passion with which he holds together the contradictory elements of existence, his activity will depend in part on what ideas he chooses to actualize. Hence the famous definition of subjective truth: "An objective uncertainty held fast in an appropriation-process of the most passionate inwardness is the truth, the highest truth attainable for an existing individual."[160] Presumably this definition of truth would apply to all those ideals the subjective thinker might try to realize. Objectively they are uncertain, unfounded, unjustified, made actual only by people choosing to live them. But most ideals, if uncertain and unjustified, are not in themselves paradoxical, offensive to reason.

[156] *CUP*, 151; *SV*, VII, 140.

[157] "Concrete thinker" is used at *CUP*, 296. For many uses of "subjective thinker" and "existential thinker" see Chapter III of the *Postscript*, "Real or Ethical Subjectivity—The Subjective Thinker," pp. 267–322.

[158] *CUP*, 116; *SV*, VII, 105.

[159] This is the principal theme of a religious discourse published by Kierkegaard in 1847; see *Purity of Heart* (New York: Harper & Brothers, 1948).

[160] *CUP*, 182; *SV*, VII, 170.

What if one took as the *telos* of one's life an idea that was not just objectively uncertain, but impossible, contradictory, in short—a paradox? Might not one's passion be inflamed exponentially by the abrasion of such an idea, and consequently might not one's life be annealed, made fully actual, by the heat of that passion?

Here, according to Climacus, is where "Christianity fits perfectly into the picture."[161] For the focus of Christian belief is not just an objective uncertainty, but a paradox, in fact, "the Absolute Paradox."[162] The Christian believes that God—the infinite, the immortal, the omnipotent, the eternal—entered into time to suffer and die in the person of Jesus of Nazareth. This is not just an uncertainty, but is a radical impossibility. "God," Climacus points out in *Fragments,* "is a concept,"[163] and concepts do not suffer and die on crosses in obscure Near Eastern kingdoms. To believe this (which is after all the central contention of Christianity) is to believe against understanding and reason; it is to suffer the "crucifixion of the understanding"[164] on the cross of the Paradox. Yet the passion of that crucifixion will lead to a final "fixing" of the individual in existence. "In the same degree that time is accentuated," writes Climacus, "do we go forward from the aesthetic, the metaphysical, to the ethical, the religious, and the Christian religious."[165] Socrates exemplified the position of the subjective thinker in the orthodox sense, and his irony betrayed his conviction that objectively everything was uncertain. But the position of the Christian is a move beyond Socrates. For the last escape hatch out of existence—the Platonic doctrine of recollection—has been blocked by the notion of original sin. "Let us now call the untruth of the individual *Sin,*"

[161] *CUP,* 206; *SV,* VII, 193.

[162] See *PF,* Chapter III, "The Absolute Paradox: A Metaphysical Crotchet."

[163] *PF,* 51; *SV,* IV, 208.

[164] *CUP,* 531; *SV* 523. Cf. also *CUP,* 496 and 501.

[165] *CUP,* 265; *SV,* VII, 256.

suggests Climacus. "The more difficult it is made for
the individual to take himself out of existence by way
of recollection, the more profound is the inwardness
that his existence may have in existence; and when it is
made impossible for him, when he is held so fast in
existence that the back door of recollection is forever
closed to him, then his inwardness will be the most
profound possible."[166] In this way, then, "Christianity
decisively accentuates existence" by placing the individual "between time and eternity in time, between
heaven and hell in the time of salvation."[167]

It would seem that Climacus has rounded out his
vision into a complex whole. He has articulated a metaphysic that will destroy the secure and certain outlines
of bourgeois sanity. To exist is to doubt (*tvivl*), since
to be conscious is already to involve oneself in duplicity
and contradiction. Through belief (*tro*) we hold polarities together, living their contradictions, drawing from
them our passion. To exist in the most eminential
sense is to raise contradiction to its highest intensity by
attempting to live a paradox. To do this is the Christian
way. It means permitting oneself to be led through
despair (*fortvivlelse*) to faith (*tro*) in its eminential
sense. Clarity, certainty, common sense are all shattered. Our universe has become a duplicitous and
dreadful one, a land of "twos"—*tvivl* (doubt), *fortvivlelse*
(despair), *tvetydighed* (ambiguity)—where the individual's most insistent wish is to become integral, to overcome the cleavages of existence. That wish becomes
his passion (*lidenskab*) and also his suffering
(*lidelse*). In a more ultimate sense it becomes also
his salvation. For ultimately it is Climacus' vision that
the very negativity of existence—the gap between ideal
and actual, infinite and finite, universal and particular,
eternal and temporal—will permit the individual to realize actuality. With his pipeline to the imaginary finally

[166] *CUP*, 186–87; *SV*, VII, 174–75.
[167] *CUP*, 193; *SV*, VII, 181.

blocked, confined to what Climacus calls the "strait-jacket of existence"[168] with no chance of escape, his mind crucified on the cross of the Paradox, the hope is that the individual will be annealed in the fire of his suffering, and that like Abraham before him, his life will burn. "Christianity," Climacus imagines someone to remark, "has set my soul aflame."[169]

5

The other works of the pseudonymous series add nothing essential to Climacus' vision. In *Repetition* Constantine Constantius follows his imaginary "young friend" through the trauma of an unhappy love affair to the onset of a religious "repetition." In *The Concept of Dread* the pedantic Vigilius Haufniensis traces the theological category of sin to its origin in the psychological category of dread. In *Stages on Life's Way* the familiar characters of *Either/Or* appear once more, only now they make their speeches and sound their complaints against the background of an explicitly religious alternative. Although fascinating in their own right, these books only buttress and amplify the central argument that runs from *Either/Or,* through *Fear and Trembling* and *Fragments,* to its searing conclusion in the *Postscript.* It would seem, then, that in tracing the development of Climacus' vision, we have also traced the outlines of what, lacking a better word, we might call Kierkegaard's "philosophy."

This would be reassuring and correct except for one salient omission—it leaves out both Johannes Climacus and Kierkegaard. For at the end of the *Postscript* Climacus revokes it, and his revocation is followed by "A First and Last Declaration" wherein Kierkegaard revokes all the pseudonyms, including Climacus. How then are we to take these works? Do they severally

---

168 *CUP,* 172; *SV,* VII, 160.
169 *CUP,* 207; *SV,* VII, 194.

articulate a single outlook, a "philosophy"? Or as readers have we been tricked, victims of an elaborate joke?
First, to Climacus and his revocation.

"As in Catholic books," he remarks in a final appendix, "one finds at the back of the volume a note
which informs the reader that everything is to be understood comformably with the doctrine of the Holy
Catholic Mother Church—so what I write contains too
a piece of information to the effect that everything is
to be understood as to be revoked; the book, then, has
not only a Conclusion, but a Revocation."[170] He goes
on to point out that although he has in effect offered
an apology for Christianity, he himself is not a Christian but only a humorist. "My attempt," he remarks,
"is *eo ipso* without importance and only for my own
diversion."[171] The reader who has just slogged
through 550 pages of the most convoluted prose may
not greet this announcement with much equanimity,
but he cannot claim that he was not forewarned. Earlier, Climacus had made clear why he wrote the book;
it was out of boredom. He had been a student for
many years and had found his life afflicted with an
enervating "indolence," "a glittering inactivity."[172] He
had "read a lot," and then spent the rest of the day
"idling and thinking, or thinking and idling."[173] Then
it occurred to him that he might occupy his time with
an intellectual puzzle. "I thought to myself," he remarked, "'You are now tired of life's diversions, you
are tired of the maidens, whom you love only in passing; you must have something fully to occupy your
time. Here it is: to discover where the misunderstanding lies between speculative philosophy and Christianity.'"[174] What we have been reading as a serious
philosophical treatise is in fact a "thought experiment."

---

[170] *CUP*, 547; *SV*, VII, 539.
[171] *CUP*, 550; *SV*, VII, 542.
[172] *CUP*, 165; *SV*, VII, 154.
[173] *CUP*, 165; *SV*, VII, 154.
[174] *CUP*, 216; *SV*, VII, 203.

"I have nothing to do here with the question of whether the proposed thought determination is true or not," Climacus observed. "I am merely experimenting."[175]

With Climacus' laughter reverberating in our ears we can go back to the book and see it for what it is—another attempt to point the way toward salvation. Like the Judge, like Johannes de Silentio (and like too Constantine Constantius, Vigilius Haufniensis, and Frater Taciturnus), Climacus has imagined a life more lively than life, a humanity richer than human. Consider first his use of the word "existence." The existence he refers to is not the quotidian life we all know. It is an intensification of life, a concentration which makes life larger, denser, richer than anything we have ever experienced. His portrait of existence is really of an existence lit up with value; in short, it is imaginary, like the love affair the Seducer envisages but never experiences. Or consider the salvation Climacus longs for. In our bones we know that it is no more possible than the "salvation" earlier proffered by the Judge. Both picture a state where the individual is penetrated by consciousness, the Judge in his remark that "he who lives ethically . . . has penetrated with consciousness his whole concretion,"[176] and Climacus in his contention that "really to exist . . . [is] to penetrate one's existence with consciousness."[177] Both meet shipwreck on the same reef. For when the ethical man has penetrated his whole being with consciousness and so become, in a sense, pure will, at just that point must his project collapse, since will to be will requires some otherness to push against. Likewise, at just the point when the Christian has succeeded in "willing one thing," in concentrating all his mind and heart on the Medusa-like Paradox, at just that point does the scissiparity of faith collapse, humbled by the sudden absence

---

[175] *CUP*, 183; *SV*, VII, 171.

[176] *E/O*, II, 263; *SV*, II, 231.

[177] *CUP*, 273; *SV*, VII, 264.

of temptation. Just as the ethical man requires competing inclinations to be ethical, so the religious man requires distraction of mind to be religious. Remove either—that is, grant either man his "salvation"—and you are really granting him only his death.

Like the aesthete alive only in his dream of beauty, like the Judge alive only in his dream of duty, like the speculative philosopher alive only in his dream of reason, Climacus too seems to come alive only in his dream of passion. It is easy to turn his dream into a "philosophy" or even a "metaphysic." And this, sadly, is what many modern theologians and philosophers have done, using Climacus to accent their trumpetings for a new "philosophy of existence." But Climacus, at least, was not taken in by his own words, and in his humorous asides he meant to remind his readers that any alleged "philosophy of existence" must remain a contradiction in terms, another way of sneaking out the back door, a dream. The real import of these humorous asides is to remind us that he has not fallen asleep in his dream. Like all the pseudonyms before him, he keeps one eye open, reminding both us and him that what he is doing is only a diversion, a way "to occupy time." For those who would take his work as important and serious, he has only the laughing refrain, "This sounds almost like seriousness."[178]

Behind Climacus' laughter there sounds too Kierkegaard's laughter, echoing forward through the *Postscript* from the four-page "Declaration" slipped furtively into its conclusion:

> What is written therefore is in fact mine, but only insofar as I put into the mouth of the poetically actual individual whom I *produced,* his life-view expressed in audible lines. For my relation is even more external than that of a poet, who poetizes characters, and yet in the preface is himself the author. For I am

[178] This is a familiar refrain of Johannes in the *Postscript;* cf., for example, *CUP,* 163; *SV,* VII, 152.

impersonal, or am personal in the third person, a *souffleur* who has poetically produced the *authors,* whose preface in turn is their own production, as are even their own names. So in the pseudonymous works there is not a single word which is mine. . . .[179]

What are we to say of this authorship that turns out to be an extended joke? Certain critics, having grasped the point that the authorship cannot be taken as "serious" or "philosophical," have employed Climacus' own theory of "indirect communication" to explain it.

On this theory no direct communication on existential matters is possible between man and man. Since these matters must be communicated indirectly, Kierkegaard has created a "marionette theater"[180] of *personae* whose dramatizations of existential alternatives may spur the reader to personal reflection and appropriation. The real action of the pseudonyms will then be performed offstage in the privacy of the reader's study. As Stephen Crites puts it:

> In these aesthetic works Kierkegaard had to find a way of pointing to the existential movements. . . . The attempt to describe them directly would falsify what is essential. For again, as in Kierkegaard's view of art, an idea can be brought forth only in its own medium. Only in this case the medium is the temporality of human existence itself: a life time. As the Don Juan idea can only be rendered in music, and not in poetry, an existential movement can only be realized in the life of an individual.[181]

[179] *CUP,* 551 unpaginated; *SV,* VII, 545–46 unpaginated.

[180] Martin Thust applied this term to Kierkegaard's pseudonyms in "Das Marionettentheater Søren Kierkegaards," *Zeitwende,* I, No. 1 (1925), pp. 18–38.

[181] Stephen Crites, "Pseudonymous Authorship as Art and as Act," published below in this same volume, pp. 214, 216.

On this theory Kierkegaard becomes a maieutic trickster who lures his reader into the kind of "double reflection" that will permit him to discover his own "subjective truth." Kierkegaard, on this view, stands ironically, even dispassionately, outside his works, using them to manipulate his reader's subjectivity. In a nutshell, this interpretation accepts Climacus' discussion of "subjectivity" and "inwardness," and sees the pseudonymous authorship as a clever strategy for stimulating these inward changes. But Climacus' discussion is part of the joke, and Kierkegaard tells us again and again in his journal that his works are not the products of dispassionate reflection, but are wrenched from the very "abscess" of his suffering as a man.[182] Even more to the point, this theory makes one critical but erroneous assumption—namely, that there are some "existential movements" which the reader can and should make. But there's the rub. For if the pseudonymous works have shown us anything, it is that *all the so-called "existential movements" end in failure.* If failure is the outcome of all attempts to make these movements, then how can their stimulation be the aim of the authorship? It can, only if the recognition of failure and not the movements is the point. This, I suspect, is precisely the aim of the pseudonyms, not to get the reader to make some impossible "existential movements," but to make the point that all such attempts at self-direction must fail. It is *failure,* I sub-

[182] At IX A 217 Kierkegaard writes:
  When I am sunken in the deepest suffering of melancholy, one thought or another becomes so knotted up for me that I cannot loose it, and then since it is related to my own existence, I suffer indescribably. And then when a little time has past, the abscess bursts—and inside lies the richest and most wonderful material for work, and just what I need at the moment. . . .
  I suffer as a human being can suffer in indescribable melancholy, which always has to do with my thinking about my own existence. Cf. also VII[1] A 222, VIII[1] A 27, *Point of View,* 7ff., and IX A 411.

mit, the necessary failure of all human projects, that is at once the central meaning of the pseudonyms, as well as the source of their deepest religious import.

At various points in the pseudonymous authorship the reader is reminded of God's elusiveness. In the *Postscript* God is compared to an ironic writer (*pace* Climacus and Kierkegaard) who never reveals himself to his reader. "For no anonymous author," writes Climacus, "can more cunningly conceal himself, no practitioner of the maieutic art can more carefully withdraw himself from the direct relationship, than God. He is in creation, and present everywhere in it, but directly He is not there."[183] But if God is not directly apprehensible, how then can he be encountered? Under what circumstances, through what refractive lenses, is the individual permitted to see God?

In *Fragments* God is defined as "the Unknown."[184] "What then is the Unknown?" asks Climacus. "It is the limit to which reason repeatedly comes. . . . It is the different, the absolutely different."[185] God is then the unsurpassable limit against which man's reason flings itself: "Reason cannot advance beyond this point, and yet it cannot refrain in its paradoxicalness from arriving at this limit and occupying itself therewith."[186] In this instance God is defined relative to reason, but there is nothing to prevent us from generalizing the definition. For there must be a limit to every human project—to desiring, to willing, to loving, to imagining. Generalizing the definition we arrive at this result: God is revealed to man only negatively as man's limit. Man encounters God only by encountering his own finitude and incapacity. God is *deus absconditus,* never present always absent, an inhabitant of dark places, God the spider.

[183] *CUP,* 218; *SV,* VII, 204.
[184] See *Fragments,* Chapter III, "The Absolute Paradox: A Metaphysical Crotchet."
[185] *PF,* 55; *SV,* IV, 212.
[186] *PF,* 55; *SV,* IV, 211–12.

It is God who ultimately haunts the world of the
pseudonyms. He lurks not in their words, but between
their words, in their silences and failures. Theirs is
an ambience of duplicity and illusion. They are trick-
sters and liars, speaking evasively and ironically. Sometimes they stop speaking and we hear only the echoes
of laughter in a darkened room. They speak in a characteristic rhythm in which the systole of their affirmation is matched by the diastole of its revocation. After
proclaiming their vision, they so often revoke it, re-
lapsing into irony or resignation. But this revocation
is not just a maieutic device to encourage the making
of those "existential movements" none of us can talk
about. On the contrary, it is a confession of our ineradicable incapacity to pull ourselves up by our own
bootstraps. "You shut your eyes, you seize yourself
by the neck," writes Climacus jokingly of the speculative philosopher, "and then—and then you stand on the
other side."[187] But all of us know that we will never
(at least in this life) "stand on the other side." With
them we share the incapacity to live our images, to
give them being, and in our joint failure we express an
unsurpassable limit of our condition. Our finitude is
reflected back to us in the "elsewhere" character of
the image, in the evident quality that it *is not, is not
here*. This is the secret of the pseudonym's world. For
it is finally the world of human consciousness itself, and
its negativity—individual characters and whole works
pretending to be other than they are, pseudonymity
masking irony, parody piled on satire—is again that of
consciousness. What the pseudonyms illustrate is the
failure of all attempts to prevent our lives boiling off
into the imaginary. Like us, the pseudonyms never
succeed in becoming integral, never overcome a fundamental dissipation. Yet precisely in that failure can be
glimpsed, ambiguously, like a shape half-seen in a
mirror, the face of God.

[187] *CUP,* 91; *SV,* VII, 79.

Thus the full austerity of Kierkegaard's vision can only be grasped when the pseudonyms are understood self-referentially. What they seek to demonstrate is not the adequacy of a new philosophy, but the nullity of all philosophy. What they seek to exhibit is not the possibilities of a new literary genre, but the final impossibility of all genres. What they are really about is neither ethics nor aesthetics nor theology nor philosophy, but rather the imaginative act which founds all these disciplines. Since this is also the act by which the pseudonyms themselves come into being, they are ultimately about themselves. Their achievement lies in the construction of a literature of self-reference, a series of works that comment repeatedly on the imaginative act involved in their own creation. And their repeated and austere comment is that that act must inevitably end in failure. We are permitted to imagine, it would seem, precisely that which we cannot create.

THE FORK

John Updike

It is not certain that the United States needs still more
translations of Kierkegaard. The Kierkegaard bibliography in this country is already amply confusing; led
by the dauntless Walter Lowrie, a campaign of translation coincident with the Second World War endowed
the English-speaking world with almost all of the tor-
rential *œuvre* that the Danish thinker had created a
century before. Eight books, including the immense
Concluding Unscientific Postscript, were published
here in 1941 alone. The current index of books in
print lists twenty-two Kierkegaard titles, not counting
duplications and anthologies. Distributed among a number of commercial, university, and religious presses
(notably Harper, Princeton, and Augsburg) and be-
devilled by overlappings and omissions (*Stages on
Life's Way* seems to be out of print, whereas some of
the *Discourses* crop up repeatedly), the list is nevertheless the fullest outside of Germany and Denmark
itself. We lack in English only some topical and humorous trifles, and the very voluminous total of the
journals and stray papers.

The Last Years: Journals, 1853–1855 (Harper),
edited and translated by Professor Ronald Gregor
Smith, draws upon the papers from 1853 onward and
the journals from their resumption, on March 1, 1854,
after a four-month gap. This material, which represents
Kierkegaard in his most haranguing and repetitious

This essay originally appeared in *The New Yorker,* February
26, 1966, © 1966 The New Yorker Magazine, Inc. It is reprinted with the kind permission of the author and the editor,
The New Yorker.

phase, is not unknown to previous translation. The
final fifty-five pages of Alexander Dru's selection de-
rive from the same portion of the journals. Professor
Smith, though he compiles three hundred and forty
pages, omits half of what Dru includes. Absent in
Smith are some of the most pungent entries in Dru:

> Oh, Luther, Luther; your responsibility is great in-
> deed, for the closer I look the more clearly do I see
> that you overthrew the Pope—and set the public on
> the throne.

> Hypocrisy is quite as inseparable from being a
> man as sliminess is from being a fish.

> What could be more ridiculous than to use a jack
> to pick up a pin—or to make use of the eternal pun-
> ishment of hell in order to make men into that half-
> demoralized, half-honest bagatelle which is roughly
> what it means to be a man.

Professor Smith prefers the extensive to the epi-
grammatic, and he might claim that his selection emphasizes Kierkegaard's religious thought—the ideas that
were projected outward in his pamphleteering attack
upon the established Christianity of Denmark. But the
pamphlets (ten in all, called *The Instant*) and the
open letters that Kierkegaard issued have been already
rendered into English by Lowrie, under the title *Attack Upon "Christendom."* This book relates to *The
Last Years* much as the outside of a sock relates to
the inside; the pattern is not identical, but the threads
are the same. After minimizing the considerable du-
plication, the editor of *The Last Years* justifies its publication by saying, "The last years of Kierkegaard's
life saw a remarkable concentration of the motifs which
controlled his whole authorship. This comes vividly to
life in the present selection from the journals and papers of that time, and casts light on all that went
before it." True, if "concentration" is taken to mean a

narrowing. The prolix philosophizing of the "aesthetic works" and the fervent exhortation of the "religious works" have been succeeded by a third stage—an apostolic or pathological vehemence. *The Last Years* shows Kierkegaard's mind narrowed to a very hard point. More precisely, it shows his mind and life, those antagonistic twins, both narrowed to a very hard point, the point of attack, which becomes the point of vanishing.

Søren Aabye Kierkegaard (the name means "churchyard," and is pronounced "Kĕrkĕgŏr") was born in Copenhagen in 1813—"the year," he was to say, "when so many worthless notes were put in circulation." His father, Michael, was a man of great force and complexity. A shepherd lad from the desolate West Jutland heath, he had become a prosperous cloth merchant and grocer in the city, only to retire at the age of forty, perhaps to devote himself to religious brooding. Within a year of his first wife's death, Michael married a household servant, Ane Lund, who bore him a child four months after their wedding. This marriage was to produce seven children, of whom Søren Aabye (as distinguished from his older brother, Søren Michael) was the last. His father was fifty-six, his mother forty-five; the advanced age of his parents accounts in part for Kierkegaard's physical frailty, and his position as the family Benjamin for his pertness and conceit. His nickname within the family was Fork—bestowed when, rebuked for shovelling food greedily at the table, he announced, "I *am* a fork, and I will stick you." Descriptions of his childhood abound in his journals:

> I was already an old man when I was born. . . . Delicate, slender, and weak, deprived of almost every condition for holding my own with other boys, or even for passing as a complete human being in comparison with others; melancholy, sick in soul, in many ways profoundly unfortunate, one thing I had: an eminently shrewd wit, given me presumably in order that I might not be defenseless.

But many weak boys with sharp tongues are born into the world, and Kierkegaard's heightened sense of himself reaches for more:

> I am in the deepest sense an unfortunate individual who has from the earliest age been nailed fast to one suffering or another, to the very verge of insanity, which may have its deeper ground in a disproportion between my soul and my body.

And in *The Last Years,* in the last entry, within a few weeks of his death, this sense of initial misfortune attains a frightening pitch:

> Through a crime I came into existence, I came into existence against God's will. The fault, which in one sense is not mine, even if it makes me a criminal in God's eyes, is to give life. The punishment fits the fault: it is to be deprived of all joy of life, to be brought to the supreme degree of disgust with life.

His adult life consisted of a series of quixotic, or expiatory, gestures. His father wanted him to study for the ministry, so he spent his youth in frivolity, drunkenness, and dandyism. His father died, so he settled down to pass the theological examination. He fell in love with and successfully courted Regine Olsen; then he broke off the engagement and buried himself in a frenetic literary activity dedicated to her. He became, under his own name and under the open secret of his pseudonyms, the most remarkable writer in Denmark, the only author above attack by the scurrilous magazine the *Corsair;* so he incited the *Corsair* (though its editor, Meïr Goldschmidt, revered him) to attack, which it did with such success that Kierkegaard's personal life was made a torment and the name Søren became a byword for the ridiculous. Lastly, he who had long been on the verge of becoming a country parson mounted a savage attack upon organized Christianity, exhorting true Christians to abstain from the sin of church worship. He refused the Eucharist, since it could not be administered by a layman, on his death-bed.

Kierkegaard's American reputation was long deferred and is still esoteric, but in Denmark Kierkegaard was a celebrity. Indeed, he seems to have been the Benjamin of Copenhagen, the marketplace capital of a small and homogeneous country. His break with Regine was surrounded by so much gossip that it amounted to a public event. His pseudonyms, with their interlocking prefaces and compliments, must have been private jokes to a considerable group. His books, surprisingly, sold well enough to make money. During the *Corsair* persecution, his twisted back and uneven trouser legs were caricatured every week for a year, and the students at the university produced a comedy whose ridiculous hero was called Søren Kirk. Children taunted him on the streets. In his journals, he lamented, "To let oneself be trampled by geese is a slow way of dying," and complained that "when . . . I have sought recreation by driving ten or twelve miles, and my body has gradually become somewhat weak . . . when I alight from the carriage . . . there is sure to be someone at hand who is jolly enough to call me names." Astonishingly, the very name Søren, up to then the most common male baptismal name, became opprobrious, and Danish parents, according to Lowrie, took to admonishing their children, "Don't be a Søren." Though helpless under such assault, Kierkegaard was not without power. A staunch monarchist, he was on conversational terms with King Christian VIII, and Lowrie asserts that in the relationship it was Kierkegaard who "held himself a little aloof." (In his journals, Kierkegaard dryly noted, "On the whole, Christian VIII has enriched me with many psychological observations. Perhaps psychologists ought to pay particular attention to kings, and especially to absolute monarchs; for the freer a man is, the better he can be known.") Kierkegaard's satirical pen was a feared weapon. He undoubtedly ruined the life of a former friend, P. S. Møller, with a personal attack published in the newspaper *Fatherland*. So his assault upon the ecclesiastical establishment was delivered from the strength of notoriety, and, far from being the private fulminations of an obscure aesthete and mystic, was a demagogic assault, a well-publicized uproar reverberating throughout Scandinavia. (*The Instant* was immediately translated into Swedish and, not needing translation in Norway, aroused the interest of young Ibsen, to become the basis of *Brand*.) Kierkegaard's expectation of arrest and imprisonment was not fulfilled, but at his funeral a crowd of students gathered to protest the church's appropriation of the body, and a riot was barely averted. W. H. Auden, in introducing his own Kierkegaard anthology, regards *The Attack Upon "Christendom"* as not a book but an act: "What for the author was the most important book of his life is for us, as readers, the least, for to us the important point is not what it contains, but the fact that Kierkegaard wrote it."

Certainly, the journals of *The Last Years* are difficult to enjoy. How different are, say, the *Last Diaries* of Tolstoy, wherein the old man, honored all over the world, a sacred figure to his countrymen, struggles with the naïveté of a child to become good! Kierkegaard never had Tolstoy's candid willingness to learn and grow. He was endowed from birth with a somewhat elderly mind. Though he read voraciously and could be gregarious and charming, only five people seem to have really interested him: Jesus, Socrates, Hegel, Regine Olsen, and his father. Though his ability to vary and extend his voice is marvellous, a single field of ideas appears to have been in his possession since the beginning. It remained only for him to explore it and to arrive at the ultimate conclusion. One does not find in *The Last Years* those categories— "the absurd," "the leap," "dread"—that modern Existentialism has made fashionable; they were expounded

in the earlier "aesthetic works." What one does find,
theologically, is a wholehearted insistence upon the
inhumanity of God. Through the bitter clamor of these
journals—the outrageous but telling satires on bourgeois Christianity, the complaints about priests and professors and Bishop Mynster, the searching diagnoses of
Luther and Schopenhauer, the not always tender dep-
recations of women, the copious self-dramatization,
the tedious extollation of "the individual," the slashing
dismissals of "knavish religiosity," "scoundrelly posterity," and the "increasing mass of drivel which is
called science"—there sounds a note that attains a cre-
scendo in the last pages: Christianity is torture, and
God a torturer:

> In Christianity God is spirit—and therefore so im-
> mensely severe, from love: for he longs for spirit
> from man. . . . God is never so severe with those
> he loves in the Old Testament as he is with the apos-
> tles, for example, whose life was sheer suffering and
> then a martyr's death. . . . In the Old Testament,
> when the prophet is in need, God always finds a way
> out—but as for the apostle . . . there is no talk of
> unexpected help which shall bring him his strictest
> necessities; no, God just leaves him in the lurch, leaves
> him to die of hunger and thirst—it can be as severe
> as that.

> If I were a pagan and had to speak Greek, I should
> say that God has arranged everything for his own
> entertainment; he amuses himself like a man who
> puts a piece of bacon in a mousetrap and watches
> all the tricks of the mice to get the bacon out without
> being trapped—so God amuses himself at the leaps
> and springs and contortions of these millions of men
> to get hold of the truth without suffering.

> . . . What torture! If a man is really to be the
> instrument of God, for the infinite will that God is,
> then God must first take all his will from him. What

a fearful operation! And it is natural that no one knows how to examine so painfully as one who is omniscient and omnipotent. Certainly with other forms of torture there are doctors present to estimate how long the tortured man can hold out without losing his life. Yet mistakes can happen, and the tortured man can die before their eyes. This never happens with one who is omniscient.

> To be a Christian is the most terrible of all torments, it is—and it must be—to have one's hell here on earth. . . . One shudders to read what an animal must suffer which is used for vivisection; yet this is only a fugitive image of the suffering involved in being a Christian—in being kept alive in the state of death.

The vision is so terrible that Kierkegaard almost relents: "What I write is from a Christian standpoint so true, so true, and from a Christian standpoint this is how I must write. And yet I can say that what I write here tortures me to produce . . . it is repugnant to me." Again: "Ah, it is with sorrow that I write this. In melancholy sympathy, though myself unhappy, I loved men and the mass of men. Their bestial conduct toward me compelled me, in order to endure it, to have more and more to do with God."

And what is the essence of God's nature, that makes "having to do" with Him so painful? Majesty:

> Suffering, that there must be suffering, is connected with the majesty of God. His majesty is so infinite that it can be characterized or expressed only by a paradox: it is the paradox of the majesty which is bound to make the beloved unhappy. . . . Suffering depends on the fact that God and man are qualitatively different, and that the clash of time and eternity in time is bound to cause suffering.

A little later, the formula is given a personal turn:

> O infinite majesty, even if you were not love, even
> if you were cold in your infinite majesty I could not
> cease to love you, I need something majestic to love.
> . . . There was and there is a need of majesty in
> my soul, of a majesty I can never tire of worshipping.

Yet elsewhere this majesty acquires human attributes, even weaknesses. God knows sorrow. "Alas,
the more I think about it the more I come to imagine
God as sitting in sorrow, for he most of all knows
what sorrow is." God loves, out of need. "It is God's
passion to love and to be loved, almost—infinite love!—
as though he himself were bound in this passion, in
the power of this passion, so that he cannot cease to
love, almost as though it were a weakness. . . ." And:
"I know that in love you suffer with me, more than I,
infinite Love—even if you cannot change."

The paragraph preceding this last quotation is revealing:

> If my contemporaries could understand how I suf-
> fer, how Providence, if I may dare to say so, maltreats
> me, I am certain that they would be so profoundly
> moved that in human sympathy they would make an
> attempt (as sometimes happens with a child which is
> being maltreated by its parents) to wrest me free
> from Providence.

The hypothetical cruel parents return in another metaphor:

> As the child of a tight-rope walker is from his ear-
> liest years made supple in his back and in every muscle
> so that, after daily practice, he is sheer suppleness
> and can carry out every movement, absolutely every
> movement, in the most excruciating positions, yet
> always easily and smiling: so with prayer to the ab-
> solute majesty.

And in a third image, world history is likened to "the uproar and hubbub which children make in their play-room, instead of sitting still and reading their books (as their parents would like)." With these similes, we touch a central nerve of Kierkegaard's thought—the identification of God with his father, whom he both loved and hated, who treated him cruelly and who loved him.

Much is known of Kierkegaard's relation with his father, but more is unknown. Kierkegaard wrote in his journals: "Perhaps I could recount the tragedy of my childhood, the fearful secret explanation of re-ligion, suggesting an apprehensive presentiment which my imagination elaborated, my offence at religion—I could recount it in a novel entitled *The Enigmatical Family*." And another entry reads:

> It is terrible whenever for a single instant I come to think of the dark background of my life, from the very earliest time. The anxious dread with which my father filled my soul, his own frightful melancholy, the many things which I cannot record—I got such a dread of Christianity, and yet I felt myself so strongly drawn to it.

A childhood classmate later wrote, "To the rest of us who led a genuinely boyish life S. K. was a stranger and an object of compassion, especially on account of his dress. . . . This [his costume, which resembled the costume of charity schools] procured him the nick-name of Choirboy, which alternated with Søren Sock, in allusion to his father's previous business as hosier. S. K. was regarded by us all as one whose home was wrapped in a mysterious half-darkness of severity and oddity." And in his autobiographical *The Point of View for My Work as an Author*, Kierkegaard wrote, "As a child I was strictly and austerely brought up in Christianity; humanly speaking, crazily brought up. A child crazily travestied as a melancholy old man. Terrible!"

Yet the boy's relation to his father was also intimate and admiring. One of Kierkegaard's pseudonyms, Johannes Climacus, reminisces:

> His father was a very severe man, apparently dry and prosaic, but under this rough coat he concealed a glowing imagination which even old age could not quench. When Johannes occasionally asked of him permission to go out, he generally refused to give it, though once in a while he proposed instead that Johannes should take his hand and walk back and forth in the room. . . . While they went back and forth in the room the father described all that they saw; they greeted passersby, carriages rattled past them and drowned the father's voice; the cake-woman's goodies were more enticing than ever. He described so accurately, so vividly, so explicitly even to the least details, everything that was known to Johannes and so fully and perspicuously what was unknown to him, that after half an hour of such a walk with his father he was as much overwhelmed and fatigued as if he had been a whole day out of doors. . . . To Johannes it seemed as if the world were coming into existence during the conversation, *as if the father were our Lord and he were his favorite*, who was allowed to interpose his foolish conceits as merrily as he would; for he was never repulsed, the father was never put out, he agreed to everything.

I have abbreviated this often quoted passage and italicized a revealing clause. By the same light, Kierkegaard did not expect to live past the age of thirty-three (the age of Christ) and did expect his father, though fifty-seven years older, to outlive him (to be immortal). In fact, his father lived to the patriarchal age of eighty-two and Kierkegaard died when he was only forty-two,

so the premonition was in spirit correct. There is no
doubt that his father fearfully dominated the household. Incredibly, in all of Kierkegaard's writings there
is not one mention of his mother. And an age that has
been able to peruse Kafka's diaries need not be reminded that, severity aside, the *competence,* the very
wonderfulness of a father can be felt as a crushing
tyranny. "It is a fearful thing," Kierkegaard wrote, "to
fall into the hands of the living God."

To all this add a precocious compassion. In his
journals Kierkegaard writes of the perils of religious
education:

> The most dangerous case is not when the father
> is a free thinker, and not even when he is a hypo-
> crite. No, the danger is when he is a pious and God-
> fearing man, when the child is inwardly and deeply
> convinced of it, and yet in spite of all this observes
> that a profound unrest is deeply hidden in his soul,
> so that not even piety and the fear of God can be-
> stow peace. The danger lies just here, that the child
> in this relationship is almost compelled to draw a
> conclusion about God, that after all God is not in-
> finite love.

It does not seem to me contradictory to posit a
father who appears as both God and a victim of God.
Such a paradox, after all, is fundamental to Christian
theology, and Kierkegaard's imagination often returns
to the forsaken Christ's outcry on the Cross. Duplicity was the very engine of Kierkegaard's thought, a
habit he elevated to a metaphysical principle—the principle of "indirect communication," which he found
both in Socrates' intellectual midwifery and in God's
decision to embody Himself in a scorned and mocked
sufferer. In all Kierkegaard's production, nothing is
more powerful, more beautiful and typical, than the
sweeping Prelude to *Fear and Trembling,* wherein
the story of Abraham and Isaac is pursued through a

sequence of differing versions. All portray, in similar
language, Abraham and Isaac rising in the morning,
leaving Sarah, and travelling to Mount Moriah, where
God has told Abraham he must sacrifice his son. In
the first version, Abraham, whose face has shown sorrow and "fatherliness," turns away a moment, "and
when Isaac again saw Abraham's face it was changed,
his glance was wild, his form was horror. He seized
Isaac by the throat, threw him to the ground, and said,
'Stupid boy, dost thou then suppose that I am thy
father? I am an idolater. Dost thou suppose that this
is God's bidding? No, it is my desire.' Then Isaac
trembled and cried out in his terror, 'O God in heaven,
have compassion upon me. God of Abraham, have
compassion upon me. If I have no father upon earth,
be Thou my father!' But Abraham in a low voice said
to himself, 'O Lord in heaven, I thank Thee. After all it
is better for him to believe that I am a monster, rather
than that he should lose faith in Thee.'" Here, in this
shocking twist of a myth, that nerve is bared. Here, in
this play of ironies and deceits carried out under the
highest pressure of anguish, we feel close to Kierkegaard's mysterious and searing experience of his father.

A specific revelation about his father troubled Kierkegaard's young manhood and was transmuted, or absorbed, into a gnawing guilt or uneasiness that he refers
to in his journals as "the thorn in my flesh," which in
turn seems to be synonymous with his singularity, his
fate, as "the individual," to suffer a martyrdom not
incomparable with Christ's. Some crucial confidence
was imparted on his twenty-second birthday: "Then
it was that the great earthquake occurred, the frightful
upheaval which suddenly forced upon me a new in-
fallible rule for interpreting the phenomena one and
all. Then I surmised that my father's great age was not a
divine blessing, but rather a curse. . . . Guilt must rest
upon the whole family, a divine punishment must be
impending over it." The exact nature of the "earthquake" is forever buried in the portentous secrecy

Kierkegaard assigned it. Possibly the old man's confession had to do with sex. On the mere statistical records, Michael Kierkegaard seduced his housekeeper in the year of mourning his first wife, married the woman when she was five months pregnant, and fathered upon her a total of seven children, the last, Søren Aabye, being born when the parents, if not as ancient as Abraham and Sarah, were of an age when, in Lowrie's delicate phrase, "no such blessing was expected." Kierkegaard frequently speaks of his own existence as a "mistake," and in the journals of *The Last Years* this sense of himself has spread to include all humanity: "This whole human existence, dating from the Fall, and which we men are so puffed up about as a devilish *tour de force* . . . is merely the consequence of a false step." Of a hypothetical son he writes:

> Concerning himself he learns that he was conceived in sin, born in transgression—that his existence is therefore a crime, that therefore his father, in giving him life, has done something which is as far as possible from being well-pleasing to God.

His vivid, even sensual awareness of Original Sin, of life itself as a crime, may be traceable to an embarrassment he felt about being himself living proof of an elderly couple's concupiscence. He ranged from the heights of conceit to abysmal depths of shame; near the end of his life, he suffered a stroke while visiting friends and, falling helpless to the floor, rejected the attempts to lift him up by saying, "Oh, leave it [his body] until the maid clears it away in the morning." In the last journals, he thanks God "that no living being owes existence to me," urges celibacy upon all Christians, faces cheerfully the consequence that the race would die out, and asserts that "human egoism is concentrated in the sexual relation, the propagation of the species, the giving of life."

Or the "earthquake" may have been learning that his father, as an eleven-year-old boy, had cursed God. An entry in the journals of 1846 reads:

> How terrible about the man who once as a little boy, while herding the flocks on the heaths of Jutland, suffering greatly, in hunger and in want, stood upon a hill and cursed God—and the man was unable to forget it even when he was eighty-two years old.

The first editor of Kierkegaard's papers, Barfod, showed this passage to Bishop Peter Kierkegaard, the one surviving sibling, who confirmed that this was indeed his father, and that, since shortly thereafter the shepherd boy was adopted by an uncle and set on the road to prosperity, he regarded this prosperity as an inverted curse, as God's vengeance for, to quote Peter, "the sin against the Holy Ghost which never can be forgiven." It seems likely that this, and not a sexual confession, is the matter of the "earthquake." And it seems to me, furthermore, that in some sense Kierkegaard's attack upon Christendom is a repetition of his father's curse—an attack, ostensibly directed against the Danish Protestant Church, upon God Himself, on behalf of the father who had suffered, and yet also against this same father, who had made his son suffer and bound him to Christian belief.

In 1849, Kierkegaard wrote in his journals, under the heading *Something about myself which must always be remembered:* "If, with my imagination, and with my passions, etc., I had been in any ordinary human sense a man, then I should certainly have forgotten Christianity entirely. But I am bound in agonizing misery, like a bird whose wings have been clipped, yet retaining the power of my mind undiminished, and its undoubtedly exceptional powers." And the pamphlets comprising *The Attack* have been, in every language except English, the first things by Kierkegaard to be translated, as anticlerical, anti-Christian literature.

The "Christendom" Kierkegaard denounced was popularly taken to be synonymous with Christianity, and perhaps it was. It is hard to account otherwise for the strange qualities of the attack as found in *The Instant* and in these journals. Are specific abuses, as in Luther's attack upon the Papal church, named? No: "Luther nailed up ninety-five theses on the church door; that was a fight about doctrine. Nowadays one might publish one single thesis in the papers: 'Christianity does not exist;' and offer to dispute with all parsons and dons." This is from a journal of 1851; by 1854, Kierkegaard had developed a piercing critique of Luther, stated wittily as:

> Luther suffered extremely from an anxious conscience, he needed treatment. Very well: but is that a reason for completely transforming Christianity into a matter of calming anxious consciences?

Kierkegaard does not want consciences to be calmed, he wants them to be exacerbated by the truth about Christianity. "My task is to put a halt to a lying diffusion of Christianity, and to help it to shake off a mass of nominal Christians." And what is the truth about Christianity?

> The ideal means hatred of man. What man naturally loves is finitude. To face him with the ideal is the most dreadful torture . . . it kills in him, in the most painful way, everything in which he really finds his life, in the most painful way it shows him his own wretchedness, it keeps him in sleepless unrest, whereas finitude lulls him into enjoyment. That is why Christianity is called, and is, hatred of man.

Now, is such advocacy not a hidden prosecution? It may be argued that harsh words were a needed corrective to an existing complacency and that the New Testament itself is sternly world-denying. But I notice that, just as liberal apologists are troubled to explain

away the "hard" sayings of Jesus, Kierkegaard is embarrassed by the Gospels' softer moments—the genial
miracle at the wedding of Cana, the sufferance of little
children, the promise to the thief on the cross. Kierkegaard says, "Men live their life in the strength of the
assurance that of such as children is the kingdom of
God, and in death they look for consolation to the
image of the thief. That is the whole of their Christianity, and, characteristically enough, it is a mixture of
childishness and crime." Surely here he is attacking
something essential to Biblical teaching—the forgiving-
ness that balances majesty. He seems impatient with
divine mercy, much as a true revolutionary despises
the philanthropies whereby misery is abated and revolution delayed. The "Christendom" he attacks has
strangely little substance, apart from the person of
Bishop Mynster, his father's pastor, who is criticized
only for his urbanity and eloquence and his refusal to
confess that "what he represented was not really Christianity but a milder form of it." Indeed, the whole attack is an invitation to the Church to commit suicide:
"Yes, truly, suicide, and yet an action well-pleasing to
God." Any specific reform—a revival of monasteries,
an abolition of "livings"—he explicitly disavows. The
one concrete result he expects from his attack is his
own imprisonment and death. Though the Church's
functionaries barely troubled to respond even in writing, he did die. He suffered his fatal stroke while returning from the bank with the last scrap of his fortune.
He had nowhere further to go, and his death, whose
causes eluded diagnosis, seems willed.

In the hospital, he told his only intimate friend, the
pastor Emil Boesen, "The doctors do not understand
my illness; it is psychic, and they want to treat it in
the ordinary medical way." His conversations with
Boesen, a kind of continuation of the journals (printed
as such by Dru), have a relaxed sweetness; his terrible "task" is done, and he is happy that so much
in his life has "come out right" and melancholy that

he cannot share his happiness with everyone. He refuses to put flowers sent him into water: "it is the fate of flowers to blossom, smell, and die." Of *The Instant,* whose tenth number lay unpublished on his desk, he said, "You must remember that I have seen everything from the inmost center of Christianity, it is all very poor and clumsy. . . . I only said it to be rid of evil, and so to reach an Alleluia! Alleluia! Alleluia!" This "Alleluia," it may be, could be reached only through a scandal in which, alone like a shepherd boy on the Jutland heath, Kierkegaard execrated God. At any rate, with Kierkegaard, as with Proust, we feel writing as a demon—the one way to set a bent life straight.

Kierkegaard would hardly be pleased to know that more than any other thinker of the nineteenth century —including Newman and Dostoevski—he has made Christianity intellectually possible for the twentieth. Not that the "millions of men falling away from Christianity" that he foresaw and desired has not occurred. But, by giving metaphysical dignity to "the subjective," by showing faith to be not an intellectual development but a movement of the will, by holding out for existential duality against the tide of all the monisms, materialist or spiritualized or political, that would absorb the individual consciousness, Kierkegaard has given Christianity new life, a handhold, the "Archimedean point." From Jaspers and Barth, Unamuno and Marcel, Heidegger and Sartre, his thought has filtered down through the seminaries to the laity. He has become, as he angrily predicted, the property of those men "more abominable and gruesome than the cannibals," professors and clergymen, and he is used, in the form of a few phrases or a bolder style, to prop up the feeble, always tottering faith of contemporary "Christians." He has become an instrument in the conspiracy to "make a fool of God." Those who read him eat the aesthetic coating and leave the religious pill, and "neo-Orthodox" Protestantism, his direct beneficiary, has accepted the antinomianism and ignored the savage austerity, the scornful authoritarianism. Yet Kierkegaard himself, this two-tined Fork with his trouser legs of unequal length, this man in love with duplicity and irony and all double-edged things, lived luxuriously to the last and is nowhere quite free of sophism and vanity. (His sermons, for example, so symphonic and ardent, somehow belong with the memorable sermons of fiction, like those of Father Mapple in *Moby Dick* and of Père Paneloux in *The Plague*.) In the journal of 1849 he reminded himself, "It must never be forgotten that Christ also succored temporal and worldly needs. One can also, untruly, make Christ so spiritual that he becomes sheer cruelty." If this is what Kierkegaard seemed to do in the end, he also remembered that infinite majesty infinitely relents. Late in *The Last Years* we find this surprising entry: "For with such clarity as I have, I must say I am not a Christian. For the situation as I see it is that in spite of the abyss of nonsense in which we are caught, we shall all alike be saved."

PSEUDONYMOUS AUTHORSHIP AS
ART AND AS ACT

Stephen Crites

Johannes Climacus, smoking his cigar in the Frederiksberg Garden and like many a young pseudonym pon-
dering what he should do with his life, determined at
length to become an author. Furthermore, he decided
that in an age when everyone seemed bent on making
life easier for people he would become the sort of
author who makes life difficult for them.[1] Readers of
his *Philosophical Fragments* and *Concluding Unscientific Postscript* might agree that he succeeded.

Johannes was himself the poetic creation of another
author, who also wanted to make life difficult. More
than that, Søren Kierkegaard frequently attests in his
journals that he wishes to be an author for whom writing is a kind of action. But one must be prepared for
paradoxes in dealing with Kierkegaard. The way he
set about writing, at least in the pseudonymous works,
seems at first glance quite the opposite of what he him-

This essay was written especially for this volume.

[1] *Concluding Unscientific Postscript*, Swenson and Lowrie tr.
(Princeton: Princeton University Press, 1944), pp. 164–67
(*Samlede Værker*, udgivet af A. B. Drachmann, J. L. Heiberg
og H. O. Lange [Gyldendal, 1962–64], bd. IX, pp. 154–57).
I will cite the most recent Danish edition of Kierkegaard's
works (hereafter as *SV*) along with the standard English translation, partly for the convenience of readers able to use the
Danish text, partly because I have generally translated quoted
passages afresh from the Danish. While I have consulted the
standard English translations, quotations offered here will generally differ in some degree from their rendering in the English
version cited.

self regarded as action. He devised ingenious methods for withdrawing personally from these works, not only enveloping the writings themselves in pseudonymous mystifications but also projecting a public image in the way he comported himself that was designed to appear out of keeping with his literary enterprise.[2] On the other hand, although he created these books as works of art, he designed them to perform a function contrary to his own conception of the function of art. These paradoxes with respect to action and art are joined in his strategy of "indirect communication."

We will not rehearse the many things Kierkegaard had to say on the subject of indirect communication in his journals and elsewhere, though some of these hints have guided our pursuit. We will search out Kierkegaard's designs through the works themselves, to discover the sort of action he was attempting to perform in them. We can say at once that it was an act directed at his reader, and implicit in this act was a conception of the human form of consciousness to which this peculiar act of communication was addressed.

1

The Lure of Possibility

The pseudonymous writings develop, among other things, Kierkegaard's famous notion of the "stages" or "spheres" of life. Part of our task will be to search out what these "stages" represent. One thing they are not: they are not a rigid descriptive scheme for classifying human types. They are not properly descriptive at all, and besides Kierkegaard certainly thought one could have all his credentials in order as a member of the human race without being either an aesthetic, an eth-

---

[2] *The Point of View for My Work as an Author,* Lowrie tr. (London, New York, Toronto: Oxford University Press, 1939; *SV,* XVIII), Chapter 2.

ical, or a religious man. Granted that he might be a rather poor sort of specimen in Kierkegaard's view if he could not recognize himself reflected in any of the stages; still he would exhibit certain general features that belong simply to man as man.

The dialectic of the stages itself presupposes that there are such general features of the human form of existence. Kierkegaard assumes that human beings are subject to a peculiar form of becoming. The closest he comes to arguing the point is in *The Concept of Dread,* where he distinguishes the fully "tensed" temporality of past, present, and future which qualifies a human form of existence from the indefinite succession to which all physical things are subject.[3] Without lingering over the difficult details of that argument, we may simply say that human beings have a form of consciousness capable of entertaining possibilities. They do not exist purely in a succession of external changes and movements. Nor are they merely sensitive instruments registering simultaneous happenings in their vicinity. They are spatially and temporally located along with other physical realities, but they remember, they anticipate, they scheme, they fear, they fantasize: they ventilate their localized reality with myriad forms of possibility. A man does not merely recall earlier experiences, but reconstructs the materials of memory as pure possibilities upon which he can exercise abstract reflection; both the pursuit of knowledge and the play of imagination require this capacity to recollect what has been experienced and learned. And besides this plasticity of memory is the capacity to anticipate possibilities not yet realized. One fears and hopes, or one yearns for

[3] *The Concept of Dread,* Lowrie tr. (Princeton: Princeton University Press, 1944), pp. 73–83 (*SV,* VI, pp. 170–80). I have analyzed this difficult section in some detail in Chapter 3 of a monograph entitled *In the Twilight of Christendom: Hegel vs. Kierkegaard on Faith and History* (Chambersburg, Pa.: American Academy of Religion, Studies in Religion Number Two, 1971).

possibilities beyond any reasonable hope and is terror-
ized by possibilities beyond any reasonable fear, possibilities changing their shape without limit before the
mind's eye. But there is a still more powerful force of
possibility pressing upon consciousness: the conscious
human being projects possible courses of action in
which he invests the weight of his reality. He will
change the situation in which he finds himself, and in
the process he will himself undergo a metamorphosis.
This protean, self-formative power of the conscious
self is what gives rise to the distinctively human form
of temporality. Within a conscious present the past
recollected and the future anticipated or projected are
distinct modalities. The discrimination between them
can be obscured only if the conscious present is itself
in some manner effaced. That, too, is a possibility of
consciousness, as we shall see. Every psychic transformation, including those reflected in Kierkegaard's
"stages," presupposes the human capacity to pursue
the lure of possibility.

Human becoming is not merely the actualization of
inherent potentialities, like the maturation of a tree. As
members of a biological species human beings do of
course share in that natural process. But concurrent
with it is this form of becoming that owes more to the
fevers of the imagination than it does to natural growth
and decay. Furthermore, the form a man's life actually
assumes will not necessarily be what he has projected
in his imagination. The conversion of possibility into
actuality is again not so simple. As often as not his
actual project will be a parody of his conscious intentions. Kierkegaard had a particularly keen eye for the
futility and the comic vanity of human projects. Yet
the projects that issue in actual human careers in existence, thwarted and misshapen as they may be, can
only have been hatched by creatures driven by the lure
of possibility. The capacity to pursue the possible was
in Kierkegaard's view the source of all human achievement, which he thought generally modest, as well as

the source of the follies and depravities, which he thought were colossal. The artist, the builder, the statesman, the lover drink from the same effervescent brew as the hypocrite, the seducer, the self-deceived fanatic. Both the heights and the depths of human existence are aerated with possibility.

Dread (*angest*) is a man's awakening to his own aerated existence, the premonition of his own protean powers. It is distinguished from fear primarily by the fact that fear is the recoil from threatening possibilities that lie outside a man's own conscious power, while dread is generated in him by the prodigious possibilities inherent in his own capacity to act. A man on the edge of a cliff may fear that an avalanche or an accidental misstep will send him to his doom. But if it should occur to him that he might be seized by a mad impulse to throw himself off deliberately, he is instantly in dread of that inner possibility. Not that we dread only disasters. Indeed, what we dread always attracts as much as it repels. A young boy or girl dreads his sexual awakening. A great actor or actress will be in dread as he waits to go onstage, not because he fears failure, but because only the "tension" of the stage will release his full powers as an artist. "For the more powers he possesses, the greater is his dread so long as he is outside the tension which exactly corresponds to his powers."[4] Beyond all such special cases, however, is the central theme of *The Concept of Dread:* that in every child of Adam dread forebodes his own fall into sin. But dread is the premonition of forbidden possibilities only because it is a man's awakening to a power of action that has no fixed bounds. "Dread is freedom's possibility," again in a peculiarly human sense: a man is chilled and exhilarated to discover that he is able to project his own path. Although he is an altogether finite creature, he does not simply choose one path among

[4] *Crisis in the Life of an Actress and Other Essays on Drama,* Crites tr. (London: Collins; New York: Harper Torchbooks, 1967), p. 78 (*SV,* XIV, p. 114).

others but makes his own path, being himself formed
in the process. He does not merely become, but becomes himself. The self he is to become is not pre-
determined, but will be formed by his own act of becoming. Even what is forbidden is possible. Dread is
a man's awakening to this power of self-formation.

> If a man were a beast or an angel he would not
> be able to dread. Since he is a synthesis, he can
> dread, and the deeper he dreads the greater the man.[5]

The beast is presumably untroubled in his fleshly immediacy, the angel serene in his contemplation of timeless possibility. But to be a "synthesis" of the finite and
the infinite, in time and in flesh to be broken open by
possibility, is to be in dread.

Kierkegaard frequently asserts that man is such a

---

[5] *The Concept of Dread,* p. 139 (*SV,* VI, p. 234). Though
Kierkegaard thought this "synthesis" distinguished human beings from animals, the point is simply to identify the sort of
creature a human being is. To the extent that, say, one of our
simian cousins should be able to entertain possibility in this
sense, we might just to that extent welcome him into the brotherhood of dread. Kierkegaard would likely have resisted that suggestion, but it is important in such cases to distinguish between
the essential lines of his analysis and extraneous beliefs he
may have held.

We might forestall another false issue by pointing out that
the freedom of which Kierkegaard speaks here has little to do
with the metaphysical problem of freedom and determinism
as it has generally been posed among Anglo-American philosophers. Though he did on occasion address himself to the
metaphysical question (e.g., arguing in the Interlude to *Philosophical Fragments* that a possibility cannot be actualized by
necessity), his point here is phenomenological rather than metaphysical: that in practical affairs consciousness distinguishes the
indeterminate possibility of the future from the determinate
reality of the past. Such futurity is an irreducible mode of
human consciousness regardless of any metaphysical issue concerning causal connections between earlier and later events.

synthesis. He does not mean that there is an infinite part of a man that is exempt from the finite conditions of his life. His consciousness is as conditioned as his metabolism. But when possibility breaks in upon it, even the most firmly fixed conditions of his existence become problematical to him, he takes up an attitude toward his existence or even against it.

> One sticks one's finger into the soil in order to smell out what country he is in. I stick my finger into existence—it smells of nothing. Where am I? What does it mean: the world? What does that word signify? Who has tricked me into the whole thing and now leaves me stranded there? Who am I? How did I come into the world? Why was I not consulted. . . .[6]

A person who has been shaken into asking such questions remains as locked into his reality as ever, but the fact that it has come to seem arbitrary to him is a sign that it has been set in the face of possibility. Even if no possibility that such a man entertains is itself unconditional, absolute, divine, still every possibility that breaks in on him is the wedge of an infinite field of possibility, infinite in the sense that no definite limit can be imposed that it cannot in principle overflow. He may know that his thought is sheerest fantasy, and yet be shaken by it into a restlessness that gives him no peace to pursue his more reasonable projects. Kierkegaard is well aware that such dread can be simply immobilizing. At the same time, it is "freedom's possibility" that enables a life of the spirit to take wings in a man.

> He who is formed by dread is formed by possibility, and only he who is formed by possibility is

[6] *Repetition,* Lowrie tr. (Princeton: Princeton University Press, 1946), p. 114 (*SV,* V, p. 171).

formed according to his infinity. Possibility is therefore the weightiest of all categories.[7]

In the context, Kierkegaard is leading up to his conclusion, that if the awakening to infinite possibility in dread is not short-circuited or repressed it may deliver the awakened man over to faith.

But the dazzle of this apologetic conclusion should not blind us to the darker side of the analysis on which it is based. Kierkegaard's concept of dread has, after all, been his most seminal insight among existentialist writers of the twentieth century, but not many of them seem to have been led by it into the arms of God. Perhaps none of his ideas is so distinctively modern, or so bleak. Leaving aside the resolution of the impasse through faith, this analysis implies that human beings are driven to distraction by possibility. They are obsessed by visions thrown up by their own minds. Even their obsessions collide with other obsessions, and the simplest bodily needs are so inflamed by the fevers of the imagination that they cannot be satiated. For consciousness is aswarm with schemes, dark fantasies, sublime aspirations, memories, hopes, and the doodles of a thousand aimless thoughts. The momentum of any project can be sustained only through the most compulsive exercise of will, struggling endlessly against distracting possibilities.

The obvious solution would be for people to face up to their reality. But precisely our reality as conscious beings is suffused with possibility. It is not a fixed or stable "state" at all, but a becoming. Self-knowledge cannot be a matter of having accurate information about a given reality of the self. On the contrary, the way we understand ourselves enters essentially into the formation of the self. Again, the point is not simply that a man is what he thinks he is. There is, to be sure, a "given" aspect to a human life: a person's biological constitution, his social background, his mother tongue,

[7] *Concept of Dread*, pp. 139–40 (*SV*, VI, p. 235).

his personal past, the larger history of which he is a part, and so on. That is why, Kierkegaard argues in *Sickness unto Death,* a man cannot in fact succeed in pursuing a purely ideal possibility: not willing to be the self he is turns out to be a form of despair. On the other hand, a man is also driven to despair if he attempts to be simply the self he is, keeping possibility at bay. There is no way short of lobotomy for consciousness to rid itself of possibility. So consciousness swings despairingly between its finite givenness and its infinite possibility, without being able to achieve an integrated life.

In fact, the combined arguments of Kierkegaard's two "psychological" works, *The Concept of Dread* and *The Sickness unto Death,* add up to a dismaying conclusion: that a human life consists generally in a series of failed projects, each doomed from the outset by its own inherent contradictions or by the incapacity of creatures who are themselves bundles of contradictions to sustain them. The peculiar temporality that holds the promise of a life of spirit has the more usual consequence that every project begins in dread and ends in despair.

2

An Age of Dissipation

There are other ways of putting the cheerless conclusions to which Kierkegaard has led us. Extending a homely old expression for a dissolute life, for example, we might say that human beings tend to dissipate. They lack integrity: they are unable to integrate their aims and their powers into a morally purposeful unity. We will try in subsequent sections to show how Kierkegaard's "indirect," pseudonymous literature is designed to be of help to a reader who is struggling to pull himself together. But as one might expect, we generally find Kierkegaard's most explicit comments on the prob-

lem of dissipation in the "edifying" (literally, "upbuilding") works in which he addresses the reader much
more "directly," speaking in his own name and with
his own voice. For in these works he diagnoses, he
exposes self-deceptions, he accuses, chasing the reader
like the hound of heaven from every cave and hedge of
illusory security. Written "for self-examination," these
works are full of terms and metaphors signifying the
diverse forms of dissipation.

Drunkenness, for instance, was one of his favorite
metaphors for the human condition. Kierkegaard liked
to quote Luther's saying: "The world is like a drunken
peasant; when you help him up on one side of the
horse he falls off on the other side."[8] Intoxicated with
possibility, people stumble without being able to sustain any direction for more than a step or two, heads
swirling in a bewildering haze of indistinct inklings;
and to the extent that speech lacks the psychological
resonance of integrated personality it becomes so much
driveling at the mouth. People make a show of sobriety
by employing the usual methods: they hold onto something to steady them, or walk close to the buildings
along the street. Social pressure, the force of custom,
the necessity of earning a living are the kinds of external supports that hold them together in an appearance of sobriety. But one shuns situations in which he
would have to walk out in the open, supported by his
own powers alone, for then he could not conceal his
shaky condition.[9]

Again, the phenomenon of the divided mind and
the fragmented purpose receives one of its richest treat-
ments in a collection of ethico-religious discourses devoted to the thesis that "purity of heart is to will one
thing." Here our hound of heaven tracks down the

---

[8] *For Self-Examination; Judge for Yourselves!* and *Three
Discourses,* Lowrie tr. (Princeton: Princeton University Press,
1944), p. 49 (*SV,* XVII, p. 68).

[9] Ibid., pp. 129–30 (*SV,* XVII, pp. 146–47). The passage
cited is from a Christian discourse on "Becoming Sober."

manifold devices of "double-mindedness." He argues that the inability to will one thing, any state in which intention constantly breaks apart into conflicting impulses, is a form of despair. For "what is it to despair other than to have two wills!"—each forever thwarted by the other.[10] The hopelessly divided man takes refuge in "busyness," scurrying from one project to another in a mad scattering of his energies unconsciously designed to ward off the quiet hour when he would have to face his despair.

Though this predicament is never quite so fully or "directly" laid out in Kierkegaard's pseudonymous literature, there are hints of it everywhere. The "movement" of faith is often presented as the most radical antidote to it, since faith is a single unconditional passion, the momentum of which draws the dissipated energies and fragmentary possibilities of the self into a unity. When Johannes de Silentio sets out to draw his portrait of the knight of faith, he begins by carefully contrasting him to the dissipated man:

> The knight will in the first place have the power to concentrate the whole content of life and the whole significance of actuality into one single wish. If a man lacks this concentration, this intensiveness, if his soul is from the beginning scattered into the multifarious, then he never comes to make the movement, he will trade shrewdly in life like the financiers who invest their capital in a variety of stocks so as to gain on one when they lose on another—in short, he is no knight. In the next place, the knight will have the power to concentrate the result of the whole operation of thought into one act of consciousness. If he lacks this intensiveness, if his soul is from the

[10] *Purity of Heart Is to Will One Thing,* Douglas V. Steere tr. (New York: Harper & Brothers, 1938; Harper Torchlight Edition, 1956), pp. 59–61 (*SV,* XI, pp. 34–35). This work is really the first part of Kierkegaard's *Opbyggelige Taler i forskjellig Aand.*

> beginning scattered into the multifarious, he will
> never be able to make the movement, he will con-
> stantly be running errands in life, and will never
> enter into eternity; for even in the moment when
> he is closest to it he will suddenly discover that he
> has forgotten something for which he must go back.[11]

Busyness, running errands in life, double-mindedness,
the divided will, dissipation into the multifarious,
drunkenness and the strain of concealing it: these
are the kinds of images Kierkegaard employs to describe the despairing condition in life. But again we
must remind ourselves that this condition stems from
the prodigious power of consciousness to grasp the
possible, and this power is in itself far from being a
curse. The knight of faith exhibits it in the highest
degree, and is unimaginable without it. He, too, experiences dread, and lives in lyrical expectation of a possibility so extraordinary that one would normally call it
an *im*possibility.[12] Yet the same power that in him
gives rise to an integrating passion leads others to personal disintegration.

We have suggested that this image of dissipated man,
if not the knight of faith, is distinctively modern. At
least, as Kierkegaard himself expected, this image has
evoked the clearest shock of recognition among his
most self-consciously "modern" readers. Kierkegaard
did often think, in the Hegelian manner, of consciousness as being subject to historical conditions; while he
sometimes denounced such historicism loudly, one
finds hints of a conception of the history of consciousness in his works.[13] And it did seem to him that the
image of dissipated man was particularly manifest in

[11] *Fear and Trembling,* Lowrie tr. (Princeton: Princeton
University Press, 1941), pp. 59–60 (*SV*, V, pp. 40–41).

[12] Ibid., pp. 18–20, 35, 61 (*SV*, V, pp. 18, 28, 41–42).

[13] See, for example, the essay on "The Ancient Tragical Motif as Reflected in the Modern" in *Either/Or,* David F. and
Lillian M. Swenson and Walter Lowrie tr., with revisions by

the educated modern European. Of course the basic analysis of the temporal tension of consciousness lured by possibility was intended to be applicable to any human form of existence. But in more strictly traditional societies its most baleful manifestations had been to some extent restrained by the authority of tradition itself, reinforced by public institutions. And then the physical hardship of people's lives had kept them rooted in certain elemental simplicities of sky and soil, vitality and suffering, patience and passion. Kierkegaard seemed to think these restraints still operated among the simpler "common" people with whom he liked to stop and chat on his daily round through the streets of Copenhagen. They may not have been knights of faith, but they were decent folk, and never too

---

Howard A. Johnson (Garden City, N.Y.: Doubleday Anchor Books, 1959), Vol. I (*SV*, II). Also the distinction between the modern "spiritlessness" (in Christendom) and the premonitions of spirit among the Greeks in *Concept of Dread*, pp. 83–86 (*SV*, VI, pp. 181–83), or the analysis in *The Present Age*, on which we will comment below.

A Hegelian notion of the history of consciousness most clearly informs Kierkegaard's master's thesis, *The Concept of Irony*, Lee M. Capel tr. (Bloomington & London: Indiana University Press, 1968; *SV*, I). In particular, he takes up the special position of Socrates in world history, in relation to the decline of traditional Greek culture and the rise of the Sophists (see Part I, Chapter 3). That example is of interest in the present connection since it seems in some respects to parallel Kierkegaard's sense of his own situation: a traditional order of consciousness has been dissipated, accompanied by the halfway measures of modern sophistry, which is adept at attacking the ruins of the old order without being able to rid itself of its own dogmatic ("positive") assumptions. There is evidence that Kierkegaard identified his own work as an author with the Socratic venture, at least in earlier phases of his writing career: that just as, according to his interpretation, the negating force of Socratic irony had demolished the "positive" illusions of the Sophists, so Kierkegaard's pseudonymous works were designed as exercises in irony that would expose the self-deceptions of "modern" thought and culture.

"busy" to pass the time of day with an entertaining stroller. No doubt Kierkegaard was subject to the hyperreflective man's romantic wistfulness toward peasant simplicity. At any rate, the surgical edge of his analysis was directed primarily at the "modern" men who shared more or less his own background. He did, to be sure, seem to think, perhaps too optimistically, that his "edifying" literature was largely accessible to even the simplest reader; and at the same time he addressed a collection of his Christian discourses to a "sufferer, who is perhaps also running wild in many thoughts."[14] But the pseudonymous literature was designed for the cultivated moderns in whom the old restraints no longer functioned at all. Released both from the struggle for survival and from the weight of traditional authority, the modern man was one in whom the sluices had been opened and consciousness had been inundated by the flood of possibility.

That is the sense in which Kierkegaard characterized "the present age" as pathologically reflective, and insisted that what the age lacked was not reflection but passion.[15] For once reflection has been flooded by limitless possibility, every constraint, every certainty, every taboo is washed away. That seems liberating enough. But on the other hand, any purpose that might have drawn the self together in passion has also been carried away in the flood. Opinions, programs, and critiques proliferate; since they are all spun out of pure

[14] The Preface to *The Gospel of Suffering*, A. S. Aldworth and W. S. Ferrie tr. (London: James Clarke & Co., Ltd., 1955), p. 9 (*SV*, XI, p. 201). This work, the third part of the *Opbyggelige Taler i forskjellig Aand*, is offered in the hope that the sufferer may find in it "a guiding track among the many thoughts."

[15] *Fear and Trembling*, p. 59n (*SV*, V, p. 40n). Kierkegaard spelled out this diagnosis in a long book review published in his own name, the latter part of which has been translated under the title *The Present Age*, Alexander Dru tr. (New York: Harper Torchbooks, 1962).

possibility their supply is inexhaustible. But the dialectic of possibility is infinite. Every thesis evokes its
antithesis. There can be no conclusion or resolution.
Kierkegaard liked to use the metaphor of sewing without knotting the thread: the more diligently one stitches
the faster the fabric comes loose at the other end. Or
a man is like a shopper in the open market so befuddled
by the contending shouts of an army of hawkers that
he cannot decide what to buy. Yet when Kierkegaard
urges that passion is needed to resolve this impasse, he
is not recommending a mindless burst of emotion, nor
is he attacking reflection as such.

> Reflection is not the evil, but a standing state of
> reflection and a standstill in reflection are the fraud
> and the corruption, which by transforming the con-
> ditions for action into means of escape lead to dis-
> sipation.[16]

Reflection is necessary for any resolute decision to
act. But because a passionless reflection is suspended
among its contending perturbations, it immobilizes any
impulse to act at all.

This paralyzing reflection does, to be sure, have consequences. It does undermine the existing order and its
institutions, but only passively. They are criticized, confronted with a thousand alternative possibilities, and
no reason can be found why they should exist rather
than some other that might be imagined. All commitment to the existing order is drained away. But there
can be no commitment to any alternative either, at
least not to the extent that revolutionary action would
require. So by "a dialectical sleight of hand," a passionless reflection "leaves everything standing but cunningly tricks it out of its significance."[17] The trick
also recoils on the magician, however: for since a man's
individuality is formed by his action, his cunning avoid-

[16] *The Present Age,* p. 68 (*SV*, XIV, p. 88).
[17] Ibid., p. 42 (*SV*, XIV, p. 71).

on reduces him, too, to a mere semblance,
uncoordinated energies.

of course busy activity in abundance. But
tivity without anyone who acts, it amounts
mostly to "flirtation," to "chatter," to the uproar of
crowds. The dissipation introduces an ambiguity at the
motivational roots of behavior. People may offer reasons for what they are doing, but their motives are sel-
dom so clear as these reasons suggest. The façade of
clear purpose conceals the ambiguity from others and
perhaps from themselves.

> Is it the livelihood, the career, that inspires the
> candidate in theology, or is it Christianity? One can-
> not tell. He takes the livelihood, he *insists* that it is
> Christianity. Is it the livelihood, the career, that in-
> spires the academic candidate, or is it learning? One
> cannot tell. He takes the livelihood, becomes a pro-
> fessor, he *insists* that it is learning. Is it the number
> of subscribers that inspires the journalist, or is it the
> cause? One cannot tell. He gathers the subscribers
> in droves, he *insists* that it is the cause. Is it love of
> the masses that moves a man to place himself at
> the head of the crowd? One cannot tell. He takes
> advantage of standing at the head of this force, that
> is easy to see, he *insists* that it is out of love.[18]

Conscious hypocrisy is not necessarily the target here.
Kierkegaard did not generally bother to analyze any
such gross pathology of the spirit. But his works,
early and late, probe the manifold forms of self-
deception. The problem of the self-deceived man is not
simply that his professions do not correspond to his
real motives, but that his professions conceal the fact
that he has no clear motives at all, but only a muddy
confusion of desires. He is absent to himself.

[18] *For Self-Examination* etc., pp. 138–39 (*SV*, XVII, p. 155).
Cf. *The Present Age*, pp. 68–83 (*SV*, XIV, pp. 88–99).

3

The "Stages": A Provisional View and Some Problems

The view of the human predicament we have attempted to sketch was what set Kierkegaard his task in the pseudonymous authorship. This body of work was designed particularly for those suffering from the modern exacerbations of that predicament, including Kierkegaard himself. For without delving into his private life, about which quite enough has been written, we need only mention what is obvious to any reader of his journals: that he found in himself a prime embodiment of the impasse he was at such pains to identify and to struggle against as a writer. In fact, as he was well aware, the greater irony is that he should have chosen this way of carrying on the struggle. For almost ten years he virtually lived at his writing desk, pouring out thoughts and images, poetic possibilities and dialectical puzzles, creating a body of work so substantial that only the most compulsive diligence could have accomplished it in that period of time. During the same period, and for some years before and after, he occupied much of his remaining time and energy writing privately in his notebooks, filling so many pages that even the twenty-odd folio volumes of the modern Danish edition of his journals and papers cannot include them all. The almost embarrassing amount that we know about Kierkegaard's personal life should not obscure its most conspicuous and perhaps most important feature, that during his maturity he spent most of the hours and days of that lifetime applying ink to paper, that he lived in his thoughts, thus exemplifying in highest degree the "age of reflection" he attacked.

It cannot be said, however, that he lacked passion. But if passion is indeed the steady ardor that concentrates a man's powers into a sustained course of action, then Kierkegaard's passion had to be expressed in his writings or nowhere. He did not just happen to become a writer. He was on the one hand trapped in reflection, possessed by his thoughts. He could not escape his own imagination. On the other hand, that is why ideas and images flowed with such ease and originality that he had to marvel at it himself. When he spoke so frankly about his own genius, he had in mind the root sense of the term, "genius" as a kind of familiar spirit, a "genie," an amiable but persistent demon that could not be got rid of. There was no getting the genie back into the bottle. One had to summon the passion to take control of it; otherwise one would be destroyed by it. Since Kierkegaard's genius demanded constant exercise, the only way to keep it in hand was to put it to work. That is why Kierkegaard had to write. But in his work he would harness his genius to passion's own task of integrating a life caught in the centrifugal forces that threaten it with dissipation: the very problem out of which his own compulsion to write had arisen. For him and for the "modern" readers to whom his works were addressed, a way had to be found through the impasse into which the fevers of the imagination had led them. Consciousness having once taken flight into possibility, there was no way back into a simpler, less troubled way of dwelling in the world. Reflection must come to terms with its own predicament, fighting fire with fire, inflaming the fevers of the imagination to the point of crisis. Kierkegaard's pseudonymous writings are designed not only to provoke such a crisis but also to help reflection through it, in order that reflection can recover its purposeful function in a man's life.

All of these writings are directly or indirectly devoted to the rendering of Kierkegaard's so-called stages. These stages are not really a progressive series of steps, like degrees in a lodge, through which one might be expected to pass. On the contrary, they are sharply discriminated alternatives. They represent possible ways of life, and each is set forth with enough richness, concreteness, and dialectical precision to give it clarity as a kind of model. To speak of models can be as misleading as to speak of stages, though. Certainly these models are not general types; each is presented in a sharply individuated way. Still less is any model put forth as a kind of pattern that a man might be able simply to apply in his own life. But they are representations of the different ways the pursuit of possibility might function in creating an individuality rather than dissipating it. In fact, each stage or model could also be called a richly rendered life-possibility. The works in which they appear engage the imagination in its own medium, in the medium of possibility. They cannot rid the imagination of the lure of possibility, but in each work possibility is employed to force an issue, to create a crisis, to press for a decision. Imagination continues to function in its own aether, but to the extent a reader's imagination is engaged by these particular models he is helped to develop a certain lucidity in finding his own way through the maze. For the reader as well as for the author whom he never directly meets in these works, possibility is called into service as a guide for a career in existence.

But when we turn from this provisional interpretation of the stages to the pseudonymous works themselves in which the stages are developed, we encounter difficulties. The stages turn out to be elusive, by no means as clearly marked out as we have been led to expect.

The aesthetic, the ethical, the religious. Those are said to be Kierkegaard's stages. But there is not a single work in which this threefold scheme is unambiguously set forth as the definitive rendering of the stages. When in the *Concluding Unscientific Postscript* Johannes Climacus wishes to single out the Christian religiosity for special consideration, he calls it "religion B" to differentiate it, not simply in degree but in kind, from an "immanent" and unparadoxical form of religious life. And while this division into religion A and B

corresponds in certain respects to the distinction made
in *Fear and Trembling* between the "knight of infinite
resignation" and the "knight of faith," the correspond-
ence is by no means complete or exact. For *Fear and
Trembling* treats a different problem than the *Postscript*
does, is written from a different point of view, is attributed to a different pseudonym. For while the Abraham of *Fear and Trembling* is a revealing image of a
life of faith and surely behaves as paradoxically as one
might wish, he is not, after all, being represented as
any sort of proto-Christian. So in these two works we
find two quite different ways of discriminating between
religious ways of life. In the *Postscript,* furthermore, to
the fourfold tabulation of the stages (aesthetic, ethical,
religion A, religion B) there are added the two intermediate stages of irony and humor. In a footnote
Johannes Climacus arranges the stages still a little differently and comes up with a sevenfold scheme.[19] We
could raise the count even higher if we follow Judge
William, the ethical pseudonym, and begin distinguishing stages within the aesthetic alone.[20] So there seems
in principle no end to the exfoliation of Kierkegaardian
stages.

On the other hand, in certain respects one best
grasps the intent behind the notion of the stages in re-
ducing the scheme to the distinction between the aesthetic and the existential, regarding the ethical and religious spheres as existential discriminations.[21] For the

[19] *Concluding Unscientific Postscript,* p. 473n (*SV,* X, p.
204n).

[20] *Either/Or,* II, pp. 185–92 (*SV,* III, pp. 170–76). The
Judge delineates four stages within the aesthetic domain.

[21] That is the way I treated the notion of the stages in the
relevant section of the introduction to my translation of *Crisis
in the Life of an Actress,* pp. 19–28. Since my purpose in that
introduction was to treat Kierkegaard's aesthetics and to show
how his aesthetics were related to aspects of his authorship as
a whole, the present essay may be regarded as a kind of sequel
to it.

distinction between experiencing and deciding, apprehending and acting, is so fundamental to any scheme of the stages that the coherence of the pseudonymous authorship depends on it; and this fundamental distinction, which discriminates the aesthetic from the existential sphere, is obscured by threefold or more elaborated renditions of the stages. Only when a man answers Judge William's call and chooses the either/or, i.e., chooses to *choose*,[22] are the existential choices brought into play at all. Of course, the Judge himself tries to compress the religious into the ethical, which is to make the existential sphere as a whole coterminous with the ethical. That is why this fundamental distinction is brought to such luminous clarity in his essays in *Either/Or*. But in *Stages on Life's Way*, which also contains an essay by the Judge, we find him struggling with the abrasive claim of the religious as it breaks away from the confines of the ethical.

In fact it would seem that in the *Stages*, if anywhere, we do find the familiar threefold scheme. That would certainly be so if we could interpret the first two parts of *Stages* as simply a reprise of the problem of *Either/Or* with some added embellishments, and then could interpret that long, agonizing diary "'Guilty?/Not Guilty?'" as the simple addition of a third possibility, a religious stage, to the scheme of *Either/Or*. Since not much depends on the point here, we are content to leave those who read the *Stages* that way unshaken in their errors. If the matter were put to argument, though, I should wish to argue that the surface similarities of *Either/Or* and *Stages* are altogether deceptive, and that the dialectical tensions of the two works

[22] *Either/Or*, II, pp. 170–82, 215–20 (*SV*, III, pp. 157–67, 196–200). The Judge argues that the aesthetic life is defined negatively by the refusal to choose at all. However much energy is required for experiencing and comprehending, the self remains essentially passive in these aesthetic pursuits. It does not take up the active relation to itself that is the hallmark of the existential movements.

are in fact quite different. In *Stages* the Judge is put
on the defensive from two sides, and the upshot is that
the sort of Hegelian ethical position he defends is reduced to a transitional or intermediate moment at best.
"For," as Frater Taciturnus declares in the concluding
essay of the book, "the poetic is glorious, the religious
is still more glorious, but whatever falls between them
is prattle, however much talent is wasted on it."[23] So
at least from the Frater's point of view, the scheme of
the stages is again dyadic, only now the fundamental
either/or comes out this way: either the aesthetic or
the religious in at least some inchoate form.

Again, if the paradoxical faith in what Johannes
Climacus takes to be its full Christian sense is thrust
into the foreground, we are confronted with another
dyad. That is the scheme we are presented with with
terrible simplicity in *Philosophical Fragments:* the
paradoxical faith vs. the aesthetic-ethical-philosophical
alternative of Socratic recollection. For once the category of faith in the absolute paradox is rigorously enunciated, all the intervening stages lose their sharpness
of definition in this new light. They are reduced to
more or less complex modes of aesthetic recollection,
and we are left with the simple alternatives: Socrates
or Christ—either/or!

Now in ringing the changes on these various ways
of rendering the stages I have not meant to charge
Kierkegaard with carelessness or inconsistency. Neither
do I think that any version can be taken as somehow
definitive, the privileged rendering of the stages for the
pseudonymous authorship as a whole. Each work
stands on its own. The reader is left alone with each
work to draw his own conclusions in relation to its
context and its specific problem. With respect to the
notion of the stages, the context of the work in hand
is everything. That is not to deny that for Kierkegaard

[23] *Stages on Life's Way,* Lowrie tr. (Princeton: Princeton
University Press, 1945), p. 375 (*SV*, VIII, p. 212).

himself the stages add up in a particular way, that the pseudonymous writings as a whole have a kind of superstructure that is perhaps most clearly disclosed in the *Postscript*. Temporality and individuality are heightened with each successive stage. But so far as any particular work is concerned, the superstructure is extraneous. The *Postscript* is itself, after all, simply one of the pseudonymous works, with its own point of view. And as we shall see, it is essential to the very notion of pseudonymous authorship that Kierkegaard should regard himself as occupying no more than the position of one of its readers.

The variations in the rendering of the stages should alert us to the fact that the design of the pseudonymous authorship is indeed a good deal more artful than it appears at first glance. Each work stands as an aesthetic whole in itself. Kierkegaard speaks of all his pseudonymous writings as aesthetic works. Each is a distinct work of art. At the same time, Kierkegaard speaks of these writings as existential communications. They pass between his own lifetime and the lifetime of his reader, and communicate something of existential significance about how a lifetime might be projected. Therein, in fact, lies another paradox: that these communications in which Kierkegaard set out to evoke the existential categories in their opposition to the aesthetic were themselves self-consciously aesthetic works.

The remaining sections of this essay will draw out this paradox and show how Kierkegaard went about resolving it.

4

Kierkegaard's Conception of a Work of Art

An aesthetic work, as Kierkegaard understood it,[24] is the embodiment of an ideal form, its presentation

[24] For a more detailed treatment of Kierkegaard's aesthetics, I again refer the reader to my introduction to *Crisis in the Life*

to consciousness in an appropriate sensuous medium.
The appropriate medium is the one in which that particular ideal form can be brought to full manifestation.

An ideal form or an idea is a pure possibility, but
it is not necessarily an intellectual object, i.e., it is not
necessarily an object of pure thought. For example,
in his celebrated essay on Don Juan, Kierkegaard argues that the Don Juan idea, the "sensuous-erotic,"
cannot be brought to expression in the more reflective
media of literature and drama, and analyzes the alleged
limitations of the versions by Byron and Molière to
support his point.[25] However successful such works
may have been in other respects, not even such masters
of language could render the essential Don Juan idea,
because language is too discursive a medium to embody the sensuous immediacy of this particular idea.
Here, Kierkegaard argues, music is the appropriate
medium. That does not mean merely that the Don Juan
idea has been fully understood all the while, while
artists tried it out in different media to see which might
fit it best. Kierkegaard means that the Don Juan idea
had never been fully grasped until it was rendered by
Mozart. Until then people had only groped for it. Even
after it has been rendered musically we cannot understand it reflectively, in thought or word. The idea and
its medium remain inseparable. Kierkegaard can write
about Don Juan, but he does not confuse this assign-
ment with the actual rendering of Don Juan. In Mozart's opera we apprehend it in the only way we can,

---

of an Actress, particularly pp. 28–36. An important critical
work on the subject is that of Theodor Wiesengrund-Adorno,
Kierkegaard: Konstruktion des Ästhetischen (Tübingen: Verlag
von J. C. B. Mohr [Paul Siebeck], 1933).

[25] *Either/Or,* I, pp. 102–14 (*SV,* II, pp. 98–109). The long
article on Don Juan from which this section is cited was Kierkegaard's most ambitious work on aesthetics proper. He later
returned to the subject in a little essay entitled "A Passing
Comment on a Detail in *Don Juan,*" one of the "other essays
on drama" translated with *Crisis* etc.

musically. That is why this opera is a classic: an idea comes fully to expression in its own medium, and music finds in this idea its own essential subject.

But there are of course other ideal forms that could only be rendered clumsily if at all in music or graphic art, because they require the reflective medium of language for their presentation to consciousness. Here Kierkegaard is in his own element. In conscious contrast to Don Juan, whom he could only talk about, is Johannes the Seducer, Kierkegaard's own poetic creation whom he could actually *present* within the pages of the same volume of *Either/Or*. For unlike the sensuous immediacy of the Don Juan idea, an eroticism that is a sheer force of nature, Johannes is a reflective seducer who strives with a certain fastidious craftiness to manipulate his Cordelia into a state of pure poetic lyricism. "Light have I made her, light as a thought, and now should this, my thought, not belong to me!" he exclaims as his project nears its consummation, worrying that some accident may yet spoil the poem he has made of their love affair.[26] The idea of this sort of seducer can only be rendered in language, since a bizarre sort of poetic reflection is its essential meaning. Kierkegaard's "Diary of the Seducer" is its adequate presentation to consciousness, since it enables us to follow every turn in the mad dialectic of the seducer's devices, and that dialectic is his idea.

It is a matter of great importance to Kierkegaard's aesthetics that neither Don Juan nor Johannes is or can be a living personality. Each is a pure idea that has found its proper aesthetic medium, and its sole reality is in that medium. That is not to say that aesthetic ideas have no relation to real life. The sensuous-erotic does, after all, inhere in everyday life and loin, but always compounded with complicated personal and social factors. What we do not experience every day or any day is pure sensuous eroticism with all extraneous

[26] *Either/Or*, I, p. 433 (*SV*, II, p. 404).

factors pared away—except in Mozart's *Don Juan!* And there we experience it as listeners caught up in it musically, at a great distance from its twitches in our own lives. Similarly with Johannes' idea, which we can experience in its purity only through the words of his diary.

In a successful work of art the idea is presented to consciousness in its timeless ideality, its luminous clarity, and its completeness. That, on Kierkegaard's terms, is why it is so satisfying. For if the human condition in real life is anything like Kierkegaard conceived it, it is the opposite of art. In its normal experience consciousness finds everything to be fleeting, unclear, and incomplete. Nagged by gritty realities, baffled by the heady play of confused and contradictory possibilities, consciousness finds a profound rest in a work of art. Here possibilities achieve luminosity and closure. Here at last is a project brought to satisfying conclusion. One can repose in it, enjoy it, turn it round and round, for it is solid and whole.

This view of art is not as soporific as it may appear. There certainly is on Kierkegaard's terms a proper excitement to be found in art, and also a purified reflection of the reality we inhabit. Art is a source of insight in an otherwise confusing life. It may even horrify us, but there is satisfaction in the lucidity with which it enables us to confront even the tragic or the grotesque. Kierkegaard insists, in fact, that we can be excited or illuminated by a work of art only because we are first able to find repose in it. If an artist is not able to become so thoroughly the servant of his idea that we catch no glimpse of his private human frailty in his presentation, if we are allowed to sense that his achievement depends on a series of accidents that another accident may spoil, then according to Kierkegaard the aesthetic experience is itself made too insecure for us to be either stirred or enlightened by it. He insists for instance that an actress who renders the idea of youthful exuberance on the stage must induce in her audience a sense of absolute trust that her vitality is boundless. That is of course an illusion, the illusion of the stage, that has nothing to do with the private feelings of the actress, who may be quite old and tired. To body forth her idea within the frame of that illusion she must project an exuberance that can never flag.

> Let us take an example from immediate comedy, from whimsey. On a night when you see Rosenkilde come on the stage, as if straight from the infinite and with its swiftness, possessed by all the whimsical muses, when at the first sight of him you find yourself saying, "Well, this evening he's blowing up a regular storm": then you feel *eo ipso* indescribably soothed. You heave a sigh and settle down to relax; you assume a comfortable posture, as if you intended to remain sitting for a long time in the same position; you almost regret not having brought some food along, because the situation induces such trust and assurance, and therefore such tranquility, that you forget that it is only a matter of an hour in the theater. . . . It is usually said that a comedian must be able to make the audience laugh, but it might be better to say that he must first and foremost be able absolutely to soothe, for then the laughter will follow of itself.[27]

The trust and repose induced by a work of art are necessary if it is to communicate any sort of ideal content, because without this tranquility the consciousness of the spectator cannot suspend its own fundamental restlessness. The ideal possibilities manifested in art are illuminating just because they contrast so sharply with our own fragmentary and entangled possibilities.

[27] *Crisis in the Life of an Actress*, pp. 75–76; cf. pp. 89–91 (*SV*, XIV, pp. 112–13, 122–24). Cf. *Repetition*, pp. 54–55, 61–66 (*SV*, V, pp. 141, 145–47).

5

Aesthetic Rest vs. Existential Movement

The ideality bodied forth in a work of art is always an abstraction from experience. It arises out of the temporality of experience, but it achieves a purified form as a self-contained possibility, free of temporality. That is why both the artist and his audience are able to come to rest in it. At least for this ideal moment of experience a man achieves integration, his consciousness drawn together by its concentration on a single purified possibility. Kierkegaard speaks of this moment of repose in ideal possibility as a recollection, in a sense of the term derived from Plato: here temporal reality is recollected, assimilated to atemporal forms that are logically prior to it. The recollected possibilities are logically prior in the sense that they give intelligible meaning to the reality of experience.

This important function of art is also performed by other operations of the mind and the imagination. Therefore Kierkegaard sometimes employs the term "aesthetic" in an extended sense that includes science and philosophy as well as art. For the cognitive grasp of an object, whether a purified object of experience or an ideal, logico-mathematical object, also enables consciousness to suspend its bewildering temporal peregrinations and to come to a satisfying moment of clarity. All knowledge is recollection.

Now when Kierkegaard says that his pseudonymous writings are all aesthetic works, he means that they are all works of art and reflection. They are generally aesthetic in both the primary and the extended sense. Both his poetic gifts and his dialectical powers are exercised in each of these works, though one or the other usually predominates. In any case, consciousness is engaged recollectively by the work, is brought to rest in it, and only if it is engaged in this way can anything else follow.

But then Kierkegaard also uses the term "aesthetic" in another extended sense, to signify a particular way of life or a general outlook that may be realized in a number of specific life-styles. An artist or thinker is not necessarily an "aesthetic man" in this sense; the aesthetic repose afforded by knowledge and art is fortunately available to anyone able to master its disciplines and summon the concentration it requires, whatever his way of life. And on the other hand the aesthetic man is not necessarily an artist or thinker by profession. The aesthetic way of life is a strategy for giving life coherence of a sort. It is a strategy modeled on the work of art, extending that model so far as possible to one's experience as a whole. Here Kierkegaard has in mind the romantic ideal of making life into a work of art. One becomes a collector of interesting experiences, or a contriver of them, actively seeking them out, and one seeks to give them satisfying form in the way they are grasped by consciousness. Since recollection is the aesthetic category, one lives recollectively. Like a novelist who looks for adventures to provide him with material for his novels, the aesthete attempts to get the better of life's turmoils and traumas by transmuting his whole experience into the ideality of recollection. As we are told in one of the diapsalmata:

> To live in recollection is the most complete life conceivable, recollection satisfies more richly than all reality, and has a security that no reality possesses. A recollected life-relation has already passed into eternity and has no more temporal interest.[28]

[28] *Either/Or*, I, pp. 31–32 (*SV*, II, p. 35). This theme is developed poetically in *Repetition*, where its darker side is revealed: a young poet in love already "recollects" his whole future life with his sweetheart, imagining himself as an old man looking back and recalling these first days of his love. His "confidant," Constantine Constantius, remarks that "He was basically finished with the whole relationship. Just as he is

The aesthetic way of life is in fact a self-negating project, a project to end all projects: its aim is to overcome within consciousness the temporality of consciousness itself. For temporality is chaotic or boring or both. The aesthete pursues the "interesting," and to be interesting an experience or a reflection must be lifted out of the relentless movement of lived time. For the interesting attracts the aesthete's attention, allows his consciousness to come to rest in it in a way that integrates consciousness itself. Consciousness so concentrates its otherwise dispersed powers on the interesting object that its own temporality is suspended.

Two kinds of objects are interesting, the momentary and the timeless. What is momentary engages our interest because it affords an intensity of experience that blots the future and the past out of consciousness in the total demand of the moment. The self is momentarily integrated with maximum intensity, concentrated in its experience. One of the most lyrical of the diapsalmata evokes such a moment. Walking down the street on a winter's day we are suddenly brought up short by a strain from Mozart. It turns out that it is being played by a couple of blind street musicians, who are minutely observed in a single glance, raggedly bundled up against the cold.

> A few of us who admired these strains gradually gathered, a postman with his mailbag, a little boy, a servant girl, a couple of roustabouts. Elegant carriages rolled noisily by, workingmen's wagons

---

beginning he has made such a tremendous stride that he has leaped over his whole life. Though the girl should die tomorrow it will produce no essential difference. . . . Recollection has the great advantage that it begins with the loss, and so it is secure, for it has nothing to lose." *Repetition*, p. 12; cf. pp. 90–93 (*SV*, V, pp. 119–20, 160–61). Recollection is developed as a philosophical theme in the *Fragments* and *Postscript*, where it is treated as the Socratic mode to which the Christian "leap" is counterposed.

drowned out these strains, but they still glittered forth in snatches. Unlucky pair of artists, do you know that these tones have all the world's glories hidden away in them?—Was it not like a lovers' meeting![29]

But it is not only in such little momentary ecstasies that time is suspended for consciousness. At the other pole of the aesthetic is reflection, the contemplation of abstract possibility or logical necessity, or the contemplation of reality under the aspect of eternity. "It is not only in isolated moments that I contemplate everything *aeterno modo,* as Spinoza says, but I am constantly *aeterno modo.*"[30] Again, "Tautology is and remains the highest principle, the highest axiom of thought. . . . It is not so poor but that it can fill out a whole lifetime."[31] Again, the point is to suspend the temporality of experience, and so the temporality of the conscious subject of experience. Immediacy and reflection, the momentary and the timeless, are at opposite poles, but both have the effect of lifting consciousness out of time. They are the aesthetic polarities, in which everyone can find occasional repose; but they are also the two modes of the aesthetic way of life, which pursues the interesting. Only what is atemporal is interesting. Love's momentary consummation is interesting, and the idea of the eternal feminine is interesting; but marriage, a constancy in time, is boring. A mystical ecstasy is interesting, and philosophical contemplation is interesting, but a vocation is another of those boring constancies in time that are to be avoided.

Kierkegaard's existential categories, however, the variously projected ethical and religious modes, deal in precisely those temporal constancies that are dismissed by the aesthete as boring. Furthermore, in the pseudonymous works the aesthetic functions primarily as the backdrop against which to manifest the existen-

[29] *Either/Or,* I, pp. 29–30 (*SV,* II, pp. 32–33).
[30] Ibid., pp. 37–38 (*SV,* II, p. 40).
[31] Ibid., p. 37 (*SV,* II, p. 39).

tial categories. It is easy enough to define the resulting
tension in general terms: *Like* the aesthetic repose,
the existential movement aims at an integration of conscious life, deliverance from the "drunken" confusion
of consciousness. But *unlike* the aesthetic, the existential integration occurs through a projection into temporality through action. That is, both the aesthetic strategy
and the existential movement proceed from the impasse created by our peculiarly human temporality.
The aesthetic strategy, however, proceeds by negating
that temporality, the existential movement by intensi-
fying it and through passion giving it a form that is
itself temporalized. Hence the distinctions within the
existential itself: the diverse existential movements are
the different temporal forms into which the self's becoming can be projected. These forms of temporality
therefore imply diverse kinds of individuality. The aesthete achieves a kind of integration of experience, but
not an individuality, because he refuses to commit
himself to a career in time. In the terms in which Judge
William belabors the young aesthete, he does not
choose to choose. He comes to *rest* in apprehending
the immediate or the timeless, but he refuses to make
the *movement* of self-formative act. Aesthetic apprehension wrests ideal possibility out of the actual
through recollection. Existential movement projects a
chosen possibility into the real world through action.

It should now be clear why the pseudonymous authorship was such a paradoxical undertaking: in these
aesthetic works Kierkegaard had to find a way of
pointing to the existential movements. That would not
have been so difficult if he had been content simply to
offer a schematic account of the existential categories
and to differentiate them from the aesthetic, as we have
just done at a very general level. But his plan was much
more ambitious. He wanted to reflect the existential
character of those movements in the very form of presentation. Indirectly, telegraphically, he would communicate the existential movement itself to his reader

by means of a medium alien to it, would communicate it not so much *in* as *through* the aesthetic work. By way of a timeless medium of art and reflection he would evoke the sense of living time. That creates the basic dialectical tension in each of these writings.

6

The Pseudonymous Theater

Kierkegaard steadily insists that his pseudonymous works teach no doctrines, impart no objective knowledge. It does not follow that they have no content. One finds philosophical arguments, the posing of dialectical puzzles, stories, lyrical flights, psychological investigations, spiritual inquisitions, and a constant counterpoint of wit. There seem to be a good many assertions and exhortations besides.

But each of these works is deliberately ambiguous, ironical. What it says is never simply what it means. In fact, what it says is above all negated by the fact that nobody says it.

For each work is a quasi-theatrical production. It takes place on a stage, an old-fashioned proscenium, as it were, a self-enclosed frame of aesthetic illusion from which no actor comes skipping out in the modern manner to nuzzle and harangue the audience or to assure it that there is after all a man under the greasepaint. The frame is the device of pseudonymity. Each writing is attributed to a Johannes de Silentio, a Constantine Constantius, a Vigilius Haufniensis. In some cases there is a pseudonymous editor as well, a Victor Eremita, a Hilarius Bookbinder, assembling the works of other pseudonyms. Each of them is a fantastic creature, a creature of fantasy, an evident fiction. This is not a "realistic" theater; its pseudonymous authors and actors are not copies of real men. To be sure, an illusion of individuality is to some extent sustained by the fact that each speaks with a distinctive voice.

He not only represents a definite point of view but
reflects his point of view in the style and tone of his
language. That is the supreme achievement of Kierkegaard's poetic gift. Constantine Constantius chooses
his words between thoughtful sips of good wine, his
young poet declaims in fits of lyric desperation; Judge
William's tone is earnest, firm, good-natured but hu-
morless, yet beneath the prosaic surface one senses a
quiet and constant ardor; Vigilius Haufniensis writes
the sort of prose one would expect to meet in an aca-
demic journal; Johannes de Silentio intones as if from
the bottom of a deep well. Anyone who has lived with
these authors for a while would recognize the voice of
any of them after three sentences, in exactly the way
that he would recognize Falstaff or Goethe's Mephi-
stopheles. But he would not mistake them for the voices
of real human beings. They are altogether theatrical
creations. They are sheer personae, masks without actors underneath, voices. William Afham, who has recollected for us the symposium on love in Part I of the
Stages, speaks for himself only at the end and only
to request that nobody make any inquiries about him.
But just in case anyone should ask, he explains in a
little spoof of Hegel that

> I am pure being, and therefore almost less than
> nothing. I am the pure being that is along every-
> where but am still not noticeable because I am con-
> stantly *aufgehoben.* I am like the line that has the
> mathematical problem above it and the answer be-
> low; who bothers about the line? Of myself I am not
> capable of anything at all. . . .[32]

That is essentially true of all the pseudonyms, though
most of them are not so self-effacing about it.

For unlike William Afham, most of the pseudonyms
are situated in definite points of view. They represent

[32] *Stages on Life's Way,* p. 93 (*SV,* VII, pp. 79–80).

animated life-possibilities. But in every case the point of view from which the work is written is itself transcended within the work, *"aufgehoben"* or at least rendered problematical, its limitations revealed. And yet that *aufgehoben* point of view, the possibility represented by the pseudonymous author, is the standpoint from which the whole problem of the work is treated. Every pseudonym occupies a specific position which like a mirror reflects its problem according to its angle of vision. Hence the quite different ways of conceiving the stages themselves, as we have observed. Every scheme or problem treated earlier is transformed when Kierkegaard projects his imagination into the frame of another pseudonym. And any existential movement treated in a particular work is presented as it is viewed from the pseudonymous author's angle of vision, generally glimpsed as it moves out of his field of vision altogether.

Repetition is a clear example. The book is written from the point of view of the aesthete and "psychologist" Constantine Constantius. After recounting his own humorously futile efforts to achieve repetition, however, he concludes that it is "too transcendent for me." Repetition "is and remains a transcendence," and "A religious movement I cannot make, it is against my nature."[33] But Constantine's young friend, the poet, does in some sense make this movement, so Constantine thinks at any rate, though it is always given an essentially poetic expression in the book. There are occasional hints about the meaning of repetition, but we are never permitted to see the movement itself except in the distorting mirror of the aesthetic. Constantine speaks of the affair as a "wrestling match" or a "breaking" (*brydning*): "the universal breaks with the exception, breaks with it in strife, and

---

[33] *Repetition*, pp. 95–105 (*SV*, V, pp. 161–62). Cf. *In the Twilight of Christendom*, Chapter 3, where I have attempted to interpret the category of repetition in its contrast to recollection.

strengthens it by this breaking."[34] This break is what
we are permitted to see in the book, but as it occurs
the young man breaks out of the aesthetic frame of the
book as well, and is lost from view. Constantine, who
has supplied that frame, has functioned in a "purely
aesthetic and psychological" way; and yet he has been
a "serving spirit" in the enterprise.

> Every move I have made is purely to shed light
> on him; I have constantly had him *in mente,* every
> word of mine is either ventriloquism or is said in
> relation to him. Even where joking and playfulness
> seem to tumble heedlessly, they take heed of him;
> even where everything ends in melancholy, it is a
> signal concerning him. . . . So I have done for him
> what I could, just as I now strive to serve you, dear
> reader, by again being something else.[35]

The pseudonym and his book constitute a mirror reflecting from its angle and within its frame the existential movement as it breaks away. This mirror is
also held up to the reader, who through the aesthetic
medium is essentially left alone with the existential
movement itself and whatever claim it may make on
him. The aesthetic medium is purely dialectical: it is
simultaneously presented and obliterated. Like William Afham's line between the problem and its sum,
the pseudonymous work is nothing at all in itself, yet
it serves to put the reader into touch with a possibility
that cannot be directly presented, because it can only
come forth in its truth in an actual lifetime.

A similar self-negation occurs in all the pseudonymous works, pointing to the existential movement but
letting it break out of its aesthetic frame. In *Fear and
Trembling,* subtitled "A Dialectical Lyric," the dialectical and the poetic are indeed fused to the highest de-

[34] Ibid., p. 152 (*SV,* V, pp. 190–91).
[35] Ibid., pp. 154–55 (*SV,* V, p. 192).

gree Kierkegaard ever achieved; in that respect it is the work that most perfectly expresses his special genius. Yet, as in *Repetition* and most of the other pseudonymous works, his name does not even appear on the title page. It is another purely aesthetic work, but again the possibility it holds out is never directly manifest in the way Kierkegaard thought an ideal possibility is normally manifest in a work of art. For again it is a possibility that can only be realized in a human lifetime, and not in a work of art. The possibility is faith. But while Abraham is the father of faith, he cannot be presented as an archetype or a paradigm of faith, one cannot become a knight of faith by doing what Abraham did. For faith is again a singularity that breaks with the universal. Johannes de Silentio, on the other hand, does represent a prototypical religiosity. He represents resignation as a universal or paradigmatic possibility. The book is written from his point of view, and within that point of view he celebrates Abraham, marvels at Abraham, whom he repeatedly confesses he cannot understand at all.

In the more strictly philosophical or psychological works this dialectic is still operative, except that a paradoxical category rather than a poetically projected character is made to break away from the standpoint of the work. In *The Concept of Dread* the dogmatic category of sin is obliquely disclosed by dread, a psychological category, but it is disclosed only as it breaks out of dread. In *Philosophical Fragments* the terms signifying the Socratic mode continue to be employed in the paradoxical "thought experiment" until they turn into their opposites. For example, the idea of the Socratic teacher is straightforward, but in the experiment we project a teacher who himself is the teaching; error becomes a willful error; knowledge becomes, not the recollection of truth immanent in the learner, but a leap tantamount to being born a second time; eternal divinity becomes the God in time; and so on. The Socratic meaning of every term is strained until

220   Stephen Crites

it breaks. Though the pseudonym, Johannes Climacus, conducts the whole experiment from a Socratic
point of view, un-Socratic expressions keep breaking
out of the Socratic terms he employs: the savior, sin,
faith, etc. The same is true in the *Postscript,* but in
this case Johannes goes much further into the dialectics of the break and into the explication of the Christian categories, though still from a Socratic angle of
vision. As for what Johannes himself may think of the
results of his experiment, he has told us plainly in the
preface to the *Fragments* that it is none of our business
and makes no difference in our consideration of the
problems raised. Certainly he has presented no defense
of Christianity, and Kierkegaard liked to point out that
the view of the Christian possibility presented in the
Fragments and *Postscript* would provide at least as
serviceable a basis for attacking it as defending it—an
option that his modern readers have been quick to
exercise. In any case, this Socratic analysis cannot be
confused with an act of faith, as Johannes is at pains
to point out; and nothing but the act of faith would
be a Christian expression of Christianity. The *Fragments* and *Postscript* are simply the performances of
Johannes Climacus in our little theater. When the curtain rings down Johannes disappears with his heavy
philosophical books into the aesthetic aether, just as
Constantine Constantius did with his slender bit of
poetry. In an appendix to the *Postscript,* Johannes
even declares that everything in the book "is to be
understood in such a way that it is revoked; that the
book has not only a conclusion but a revocation."[36]
Of this revocation we shall have more to say presently.
It is already extraordinary enough that Kierkegaard
should have carried his ironical devices so far as to
revoke his chief philosophical work. He could regard
even this book as a veil of illusion through which
something was being communicated that the book had
to leave unsaid.

[36] *Concluding Unscientific Postscript,* p. 547 (*SV,* X, p. 280).

If we continued calling the role of the pseudonyms we would discover that the dialectic of revocation and breaking away takes diverse forms. But always the work is suffused with double meaning. Sometimes this double meaning is achieved by presenting two or more pseudonyms (*Either/Or, Stages*), each sustaining a point of view that is consistent and complete in itself, but letting them collide in irreconcilable conflict. Each can resolve the issue, but purely on his own terms, which are cast in doubt from the point of view of the other pseudonyms.[37] For with respect to existential conflicts Kierkegaard denies that there is a general, un-situated, "objective" standpoint from which the issue could be resolved. That is the point of his attack on Hegelian "mediation" as he understood it. So there are no really coercive conclusions in any of the pseudonymous works. Every apparent conclusion is merely that implied by the standpoint of the pseudonym, and even it is called into question within the work as a whole. Kierkegaard does not deny that reasonably secure conclusions can be reached regarding matters of fact, or regarding abstract logical or mathematical possibilities. But here the question concerns possible ways of life, the way a man should project his own future, and that is not an issue that can be settled within an aesthetic frame. Like a literary treatment of a musical

---

[37] If one supposes that Judge William necessarily wins the palm in *Either/Or*, it should be noted how often the Judge expresses his exasperation at the ability of the quick-witted young aesthete to turn every question around. Also perhaps relevant to the Judge's efforts is a little passage in "The Rotation Method," where the aesthete describes his strategy for enduring the tiresome philosophical lectures of a certain gentleman: since in the heat of these earnest lectures the gentleman always perspired copiously, the aesthete learned to divert himself by observing the beads of sweat coursing from the gentleman's brow to the tip of his nose. *Either/Or*, I, p. 295 (*SV*, II, p. 276). If the aesthetic and the ethical did not reach a standoff in the book, the reader would not be confronted with a genuine either/or, and that is the whole point!

idea, the medium would break down in the attempt. What takes place on the stage of our little theater is always "interesting," but to the extent that we do in fact become interested in it we discover that the essential action is being conducted offstage.

7

The Author's Act and the Reader's Burden

There is one document in which a pseudonym who may be presumed to represent a religious movement is allowed to speak entirely for himself. That is the long diary entitled "'Guilty?/Not Guilty?'" that appears in the third part of *Stages on Life's Way*. As in other cases, the existential movement represented in the diary is also reflected off the points of view of other pseudonyms, including that of the "psychologist," Frater Taciturnus, whose commentary on the diary concludes the book. It is Frater T., in fact, who interprets the diary as clearly representing some sort of inchoate religious movement. But in this case the subject of the movement is not merely glimpsed as he disappears beyond the horizon of his commentator, as in *Repetition* and *Fear and Trembling*. He also speaks for himself, indeed speaks at length and in the sort of total intimacy that the diary format allows. In this one case we seem to be permitted an interior view of an existential movement, and from this vantage point the meaning of the movement is by no means as clear as the commentary makes it seem. As the title suggests, the young diarist is in a state of fundamental conflict about the meaning of what he has done, which his many anguished pages of reflection serve to clarify but which no amount of reflection can seem to resolve. Outwardly, his abandonment of his lady love would in many respects have resembled the conduct of that other diarist, Johannes the Seducer, whose diary this one is clearly intended to parallel. Inwardly the situation is totally different.

The diarist behaved as he did out of an obscure sense of a kind of religious vocation that seemed to preclude marriage. But we leave him in a state of total uncertainty whether he has indeed received such a calling or whether he has been undone by some dark morbidity. He even keeps alive a strange hope that he may yet in some unimagined manner receive his beloved back again. It is possible that he is indeed embarked on a religious movement, as Frater T. insists, but if so it is clear that he offers the reader no simple paradigm of such a movement. Again, though in a new way, Kierkegaard has invested the existential movement with double meaning.

The closest the young diarist comes to a conclusion is expressed in this comment:

> I have never been able to understand it in any other way than this, that every man is essentially assigned to himself, and that apart from this there is either an authority such as that of an apostle—the dialectical determination of which I cannot comprehend, and meanwhile out of respect for what has been handed down to me as holy I refrain from concluding anything from my non-understanding—or there is chatter.[38]

That, in the end, represents the standpoint of Kierkegaard's authorship as a whole. Some of the later works, written in his own name, do attempt to bring out what it would mean for an individual to live under apostolic authority. But the pseudonymous writings are designed to throw every reader back on his own resources. There is not even an actual author to lay any claim on him. They assign him to himself.

The pseudonymous works present their life-possibilities in this elusive form in order to evoke in the reader a movement that is entirely his own. They

[38] *Stages on Life's Way*, p. 314 (*SV*, VIII, p. 148).

are not cookbooks that he could follow in concocting a
novel but pretested pattern for his life, like an exotic
soufflé. But each work is in its own way designed to
create a quiet crisis in the life of a reader that can
be resolved only by his own decision. To a reader
bewildered by the riot of possibility they also offer an
oblique aid in recognizing and nurturing a possibility
that he might be able to make his own.

While these works may encourage a man in whom
a decision may be stirring, it is obvious that no book
can force a man to decide. Kierkegaard was not one
to underestimate the potential complacency of a reader.
The resources of human torpor seemed to him to be
perfectly awesome. That is why he regularly distinguished between the "real reader" of his books and
others who might chance to turn their pages. The page
turners might scrutinize them either superficially or
carefully. That was not the point of the distinction.
The reason he regarded the professors as his particular
nemesis was that they would perhaps be careful page
turners, looking for ideas to merchandise in their own
books and lectures, without ever being "real readers"
at all. Kierkegaard found artful ways of distinguishing
between the readers and the page turners. He quotes
a motto from Lichtenberg as the superscription to the
first part of *Stages on Life's Way:* "Such works are
mirrors: when an ape peers in no apostle can look
out." He frequently appends little letters to his
"reader," as in *Repetition* where his pseudonym tells
this reader that the book has been written after the
manner of Clemens Alexandrinus, who wrote "in such
a way that the heretics could not understand it."[39]
That particular letter is preceded by a kind of envelope,
taking up a whole page, addressed "To the Honorable
Mr. N.N., this book's real reader."[40] When other
works were addressed to "that individual" the intent
was the same, for only the reader who permitted him-

[39] *Repetition,* p. 149 (*SV,* V, p. 189).
[40] Ibid., p. 147 (*SV,* V, p. 187).

self to be singled out by the book for a movement into individuality was its "real reader." For the books are so designed that their real resolution can only be carried out by the reader.

This way of presenting the existential categories, essentially shifting the burden of each book onto the reader, was not a mere literary conceit on Kierkegaard's part. That was the way it had to be done, given his view of the existential categories. They refer to movements in existence. The attempt to describe them directly would falsify what is essential. For again, as in Kierkegaard's view of art, an idea can be brought forth only in its own medium. Only in this case the medium is the temporality of human existence itself: a lifetime. As the Don Juan idea can only be rendered in music, and not in poetry, an existential movement can only be realized in the life of an individual. One can talk *about* it, of course, and Kierkegaard devoted great ingenuity to finding ways to do so. But what is talked *about* never comes forth in its truth in the literary treatment. "Truth is subjectivity": the point of that much-misunderstood slogan is simply that an existential truth has a conscious human temporality for its medium, and not propositions, images, or any other aesthetic form. It is not an object of reflection, in which consciousness comes to rest, but the movement of a conscious life projected toward the future. Only in that medium can it come to clarity. To use one of Kierkegaard's favorite expressions, the idea becomes clear only when the individual becomes "transparent" to it.

We recall that Johannes Climacus concluded his big philosophical work, the very one in which he had enunciated the idea that "truth is subjectivity," by revoking the whole book. For to explain philosophically what was meant by this slogan was not the same as realizing a subjective truth! The revocation appears in an appendix significantly entitled "For an Understanding with the Reader." Johannes goes on to imag-

ine the sort of reader who would fulfill his heart's
desire, and even offers a eulogy for such an imaginary
reader. He would read every line with care and would
be able to "hold out just as long as the author." But
then this reader

> can understand that understanding is revocation, un-
> derstanding for him as a solitary reader is indeed
> precisely the book's revocation, he can understand
> that writing a book and revoking it is something dif-
> ferent than not writing it at all.[41]

The reader who has absorbed the contents of the
book will understand that the time has come for his
move. That will be the real conclusion of the book, the
only subjective truth it can have, and will be at the
same time the revocation of the book as an aesthetic
representation of existential movements. In other
words, the contradiction between the aesthetic medium
and the existential import of the book will be resolved
when the reader is moved to act: then the book's idea
will have found its own medium.

The *Postscript* has another appendix, this one written in Kierkegaard's own name. He assumes legal
responsibility for the whole pseudonymous authorship.
But he makes it clear that he regards his position as
author of these works as a kind of legal fiction, and
insists that his only essential position is as one of the
readers to whom they are addressed.

> So in the pseudonymous books there is not a single
> word of my own; I have no opinion of them except
> as a third person, no knowledge of their meaning
> except as a reader, not the remotest private relation
> to them, since it would be impossible to have that
> toward a doubly-reflected communication. A single
> word from me personally in my own name would

[41] *Concluding Unscientific Postscript*, p. 548 (*SV*, X, p.
281).

be a presumptuous self-forgetfulness, which by that one word would make me guilty, dialectically viewed, of essentially annihilating the pseudonyms.[42]

The detachment of these "communications" from any communicator had sometimes been reinforced within the works themselves by having a pseudonymous editor offer outlandish accounts of how he came upon these writings: he fished the box in which they were contained out of a lake, he found them accidentally in a secret drawer of an ancient desk, etc. Furthermore, Kierkegaard seems personally to have indulged in a good deal of ingenious if slightly ludicrous play acting in his public demeanor in order to disown them. For that seemed to him to be a way of supporting their essential function. He thrust the pseudonymous writings away from himself so that they could float as pure aesthetic objects, entirely at the reader's disposal.

That was what it meant for Kierkegaard to communicate "indirectly." He considered that these devices served, just by means of the great aesthetic distance they produced, to make this authorship a form of action on his part, in which his own lifetime telegraphically addressed the lifetime of the reader. The effect of this action depended entirely on the reader. But precisely by placing the burden on the reader in this way, Kierkegaard would fulfill his peculiar vocation as a writer: to communicate the sort of possibility that could only be forged out of a lifetime. Just this act of communication, however, precluded any personal connection between author and reader beyond the most polite tip of the author's tall hat by way of encouragement. The intentions of the author, and what-

---

[42] "A First and Last Declaration," appended to the *Postscript*, p. 551 (*SV*, X, p. 286). The declaration as a whole is an excellent statement of Kierkegaard's design in the pseudonymous works, and has served as a guide to the interpretation offered in this essay.

ever use he himself might be able to make of these
little theatrical productions in finding his way to some
kind of individuality, were irrelevant to this act of
communication.

> What is indirect is to place dialectical contrasts
> together—and then not one word concerning [the
> author's] personal understanding.
> What is more indulgent in the more direct com-
> munication is that there is in the communication a
> craving to be personally understood, a fear of being
> misunderstood. The indirect is sheer tension.[43]

The final irony of the pseudonymous writings is that
Kierkegaard finally found himself unable to sustain
this tension. In the end he did worry about being mis-
understood, worried about it a great deal, and finally
could not stand it. In his last years he kept interpreting
the pseudonymous works, lest the reader miss the
Christian point of the whole. *The Point of View for
My Work as an Author,* subtitled "A Direct Communication" and "A Report to History," was only his most
elaborate attempt to explain himself. And then he
died leaving his journals and papers behind, deliberately addressed to posterity. Otherwise we surely would
not understand Kierkegaard and his intentions as well
as we do. But with these disclosures the whole delicate screen of indirect communication was torn aside.
The author appears during each performance offered
in his little theater, and his admirers hoist him on the
stage to give a running explanation of the piece being
performed. Despite his horror at the thought that his
work would spawn a flourishing field of Kierkegaard

[43] *Søren Kierkegaard's Journals and Papers,* Hong tr.
(Bloomington and London: Indiana University Press, Vol. I,
1967), p. 318 (*Papirer,* X³ A 624).

scholarship, despite his clear sense that that would be the final misunderstanding, he brought it on himself, and made it almost impossible to read his works as he had intended.

But who knows? Perhaps when the possibilities of Kierkegaard scholarship have been exhausted, when the last detail of the affair between Søren and Regine has been ferreted out, when the Kierkegaard encyclopedias and concordances have been safely embalmed in the upper stacks and the dust has settled so thick on the multi-volume editions of the *Journals* that only archaeologists have access to them, when the American-Scandinavian Foundation is a thing of distant memory —perhaps then a young student, if there still are students, will chance to come upon *Either/Or* with his earphones off, or an older man still vigorous on early retirement and with time on his hands will chance to flip the wrong switch of his microfiche machine and find himself reading how Johannes Climacus, smoking his cigar in the Frederiksberg Garden and wondering what to do with his life, decided to become an author who would make things difficult for people. And who knows? perhaps Kierkegaard will yet find his reader.

THE SINGULAR UNIVERSAL

Jean-Paul Sartre

The title of our colloquium is "Kierkegaard Living."
It has the merit of plunging us into the heart of the
paradox, and Søren himself would smile. For if we
had come together to speak of Heidegger, for example,
no one would have dreamed of dubbing our meeting
"Heidegger Living." Kierkegaard living means, then,
"Kierkegaard dead." And not just that. It means that
he exists for us, that he is the object of our discourse,
that he has been an instrument of our thought. But,
from this point of view, one could use the same expression to designate anyone who, having died, later entered the culture. To say, for example, "Arcimboldo
Living,"[1] since surrealism allows us to reappropriate
this painter and illumine him anew, is to make of him
an *object* in what Kierkegaard called the *world-
historical*. But, precisely, if Søren seems to us like a
radioactive isotope, whatever its potency and its viru-
lence, he is no longer this living being whose subjectivity appears necessarily, insofar as it is lived, as other
than what we know of it. In short, he founders in
death. This historical scandal that the abolition of the
subjective provokes in a subject of history—and the

This paper was delivered by the author on the occasion of
an international colloquium entitled "Kierkegaard Living," held
in Paris by UNESCO April 21–23, 1964, to celebrate the 150th
anniversary of Kierkegaard's birth. It has been translated from
the French by Peter Goldberger whose notes accompany the
text. It is reprinted with the kind permission of the copyright
holder, UNESCO.

[1] Giuseppe Arcimboldo (c. 1530–93) painted faces and figures ingeniously fashioned of fruits, vegetables, plants, and
animals (tr. note).

becoming-an-object of that which was an agent—explodes with regard to all who have disappeared. History is punctured. But nowhere is it more obvious than in the case of the "knight of subjectivity." Kierkegaard is the man who posed for himself the question of the historical absolute, who underlined the scandalous paradox of the apparition and abolition of this absolute in historical time.

If we cannot revive the martyr of inwardness except in the form of an object of knowledge, a determination of his praxis will escape us forever: the living effort to escape knowledge by the reflective life, his pretension of being, in his singularity, at the heart of his finitude, the absolute-subject, defined in inwardness by his absolute relation with being. In other words, if death is historically the simple passage of the interior to exteriority, then the title "Kierkegaard Living" is no longer justified. And if something remains for us of this life which, in its time, in its place, has been ended, then Kierkegaard is himself the scandal and the paradox. Unable to be understood except as this immanence which for forty years never stopped designating *itself* as such, either he vanishes forever, and the world was rid, in 1856, of *nothing;* or else the paradox revealed by this dead man is that a historical being, beyond his abolition, can still communicate as a non-object, as an absolute subject, with the generations that follow his own. That which will hold our attention, then, is not the religious problem of Christ become man or the metaphysical problem of death, but the strictly historical paradox of survival. We shall examine our knowledge of Kierkegaard in order to find out what it is of a dead man that escapes into knowledge and survives *for us* after his time; we shall ask ourselves if this presence, inaccessible to knowledge properly so called, the subjectivity of another being, nevertheless is given to us by some other means. Either history comes to a close in the knowledge of death, or the historical survival of the subjective should change our conception of history. In other words, Kierkegaard, today, this twenty-fourth of April, 1964, is dissolved by the enzymes of knowledge or persists to manifest for us the still virulent scandal of what one might call the transhistoricity of the historical man.

He put the fundamental question in these terms: "Is a historical point of departure possible for an eternal consciousness; how can such a point of departure have any other than mere historical interest; is it possible to base an eternal happiness upon historical knowledge?"[2]

And, of course, what he takes aim at here is the scandalous paradox of the birth and death of God, of the historicity of Jesus. But we must go further, for, if the answer is yes, the transhistoricity pertains, just as well as to Jesus, to Søren, his witness, and to us, the grandnephews of Søren. And as he says himself, we are all contemporaries.[3] In one sense to say that is to leap over history. Nevertheless, history exists, and it is man who makes it. Thus posteriority and contemporaneity imply and contradict one another. For the present, we can go no further. We must then return to Kierkegaard and examine him as a privileged witness. Why privileged? I think of the Cartesian proof of the existence of God from the fact that *I exist with the idea of God*. Kierkegaard is a singular witness, or as he says, "the Exception,"[4] by virtue of the *redoubling* in himself of the subjective attitude. He is for us an object of knowledge as the subjective witness to his own subjectivity, that is, as the existent announcer of existence by his own existential attitude. Thus he

[2] This question appeared as the epigraph to SK's *Philosophical Fragments* (tr. note).

[3] SK often discussed the contemporaneity of all believers in Christ. See especially *Philosophical Fragments*, Chapter 4, *Training in Christianity*, passim, and *Attack Upon "Christendom,"* p. 242 (tr. note).

[4] SK refers to the "extraordinary" or to the "exceptional" in the *Papirer* at VII[1] A 173–74, VIII[1] A 202, *inter alia* (tr. note).

becomes both the object and the subject of our study. We should take this subject-object insofar as he manifests a historical paradox which goes beyond himself. We shall question his testimony insofar as in its historicity—he said such-and-such a thing at such-and-such a time—it goes beyond itself and causes the object-subject paradox to burst into history. In integrating *his* words into our language by translating him with *our* words, will knowledge find its limits and, by a paradoxical reversal of meaning, indicate the signifier[5] as its silent foundation?

In principle, everything can be *known* about him. No doubt he keeps his secrets well hidden. But one can come just to the point of uncovering them, force statements from him, and interpret them. The problem becomes: when all is *known* about the life of a man who refuses to be an object of knowledge and whose originality rests precisely in that refusal, is there an irreducible remainder? How can one capture it and think it? The question has both a prospective and a retrospective side. One can ask: what is it to live when the essence of these determinations has been foreseen? For the singularity of the Kierkegaardian adventure is that just as it is taking place, it unmasks itself to itself as known in advance. Thus the adventure lives in knowledge and against it. We must take into account that this opposition of foresight and lived experience was embodied around 1890[6] in the

[5] The signifier (*le signifiant*) and the signified (*le signifié*) are technical linguistic terms developed by the pioneering Swiss linguist Ferdinand de Saussure (1857–1913) to indicate the two parts of a "linguistic sign." The signified, in the words of the contemporary American linguist Mario Pei, is "the concept or object which is phonetically symbolized by the spoken word." Pei defines the signifier as "the sound-image or linguistic symbol which stands for an object or concept in the common mind of the speaking community" (tr. note).

[6] The date 1890 appears in the French text, but it is most likely a misprint for 1840, when SK was reacting against the "dead determinacies" of Hegel's system (tr. note).

opposition of Hegel and Kierkegaard. Hegel has disappeared; his system remains. Søren, whatever he may do, moves within the limits of the unhappy consciousness;[7] that is, he can realize only the complex dialectic of the finite and the infinite. He will not be the one to overcome it. Kierkegaard knows that he is already located within the system, knows Hegelian thought, and is not ignorant of the interpretation given *in advance* to the movements of his life. Trapped, held in the beam of the Hegelian projector, he must vanish into objective knowledge or else show his irreducibility. But, precisely, Hegel is dead, and this death denounces knowledge as dead knowledge or knowledge of death. And Kierkegaard testifies by his simple life that all knowledge of the subjective is in a certain sense a false knowledge. Foreseen by the system, he discredits it entirely by not appearing *in it* as a moment to be overcome, in the place where the master put him, but simply, on the contrary, as a survivor of the system and of the prophet, who, despite the dead determinations of the prophecy, ought to live this foreseen life as if it were at the beginning indeterminate and as if the determinations only produced themselves in free non-knowledge (*non-savoir*).

The new aspect of this complex of problems (*problématique*) that Kierkegaard reveals to us is that he does not contradict in his personal life the content of knowledge, but that he discredits the knowledge of the content. And in denying the concept by the same means whereby he *realizes* the prescriptions of it in another dimension, he is entirely penetrated by the light beams of knowledge—for the others, and for himself who knows Hegelianism—yet, at the same time,

[7] Hegel explained the "unhappy consciousness" as "the Alienated Soul which is the consciousness of self as a divided nature, a doubled and merely contradictory being." See G. W. F. Hegel, *The Phenomenology of Mind*, trans. J. B. Baillie (New York: Harper & Row, Torchbooks, 1967), p. 251 (tr. note).

he remains entirely opaque. In other words, this pre-existent knowledge reveals a being at the heart of future existence. Thus, thirty years ago, the contradictions of colonialism constituted to the generation of colonials being born an existence of misfortune, of anger and blood, of revolt and struggle; some of the best-informed of the oppressed and of the colonists knew it. And, to take an entirely other example, a position created high or low on the social ladder creates a destiny, that is, a future but foreseeable being for him who will fill it, even though this destiny, if there is more than one applicant, remains for each a *possibility of being*. And, in the strict particularity of private life, the structures of a defined family (as a certain case of an institution produced by the movement of history) permit the analyst, in theory at least, to foresee this being: a destiny (to live and to undergo) that will be a certain neurosis in the child who is born in this milieu. Kierkegaard *foreseen* by Hegel is but a privileged example of these ontological determinations which exist before birth and are left to be *conceptualized*.

Søren identifies himself with the problem because he is conscious of it. He knows that Hegel, in designating it as an isolated moment in universal history, grasps it as already overcome, that is, as a "schematism" to be filled with his life, the Error (*non-vérité*) that he is from the outset as a truncated determination. But, precisely, the Hegelian designation comes to touch him like the light from a dead star. And the Error has to *be lived through,* so it pertains also to subjective subjectivity. Also he can write in the *Fragments:* "My own Error is something I can discover only by myself, since it is only when I have discovered it that it is discovered, even if the whole world knew of it before."[8] But discovered, my Error becomes, at least in the immediate sense, my Truth. Thus subjective truth exists.

[8] SK, *Philosophical Fragments,* trans. David Swenson (Princeton: Princeton University Press, 1962), p. 17 (tr. note).

It is not *knowledge,* but self-determination. It will be
defined neither as an extrinsic relation of understanding to being, nor as the internal mark of a calculus of
adequacy (*adéquation*), nor as the indissoluble unity
of a system. "Truth," he says, "is the act of freedom."[9]
I would not know how *to be* my own truth even if the
premises were given me in advance. To unveil it is to
produce it, or to produce myself as I am, to be for myself what I have to be.

What Kierkegaard illuminates is that the opposition
of non-knowledge (*non-savoir*) and knowledge is that
of two ontological structures. The subjective has to
be what it is; it is a singular realization of each singularity. One would have to ask Freud for the best commentary on this remark. Indeed, psychoanalysis is not
knowledge nor does it pretend to be, except when it
risks hypotheses about the dead, and when death thus
leads it to become a science of death. It is a movement, an interior labor which all at once uncovers it
and progressively renders the subject capable of with-
standing it. So that at the limit—otherwise ideal—of this
becoming, there is adequation (*adéquation*) between
what the being has become and the truth it was. Truth
is the unity of the conquest and the conquered object.
It changes without learning anything and appears only
at the end of a transformation. It is a non-knowledge
(*non-savoir*) but an effectivity (*effectivité*), a putting
into perspective that is present to itself insofar as it
realizes itself. Kierkegaard added that it is a decision
of authenticity; it is the refusal of flight and the will
to return to oneself. In this sense *knowledge* cannot
take into account this obscure and inflexible *movement* by which scattered determinations are elevated
to Being and reunited in a tension that confers on them
not significance but a synthetic meaning. The ontological structure of subjectivity escapes to the extent that

[9] I have been unable to locate the source of this quotation
(tr. note).

subjective being is, as Heidegger said so well, in question in its being, insofar as it *is* never but in the mode
of having to be its being.

From this point of view, the moment of subjective
truth is a temporalized but transhistorical absolute.
Subjectivity is temporalization itself; it is *what happens to me,* that which cannot be except in happening.
It is myself to the degree that I can be born only to
adventure—and that, as Merleau-Ponty said some-
where, short as my life may be, I will *at least* die. But
it is also myself to the extent that I attempt to retake
control of my own adventure in assuming (we shall
return to this) its original contingency in order to establish it in necessity, in short where *I* arrive myself.
Treated in advance by Hegel, subjectivity becomes a
moment of objective mind, a determination of the culture. But if nothing of lived experience (*le vécu*) can
escape knowledge, its *reality* remains irreducible. In
this sense, lived experience, as concrete reality, is
posed as *non-knowledge* (*non-savoir*). But this negation of knowledge implies the affirmation of oneself.
Lived experience recognizes itself as a projection in
the realm of significance, but at the same time it does
not recognize itself there, since, in this realm, a set
forms which aims ineffectually at the objects, and because, precisely, it is not an object. It is doubtless one
of the constant preoccupations of the nineteenth century to distinguish being from the knowledge one has
of it, in other words to reject idealism. That for which
Marx reproaches Hegel is not so much his point of
departure as the reduction of being to knowledge. But
for Kierkegaard—and for us today considering the
Kierkegaardian scandal—it is a question of a certain
ontological area where being claims at once to escape
knowledge and to be reached itself. Waelhens says
quite well: "No longer an *explanation at a distance,*
philosophy (for Kierkegaard, Nietzsche, and Bergson)
claims to be henceforth *one* with experience; not content to throw light on man and his life, it aspires to

become this life, arrived at perfect self-consciousness. It seemed that this ambition entailed for the philosopher the obligation of renouncing the ideal of philosophy as a rigorous science, for in its roots this latter ideal is inseparable from the idea of an uncommitted spectator."[10]

In short, the determinations of lived experience are not simply heterogeneous with knowledge, as the existence of the talers was for Kant with the concept of taler and the judgment that puts the two together.[11] It is the very way that they touch each other in the redoubling of the presence to itself which reduces knowledge to the pure abstraction of the concept, and, in a first moment at least—the only one that Kierkegaard described—makes the subjectivity-object an objective *nothing* in relation to subjective subjectivity. Knowledge itself has being; understandings are realities. Now, for Kierkegaard, in the very time of his life, there is a radical heterogeneity between the being of knowledge and that of the living subject. Thus one might put the determinations of existence into words. But *either* this designation is nothing but a place-marker, a set of references with no conceptualization, *or* the ontological structure of the concept and of the conceptual connections—that is, the objective being, the being in exteriority—is such that these references, taken as notions, can only engender a false knowledge when they claim to be knowledge of being in its inwardness. Living, Kierkegaard lives the paradox in passion: he wants passionately to designate himself a transhistorical absolute; by humor, by irony, he shows himself and hides at the same time. It is not true that he refuses to communicate; he simply remains *secret* in the communication itself. His mania for pseudonyms is a systematic disqualification of his *own name*. Even to *call him up* as a person before the tribunal of others

[10] I have been unable to locate this citation (tr. note).

[11] Immanuel Kant employed the example of the talers (or dollars) in *The Critique of Pure Reason*, A599 (tr. note).

requires a multiplicity of mutually contradictory appellations. The more he is Climacus or Vigilius Haufniensis, the less he is *Kierkegaard*, this Danish citizen, inscribed on the registers of the civil state.

That is fine as long as he lives. He informs by his life against the predictions of a dead man which are a knowledge of death. That is to say that he constructs himself constantly while writing. But on the eleventh of November, 1855, he dies, and the paradox turns against him without ceasing to be scandalous *for us*. The prophecy of one dead condemning one living to an unhappy consciousness and our knowledge of the living one, now dead, reveal their homogeneity. In fact, it is in our own time that Käte Nadler—to cite but one example—applies to the late Kierkegaard, in analyzing him, the predictions of the late Hegel.[12] A dialectical pair forms, of which each term informs against the other: Hegel foresaw Kierkegaard in the past, as a passed moment; Kierkegaard made the internal organization of the system lie in showing that the passed moments are preserved, not only in the *Aufhebung* that maintains them while transforming them but also in themselves, without any transformation, even if they can be reborn, creating by their lone appearance an antidialectic. But if he dies, Hegel recovers possession of it. Not *within the System*, which falls apart before our eyes as a set totality of knowledge and which, in the form of a system, is *completed* by the very movement of history—but by the simple fact that the late Kierkegaard becomes *for us* homogeneous with the descriptions that Hegelian knowledge gives of him. It remains the case, of course, that he has contested the entire system by appearing in a place not designated for him, but because the system

[12] See both Käte Nadler, *Der dialektische Widerspruch in Hegels Philosophie und das Paradoxon des Christentums*, Phil. Diss. Kiel 1931 (Leipzig: Felix Meiner, 1931), pp. viii–143 and her "Hamann und Hegel," *Logos* 20: 1931, pp. 259–85 (tr. note).

itself is an object of knowledge, and as such is contested, this anachronism brings us nothing really new. By way of contrast, the knowledge that *we* have of him is knowledge of a dead man, hence knowledge of death; as such he rejoins Hegelian intuition which produced and conceptualized a future death. In ontological terms, the prenatal being of Kierkegaard is homogeneous with his posthumous being, and existence seems a means of enriching the first until it equals the second: a provisional distress, an essential means of going from one to the other, but, in itself, a fever inessential to being. The notion of unhappy consciousness becomes Søren's unsurpassable destiny, the generality which envelops our more particular understandings of his dead life. Or, if you like: to die is to restore oneself to being and to become an object of knowledge. There at least is the lazy conception that aims to close the breach. Is it right? Shall we say that death puts an end to the paradox by denouncing it as a purely provisional appearance, or, on the contrary, that it pushes it to the extreme and that, since we die, all history is paradoxical, an unsurpassable conflict between being and existence, between non-knowledge (*non-savoir*) and knowledge? Kierkegaard's merit lies in posing the problem *by his very life*. Let us return to him.

Let us first observe that between him and us history *has taken place*. No doubt it continues. But its richness puts between him and us an *obscure density,* a distance. The unhappy consciousness will find other incarnations, of which each one will contest it by his life and confirm it by his death, but not one of them will reproduce Kierkegaard by any sort of resurrection. Knowledge is based here on non-coincidence. The poet of faith left writings. These writings are dead if we do not breathe our life into them, but they come back to life at first as having been written over yonder, once upon a time, with the means at hand, and responding only partially to our present needs: unbelievers will rule that *Kierkegaardian proof is not convincing*. Theologians, in the very name of dogma, will be able to declare themselves unsatisfied, to find the attitude and declarations of the "Poet of Christianity" insufficient and dangerous. They will hold against him, in the name of their own vows, in the very title of *poet* he gives himself, his not having left what he himself calls the "aesthetic stage." Atheists will be able *either*—a formula dear to him—to refuse all relation to this absolute and to opt firmly for a relativism, *or* to define the absolute *in some other way* in history, that is, to see in Kierkegaard the witness of a false absolute or the false witness of the absolute. The believers, they will declare that the absolute he aims for is truly that which exists, but that the relation of historical man to transhistoricity, at least Kierkegaard would want to establish it, is turned aside, is lost despite itself in the skies of atheism. In both cases, the attempt is denounced as a *failure*.

There is more: the failure is *explained*. Variously, it is true, but by convergent approximations. Mesnard, Bohlen, Chestov, Jean Wahl agree in emphasizing the psychosomatic spirit of the "thorn in the flesh."[13] That means that in Kierkegaard even lived experience (*le vécu*) is contested; by relation to the concept, life becomes the inauthentic; Kierkegaard lived badly (which means obscurely, disguised) determinations that we fix better than he. In short, for historical knowledge, one lives to die. Existence is a small surface agitation which soon calms down to allow the dialectical development of concepts to appear; chronology is founded on homogeneity and, finally, on timelessness. Every life venture results in failure for the simple reason that history continues.

[13] The "thorn in the flesh" (2 Cor. 12: 7–9) is referred to by SK in the *Papirer* (VII[1] A 126, VIII[1] A 119, VIII[1] A 156, IX A 119, IX A 208, X[1] A 560, X[1] A 643, X[2] A 20), *Edifying Discourses* (IV 61ff.), and *Concluding Unscientific Postscript* (pp. 406–7) (tr. note).

But if life is a scandal, the failure is still more scandalous. First we denounce it and describe it by collections of words which aim at a certain object named Kierkegaard. In this sense the "poet of faith" is a signified: like the table, like a socioeconomic process. And death does first present itself as the subject falling into the objective absolute. But Kierkegaard in his writings—today inert or living in our life—proposes an inverse word usage; he seeks a dialectical regression from the signified and meanings (*significations*) to the signifier. He presents himself as a signifier and refers us at once to the transhistoricity of signifiers. Should we deny this regression a priori? It is to constitute ourselves as relative. Relative to history if we are non-believers; relative to dogma and mediated by the Church if we believe. Now, if this is the case, then all must be relative, in us and in Kierkegaard himself, *except his failure.* For the failure can be *explained,* but not *resolved;* as non-being, it has the absolute character of negation. Indeed, historical negation is, even at the heart of a relativism, an absolute. It would be a negative absolute to declare: at Waterloo *there were no* fighter planes. But this negative declaration would remain formal. The two sides being equally without fighter planes and not even in a position to miss them, this ineffectual absence is reduced to a formal and uninteresting position, marking only a *temporal distance.* Only there are other negative absolutes, and these are concrete: it is exact to say that Grouchy's army *did not* rejoin the Emperor,[14] and this negation is historical in the sense that it reflects the failed attempt of an army officer, the enemy's fear turned to satisfaction. It is effectual in the sense that the delay of Grouchy most probably *decided* the battle. Hence it is an absolute, an irreducible but concrete absolute. Thus of the failure: from the fact that an expectation

---

[14] Emmanuel de Grouchy (1766–1847) was a general under Napoleon at Waterloo (tr. note).

has not been realized in objectivity, it refers back to subjectivity. Or, more exactly, the interpretations of the failure aim by moderated negations—he didn't consider . . . he couldn't conceive at the time, etc.—to reduce it *to the positive,* to erase it before the affirmative reality of the Other's victory, whatever it may be.

But at once this relative positivity slips back and uncovers what no knowledge could express directly—because no historical development could salvage it: the failure lived in despair. Those who died of dread, of hunger, of exhaustion, those conquered and executed are wounds of knowledge insofar as they have existed. Subjectivity is *nothing* for objective knowledge since it is non-knowledge (*non-savoir*), and yet the failure shows that subjectivity exists absolutely. Thus Søren Kierkegaard, conquered by death and taken up again by historical knowledge, triumphs at the very moment he fails, by showing that history cannot take him up again. Dead, he remains the unsurpassable scandal of subjectivity; known to his bones, he escapes history by the very fact that it constitutes his defeat and that he lived the latter by anticipation. In short, he escapes history because he is historical.

Can one go further? Or must one think simply that death steals the agents of past history absolutely from the historian? For knowledge, one must examine *what is left* of Kierkegaard, his verbal remains. For he is constituted in his historicity as an absolute contesting the historical knowledge which was to penetrate him after his death. But this examination is of a particular type; it is itself a paradox. Kant puts himself in the realm of knowledge to test the validity of our understandings. We can come to him, we the living, across the realm of knowledge, to examine his words with words, question him on concepts. But Kierkegaard steals language from knowledge to use it against knowledge. If we come to him, as we are constrained to do, across the realm of knowledge, our words meet his and are disqualified in disqualifying them. Our use of the word and his are heterogeneous. Thus the message of this dead man is scandalous by itself, since we cannot consider this residue of a life as a determination of knowledge. On the contrary, the paradox reappears since thought, verbally expressed, forms itself in the bosom of knowledge as irreducible non-knowledge. From there, either our examination ends, or else it changes and becomes itself a question of non-knowledge. That means that the questioner is challenged in his being by the questioned. Such is the fundamental virtue of this pseudo-object we call the work of Kierkegaard. But let us push the examination to the very moment of metamorphosis.

This philosopher is an anti-philosopher. Why does he refuse the Hegelian system and, in general, all philosophy? Because, he tells us, the philosopher searches after a first beginning. But why, one will ask, does he who refuses beginnings take Christian dogmas as a point of departure? For to accept them a priori without even testing their validity is to make them uncontested principles of thought. Isn't there a contradiction? And doesn't Kierkegaard, without having himself established a solid beginning, take another's beginning for the origin and foundation of his thought? And, without testing it critically, without doubting it until it can no longer be doubted, doesn't it retain, even in his most intimate thought, the character of alterity?

This is just the unjust question knowledge asks of existence. But through Kierkegaard's pen, existence answers by rejecting knowledge's suit. To deny dogma, he says, is to be mad and proclaim it. But to prove dogma is to be stupid: while one wastes one's time proving the immortality of the soul, living belief in immortality withers. Pushing things to their absurd conclusion, on the day when immortality is irrefutably proven no one will believe in it any longer. Nothing helps one understand better that immortality, even proven, cannot be an object of knowledge, but that it is a certain absolute relation of immanence to transcendence that cannot be established except in and through lived experience (*le vécu*). And surely, that will do for believers. But for myself as a non-believer, that means that the true relation of man to his being cannot be lived, in history, except as a transhistorical relation.

Kierkegaard answers our question by refusing philosophy, or rather by changing radically its end and aims. To seek the beginning of knowledge is to affirm that the foundation of temporality is precisely atemporal and that the historical person can break away from history, desituate himself, and relocate his fundamental atemporality by the direct vision of being. Temporality before the means of atemporality. And, most certainly, Hegel was aware of the problem, since he put philosophy at the end of history, as having-become-truth and as retrospective knowledge. But, precisely, history is not finished, and this atemporal reconstitution of temporality, as the unity of the logical and the tragic, becomes in turn an object of knowledge. From this point of view, in the beginning of the Hegelian system there is not being at all, but the person of Hegel, such as it has been made, such as it has made itself. An ambiguous discovery which, from the point of view of knowledge, can lead only to skepticism.

To escape this conclusion, Kierkegaard takes as his point of departure the *person* seen as non-knowledge (*non-savoir*), that is, as he produces and uncovers, at a certain moment of temporal unfolding of his life, his relation to an absolute which is itself inserted in history. In short, Kierkegaard, far from denying the beginning, witnesses for a beginning in life.

How do we conceive, in the realm of history, of this historical situation not contesting the pretension of the thinker to unveil the absolute? How can a thought that has *appeared* bear witness for itself further than its *abolition*? That is the question he poses in the *Philosophical Fragments*. Of course, this para-

dox is at first religious, eminently so. The apparition
and abolition of Jesus is the cause of it. Or, just as
well, the transformation of a sin—Adam's—into original
and hereditary sin. But it is also the personal problem
of the thinker Kierkegaard: How does one ground the
transhistorical validity of a thought that is produced in
history and that disappears in it? The answer lies in
"reduplication": the insurpassable cannot be knowledge, but the foundation in history of an absolute and
non-contemplative relation with the absolute which is
realized in history. Instead of knowledge dissolving
the thinker, it is the thinker who bears witness for his
own thought. Or, to bear witness for it is one and the
same thing. But these ideas are obscure and can appear to be a verbal solution insofar as one does not
understand that they proceed from a novel conception
of thought.

The thinker begins as one is born. It is not a refusal but a displacement of the beginning. Before birth
there was non-being, there is the leap, then, born to
itself the child and the thinker find themselves situated
immediately in a certain historical world that has made
them. They reveal themselves as a certain adventure
of which the point of departure is a set of socioeconomic, cultural, moral, religious, and other relations
which will be pursued by whatever means are at hand,
that is, as a function of these same relations, and
which will progressively be registered in this same set.
The beginning is reflective: I saw, I touched the
world; I see myself, I touch myself, who touches and
sees surrounding things; and I reveal myself as a finite
being invisibly conditioned, even in my touch and my
vision, by these same things I touch and see. Against
Hegel's fixed and inhuman beginning, Kierkegaard
proposes a moving start, conditioned and conditioning,
of which the foundation is much like what Merleau-
Ponty calls envelopment. We are enveloped: being is
behind us and in front of us. The seer is visible and
sees only by virtue of his visibility. "The body," says

Merleau-Ponty, "is trapped in the thread of the world, but the world is made of the stuff of my body."[15] Kierkegaard knows himself to be enveloped; he sees Christianity and especially the Christian community of Denmark with the eyes that this very community has made for him. A new paradox: I see the being who made me; I see it as it *is* or as it made me. For "survey thought" nothing could be simpler: without quality, the understanding seizes the objective essence without its own nature's imposing particular deviations. And for idealist relativism, there is no difficulty either: the object fades away; what I see, being the effect of the causes which modify my vision, contains no more than my determination by these causes. In either case, being is reduced to knowledge.

Kierkegaard rejects both solutions. The paradox, for him, is that one discovers the absolute in the relative. A Dane, son of a Dane, born at the beginning of the last century, conditioned by Danish history and culture, he discovers Danes his contemporaries, formed by the same history and by the same cultural traditions. At the same time, besides, he can *think* the historical traditions and circumstances that produced them all and produced himself. Is there deviation or appropriation? Both. If objectivity should be unconditioned knowledge, then there is no real objectivity. To see the environment, here, is to see without seeing, to touch without touching, to have by oneself an a priori intuition of the other and, at the same time, to capture it by following common presuppositions that one cannot entirely bring to light. My neighbor is dark in broad daylight, separated from me by his apparent resemblances; nevertheless, I sense him in his profound reality when I become deeper to the point of

---

[15] Cf. Maurice Merleau-Ponty, *The Phenomenology of Perception,* trans. Colin Smith (London: Routledge & Kegan Paul; New York: The Humanities Press, 1962), p. 214. "The sensible [world] gives back to me what I lent to it, but this is only what I took from it in the first place" (tr. note).

finding in myself the transcendent conditions of my own reality. Later, much later, the presuppositions inscribed in things will be correctly transcribed by historians. But, at this level, the reciprocal comprehension that supposes a common envelopment will have disappeared. In short, contemporaries understand each other without knowing each other; the future historian will know them, but his most difficult task—bordering on impossibility—will be to understand them as they understood one another.

In fact—and Kierkegaard is aware of it—the experience which returns after the leap is understood more than it is known. That means that it remains in the realm of the presuppositions which ground it without coming to elucidate them. The source of this beginning? The dogmas. A certain religion produced Kierkegaard; he cannot pretend to emancipate himself from it in order to climb beyond it and see it constituted historically. Let us understand, however: other Danes, from the same society, from the same class, became unbelievers, but even these could not help but make their irreligion the challenge or contestation of *these* dogmas, of this Christianity which had produced them, and thus of their past, of their religious childhood, and finally of themselves. That means that they remained complete with their faith and their dogmas in the vain negation that they exercised on them, using other words to designate their demand for an absolute. Their atheism was in fact a Christian *pseudo-atheism*. Indeed, the envelopment decides the limits between which the real modifications are possible. There are times when disbelief can only be verbal. Kierkegaard, for having doubted in his youth, is more consequential than these "freethinkers"; he recognizes that his thought is not free and that religious determinations will follow him whatever he may do, wherever he may go. If Christian dogmas are for him, in spite of himself, irreducible, it is perfectly legitimate that he put the beginning of thought at the moment when it turns on them to get hold of its roots. A doubly historical thought: it seizes the envelopment as a conjuncture; it is defined as the identity of the beginning of thought and of the thought of the beginning.

If it is thus, what becomes of the universality of historical determinations? Must we absolutely deny the social sphere, its structures, its conditioning, and its evolution? Not at all. We shall see that Kierkegaard bears witness to a double universality. The revolution is that historical man, by his anchoring (*ancrage*), makes of this universality a particular situation, and of common necessity an irreducible contingency. In other words, far from the particular attitude being a dialectical incarnation of the universal moment, as in Hegel, the person's anchoring makes an irreducible singularity of this universal. Did not Søren once say to Levin: "How lucky you are to be a Jew; you escape Christianity. If I had been born as you, I would have enjoyed quite a different life."[16] An ambiguous remark, for he often reproaches the Jews for being inaccessible to religious experience. No doubt the truth is dogma, and the Christian who is not religious remains inauthentic, outside himself, lost. But there is a sort of humble birthright which in the case of a Jew, a Moslem, or a Buddhist means that the accident of being born here rather than there becomes law.

Inversely, the profound reality of Kierkegaard, the fabric of his being, his torment, and his law appear to him at the very heart of their necessity like the accident of his facticity. Again this contingency is common

---

[16] In a letter to H. P. Barfod dated September 12, 1869, Pastor A. F. Schiødte wrote of SK: "He once said to Levin, that it was a bit of luck for him, Levin, that as a Jew he was *free of Christ*. For if he, Kierkegaard, was free of Christ, then he would have lived in a completely different way, would have enjoyed life and gotten along quite well." Excerpts from this letter have been published in Steen Johansen, *Erindringer om Søren Kierkegaard* (København: Steen Hasselbachs Forlag, 1955), pp. 24–25, 42–43, 44 (tr. note).

to all members of his society. He discovers others there which are only his own. He writes in 1846: "To believe is to become light thanks to a considerable weight one takes on; to be objective is to become light by throwing off the burdens. . . . Faith is an infinite weight and its altitude the effect of an infinite weight."[17] The allusion is clear to what he calls elsewhere the "thorn in the flesh." Here we have a pure contingency, the singularity of his conditionings. Søren's unhappy consciousness is produced by chance determinations for which Hegelian rationalism does not account: a somber father, convinced that a divine curse would reach him through his children; the mourning clothes that seem to confirm these prospects and end by convincing Søren he would die by the age of thirty-four; the mother, servant and mistress, whom he loves insofar as she is *his* mother and of whom he disapproves insofar as she is established as an intruder in the home of a widower and as she bears witness to the carnal waywardness of the father; etc. The origin of the singularity is the most radical accident: if I had had another father . . . if my father had not blasphemed, etc. And this prenatal accident is found again in the person himself and in his determinations: the thorn in the flesh is a complex disposition of which we do not know the true secret. But all authors agree on finding in the secret, as its center, a sexual anomaly. A singularizing accident, this anomaly *is* Kierkegaard; it *makes* him. Incurable, it is insurpassable. It produces his most intimate self as a pure historical contingency that might not have been and in itself signifies nothing. Hegelian necessity is not denied, but it cannot be embodied without becoming a singular and opaque contingency. In an individual, reason in history is irreducibly lived as folly, as interior accident, expressing accidental encounters. To our examination,

[17] I have been unable to locate the source of this quotation (tr. note).

Kierkegaard responds by unveiling another aspect of the paradox: there is no historical absolute but that rooted in accident; by the necessity of anchoring, there is no incarnation of the universal but in the irreducible opacity of the singular. Is it Søren who *says* that? Yes and no: in truth he *says nothing* if "says" is equivalent to "means," but his work refers us, without speaking, to his life.

But here the paradox returns: for to live the original contingency is to surpass it. Man, the irremediable singularity, is the being through whom the universal comes into the world, and the constitutive accident, as soon as it is lived, takes the form of necessity. We learn in Kierkegaard that lived experience (*le vécu*) is made up of non-significant accidents of being insofar as they are surpassed toward a meaning they lacked at the start. I shall call these the singular universal.

To decipher this message better, let us return to that notion of sin which stands at the center of his thought. As Jean Wahl said very well, Adam is in a preadamic state of innocence, that is, of ignorance. Nevertheless, although the self does not yet exist, this being already contains a contradiction. At this level the mind is a synthesis that unites and divides; it reunites body and soul and, at the same time, gives rise to the conflicts which oppose them. Dread appears as the internalization of being, that is, of its contradiction. In other words, being has no inwardness before dread. But since mind can neither flee nor accomplish itself, since it is a dissonant unity of the finite and the infinite, the possibility of choosing *one* of the terms—the finite, the flesh, in other words, the self that does not yet exist —is manifested as dread, at the moment when the divine Shalt Not echoes. But what is this Shalt Not? In truth communication is not possible—no more than between Kafka's Emperor and this subject he wants to touch but whom his message does not reach.[18] But

[18] In Franz Kafka's piece "An Imperial Message" (which appears in the collections *A Country Doctor* and, as a passage

Kierkegaard gave the Shalt Not its true value when he
refused the serpent the power to tempt Adam. If one
eliminates the Devil, and if Adam is not yet Adam,
who can forbid and at the same time suggest to the
preadamite that he *make himself* Adam? God alone. A
curious passage from the *Journal* helps us understand:

> Omnipotence . . . should make things dependent.
> But if we rightly consider omnipotence, then clearly
> it must have the quality of so taking itself back in
> the very manifestation of its all-powerfulness that the
> results of this act of the omnipotent can be inde-
> pendent. . . . For goodness means to give absolutely,
> yet in such a way that by taking oneself back one
> makes the recipient independent. . . . Omnipotence
> alone . . . can create something out of nothing which
> endures of itself, because omnipotence is always tak-
> ing itself back. . . . If . . . man had even the least
> independent existence (in regard to *materia*) then
> God could not make him free.[19]

The preadamic state of innocence is the last moment of dependence. At this moment God withdraws
from His creature as the ebbing tide uncovers a bit of
jetsam, and by this movement alone He creates dread
as the possibility of independence. That means He

---

in the title story, *The Great Wall of China*) the dying Emperor
sends a message to "you, the lone individual, the meanest of
his subjects." The messenger sets off immediately, but he must
travel through the crowds at the deathbed, through the cham-
bers and down the stairs of the inner and outer palaces, through
the courtyards—"and so on for thousands of years"—out the
gate—"never, never can this happen"—through the capital city—
"No one can force a way through that, least of all with a message from a dead man.—But still you sit by your window and
dream it all true, when evening falls" (tr. note).

[19] SK's *Papirer*, VII[1] A 181; cf. Alexander Dru, ed. and
trans., *The Journals of Kierkegaard* (London: Oxford University Press, 1938), entry #616 for the year 1846 (tr. note).

makes Himself at once He who forbids and He who tempts. Thus dread is the abandonment of being to the forbidden possibility of choosing one's finitude by a sudden withdrawal of the infinite. It is the internalization of this abandonment, and draws to a close by the free realization of the sole possible of Adam abandoned which is the choice of the finite. At the moment of sin, there is restitution of the original being as *meaning*. Being was the contradictory unity of the finite and the uncapturable infinite, but this unity resided in the refusal of ignorance. Sin as *re-externalization* makes the constituent contradiction reappear. It is the determination of it: the self and God appear. God is infinite withdrawal, but immediately present insofar as sin bars the way from all hope of retreat. The *self* is the chosen finitude, that is, nothingness affirmed and delimited by an act; it is determination conquered by defiance; it is the singularity of extreme distancing. Thus the terms of the contradiction are the same, and yet the *state* of ignorance and sin are not homogeneous: the finite is constituted as lost infinity, freedom as *necessary* and irremediable grounding of the constitution of the *ego*. Good and evil appear as the meaning of this externalization of inwardness which is sinful freedom. Everything happens as if God *needed sin* in order that man might produce himself before Him, as if He gave him life in order to take Adam out of ignorance and *give* man *some* meaning.

But we are all Adam. Thus the preadamic state is nothing but one with the contingency of our being. For Kierkegaard, it is the disunited unity of the accidents that produce it. In this sense, sin will be the *institution* of Kierkegaard as the surpassing of these scattered givens *toward a meaning*. The beginning is the contingency of being; our necessity only appears by the act which assumes this contingency in order to give it its *human meaning,* that is, in order to make of it a singular relation to the All, a singular embodiment of the progressive totalization that envelops and produces it. That Kierkegaard saw well: what he calls sin is on the whole the surpassing of the *state* by freedom and the impossibility of retreat. Thus the course of the subjective life, what he calls passion—and Hegel called *pathos*—is nothing other than freedom registering the finite and lived in finitude as inflexible necessity.

If I wished to summarize what his non-significant testimony brings to me, a twentieth-century atheist who does not believe in sin, I should say that the state of ignorance represents for the person being in exteriority. These exterior determinations are internalized to be re-externalized by a praxis which *institutes* them while objectifying them in the world. That is what Merleau-Ponty said when he wrote that history is the realm where "a heavily burdened form of contingency suddenly opens a future cycle and commands it with the authority of the established."[20] This future cycle is *meaning;* in the case of Kierkegaard it is the self. Meaning can be defined as the future relation of the established to the totality of the world, or, if one prefers, as the synthetic totalization of the scattering of the accidents by an objectifying negation, which inscribes them as the freely created necessity in the very universe where they scattered, and the presence of the totality—totality of time, totality of the universe—in the determination that denies them while posing itself for itself. In other words, man is the being who transforms his being into *meaning,* the being by whom *some meaning* comes into the world. Meaning is the singular universal: by his *self,* the practical assumption and surpassing of being as it is, man restores unity of envelopment to the universe by etching it on future

[20] Cf. Merleau-Ponty, op. cit., p. 449. "Now if it is true that history is powerless to complete anything independently of consciousnesses which assume it and thereby decide its course, and if consequently it can never be detached from us to play the part of an alien force using us for its own ends, then *precisely because it is always history lived through* we cannot withhold from it at least a fragmentary meaning" (tr. note).

history in the being which surrounds it as a finite determination and as hypothetical. Adam is temporalized by sin, the necessary free choice and radical transformation of what he is; he makes human temporality enter into the universe. That clearly signifies that freedom *in each man* is the ground of history. For we are all Adam in that each of us commits for himself and for all a singular sin, that is, that finitude is for each both necessary and incomparable. By his finite action, the agent causes the course of events to deviate, but only in conformity with what this very course should be. In effect, man is the mediation between after-the-fact transcendence and advance transcendence, and this double transcendence is made one. Also one might say that through man the course of events deviates by itself in its own deviation.

Kierkegaard here reveals to us the foundation of his paradox and ours—which are one. Each of us, in his very historicity, escapes history to the very extent to which he makes it. Historic to the extent that others also make history and make me, I am a transhistorical absolute through that which I make of what the others make, of what they have made of me, and of what they will make of me later, that is, through my historiality (*historialité*). It is still necessary to understand clearly what the myth of sin brings to us: the *institution* is singularity become law for others and for myself. Kierkegaard's work is himself as universal. But furthermore, the content of this universality remains his contingency, even elected and surpassed by the choice he made of it. In short, it is a two-sided coin. By its meaning it raises contingency to concrete universality; that is the *obverse,* luminous and yet unknowable—to the extent that knowledge refers to the "world-historical" in the mediation of the *anchoring* (*ancrage*). By its dark *reverse,* it refers to the contingent set, analytic and social givens that define Kierkegaard's being before his *institution.*

In that way, two errors of method are revealed.

Through one—world-historical—the Kierkegaardian
message would be defined in its abstract universality
and as a pure expression of general structures; that
would be, for example, as the Hegelians put it, the
unhappy consciousness, an incarnation of a necessary
moment of universal history, or else—as Tisseau[21]
would have it—a radical definition of faith, an appeal to
all Christians launched by a true Christian. Through
the other error, the simple effect or the simple trans-
mission of the original accidents would be seen in his
work; that is what I shall call "analytical skepticism."
It is based on the belief that *all the childhood* of Kierkegaard is present in his work as the basis of the singularity, and that, in one sense, there is nothing more
in written books than the institution of a life. Søren's
works are rich in Freudian symbolism, it is true, and
an analytical *reading* of his texts is perfectly possible.
I shall say as much for what I shall call "skeptical
Marxism," which is to say a bad Marxism. Although
the good is mediated, there is without a doubt a radical
conditioning of Kierkegaard by his historical milieu.
His disdain for the masses and his aristocratic attitudes
leave no doubt—no more than his financial relationships—of his social origins or of his political positions
(for example, his taste for absolute monarchy), which,
although masked, come up everywhere and obviously
establish his ethical and religious positions.

But precisely, Kierkegaard teaches us that the self,
the act, and the work, with their shadowy side and

[21] Paul-Henri Tisseau has translated into French SK's "In
Vino Veritas" (1933), *Repetition* (1933), *The High Priest—
The Publican—The Woman That Was a Sinner—Three Dis-
courses at the Communion on Fridays* (1934), *The Lilies of
the Field and the Birds of the Air* (1935), *The Concept of
Dread* (1935), *Fear and Trembling* (1935), "Purity of Heart
Is to Will One Thing" (1935), *Training in Christianity* (1936),
Prayer and Fragments on Prayer, from the *Journal* (1937),
Christian Discourses (1952), "Diapsalmata" (1963), as well
as two collections and a biography (tr. note).

their light side, are perfectly irreducible to one or to the other. All shadow is in the light because it is *instituted*. It is true that every act and every writing express the whole self, but it is because there is a homogeneity of the self-as-institution and the act-as-legislator. It is impossible to put the general *at the base;* that would be to forget that it is general in the world-historical sense—for example, relations of production in Denmark in 1830—but that it is lived as a non-significant accident by each person; it is to forget that the person is inserted there by accident. By the fact that he singularly expresses the universal, he singularizes all history, which becomes at once *necessity* —in the same fashion that objective situations are self-controlled—and *adventure,* because he is always the general, resented and instituted as an at first non-significant particularity. Thus the person becomes the singular universal by the presence within him of agents which are defined as universalizing singularities. But inversely, the shadowy side is already light because it is the moment of the internalization of exterior accidents. Without this pre-instituting unity, one falls back into scattering; too often psychoanalysis reduces sense to nonsense, because it refuses to see the irreducibility of the dialectical steps. But Kierkegaard showed, perhaps for the first time, that the universal enters into history as the singular, to the extent that the singular installs itself there as universal. Under this novel form of historiality we again find the paradox which takes here the insurpassable aspect of an ambiguity.

But as we have seen, the *theoretical* aspect of Kierkegaard's work is pure illusion. When we *encounter* his words, they suddenly invite another use of language, that is, of our own words, since they are the same. They refer in his writings to what is named, or, according to his own declarations, to the "categories" of existence.[22] But these categories are neither principles,

<hr/>

[22] See *Concluding Unscientific Postscript*, p. 101, *inter alia* (tr. note).

nor concepts, nor the makings of concepts. They appear as lived relations to the totality, which one can reach by following the word along a regressive aim which leads back from the speech to the speaker. That means that not one of these combinations of words is *intelligible,* but that they constitute, by the very negation of every effort to know them, a reference to what grounds the effort. Kierkegaard uses irony, humor, myth, and non-significant phrases to communicate indirectly with us. That means that his books, if one assumes before them the habitual attitude of the reader, form, by their words, pseudo-concepts which are organized before our eyes as false knowledge. But this false knowledge denounces itself as false at the instant it is constituted. Or rather it is constituted as knowledge of a pretended object that can only be subject. Kierkegaard uses objective and objectifying sets *regressively,* so that the self-destruction of the language necessarily unmasks the one who uses it. The surrealists thought they would unmask being in this way, by lighting fires in the language. Still, being was, for them, *in front of their eyes;* if the words burned—whatever they were—being would be uncovered to infinite desire as a surreality which was also, in the end, a non-conceptual surobjectivity. Kierkegaard constructed language so as to present, in false knowledge, lines of force which, in the pseudo-object constituted, give possibilities of a return to the subject; he invents regressive enigmas. His verbal constructions are rigorously logical. But the very abuse of this logic always runs into contradictions or indeterminacies which imply a reversal of orientation for our point of view. For example, as Jean Wahl has made us aware, this simple title *The Concept of Dread* is a provocation.[23] Dread, for Kierkegaard, cannot in any case be the object of a concept, and, to a certain degree, insofar as it is at the source of the

---

[23] Jean Wahl, *Études Kierkegaardiennes,* Bibliothèque d'Histoire de la Philosophie, 2e edition (Paris: Librarie Philosophique J. Vrin, 1949), p. 213 (tr. note).

temporalizing free choice of finitude, it is the non-conceptual foundation of all concepts. And each of us ought to be able to understand that the word "dread" is a universalization of the singular, hence a false concept, since it awakens universality in us insofar as it refers to the unique, its foundation.

It is in using the words in their countersense that one can reach Kierkegaard in his lived and vanished singularity, that is, in his instituted contingency. Excluded, corrupted, useless, victim of the curse he believed his father had brought down on the whole family, his finitude can be described as impotence and as alterity. He is *other* than *all* the others, other than himself, other than what he writes. He institutes his particularity by the free choice of being singular; that is, he establishes himself at that ambiguous moment when internalization, future externalization writ large, is suppressed so that the latter can be born. Kierkegaard's option, fearing alienation in registering himself in the transcendence of the world, is to identify himself with this dialectical step, nearly the perfect *secret place*: most certainly, he cannot avoid being externalized, for internalization can be nothing but objectifying; but he does his best to see that the objectification does not define him as an object of knowledge; in other words to see that his personal registration in the real, far from summarizing him in the unity of current history, remains *as such* indecipherable and refers to the inaccessible secret of inwardness. He is brilliant at a party, laughs, makes others laugh, and jots in his notebook: I want to die.[24] He makes them laugh because he wants to die; he wants to die because he makes them

[24] SK wrote in his *Journal:* "I have just returned from a party of which I was the life and soul; wit poured from my lips, everyone laughed and admired me—but I went away—and the dash should be as long as the earth's orbit————————————————and wanted to shoot myself." *Papirer,* I A 161, cf. Dru, op. cit., entry #53 for April 1836 (tr. note).

laugh. Thus the exteriority—the brilliant conversation-
alist—is deprived of meaning, *unless* one sees in him
the intentional contestation of all action reduced to its
objective result, *unless* the *meaning* of all manifestation is precisely incompletion, non-being, non-
significance, and he requires those who wish to decipher
him to return toward the inaccessible source: inwardness. Kierkegaard institutes his accidents by the choice
of becoming the knight of subjectivity.

Dead, Søren enters into knowledge as a bourgeois
who came to Denmark during the first half of the last
century and who was conditioned by a definite family
situation, an expression of the movement of history in
its generality. But he enters into knowledge as unintelligible, as a disqualification of knowledge, as a virulent lacuna which escapes the concept and consequently escapes death. Here we are back at our original
question. We were asking: what prevents the late Kierkegaard from becoming an object of knowledge? The
answer is that he was not one when he was alive.
Death, which we took to be the metamorphosis of
existence into knowledge, Kierkegaard shows us as
radically *abolishing* the subjective, but without changing it. If Kierkegaard, in the first instance, can appear
as a bundle of understandings, it is because the *known*
is not challenged in any immediate way by lived experience (*le vécu*). But soon it is knowledge which
challenges itself radically in the pseudo-object that this
dead man is to us. It discovers its own limits and that
the aimed-for object is stolen away without ever being
able to be given as an autonomous determination of
the exterior.

The paradox, at this level, takes on a new aspect:
can one go beyond the contestation of knowledge by
itself? Can one go beyond it in the face of the living
being who bears witness to its secret? Can one go
beyond it when this living being has been abolished?
To these questions, Kierkegaard gives one and the same
answer: the regression of the signified to the signifier

cannot make an object of any intellection. Nevertheless, we can catch hold of the signifier in its real presence by what he calls the *understanding*. And the
knight of subjectivity does not define comprehension,
and he does not make of it a new act. But, by his work,
he *gives* his life *to be understood*. We in 1964 encounter him in history, a history made as an *appeal
to the understanding*.

But does anything remain to be understood if death
is abolition? To that, Kierkegaard responded with the
theory of "contemporaneity." Before Søren, the dead
man, there remains something to be understood: ourselves. Søren encountered the same paradox which
confronts us with regard to him—the living dead man
—with regard to Jesus, from Adam on. And his first
answer is that one understands what one becomes. To
understand Adam is to become Adam. And most certainly one cannot become Christ, much less understand his unintelligible message, without a single temporal mediation by becoming the man to whom the
message is directed, by becoming a Christian. Thus
Kierkegaard is living if we can become Kierkegaard,
or if, inversely, in death he continues to have himself
instituted through the living by borrowing from them
their life, by slipping himself into their life and nourish-
ing his singularity on ours. Or, in other words, if he
appears at the heart of knowledge as the perpetual
denouncer, in each, of non-knowledge (*non-savoir*),
of the dialectical step where internalization blends into
externalization, in short, of existence.

Yes, says Kierkegaard. You can become me, because I can become Adam. Subjective thought is the
reflective capture of my being-an-event, of the adventure that I am and that leads me necessarily to become
Adam, that is, to recommence original sin in the very
movement of my temporalization. Sin is choice. Each
man is at once himself and Adam recommenced to the
very degree that Kierkegaard is at once himself and
his father, the blasphemer whose blasphemy he as-

sumes by his own sin. All sin is singular insofar as it
institutes a unique person under particular conditions,
and, at the same time, it is *sin itself* in its being the
universality of sin as contained in the singularity of
choice. Through choice, each man is always becoming
all mankind. Each one moves history forward by beginning it again, and also by being, in advance in himself, the new beginnings yet to come. From this point
of view, if Kierkegaard can become Adam, it is because
Adam was at the heart of his sinful existence already
the premonition of a future Kierkegaard. If I can become Kierkegaard, it is because Kierkegaard was in
his being already a premonition of us all.

If we take up the question again in the very terms
in which we posed it, it comes to this: Kierkegaard's
words are our words. To the degree that, in the midst
of knowledge, they become non-knowledge and are
referred by the paradox from the signified to the signifier, we are the signifier that they reveal regressively.
Reading Kierkegaard I climb back as far as myself; I
want to catch hold of him, and it is myself I catch.
This non-conceptual work is an invitation to understand myself as the source of all concepts. Thus the
knowledge of death, in finding its own limits, does not
emerge into absence; it comes back to Kierkegaard,
myself. I discover myself as an irreducible existent,
that is, as freedom become my necessity. I understand
that the object of knowledge *is* his being in the tranquil
mode of perpetuity, and at the same stroke that I am
a non-object because I have to be my being. Indeed,
my being is a temporalizing, hence a submitted choice,
but the nature of this submitted being is to be submitted *in freedom,* hence to have to continue to choose.

Kierkegaard is restored as my adventure not in its
unique sense, but on the level of my being-an-
adventurer, insofar as I have to be the event that happens to me from outside. Insofar as history, universal-
ized by things, carriers of the mark of our action, becomes, by each new human birth, a singular adventure

and folds its universality back into itself, Søren, dead, can be living, because in advance he was I who was not yet, since I begin him again under other historical conditions. And, curiously, this relationship of reciprocal inwardness and immanence between Kierkegaard and each of us is not established in the relativity of circumstances but on the very level where each one is an incomparable absolute. The common and each time singular reality, it is the words that make it clear to us, inverted signs, tools of indirect communication that refer me to myself because they refer uniquely to him.

Kierkegaard lives because, refusing knowledge, he reveals the transhistorical contemporaneity of the dead and the living; that is, he reveals that each man is all mankind as the singular universal; or, if one prefers, because he manifests, against Hegel, temporalization as the transhistorical dimension of history. Humanity loses its dead and begins them again absolutely through the living. He is not I, however, who am an atheist. Nor some Christian who tomorrow will reproach him for his negative theology. Let us say that he was, in his own time, a *unique* subject. Once dead, he only comes back to life by becoming a *multiple subject,* that is the internal connection among our singularities. Each of us *is* Søren as adventure. And each interpretation, contesting the others, assumes them all the while as its negative depth. Each, inversely, is contested but assumed by the others to the degree that, refusing to see in them a full reality or a knowledge concerning reality, the others conceive its possibility by relating to the possibility Kierkegaard has of supporting several interpretations. Indeed, difference of opinion, contradiction, and ambiguity are precisely the determined qualification of existence. Thus Kierkegaard's depth, his manner of remaining *other* within me, without ceasing to be mine, is today's Other, my real contemporary who is the foundation of it. Inversely, he is the denunciation in each of the ambiguity

in himself and in others. Comprehensible in the name
of each ambiguity, he is our multiple and ambiguous
link, our existential relation, between contemporary
existents as such, that is, as lived ambivalences. He
resides in history as the transhistorical relation between contemporaries caught in their singular historiality (*historialité*). In each of us he gives and refuses
himself, as he did during his life. He is my adventure
and remains, for the others, Kierkegaard, the Other,
at the horizon—a witness for that Christian that faith
is an ever periled becoming, a witness for me that
becoming-an-atheist is a long and difficult undertaking,
an absolute relation with those two infinites, mankind
and the universe.

Every undertaking, even triumphantly carried out,
remains a *failure,* that is, an incompletion to complete.
It lives because it is open. The failure here is clear.
Kierkegaard shows historiality, but misses history. Set
against Hegel, he was employed too exclusively in returning his instituted contingency to the human adventure, and because of this fact, he neglected the praxis
that is rationality. By the same stroke, he denatured
knowledge, forgetting that the world we know is the
one we make. The anchoring (*ancrage*) is a fortuitous
event, but the possibility and rational meaning of this
accident is given in the general structures of envelopment that ground it and that are themselves the universalization of the singular adventures by the ma-
teriality where they inscribe themselves.

Kierkegaard is living in death in that he affirms the
irreducible singularity of each man to history, which
nevertheless conditions him rigorously. He is dead, in
the very bosom of the life that he continues through
us, insofar as he remains an inert examination, an open
circle which requires closing by us. Others, in his time
or shortly after, were further along than he, showed
the completed circle by writing: "Men make history
on the base of anterior circumstances."[25] In these

words, there is and is not progress beyond Kierkegaard, for this circularity remains abstract and risks excluding the human singularity of the concrete universal inasmuch as it fails to integrate Kierkegaardian immanence with the historical dialectic. Kierkegaard and Marx, these living dead condition our anchoring and make themselves, separately, our future and our future task: how to conceive history and the transhistorical absolute to restore, in theory and in practice, their full reality and their relation of reciprocal inwardness to the transcendent necessity of the historical process and to the free immanence of a constantly rebegun historization. In short, how to uncover in each conjuncture, indissolubly tied together, the singularity of the universal and the universalization of the singular.[26]

[25] In "The Eighteenth Brumaire of Louis Bonaparte" (1869), Karl Marx wrote: "Men make their own history, but they do not make it just as they please; they do not make it under circumstances chosen by themselves, but under circumstances directly encountered, given, and transmitted from the past." Karl Marx and Friedrich Engels, *Basic Writings on Politics and Philosophy*, ed. Lewis S. Feuer (Garden City: Doubleday & Co., Anchor Books, 1959), p. 320 (tr. note).

[26] I am grateful to Françoise Rosset and Richard Raskin for their assistance in preparing this translation and notes (tr. note).

THE LOSS OF THE WORLD IN
KIERKEGAARD'S ETHICS

Louis Mackey

Any inquiry into the metaphysical foundations of Kierkegaard's ethics runs into the unique hermeneutical problem posed by his method of indirect communication. On his own admonition, Kierkegaard's books, even those that are richest in theoretical content, are not to be read as doctrinal compendia or philosophical essays. In his ethical writings Kierkegaard offers no system of norms, values, or precepts. Except incidentally, and then usually in a polemic interest, there is no analysis of moral phenomena as such. Certainly there is no explicit concern for the metaphysical basis of ethics. There is only a strategy, calculated, as he put it, "to make aware."[1] His utterances on ethics are the tactics of that strategy. They are elements in a rhetoric of edification, whose meaning is not enclosed within them as their content, but projected beyond them as their effect on the reader.

The effect intended by Kierkegaard's rhetoric is a certain self-relationship ("subjectivity" or "inwardness"), which cannot be formulated and given out as doctrine or information, but which the reader is required to achieve on his own. The books provide only the occasion, the impetus, and the demand. For ex-

---

This essay appeared originally in *The Review of Metaphysics*, June 1962, Vol. XV, No. 4. It has been revised by the author for inclusion in this volume. It appears with the kind permission of the author and the editor of *The Review of Metaphysics*.

[1] See, among many references, Søren Kierkegaard, *The Point of View* (London, 1950), pp. 138, 155; and Alexander Dru, *The Journals of Søren Kierkegaard* (London, 1938), No. 1001.

ample, the proposition "Truth is subjectivity"[2] is not a philosophical indicative, but a rhetorical imperative. Translated into the language of personal address, it says: "You reader! Whatever you believe, whatever you claim to know, remember in fear and trembling that you hold this faith and stake this claim solely on the strength of your own freedom to do so, with no guarantee more ultimate than your own decision, at your own risk, and on your own responsibility!" This charge to the reader, which is the real and indirect import of "Truth is subjectivity," is as far as it could be from the epistemological relativism which the proposition immediately suggests. What the reader is to get from "Truth is subjectivity" is not the comforting assurance that "it doesn't matter what you believe," but rather the existential terror—that glimpse of the abyss which is itself a confrontation with the Absolute—that ensues when "the uncertainty of all things is thought infinitely."[3]

It is possible and salutary to read Kierkegaard as he meant to be read, to let the rhetoric have its effect without bothering one's head over metaphysical doubts. And yet Kierkegaard could not really hope that his half-learned readers would refuse to lay their dialectical hands on his work.[4] Precisely because of their rhetorical indirection, his writings do not preclude but demand philosophical interpretation and criticism. Every sustained act of rhetoric, insofar as it projects a determinate state of affairs as its meaning and satisfaction, also structures by implication the universe which makes possible both that state of affairs and the practice of the rhetoric demanding it. The purpose of this paper is to evaluate the suggestion of *acosmism* that is found in the ethical writings of Kierkegaard, especially the

[2] Kierkegaard, *Concluding Unscientific Postscript* (Princeton, 1944), pp. 179ff. This book will be referred to hereafter as *CUP*.

[3] *CUP*, p. 80.

[4] *CUP*, "A First and Last Declaration," unpaged (= p. 554).

Concluding Unscientific Postscript. For this purpose it is not sufficient to understand the end intended by Kierkegaard's program. It is also necessary, over Kierkegaard's objections, to investigate the metaphysical groundwork by which both program and end are sustained.

———————

The problem of acosmism is posed by two Kierkegaardian propositions central to the argument of the *Postscript.* (1) The ethical reality of the subject is the only reality. (2) All realities other than his own the subject encounters only in the mode of possibility, by thinking them.

From the *Postscript* we know that the "ethical reality of the subject" means neither the subject's inner intentions nor his external actions nor the two together, but rather the *tension* of inwardness *from* will *to* performance. To exist as a human being means *to be between* (*inter-esse*) thinking and being.[5] The reality of the individual is his *interest* in existing, his passionate *concern,* as he stands in the crisis of decision, *to move from* possibility (thinking) *to* action (being). It is only his own reality in this sense to which the individual has direct access *as* reality. Other realities he can relate to only cognitively or aesthetically, by translating them into possibilities.

The combination of propositions (1) and (2) seems to imply an acosmism—a worldlessness of the individual—that borders on solipsism.

Yet these propositions, like "Truth is subjectivity," must not be taken casually at face value. For we know that the face of any Kierkegaardian utterance is likely to be a pseudonymous persona whose words have a rhetorical significance different from the meaning they directly assert. That this is the case here is indicated

[5] *CUP,* p. 279.

by the one passage in his works in which Kierkegaard shows himself sensitive to the suggestion of acosmism and counters it in advance:

> To grant thinking the supremacy over all else is gnosticism; to make the ethical reality of the subject the only reality might seem to be acosmism. That it will seem so to a busy thinker who is out to explain everything, a nimble wit who speedily traverses the entire world, proves only that he has a very limited conception of what the ethical means to the subject. If ethics were to take the whole world away from such a busy thinker and let him keep only his own self, presumably he would think: "Such a trifle is not worth keeping, let it go with the rest!" And so—that is acosmism. But why will such a busy thinker speak and think so disrespectfully of himself? If the sense were that he should give up the whole world and be content with another man's ethical reality, then he would be right to regard it as a poor trade. But his own ethical reality should, ethically, mean more to the individual himself than heaven and earth and all that therein is, more than the 6,000 years of world-history, more than astrology, veterinary science, and everything that the age demands—which aesthetically and intellectually is a monstrous vulgarity. If this is not the case, then so much the worse for the individual himself, for then he has nothing at all, no reality at all. For to all else he has only a possibility-relationship at the very maximum.[6]

The suggestion then is not so much wrong as it is irrelevant and improper. The question of the *reality* of the world, whatever interest it may have for the disinterested science of metaphysics, is *irrelevant* to

[6] *CUP*, p. 305. I have slightly altered the existing English translation. This passage is found at p. 331 of Vol. VII of the second Danish edition of Kierkegaard's *Samlede Vaerker*, hereafter referred to as *SV*.

the ethical concern of the individual. Because it is irrelevant it is also *improper* to raise the question of acosmism. Such questioning is a dangerous distraction —a "parenthesis"—that tempts the individual to forfeit the only reality to which he has entry and for which he is responsible, for the sake of an impressive but illusory pursuit of mere possibilities.

No one who knows the devastation Kierkegaard's own nimble wit can work would lightly put himself in the place of that busy thinker who is here castigated. Yet the sense of Kierkegaard's polemic is not wholly clear without further analysis. The precise respect in which the reality of the world is ethically irrelevant needs to be defined.

It is evident from his works at large that Kierkegaard does not intend to *deny* the reality of the world. When he does touch in passing on metaphysical problems, his most obvious affiliation is with the Greeks, whose "honest" realism he contrasts with the "mendacious" idealism of Hegel. It is not always clear whether his orientation is Platonic or Aristotelian or that of an orthodox creation-doctrine combining elements of both. But it is clear that he means to defend the reality of an objective world-order against skeptical and sophistical intrusions.[7] *Metaphysically,* and *with respect to the extra-subjective realm,* Kierkegaard tends to make the larger assumptions of classical realism. Not that he tries to establish the truth of these assumptions by argument; for the most part they stand in the background of his writing, as "beliefs-which-it-is-not-necessary-to-call-into-question."

But the fact that such metaphysical questions never become matters of importance to Kierkegaard is itself significant. In spite of his devotion to the Greeks and his implicit realism, Kierkegaard can write:

Instead of conceding the contention of Idealism, but in such a way, be it noted, that one dismisses as

[7] Cf. Kierkegaard, *Philosophical Fragments* (Princeton, 1944), pp. 30, 29–38 passim; also *CUP,* pp. 293–95.

a temptation the whole question of actuality (of an elusive *an-sich*) in relation to thought, which like all other temptations cannot be overcome by giving way to it; instead of putting an end to Kant's misleading reflection, which brought actuality into relation with thought; instead of referring actuality to the ethical, Hegel went further. He became fantastic and vanquished the *skepsis* of Idealism with the help of pure thought, which is an hypothesis and, even if it does not so declare itself, fantastic. And this triumph of pure thought (that in it thought and being are one) is something both to laugh at and to weep over, for in pure thought the question of the difference between thought and being cannot actually be raised at all. —That thought has reality was assumed by Greek philosophy without further ado. By reflecting on the matter one would have to come to the same result; but why confuse a thought-reality with actuality? A thought-reality is a possibility, and thought must simply dismiss every further question concerning its actuality. . . . A skepticism which attacks thought itself cannot be stopped by thinking it through, for this would have to be done by thought, which is on the side of revolution. It must be broken off. To answer Kant within the fantastic shadow-play of pure thought is precisely not to answer him. The only *an-sich* that cannot be thought is existing, with which thought has nothing to do at all.[8]

---

[8] *CUP*, p. 292; *SV*, Vol. VII, pp. 316–17. I have altered the existing English translation of this passage in the direction of a more literal rendering. The word I have translated "actuality" is *virkelighed*. This word is rendered "reality" in the existing translation, and appears as such everywhere else in this paper in phrases like "the ethical reality of the individual." I have kept "reality" for the most part because it is the word most familiar to English-speaking readers of Kierkegaard. But in this passage Kierkegaard distinguishes *virkelighed* from *realitet* (as in "thought-reality"): *virkelighed* is actuality as distinct from possibility; *realitet* is a generic term including possibility. The existing translation is obliged to render *realitet*

Kierkegaard believed that Kant's critical idealism
had instituted a skepticism which attacked the validity
of thought. His belief is not difficult to understand if
we recall several features of Kant's philosophy. Existence in the categorial sense, as a pure concept of
the understanding, is constitutive of phenomenal
(= thought)-reality only, and not of actuality *an-sich*.
Kant asserts that the *existence* of the *Ding-an-sich* can
be known, though by what Kantian mechanism it is
apprehended is not clear. In any case, the *nature* and
meaning of existence in this non-categorial sense—that
anything is at all—is not open to philosophical inquiry.
We cannot, Kant says, ask to know the conditions of
the actuality of experience, only the conditions of its
possibility.

There are then two senses of existence in Kant's
critical philosophy: categorial existence, a constituent
of any possible experience; and actual, non-categorial
existence *an-sich*, which we must acknowledge as a
fact, but with which, as Kierkegaard says, thought has
no further dealings.

Kant's view of the existence of the human self de-
rives from his view of existence in general. I can know
the phenomenal existence of the phenomenal self; the
transcendental unity of apperception, though not properly and substantially a self, is a—or rather *the*—condition of the possibility of all experience, including the
experience of the phenomenal self. But the actuality
of the self in any further sense is beyond investigation.
For theoretical reason, it is a mare's-nest of pseudo-
syllogisms. For practical reason, it is an item, not of
knowledge, but of faith. The self, so apprehended, is
the one *Ding-an-sich* to which we have access, though
not theoretical access. Actuality is for Kant, though
in a rather different sense than for Kierkegaard, "referred to the ethical."

---

in this passage by "validity," which is misleading. In any case,
"actuality" in this citation is to be understood as synonymous
with "reality" elsewhere in this paper.

Something like this seems to have been Kierkegaard's understanding of Kant. And for Kierkegaard these considerations were decisive. All thinking necessarily makes the assumptions of Greek realism. But all that Greek realism actually assumes is that the object of thought is "real" *as an object of thought:* it is an *essential possibility.* No more than this can or need be assumed for the purposes of theoretical understanding. Existential reality—the actual existence of these essences, thought-realities, or possibilities—cannot be grasped by thinking. The question of actual existence cannot even be formulated as a theoretical and cognitive question. It must therefore be dismissed as a misunderstanding and a temptation.

Hegel's endeavor to think through Kant's *skepsis* is no more likely to succeed than is a squirrel's attempt to get out of his cage by going around one more time. Hegel's objection to Kant—if he knows of a reality that eludes thought, he must already be out beyond the boundaries he has assigned to thought—holds only because Kant asserts that our acknowledgment of the *Ding-an-sich* is a cognitive acknowledgment. This would be "Kant's misleading reflection, which brought actuality into relation with thought." Against such a view Hegel is right; but right only in that his idealism is thoroughgoing and consistent, not (as he believes) right in the sense that he avoids or resolves the difficulty. Hence his mendaciousness as opposed to the Greeks, who did not make the reality of the world a *theoretical* problem. The difficulty cannot be resolved, and the contention of idealism—which is in effect that *this* question of actuality cannot even arise—must be conceded. Hegel did not solve the problem of the thing-in-itself; he simply erased it. And *qua* metaphysician, in a cognitive respect, he was quite correct. He erred by presuming that he had dealt with the problem of the relation of thought and being, when in fact he had only formulated—fantastically—its unformulability.

Therefore, the skepticism which Kant introduced

into philosophy cannot be resolved. It can only be broken with. The metaphysical problem of actuality and its relation to cognition must be dismissed as a pseudo-problem, a temptation to absent-mindedness and distraction. Actuality must be referred to the ethical—to the subject's existence, his *inter-esse,* which he apprehends not by thinking it, but by existing it in passion and decision.

This is the meaning of Kierkegaard's statements, that the ethical reality of the subject is the only reality, and that to all realities other than his own he has only a possibility-relation. These propositions do not *define* a metaphysical *position;* they *disavow* a metaphysical *problem.* In this light it is clear why Kierkegaard believes that the imputation of acosmism is irrelevant to his concern and ethically improper.

However, although he believes that metaphysical questions have no bearing on ethical matters, Kierkegaard is still a realist—not only in the sense that he believes every object of thought to be real as an object of thought, but also in the more exact sense that there *are* other actualities than my own. Things in nature exist in their own way, and every other human being has his own existence in just the same way that I have mine. Kierkegaard writes books in order to communicate. The very act of communicating, no matter how indirect, implies the being of the recipient and of a world which incorporates both communicants.

Therefore, when he says that the ethical reality of the subject is the only reality, Kierkegaard means to stress that the only reality which the individual can grasp (*faa fat paa*) *as reality*—by *being* it—is his own. Other realities, men and things, he can only get hold of (*faa fat paa*) *as possibilities,* by abstracting from their actual existing.

"Possibility" in this context means *the manner of my relation to realities other than my own.* To assert that I apprehend other realities as possibilities is not to *deny,* but to *affirm,* a relationship, albeit an indirect relationship, holding among real entities. Realities other than my own *are, in themselves; to me* they *are addressed as* possibilities.[9]

From an intellectual or aesthetic point of view, other realities are grasped as possibilities to be reflectively or imaginatively entertained. They are taken objectively, as the contents of a transparent intentionality, considered "for their own sake," and not for any relevance they might have to the existential situation of the thinking and imagining individual. From the disinterested poetic and intellectual point of view, Kierkegaard says, possibility is higher than reality.[10]

From an ethical point of view, other realities are again grasped as possibilities; now, however, not as material for contemplation, but as a *demand for action,* a *claim on my freedom.* Other realities confront me ethically as opportunities—they are alternatives for action—and as requirements—they insist that, either consciously or by default, I do something about them, seize them and actualize them or let them pass. Ethically I am not disinterested, but interested. I apprehend other realities as possibilities, not "for their own sake," but exclusively because they irrupt into my situation so as to make a difference in the way I exist my actuality. Kierkegaard writes, "Ethically regarded, reality [sc.: the individual's ethical reality] is higher than possibility."[11] Intellectually and aesthetically, I abstract from my own reality in order to enjoy other realities in the mode of possibility. Ethically, I grasp other realities as possibilities in order to exist my own reality.

For Kierkegaard, the "stages on life's way"—aesthetic-intellectual, ethical, religious—are fundamentally *ways of being human.* They are similar to Heideggerian "existentials." They do not characterize man-things as attributes might characterize substances. They

[9] Cf. Per Lønning, *"Samtidighedens Situation"* (Oslo, 1954), pp. 15, 39ff.

[10] *CUP,* p. 282.

[11] *CUP,* p. 284.

are modes of existing in and by which a free being like man constitutes his own selfhood.

The key word here is *free*. I am free with respect to other realities. They do not impinge on me directly so as to make me what I am, nor do I so impinge on them. *Because* I am free, other realities become for me possibilities, things-which-*I-am-able*-to-do-something-about. I can either stand off and look at them (aesthetically-intellectually), or take them into my existence as opportunities and demands for decision (ethically). Realities other than mine *are,* and they are *related* to me. But they are related to me *externally*. They do not touch me as *realities* in such a way as to determine me. They bear on me indirectly, across the nothingness of freedom, "the alarming possibility of *being able*."[12]

Therefore, Kierkegaard would say that the isolation of the individual in his freedom is not a perverse denial of the world, but a *sine qua non* of ethics. "This is profitable preliminary training for an ethical mode of existence: to learn that the individual stands alone."[13] Deny that the ethical reality of the subject is the only reality, deny that he is related to all other realities as possibilities, and you have denied freedom. Deny freedom, and you have made nonsense out of ethics and human existence in general.

It is now clear not only why Kierkegaard regards the metaphysical question of acosmism as ethically irrelevant, but also why he believes it ethically *necessary* to recognize that individuals are isolated, each in his own subjectivity sustaining only a possibility-relation to other realities. But a further question arises: is it ethically *sufficient* to hold that the individual is related to other realities as to possibilities?

Consider a case of temptation, say the radical temptation to neglect my proper ethical concern for the sake

[12] Kierkegaard, *The Concept of Dread* (Princeton, 1957), p. 40. Hereafter referred to as *COD*.

[13] *CUP*, p. 287.

of some "objective result" my action might have, such as the esteem of posterity. Such results, Kierkegaard rightly says, I cannot guarantee by my free action alone. Factors other than my will help to decide my historical significance or insignificance. The esteem of posterity is "impossible because it is merely possible, i.e., perhaps possible, i.e., dependent upon something else,"[14] and *therefore* "it is unethical to be concerned about it."[15]

Now it may or may not be unethical for me to be concerned about the historical fate of my actions. But if it is, and if I am nevertheless tempted to such concern, then I do not believe that the temptation issues from the *impossibility* of my guaranteeing this significance to my acts. The inference: perhaps possible, therefore merely possible, therefore impossible, therefore a temptation, does not hold. No one is tempted by impossibilities or by *mere* possibilities. Men are tempted because they are involved in situations compounded of *real* relations to other men, objects, and events. If I am tempted to seek historical importance, it is because I am *really* involved in history, in the *reality* of other men and their decisions, and in the *reality* of the natural forces that help to shape history.

To be sure, I am free, and for that reason the world —with other men as members of it—confronts me as possibility. But it confronts me as *real* possibility, as possibility arising not only out of my freedom, but also out of my participation in realities other than my own. My freedom, however much it isolates me in responsibility and in risk, *does not altogether sever me from the reality of the world as such.*

If this is not the case, if there is not, e.g., something like a contingent causal relation involved when I am lured by a possibility, then the alternative is that *I tempt myself.* But this is ethical nonsense. I may of course tempt myself in particular cases; that is, I may

[14] *CUP,* pp. 121–22.
[15] *CUP,* p. 122.

fancy to myself alluring possibilities. But *fundamentally* I do not tempt myself. Self-enticement is possible only on the basis of a more radical experience of *being enticed;* otherwise temptation is an unimaginably gratuitous experimentation with possibilities. If I am totally isolated by my freedom, then the experience of temptation is illusory and the notion of temptation meaningless.

Yet something like this follows if we accept Kierkegaard's view that I am related to other realities only as possibilities. Unless I am *also* related to them directly as *realities,* I cannot be tempted.

Or take another case. Kierkegaard holds that other realities confront me ethically as demands for decision. They are possibilities which *require* me, not to perform this or that particular action, but to act in a way relevant to the alternatives they establish. Other realities address themselves to my freedom in such a way as to make a claim on me.

Suppose that on my way home I am approached by a shabby stranger who asks me for money, insisting that he needs it for some vital purpose. I may interpret him and his request in various ways, but in any event I either do or I do not give him the money. I am free, and therefore not determined to do one thing rather than the other; I can do either in an indeterminate variety of ways; but I am required to do something. Even if I view the situation aesthetically—say as material for my next novel—I still either give or do not give what is asked. The same thing is true even if I look the other way and pretend not to notice the fact that another reality has arisen in my situation and calls for action.

Now I believe that another reality, appearing before me as possibility, cannot require me to act unless this other reality and I are in the first place related as realities.

If this is not the case, then the alternative must be that *I obligate myself.* But this is ethically absurd. It is true, of course, that I can and do in particular cases imagine alternatives and determine myself to act on them. But it is also true that, however free I am, fundamentally I do not create my own possibilities and require myself to act in a way relevant to them. The very fact that alternatives are given, and that they insist, will I or nil I, on relevant action—do x or do not do x—is itself a sign that these alternatives emerge not only out of my freedom, but also out of my real community with other beings. Pure self-obligation, like pure self-enticement, is only experimentation. Freedom (the possibility-relation of Kierkegaard) and the "reality-relation" are both *necessary* conditions of ethical action; only together do they constitute the *sufficient* condition of such action.

When I run into the panhandler, the two of us participate, however slightly, in each other and in a common world. We are, however brief and transitory our encounter, really members one of another and of a larger reality that includes us both.

I believe, however, that Kierkegaard implicitly denies this. He means to say that the individual is really isolated from other beings, receiving from them neither support, insistence, opposition, nor allurement. The world is only a cluster of possibilities for him, and as such does not offer him matter, content, locus, opportunity, or exigence for action—these he must generate out of his own freedom. Kierkegaard was rightly apprehensive about the kind of objectivism that threatened to dissolve human individuality in the non-human world, the race, the state, or some other collectivity. But his fear of coalescence and his will to preserve freedom untrammeled led him to sweep away all order, participation, and community. His insistence that the question of the reality of the world is ethically irrelevant, and that only an indirect possibility-relation holds between the ethical subject and other realities, implies a sort of freedom that is separative only and is not supported by the cosmos. Kierkegaardian free-

dom—perhaps this is the influence of the romantics—
is the negative half of Augustinian freedom. As St.
Augustine learned from his own experience—an experience of painful involvement, quite unlike Kierkegaard's experience of withdrawal—it is this half of freedom which, left to itself, can only consume itself in
the pursuit of vanity. It often seems that Kierkegaardian subjectivity—the tension of inwardness within
itself—far from being concrete and existential, is but
an abstraction vibrating in a vacuum.

In any case, unless we allow that I—in my own ethical and human reality—participate in the reality of other
beings, then we are forced to the conclusion that I
create my own possibilities, tempt myself, and obligate
myself. I become my own God and my own devil. And
this, depending on one's perspective, is either foolish
or presumptuous.

In fact, it is a conclusion that, for other reasons,
would be unacceptable to Kierkegaard himself. He
jibed at Kant's conception of moral autonomy because
it led to this end.[16] Concerned as he was with religious
faith, he saw in the failure of autonomy God's opportunity. Where the human spirit recognizes itself to be a
land of emptiness and want, there God can enter in
and fill up man's need with the bounty of his own
gratuitous goodness.

For this reason, it might be objected that my previous criticism bypasses the center of Kierkegaard's
ethic. It might be protested that he *intended* really to
isolate the individual, to deprive him of the illusory
securities of community and world-order, so as to bring
him face to face with God. Community and world-
order are realities, but they are not the absolute Reality, and the individual must not rely upon them or

---

[16] Dru, *The Journals of Søren Kierkegaard*, No. 1041. On
this point and the following, see my paper "The Analysis of
the Good in Kierkegaard's *Purity of Heart*," in I. C. Lieb, ed.,
*Experience, Existence, and the Good: Essays in Honor of Paul
Weiss* (Carbondale, Illinois, 1961), pp. 261–74.

stake his existence upon them. His isolation is not so much metaphysical as it is personal and religious. And the "weakness" I have discovered in the "metaphysical foundations of Kierkegaard's ethic" is actually a deliberate, systematic, and justified tactic in the strategy of indirect communication.

If this is true, my criticism of Kierkegaard serves only to illumine and enhance his effectiveness. The rhetorician has got around the philosopher after all, and my analysis is not a diagnosis but a symptom.

Let us examine this objection. Kierkegaard's rhetoric is meant to drive the reader away from the world, to a confrontation with God. But it seems to me that there is a contradiction in Kierkegaard's account of the God-man relation. Consider his typical descriptions of this relation. God is said to be negatively present in subjectivity;[17] He is present but hidden in the world;[18] He is present whenever the uncertainty of all things is thought infinitely;[19] He is present to freedom, where freedom is conceived as infinite possibility;[20] "God *is* that all things are possible and that all things are possible *is* God."[21] In a word, God communicates with men indirectly, in the mode of possibility.[22] Every direct relation to God is branded paganism,[23] and even the Incarnate Presence of God among men is more concealment than revelation.[24]

Thus man is related to God, as to the world, by a possibility-relation. The reality of God is apprehended only in the form of negation, radical uncertainty,

[17] *CUP*, p. 52.

[18] *CUP*, p. 218.

[19] *CUP*, p. 80.

[20] *CUP*, p. 124.

[21] Kierkegaard, *The Sickness Unto Death* (Garden City, New York, 1954), pp. 173–74.

[22] *CUP*, pp. 139–40, 217–22.

[23] *CUP*, pp. 218–19.

[24] Cf. Kierkegaard, *Philosophical Fragments*, Chapter IV; also *Training in Christianity* (Princeton, 1947), Parts I and II.

dread, offense, or faith. The only "natural theology" in Kierkegaard is an extreme form of *via remotionis;* for example, his discussion in *Philosophical Fragments* of the annihilating encounter of human reason with the Absolute Paradox. Such "revealed theology" as there is is strangely lacking in an understanding of creation, redemption, grace, and sacrament; mystery and miracle—the awesome appearing of the infinite richness of the divine reality—are replaced by absurdity and paradox—the self-concealment of the divine in the form of unthinkable possibilities.

The Kierkegaardian individual, when he confronts God, meets Him by the most remote indirection, as an empty or contradictory X. The ethical reality of the individual, freedom tensed between its own passion and its own decision, is isolated not only from the reality of the world, but also from the reality of God.

I believe, therefore, that the Kierkegaardian rhetoric drives the individual, not to an encounter with the Absolute Reality and Power (*Qui Est, ipsum esse subsistens*), but only further back into his own inwardness. The effect of Kierkegaard's position is *to infinitize the freedom of the individual and thereby to absolutize human subjectivity*.

In the last chapter of *The Concept of Dread,* Kierkegaard explains the way in which dread, the experience of the nothingness of freedom, can become an instrument of salvation when taken up into an act of faith. Kierkegaard writes that

> in possibility everything is equally possible, and he who truly was brought up by possibility has comprehended the dreadful as well as the smiling. When such a person, therefore, goes out from the school of possibility, and knows more thoroughly than a child knows the alphabet that he can demand of life absolutely nothing, and that terror, perdition, annihilation, dwell next door to every man, and has learned the profitable lesson that every dread which alarms

may the next instant become a fact, he will then interpret reality differently, he will extol reality, and even when it rests upon him heavily he will remember that after all it is far, far lighter than the possibility was.[25]

And he adds that

if one is to learn absolutely, the individual must in turn have the possibility in himself and himself fashion that from which he is to learn, even though the next instant it does not recognize that it was fashioned by him, but absolutely takes the power from him.

But in order that the individual may thus absolutely and infinitely be educated by possibility, he must be honest towards possibility and must have faith. By faith I mean what Hegel in his fashion calls very rightly "the inward certainty which anticipates infinity." When the discoveries of possibility are honestly administered, possibility will then disclose all finitudes but idealize them in the form of infinity in the individual who is overwhelmed by dread, until in turn he conquers them by the anticipation of faith.[26]

It is clear from such utterances that Kierkegaard means what he says elsewhere in the same book, that "it is the supreme glory of freedom that it has only with itself to do."[27] But human freedom, thus absolutized, becomes indistinguishable from the omnipotence of God. Kierkegaardian freedom *does* generate its own possibilities; it *does* both obligate and tempt itself: how significant that Kierkegaard could "associate no definite thought with the serpent" in the myth of the Fall! For the serpent, he complains, "lets the temptation come from without."[28] Kierkegaardian

[25] *COD*, p. 140.
[26] *COD*, pp. 140–41.
[27] *COD*, p. 97.
[28] *COD*, p. 43.

freedom anguishes itself, makes itself guilty, and at last, by taking-in-advance (anticipating: *at tage forud*) all possibilities, it redeems itself from the perdition it has brought on itself. If it is not itself God, at least it has a handy purchase on the divine omnipotence.

Kierkegaard, like Hegel, operates exclusively in terms of two relations: identity and difference. Whatever is not wholly same is simply other; whatever is not wholly other is simply same. And so, for Kierkegaard as for Hegel, absolute opposition falls back into sameness. Between God (omnipotence) and man (freedom) there is an infinite gulf fixed. They have nothing in common, but for that very reason there is also nothing to distinguish them.

The absence in both Hegel and Kierkegaard of anything like a logic of analogy—a logic that recognizes multiple modes of sameness-in-difference—and the consequent lack in both of a conception such as the "chain of being" necessitate in both a collapse of the distinction between God and man. This indistinction of the finite from the infinite, a union Hegel labored consciously to achieve, occurs in Kierkegaard in spite of himself because he is enslaved to Hegel's dialectic even when he protests against it in the name of the "infinite qualitative difference."

It is not strange that Kierkegaard always formulates the relation of God and man as paradoxical identities: man's need of God is his highest perfection; the only existential evidence of God's love is suffering; the recoil of reason from God is its oneness with God's purposes; the only purity of heart is the consciousness of absolute impurity; the God-man is the historical event which on principle could not happen—and so on.

Now I do not wish to deny that there is a moment of absoluteness in human freedom: the capacity of man, recognized by Augustine and most other theologians, to utter a radical and final yes or a radical and final no to the claim and the grace of God. Nor would I deny that Kierkegaard is the connoisseur without peer of this religious crisis, with its terrible testimony to the reality of God—and its equally terrible temptation, *eritis sicut dii.* But it seems to me that his understanding of subjectivity often succumbs to the temptation, and confuses the *potentia absoluta divina* with human freedom in a way that is close to demonic.

Moreover—and this is just the other side of the demonia—his understanding of human subjectivity *trivializes existence and thereby destroys the very end his indirect rhetoric was intended to achieve.* Kierkegaard's ethical thought is involved in a basic self-contradiction: it makes impossible the very effect it was meant to establish. The Kierkegaardian individual is existentially—in his ethical reality—acosmic if not atheistic. He is infinitely free. But because it is without limitation—by the relative objectivity of the world or the absolute objectivity of God—his freedom is empty of everything but indeterminate possibilities.

In the Interlude of the *Philosophical Fragments,* Kierkegaard effectively shows that nothing really happens in a world without freedom. For if everything is necessary, then everything on principle already *is,* and the historical unfolding of events is a time lag of no essential or existential significance.

But now, from the passages just quoted from *The Concept of Dread,* with their apotheosis of freedom, the same conclusion follows. To the man educated in possibility by dread, nothing that happens in reality matters. Against a background of infinite possibility, every actuality is a matter of indifference. The man educated by dread has *so prepared himself* for *any* reality that *no* reality can overtake him and surprise him either with terror or with joy. Kierkegaard's man of faith is no less fatuous than his speculative philosopher. Both of them are fantastically outside existence. Both absolute freedom and total determinism render actuality superfluous.

This, I believe, is a contradiction in Kierkegaard's own thought, not a difficulty incident upon understanding him in a way external to his own concern. Kierkegaard begins, as we saw, by making in a large and vague way the assumptions of classical realism. It is only by means of such assumptions that he can initially dismiss all metaphysical objections as impertinent, and go on to enforce his ethical claim. His claim, however, is that the individual's inwardness is the only reality to which he has access as reality, and therefore the only reality that is ethically significant. Although the rhetoric presupposes and must presuppose a world as the condition of its own possibility, it ends by isolating the individual not *within* but *without* a world, just as effectively as if that world were not there—and indeed, for all ethical purposes it is not. The practice of the rhetoric of indirect communication demands a world; the end projected by the rhetoric—the inwardness of the individual—is worldless. But an inwardness so projected is not only in conflict with the strategy that urges it; it is at once demonic and effete. Kierkegaard's ethical thought, even in its religious dimension, rests on an acosmism as pretentious as the idealism of Hegel, an acosmism which, furthermore, drains existence of its terror, its passion, its risk, and its responsibility as surely as did the gnostic "System" against which he directed his polemic.

After all this I cannot be insensitive to the presence behind me, applauding enthusiastically and exclaiming, "Very good, young man! Very bravely protested. Why, this sounds almost like seriousness.—Just one little detail: haven't you missed the point after all? The point was really not man or God or the world or metaphysics. The point was—you. The difficulties *you* have finding a metaphysical consistency in my books. But that only shows that you are so absent-minded and fantastically *sub specie aeternitatis* that my indirect communication passed you by altogether—or else that in your own way you did get the point, however unimaginatively, but managed to turn it to your disadvantage. In which case, make the most of it. But your theoretical objections and your metaphysical contradictions don't bother me a bit."

"Now hold on there! Can you get off the hook so easily—just by saying you're not concerned? The whole point of my paper was to prove that you *must* be concerned."

"Well, I suppose if one is a serious-minded person, metaphysically and morally a responsible sort, a faithful husband and a good provider, and an ornament of his profession, one must be concerned for the implications of what he says. But suppose one is a wastrel who takes no responsibility, suppose one is a poet . . ."

And having spoken the magic word he disappears, as he always eludes any reader who wants to lay serious dialectical hands on him. Kierkegaard insists on having the last word. He *will* remain what he is, the poet of inwardness, forever vanishing behind one of an endless series of masks, never present *in propria persona* when you want to hold him accountable.

And does he not in his own way succeed in producing the effect he desires? If this analysis fails to dissect and expose Kierkegaard, is it not also true that Kierkegaard, by provoking the analysis, *has* led us through freedom to God and to an awareness of the ethical significance of the reality of the world? Such an awareness is neither given nor directly implied in his writing; quite the opposite, if the argument of this paper is valid. But is not this itself the supreme indirection of Kierkegaard, that he thrusts his readers away from him to seek the truth for themselves? By disappearing from the scene by assuming no responsibility for what he *does* imply, the poet returns his readers to their own situation and leaves them free for *any* implications.

It is not after all un-Kierkegaardian to find Kierkegaard "wrong." The nature of the "subjectivity" Kierkegaard was trying to communicate necessitated a peculiar kind of rhetoric. If poetry be defined as language centripetally drawn and self-contained, and rhetoric as centrifugal other-addressing speech, then it may be said that Kierkegaard's rhetoric had to exhaust itself in his poetry. Only the reader can address himself: subjectivity demands it.

And, finally, it must be remembered that Kierkegaard on his own admission is the "master of irony." Though he himself vanishes, his works remain to take their effect—ironically—by surviving the analysis that would destroy them.

CHRISTIANITY AND NONSENSE

Henry E. Allison

> My propositions serve as elucidations in the following
> way: anyone who understands me eventually recog-
> nizes them as nonsensical, when he has used them—as
> steps—to climb up beyond them. (He must, so to speak,
> throw away the ladder after he has climbed up it.)
> *Ludwig Wittgenstein.*

The *Concluding Unscientific Postscript* is generally regarded as the most philosophically significant of Kierkegaard's works. In terms of a subjectivistic orientation it seems to present both an elaborate critique of
the pretensions of the Hegelian philosophy and an
existential analysis which points to the Christian faith
as the only solution to the "human predicament." Furthermore, on the basis of such a straightforward reading of the text, Kierkegaard has been both vilified as
an irrationalist and praised as a profound existential
thinker who has uncovered the only legitimate starting
point for a philosophical analysis of the religious life
and a Christian apologetic.

The aim of this paper is to suggest that any such
reading involves a radical misunderstanding of Kierkegaard's intent. Given the supposition that the *Postscript* is to be regarded as a contribution to religious or
existential philosophy, the charge of irrationalism is
irrefutable. Viewed as an anti-idealistic philosophical
thesis, the "doctrine" that "truth is subjectivity" not
only leads to a consistent misologism, but also implies

This essay originally appeared in *The Review of Metaphysics*,
March 1967, Vol. XX, No. 3. It is reprinted with the kind permission of the author and the editor of *The Review of Metaphysics*.

the ultimate identification of Christianity and non-sense. However, when this result is understood in light of Johannes Climacus' (the pseudonymous author) self-proclaimed role as a humorist, and of the discussion of indirect communication and "double reflection" which is prefaced to the "argument," the doctrinal content of the work must be regarded as an ironical jest, which essentially takes the form of a carefully constructed parody of the *Phenomenology of Mind*. Moreover, the real purpose of this jest is not to convince the reader of a philosophical or religious truth, but to prevent him from theorizing, even in an "existential" sense about Christianity, and instead to help him to come to grips, in the isolation of his own subjectivity, with the question of what it means to become a Christian. Thus, far from being a contribution, good, bad or indifferent, to a philosophy of existence, the *Postscript* emerges as Kierkegaard's attempt at a *reductio ad absurdum* of any such enterprise.

1

The *Postscript* is essentially concerned with the problem of becoming a Christian. This is called the "subjective problem," and is sharply distinguished from the objective problem of the truth of the Christian religion. The latter question, which is the central concern of historical criticism and speculative philosophy, is rather cursorily dismissed with the reflection that an objective investigation of the historical claims of Christianity can never yield more than approximation (a certain degree of probability), and that any mere approximation is incommensurable with the "infinite personal interest in an eternal happiness" which characterizes a believing Christian. Furthermore, any such objective approach to Christianity is not only futile but perverse, for the disinterestedness demanded of an objective observer is diametrically opposed to the decisiveness and total commitment which constitutes the very essence of Christian faith.

This analysis of the two approaches to Christianity gives rise to the distinction between subjective and objective reflection, and it is within the framework of this distinction that the "argument" of the work unfolds. The tendency towards objective thought finds its culmination in Hegel. In the Hegelian philosophy we are shown the necessity of transcending our finite particularity and viewing things from the standpoint of the Idea. There one will come to see the unity of thought and being and the identity of subject and object. The goal of the *Phenomenology of Mind* is precisely to lead the individual along the "highway of despair," to see the inadequacy of all finite forms of consciousness, and eventually to the promised land of Absolute Spirit, where all finite oppositions are reconciled. From this standpoint it is encumbent upon the individual to "forget himself,"[1] in the sense of his finite particularity, to become disinterested in his personal existence and absorbed in the Idea.

It is precisely this viewpoint which is the main target of Climacus' attack. His basic objection, and here it must be remembered that this objection is directed as much against the Danish Hegelians, e.g., Heiberg and Martensen, as Hegel himself, is that this ultimate conformity of thought and being can never be realized by an existing human being, for it is precisely existence which keeps the moments of thought and being, of ideality and reality apart. Thus, the attempt to realize their union and to achieve the standpoint of pure thought necessarily involves the comical attempt to forget that one happens to be an existing human being. Climacus epitomizes this contention with the reflection that: "If the Hegelian philosophy has emancipated itself from every presupposition, it has won this freedom by means of one lunatic postulate: the initial transition to pure thought" (p. 279).

[1] Hegel, *The Phenomenology of Mind,* trans. by J. B. Baillie (London and New York, 1931), p. 130.

However, while the objective thinker tends to lose himself in his speculations, the subjectively oriented thinker "is essentially interested in his own thinking, existing as he does in his thought" (p. 67). This means that the subjective thinker is not concerned with the results yielded by disinterested reflection, but with the realization of the truth in his own existence. Objective reflection is concerned with "the matter at issue," i.e., whether a particular theory is true or false, but for the subjective thinker, his very subjectivity becomes "the matter at issue." Hence Climacus proclaims:

> This must constantly be borne in mind, namely that the subjective problem is not something about an objective issue, but is the subjectivity itself. For since the problem in question poses a decision, and since all decisiveness, as shown above, inheres in subjectivity, it is essential that every trace of an objective issue should be eliminated. If any such trace remains, it is at once a sign that the subject seeks to shirk something of the pain and crisis of the decision: that is, he seeks to make the problem to some degree objective. (p. 115)

With this the wedge is firmly placed between the two modes of reflection. They are not only heterogeneous, but incommensurable. Instead of the Hegelian both/and whereby the individual finds himself in the infinite after forgetting himself in the finite, Climacus offers the existential either/or wherein the forgetfulness of self, characteristic of speculative thought, is viewed as a fantastic flight from one's existential situation, and the authentic task of the subjective thinker is to "immerse himself in existence," i.e., to become increasingly conscious of his existential situation.

Climacus offers several illustrations of what he means by subjective reflection or becoming subjective, and perhaps the most illuminating of them is his analysis of the question: "What does it mean to die," wherein he clearly anticipates the well known discussion of Heidegger. Objectively, Climacus suggests, we know all sorts of things about death. We know, for instance, that we shall die if we swallow a dose of sulphuric acid or if we drown ourselves. We also know from history books that Napoleon always went about with poison ready at hand, and that in certain circumstances the Stoics regarded suicide as a courageous act. Furthermore, we are all aware of the fact that we will eventually die, and even that it might happen at any moment. Yet to possess all these items of information, to objectively recognize the inevitability and the uncertainty of death, is not to have understood it. Such understanding is radically different from understanding any item of information. It requires the ability to so exist that one regards death as an ever present possibility. This does not mean, however, that one simply acknowledges in passing that one must think about it at every moment, but that one really does so think about it. This intensity of subjective reflection is necessary according to Climacus, for

> . . . if I am a mortal creature, then it is impossible to understand this uncertainty in terms of a mere generality unless indeed I, too, happen to be merely a human being in general. . . . And if initially my human nature is merely an abstract something, it is at any rate the task which life sets me to become subjective; and in the same degree that I become subjective, the uncertainty of death comes more and more to interpenetrate my subjectivity dialectically. It thus becomes more and more important for me to think it in connection with every factor and phase of my life; for since this uncertainty is there in every moment, it can only be overcome by overcoming it in every moment. (p. 149)

2

This analysis of the two kinds of reflection leads Climacus to a consideration of the kind of truth ap-

propriate to each. From the point of view of objective
reflection, truth is viewed in the traditional manner as
the conformity of thought and being. The precise
meaning of this formula, however, is dependent upon
an understanding of "being." Here Climacus recognizes two possibilities: either "being" is understood as
real or empirical being or as ideal being. Because of
the uncertainty of all empirical generalizations (an uncertainty which is grounded for Climacus, as for Plato,
in the changing character of the world of sense), if
"being" is understood in the former sense (as empirical being) truth becomes a *desideratum,* something to
be approximated but never finally achieved by any
existing individual. (Hence "an existential system is
impossible.") If, however, it is understood in the latter
sense (as ideal being) its conformity with thought becomes an empty tautology, "an abstract self-identity."
In either case, however, the Hegelian attempt to mediate between thought and being must be rejected.
Such mediation may be valid *sub specie aeterni,* but
this is irrelevant to the poor existing individual, who
is "confined to the straitjacket of existence" and cannot attain that exalted standpoint.

What is needed, therefore, is an explanation of how
the eternal, i.e., ethico-religious, truth is to be understood by an existing individual, and this is provided
by the contention that truth lies in subjectivity. Since
objective reflection necessarily leads away from the
subject and culminates in a disinterested contemplation, a truth which is true for the subject, i.e., existentially relevant, can only be acquired through inwardness or subjective reflection:

> The subjective reflection turns its attention inwardly
> to the subject, and desires in this intensification of
> inwardness to realize the truth. And it proceeds in
> such fashion that, just as in the preceding objective
> reflection, when the objectivity had come into being,

the subjectivity had vanished, so here the subjectivity of the subject becomes the final stage and objectivity a vanishing factor. (pp. 175–76)

Now inwardness culminates in passion, and it is only in the moment of passion that an individual is able to existentially realize the union of the finite and the infinite which is the goal of the Hegelian dialectic. "In passion," Climacus contends, "the existing individual is rendered infinite in the eternity of the imaginative representation, and yet is at the same time most definitely himself" (p. 176). This unique quality of passion is grounded in its dual nature as both the culmination of inwardness and the means to self-transcendence. Because of this dual nature Climacus can regard the individual during the moment of passion as at the same time fully at one with himself and in a genuine relationship with God. This conception follows from Climacus' definition of inwardness as "the relationship of an individual to himself before God" (p. 391) and points to Kierkegaard's oft expressed conviction that man, as a "synthesis of the finite and the infinite" is only really at one with himself when he exists in full consciousness of his God-relationship. Finally, since he often describes an individual's "God-relationship" as a "possibility relationship" and God as "infinite possibility," and since he regards imagination as the organ of possibility in man, it follows that for Climacus the union of God and man, the finite and the infinite, can only take place in the imagination.[2]

From this it can be readily seen that subjective reflection provides the only possible approach to ethico-religious knowledge, which is the only knowledge that

[2] My interpretation of this passage, and especially the phrase "in the eternity of imaginative representation" (*i Phantasiens Evighed*) is indebted to Professor Louis Mackey of Rice University.

has "an essential relationship to the existence of the knower." However, whereas from the objective point of view reflection is directed towards the result of one's investigation, conceived of as a body of truth maintaining its validity apart from the individual's relationship to it, subjective reflection is directed towards the relationship itself, with the paradoxical result that "if only the mode of the relationship is in the truth, the individual is in the truth, even if he should happen to be related to what is not true" (p. 178). In other words, one can say that while objective reflection is directed towards the "what" or content of a doctrine, subjective reflection is concerned with the "how," the way in which it is existentially appropriated by the individual. Thus, it is the "passion of the infinite," or the genuineness of the commitment which is decisive, and not the specific nature of that to which one is committed. As an illustration of this Climacus utters the well-known, yet highly misleading dictum:

> If one who lives in the midst of Christendom goes up to the house of God, the house of the true God, with the true conception of God in his knowledge, and prays, but prays in a false spirit; and one who lives in an idolatrous community prays with the entire passion of the infinite, although his eyes rest upon the image of an idol: where is there more truth? The one prays in truth to God though he worships an idol; the other prays falsely to the true God, and hence worships in fact an idol. (pp. 179–80)

This statement is misleading because it appears to endorse the unqualified rejection of the "what" of belief in favor of the "how," with the obvious implication that it is better to be a "true," passionately committed Nazi than to be a lukewarm Christian. This, however, is not Climacus' intent, and he goes to great lengths to obviate any such misunderstanding. First, he endeavors to distinguish between true inwardness and madness. Climacus points to Don Quixote as the prototype of "subjective madness," and argues that the basic characteristic of such madness is the concentration of one's passion upon a particular finite object, an *idée fixe*. Thus, madness becomes characterized as an "aberrant inwardness," wherein one becomes infinitely concerned over something which is of no decisive significance. In contrast with this, true inwardness is always directed towards the infinite, i.e., towards one's God-relationship, and, Climacus concludes: "At its maximum this inward 'how' is the passion of the infinite, and the passion of the infinite is the truth. But the passion of the infinite is precisely subjectivity, and thus subjectivity becomes the truth" (p. 181).

Second, and most important, this passionate "how" is so qualified that Christianity, as the ultimate "what," becomes its only satisfactory correlate, and thus, what began as an attack upon objective reflection, ends up as a rather peculiar "demonstration" of the subjective truth of Christianity. This is not accomplished, however, by an immediate reconciliation of the "how" and the "what," the commitment and its object, but by further accentuating their opposition, thereby suggesting an eventual *coincidentia oppositorum*. The basic premise of this "argument" is Climacus' contention: "An objective uncertainty held fast in an appropriation process of the most passionate inwardness is the truth, the highest truth attainable for an existing individual" (p. 182).

This definition of truth which, Climacus tells us, is an equivalent expression for faith determines the opposition between subjective and objective reflection, "the fork in the road where the way swings off." Just as the scientific quest for objective truth requires the rejection of all subjective or private interests, so "when subjectivity is the truth, *the conceptual determination of the truth must include an expression for the antithesis to objectivity*" (p. 182). Thus, there is a direct correlation between objective uncertainty and subjective truth, the objective uncertainty serving to increase "the tension of that infinite passion which is inwardness." When systematically applied such a conception leads to a radical misologism, and as we shall see, this is precisely the direction in which the discussion proceeds.

Climacus had begun his analysis of subjectivity by arguing quite cogently that the decisiveness of religious or ethical commitment is incompatible with the disinterested reflection of objective thought. Thus, one can neither speculate one's way into Christianity, nor treat the content of Christian faith in a speculative manner, à la Hegel, without completely perverting its very essence. However, where St. Thomas Aquinas was content to point out that one cannot know and believe the same thing at the same time, and where Kant sought to deny knowledge in order to make room for faith, Climacus argues for a direct relationship between theoretical implausibility and religious faith. Thus Climacus can assert: "Faith is precisely the contradiction between the infinite passion of the individual's inwardness and the objective uncertainty." Moreover, since such objective uncertainty is the inevitable lot of all existing beings, the attempt to deny it can only be regarded as absentmindedness, and thus the true believer "must constantly be intent upon holding fast the objective uncertainty, so as to remain out upon the deep, over seventy thousand fathoms of water . . . still preserving his faith" (pp. 182–83).

Armed with this conception of truth, Climacus returns to the problem of his earlier work, the *Philosophical Fragments:* the question of the relationship between the Socratic and the specifically Christian religiosity. Both here and in the *Fragments* Socrates is viewed by Climacus as the very prototype of the subjective or existential thinker outside of Christianity. His great merit over against both Plato and the modern speculative thinkers is that he never forgets that he is an existing individual, but rather "concentrates essentially upon existence."

The heart of Socratic thought is to be found in the notion that the truth lies within. As Climacus tells us in the *Fragments*: "In the Socratic view each individual is his own center, and the entire world centers in his views, his self-knowledge is a knowledge of God" (p. 14). Thus, the task confronting a Socratic thinker is to become subjective, in the sense of continually realizing in existence his God-relationship. This, according to Climacus, is the profound significance of Socrates' doctrine that knowledge is recollection, and which clearly differentiates it from the speculative use made of that doctrine by Plato. Existentially understood it means that the knower is potentially in possession of the eternal truth, i.e., his God-relationship, and is confronted with no difficulty other than the fact that he exists. This minor difficulty, however, turns out to be decisive, and provides the clue to understanding Socrates' frequent professions of ignorance. This ignorance is viewed by Climacus as a consequence of the previously established contention that for one engaged in the business of existing, the eternal truth remains objectively uncertain. Moreover, since a total commitment is demanded to what is objectively uncertain, Climacus contends that from the point of view of the existing individual the truth becomes a paradox. This paradox was thoroughly grasped by Socrates, who totally committed himself to the truth despite his recognition of its objective uncertainty (the manner in which he faced death in the *Phaedo* being Climacus' favorite illustration), and for this reason: "Socrates was in the truth by virtue of his ignorance, in the highest sense in which this was possible within paganism" (p. 183).

But paganism is not Christianity, and although Climacus points to the analogies between Socratic inwardness and Christian faith, his main goal seems to be to show the superiority of the latter. The basic limitation of the Socratic position lies in the theory of recollection. This theory has a two-fold existential significance. First, as was shown in the *Fragments,* it clearly implies that neither an historical event nor another person can have any decisive significance for an existing individual. Since the truth lies within, one person can do no more than provide the occasion whereby another comes to recollect it (the slave boy incident in the *Meno* being the paradigm case), and thus the maieutic relationship is the highest possible between men. Second, because the truth lies within, temporal existence lacks any ultimate seriousness, for the possibility of "taking oneself back into eternity through recollection is always there" (p. 184). To be sure, Socrates with his passionate inwardness did not make use of this possibility, but according to Climacus its very presence serves to mitigate the seriousness of his inwardness.

This limitation raises the question of the possibility of a higher level of inwardness. Since the limitation of the Socratic position stems from the contention that the individual is initially in possession of the truth, any deeper expression of inwardness or subjectivity must involve a denial of this possession. However, the denial that the individual is in possession of the truth is *eo ipso* a denial of the contention that truth is subjectivity, and thus we are led by the inexorable "logic" of Climacus to the paradoxical conclusion that the deepest possible expression of the notion that subjectivity is truth, is precisely the proposition that subjectivity is untruth. This, however, is not to be understood as implying a regression to the speculative standpoint, wherein subjectivity is also untruth, for the decisive characteristic of this level of ultimate inwardness is that here "subjectivity is beginning upon the task of becoming the truth through a subjectifying process, is in the difficulty that it is already untruth" (pp. 185-86). The result is not the abandonment, but the further accentuation of existence, and hence of inwardness. The subject cannot be regarded as eternally being in untruth, as this would apparently imply that he was created thusly by God, nor does it make sense to regard the loss of the "eternal essential truth" as the result of an unfortunate accident. Thus, the only explanation for the loss is that the individual brought himself into the condition in time, by a free act. If, however, the individual has in fact cut himself off from the eternal by a free act then the pathos of his existential condition is accentuated to the utmost possible degree.

Now it just so happens that this is precisely how Christianity, with its doctrine of original sin, views the human condition. From the Christian standpoint a man is born in sin and as a sinner. Thus, in contradistinction to the Socratic man who has access to the eternal by way of recollection, the Christian is profoundly aware of his alienation from the eternal, a situation poignantly depicted in Hegel's analysis of the "Unhappy Conscience." Furthermore, Climacus reflects: "If it was paradoxical to posit the eternal truth in relationship to an existing individual, it is now absolutely paradoxical to posit it in relationship to such an individual as we have here defined" (p. 186).

However, this is exactly what Christianity proclaims to have taken place through the entrance of God into history as the Christ. Thus, if for Socrates the paradox is to be found in the relationship between the eternal truth and the existing individual, for the Christian the eternal truth itself is inherently paradoxical. This is because for the Christian the eternal (decisive truth) is precisely that the eternal truth (God) has come into being in time. Hence, what for Socrates remained an objective uncertainty is for the Christian an objective absurdity: "The absurd is that the eternal truth has come into being in time, that God has come into being, has been born, has grown up, and so forth, precisely like any other individual human being, quite indistinguishable from other individuals" (p. 188).

This absurdity is the content of the Christian faith,

the "what" corresponding to the "how" of Christian inwardness. It is the absolute paradox, or the paradox *sensu eminentiori* to which the Socratic paradox and its corresponding inwardness bear only a remote analogy. Since the starting point of the whole discussion was the affirmation of the direct correlation between objective uncertainty and inwardness, "the less objective security the more profound the possible inwardness," it would appear that it is only when the "what" becomes objectively absurd, and the more absurd the better, that the maximum degree of inwardness is attainable. Now since the requisite absurdity is found in the content of Christian faith, we are led to the conclusion that Christianity is the source of the maximum possible inwardness, and thus can be regarded as the "true" religion (subjectively understood), not in spite of, but precisely because of its objective absurdity! For, in Climacus' own words: "The absurd is precisely by its objective repulsion the measure of the intensity of faith in inwardness" (p. 189).

Despite the protest of several recent commentators this position must be regarded as radically irrationalistic.[3] The "argument" as it stands, with its explicit correlation between objective absurdity and subjective "truth" is clearly an expression of a consistent misologism or an "intellectualistic anti-intellectualism"[4] which

---

[3] Cf. the essays of James Collins, Cornelio Falio and N. H. Søe in *A Kierkegaard Critique*, ed. by Howard A. Johnson and Niels Thustrup (New York, 1962) and Heywood Thomas, *Subjectivity and Paradox* (New York, 1957). The interpretation of these commentators is also attacked along similar lines by H. M. Garelick in his *The Anti-Christianity of Kierkegaard* (The Hague, 1965).

[4] This frequently reiterated charge seems to have been most explicitly formulated in relation to the *Postscript* by Thorsten Bohlen in *Kierkegaard's tro och Kierkegaard-Studies* (Copenhagen, 1944). For a discussion of Bohlen's position see Søe's "Kierkegaard's Doctrine of the Paradox" in *A Kierkegaard Critique*, pp. 208–10. A similar position is very forcibly argued

finds its closest historical antecedent in the *"credo quia absurdum"* attributed to Tertullian. However, just as Hegel's panlogism differs from the pre-Kantian rationalism of a Leibniz or Spinoza by virtue of its dialectical structure, so Climacus' misologism can be viewed as an irrationalistic revision of the Hegelian schema. Thus, while Hegel rejects the absolute starting point of his predecessors and begins instead with the immediate, viewing absolute knowledge as the goal to be obtained through the demonstration of the inadequacy of all finite forms ("Of the Absolute it must be said that it is essentially a result."), Climacus, in his endeavor "to make the necessity of the paradox evident" (p. 191), begins with an analysis of the inadequacy of all lower stages of inwardness. This analysis, which traces the spiritual life of the individual, rather than the life of Absolute Spirit, from the lowest level, aesthetic immediacy, to the highest non-Christian expression, infinite resignation, and the consciousness of guilt before God, occupies the bulk of the *Postscript;* but its main purpose, (suggested by the name Climacus) is to lead the individual up the dialectical ladder of inwardness to the point at which he can appreciate the uniqueness and absoluteness, as well as the absurdity of the Christian faith. Hence, one can say that for Hegel's conception of the necessary advance of the Spirit to absolute knowledge, Climacus substitutes the equally necessary (albeit in a different sense) advance of subjectivity to absolute paradox.

The necessity of this advance for the spiritual development of the individual is demonstrated by means of a further comparison of the Socratic and Christian forms of religiousness, here entitled A and B, or the "religiousness of immanence" and "paradoxical religiousness" respectively. The former is characterized by a "dying away from immediacy," the repudiation,

by Richard Kroner in "Kierkegaard's Hegelverstandnis," *Kant-Studien,* Bd. 46, Heft 1, 1954–55, pp. 19–27.

or at least relativization of all one's finite concerns, and the devotion of all one's energies to the realization of one's "absolute telos," a phrase applied to both the individual's God-relationship and his eternal happiness, which seem to be identical for Climacus. Since the presupposition of this level of inwardness is the belief that the truth lies within, the individual is viewed as already potentially in possession of his God-relationship or eternal happiness, and his task is simply to transform his mode of existence so as to become in truth what he already is potentially. Hence, Climacus calls this level the "dialectic of inward transformation" (p. 494). The task of self-transformation, however, is soon shown to be far more difficult than it first appeared. Since this "dying away from immediacy" or "infinite resignation," cannot be accomplished once and for all, but must be undertaken at every instant, such a mode of existence essentially involves suffering. Moreover, since that which must be continually begun anew can never be completed, the decisive expression for this form of religiousness is the consciousness of guilt. This consciousness of guilt, the awareness of being in the wrong over and against God, is the highest development of the religiousness of inwardness, and we are thus led to the paradoxical conclusion that the deepest expression of the individual's God-relationship is to be found in the consciousness of the disrelationship.

It is at this point that the parallelism with Hegel once again becomes manifest. Just as the *Phenomenology of Mind* showed that one must traverse the "highway of despair" and experience the shipwreck of all finite forms of understanding before he is able to grasp the standpoint of the Absolute, so for Climacus, it is only the individual who has existentially striven to realize his God-relationship and has been shipwrecked upon the consciousness of guilt for whom the absolute paradox becomes meaningful. "Religiousness A," Climacus contends, "must be present in the individual before there can be any question of becoming aware of the dialectic of B" (p. 494). Only when existential pathos has reached its decisive expression in the consciousness of guilt can the venture into the absurd become an existential possibility. Just as it is the consciousness of the path which distinguishes the Hegelian conception of absolute knowledge from the dogmatic pretensions of his predecessors, for Climacus it is precisely the presence of this prior consciousness which distinguishes the venture into the absurd from superstition.

This implies that any speculative interpretation of the paradox involves a misunderstanding. The difficulty involved in becoming a Christian is not the intellectual difficulty of understanding how the eternal can be reconciled with the temporal, but the existential difficulty of committing oneself to the belief that one's eternal happiness is based upon something historical, and moreover, something historical which by its very nature cannot become historical. Such a commitment involves the complete sacrifice of one's reason, both theoretical and practical, for in addition to being inherently contradictory, the absolute paradox also violates the ethical integrity of the individual in that it places the locus of his eternal destiny in something external to him. The problem of the relationship between the ethical and the paradoxically religious modes of existence is one of the most interesting, yet generally ignored aspects of Climacus' analysis. Nevertheless he takes great pains to depict the proper relationship between them. The analogy, he argues, between faith and the ethical mode of existence is to be found in the "infinite interest" or "inwardness which distinguishes both from an aesthetic mode of existence." But the believer differs from the ethicist in being infinitely interested in the reality of another, i.e., in the fact that God has existed in time" (p. 288).

This, Climacus asserts, can only be believed against the understanding, so that the believer's task is not to understand the paradox, but to understand that it cannot be understood. However, in view of the elaborate dialectical analysis which prepares the way for the apprehension of the paradox, it would seem that this itself requires a good deal of understanding, and is well beyond the ken of the "simple believer" whom Climacus is always praising at the expense of the pretentious speculative philosopher. This is no doubt the justification for those who regard the position of the *Postscript* as an "intellectual anti-intellectualism," and Climacus himself seems to admit as much when he proclaims that it is after all necessary for the Christian to make use of his understanding, "precisely in order to believe against his understanding" (p. 504).

Thus, the dialectical ascent to faith culminates in the "crucifixion of the understanding" (p. 500). Here, at the highest level of the spiritual life we encounter a total break with immanence. The individual has gone through the process of "infinite resignation," and has come to the realization of the shipwreck of his own resources, both intellectual and moral. His consciousness of sin makes him fully aware of his alienation from God and the hopelessness of his situation. Yet he nevertheless clings passionately to the absurd, and, so Christianity tells us, finds therein his salvation.

Climacus' analysis of subjectivity has thus brought us to the point where we can indeed recognize "the necessity of the paradox" in that we can see that its acceptance through an act of faith is the only solution to the human predicament. Moreover, with this insight we are also able to apprehend the return of objectivity. The analysis of the "how" has led us inevitably to the "what" of Christianity as its only true correlate, as the only content capable of satisfying the "passion of the infinite." Objectivity and subjectivity are reconciled in the inwardness of faith in a manner strangely reminiscent of the speculative reconciliation of consciousness and its object at the end of the *Phenomenology of Mind,* and Climacus is rapidly emerging as a rather queer sort of Hegelian. The essence of Climacus' position is to be found in a passage near the end of the work where the relationship between the how and the what is explicitly formulated.

> The thing of being a Christian is not determined by the what of Christianity but by the *how* of the Christian. This *how* can only correspond with one thing the absolute paradox. There is therefore no vague talk to the effect that being a Christian is to accept, and to accept, and to accept quite differently, to appropriate, to believe, to appropriate by faith quite differently (all of them purely rhetorical and fictitious definitions); but to *believe* is specifically different from all other appropriation and inwardness. Faith is the objective uncertainty due to the repulsion of the absurd held fast by the passion of inwardness, which in this instance is intensified to the utmost degree. This formula fits only the believer, no one else, not a lover, not an enthusiast, not a thinker, but simply and solely the believer who is related to the absolute paradox. (p. 540)

With this Climacus' conviction of the uniqueness and incommensurability of the Christian faith with all other levels of inwardness receives its decisive expression. It thus is not true that it does not matter what one believes as long as one believes it with sufficient inwardness, for the only thing that can really be believed, i.e., truly appropriated with the "passion of the infinite" is the absolute paradox. This aspect of Climacus' position is clearly expressed by Kierkegaard himself, who in a Journal entry for the year 1849, writes:

> In all that is usually said about Johannes Climacus being purely subjective and so on, people have forgotten, in addition to everything else concrete about him, that in one of the last sections he shows that

the curious thing is: that there is a "how" which has
this quality, that if *it* is truly given, that the "what"
is also given; and that it is the "how" of "faith."
Here, quite certainly, we have inwardness at its maximum proving to be objectivity once again. And this
is an aspect of the principle of subjectivity which, so
far as I know, has never before been presented or
worked out.[5]

3

Viewed in the usual manner as an argument for the
uniqueness, absoluteness and "subjective truth" of the
Christian faith, Climacus' "apologetic" must be regarded as an utter failure. In terms of his misologistic
orientation the "subjective truth" of Christianity is a
function of the absurdity of its objective content. It is
only because of the "repulsion of the absurd" that
Christianity is able to intensify inwardness to the "utmost degree," and it is thus its very absurdity which
allegedly qualifies it as the only "what" corresponding
to the ultimate "how." But at this point the question
inevitably suggests itself to us in our misguided role as
objective thinkers: why this particular absurdity?
Granted, for the sake of argument, that the belief that
our eternal happiness is based upon an objective absurdity is necessary to raise the passion of the religious
individual to its highest level, but does that really serve
to prove that Christianity is the only absurdity which
can really be *believed* (in the strong Climacian sense)?
At the most this would seem to show that the passionate acceptance of Jesus of Nazareth as the Christ requires the highest level of inwardness, but so, it seems,
would the acceptance of the claim of any of an untold
number of deluded fanatics who have believed that
they were God. Moreover, if Christianity is really as
absurd as Climacus contends, if becoming a Christian

---

[5] *The Journals of Søren Kierkegaard*, ed. by Alexander Dru
(London, 1931), No. 528.

really does require a "crucifixion of the understanding,"
then it is hard to see what criteria we could find to
distinguish between this saving absurdity, and plain
"garden variety" nonsense. Once the understanding is
crucified in the radical manner which Climacus suggests, it is clearly no easy task to resurrect it.

Yet perhaps we are jumping to conclusions.
Climacus does in fact attempt to distinguish between
the absurdity of the absolute paradox and mere nonsense. The problem is discussed in passing in the *Fragments*. There he distinguishes between the paradox,
and the, to him, nonsensical belief that Christ's initial
disciples stood in a special relationship to him, that
they received the "condition," i.e., the inner witness
of the Holy Spirit which makes faith possible, directly
from him, and that they in turn were able to give this
"condition" to the next generation of disciples. This
view, which bears a curious analogy to the Roman
Catholic and Grundtvigian conceptions of the Church
as an objective authority and means of grace is distinguished from the paradox in that it is not only absurd, but self-contradictory, for it holds that "God is
the God for the contemporary, but that the contemporary is God for the third party" (p. 27). Now, this
would seem to suggest that the paradox differs from
other absurdities in not containing a contradiction, but
as we shall see, this hardly jibes with the analysis in
the *Postscript*.

Again, in the *Postscript,* Climacus endeavors to distinguish between Christian faith and superstition or
aestheticism, which may be regarded as a kind of nonsense. This is accomplished by means of an analysis
of the dialectical structure of faith in its relationship
to religiousness A:

> In case religiousness A does not come into the pic-
> ture as *terminus a quo* for the paradoxical religious-
> ness, religiousness A is higher than B, for then the
> paradox, the absurd etc., are not to be taken *sensu*

eminenti (in the sense that they absolutely cannot be understood either by clever or by stupid people), but are used aesthetically of the marvelous among other marvelous things, which are indeed marvelous, but which after all can be comprehended. (p. 496)

Thus, to base my hopes for eternity upon my red hair, believing that this color is particularly pleasing to the gods, is the lowest form of paganism, totally lacking in inwardness. It is a rather superficial application of the aesthetic category of fortune, something at which the subjective thinker who has striven with all his passion to realize his relationship to the eternal could only laugh (or perhaps cry?). Now this is quite true, but it is also the case, as Climacus points out, that Christianity itself bears "a certain resemblance" to aesthetics:

Religiousness B is discriminative, selective and polemical: only upon a definite condition do I become blessed, and as I absolutely bind myself to this condition, so do I exclude every other man who does not thus bind himself. This is the incentive to particularism in universal pathos. Every Christian possesses the pathos of religiousness A, and then this pathos of discrimination. This discrimination imports to the Christian a certain resemblance to one who is fortunate through favor, and when it is so conceived selfishly by a Christian we have the desperate presumption of predestination. (p. 516)

This resemblance is, however, according to Climacus, misleading. The fact that his happiness is based upon something historical, he contends, "makes the Christian's happiness or good fortune recognizable by suffering," and as a consequence, "the religious determinant of being God's elect is as paradoxically contrary as possible to being a Pamphilius of fortune . . ." (p. 516). But is it really? The essential difference between the Christian and the superstitious pagan is that the former believes "against his understanding" in full consciousness of its absurdity, and hence with suffering, while the latter (our red-headed Pamphilius of fortune) simply affirms his good fortune with a naive self-confidence. Now this certainly serves to distinguish between the "way" of believing or the levels of inwardness of the Christian and the pagan, but it hardly enables us to make any judgments concerning the *contents* of their respective beliefs. According to Climacus' analysis it would seem that they both believe absurdities, with the rather dubious advantage of the Christian being simply his awareness of the absurdity of his belief.

Finally, we must consider the passage in the *Postscript* where Climacus specifically endeavors to distinguish between the absurdity of Christianity and nonsense. As we have seen, Climacus argues that the proper use of understanding for a Christian is to make sure that he believes against his understanding. From this he concludes:

> Nonsense therefore he cannot believe against the understanding, for precisely the understanding will discern that it is nonsense and will prevent him from believing it; but he makes so much use of the understanding that he becomes aware of the incomprehensible, and then he holds to this, believing against the understanding. (p. 504)

This passage has been cited as evidence against the charge that Kierkegaard is an irrationalist, and it is suggested that Christianity is here distinguished from nonsense as being (in terms of the traditional distinction) above rather than contrary to reason.[6] It is clear, however, that such a contention hardly fits the argument of the *Postscript*. In addition to the fact that

---

[6] Søe in *A Kierkegaard Critique*, p. 290.

Climacus constantly emphasizes the need to believe against the understanding, rather than merely something which transcends it, the whole analysis of the *Postscript* is geared to showing the contradictory nature of the paradox. Traditionally, the realm of the *supra rationem* was held to be incomprehensible for the finite understanding, but not inherently contradictory. It was, for instance, precisely in terms of this distinction that Leibniz endeavored to reconcile faith and reason in the *Theodicée*. Climacus, however, maintains that the paradox contains not one, but two "dialectical contradictions": first the basing of one's eternal happiness upon the reality of something historical, the contradiction here being between the approximate nature of all historical knowledge, and the total commitment demanded by faith; and second, the "fact that this historical datum is compounded in a way contradictory to all thinking . . ." (p. 513).

It is true that these contradictions are called "dialectical," and the first instance at least this seems to suggest a juxtaposition of incongruous concepts, a kind of "category mistake," rather than a simple logical inconsistency. In the second instance, however, where the reference to the fact that the historical datum is one which by its very nature cannot become historical, is clearly a case of logical contradiction, and thus we are led once again to the recognition of the irrationality of the paradox.

With this we are back to our original question: If the paradox here viewed simply as "the incomprehensible" is indeed irrational and even contradictory, how is this peculiar kind of irrationality to be distinguished from mere nonsense? According to the cited passage this distinction is recognized by the understanding of the believer, but this raises two fundamental difficulties. The first is again the oft mentioned problem of criteria. Climacus has so strongly emphasized the absurdity of the paradox that it would seem that any effort to distinguish its objective content from mere nonsense is bound to fail. One could, of course, retort that these objective considerations are irrelevant, and that it is its subjective or existential significance for the believer which distinguishes the paradox from nonsense. This, however, gets us nowhere, for it amounts to the admission that *objectively* there are no criteria, and hence that the only difference between Christianity and nonsense is that the former happens to be taken seriously by some individuals while the latter is not. Moreover, we must remember that according to Climacus the distinction is recognized by the understanding. But if this is indeed the case, has not objectivity once again reared its ugly head in a decisive, albeit a perverse manner? From the standpoint of subjective reflection, with its direct correlation between subjective truth and objective uncertainty, would not the recognition, assuming it could be made, that "the incomprehensible" is not nonsense, actually serve as a check, rather than an inducement to inwardness? The only way to avoid this conclusion, and to distinguish between the paradox and mere nonsense, would be to suggest that the former is in some sense even more irrational than the latter. This would mean, however, that for the Hegelian demand to go beyond faith, Climacus is substituting the rather dubious demand to go beyond nonsense!

Secondly, and even more fundamental, Climacus' contention that the understanding will discern nonsense and *prevent* one from believing it, while a reasonable enough statement, stands in blatant contradiction to the distinction between will and intellect, subjectivity and objectivity, which is central to his whole "doctrine." In discussing the problem of historical knowledge in the *Fragments,* Climacus draws attention to the uncertainty involved in all statements about the past. Arguing against the Hegelian conception of history as the necessary process of Spirit in the world, he contends that since the past has come into existence it "has the elusiveness which is implicit in all coming into existence" and thus cannot be regarded as necessary. Now if this be the case, Climacus continues, "the organ for the historical must have an analogous structure. It must comprise a corresponding somewhat by which it may repeatedly negate in its certainty the uncertainty that corresponds to the uncertainty of coming into existence." This condition is met by faith or belief (*Tro*) because as an act of the will "there is always present a negated uncertainty, in every way corresponding to the uncertainty of coming into existence" (pp. 100–1). Furthermore, precisely the same reflection is applicable to doubt, the negative correlate of belief. According to Climacus the radical doubt of the Greek sceptics was not the result of cognition, but a free act of the will, and on this basis he argues against both Descartes and Hegel that doubt cannot be overcome by reflection but only "by a free act of the will" (p. 102). However, if belief and doubt are viewed as acts of will, and as such sharply distinguished from forms of knowledge, it seems rather difficult to see just how our understanding of anything, even nonsense, could "prevent" our belief.

Moreover, lest one suppose that our pseudonymous author has changed his position in the later work, we can readily see that the whole critique of the objective approach to Christianity in the *Postscript* is dependent upon the distinction between the decisiveness of will characteristic of Christian faith, and the disinterestedness of speculative understanding. It is on this basis that Climacus is able to argue that religious commitment (subjectivity) does not follow as a matter of course from objective considerations, but requires a "leap." But if an act of will, a religious commitment, necessarily involves a break with the understanding, how can one maintain that intellectual considerations, i.e., the recognition that something is nonsensical, can "prevent us from believing it"? If belief really is an act of the will, which by its very nature involves a "leap" beyond the understanding, then far from inhibiting belief, the recognition of the nonsensical character of a doctrine would seem to provide an inducement to inwardness, and hence be a potential source of "subjective truth." Thus, we are led to the conclusion that not only does Climacus' misologism fail to provide criteria in terms of which the understanding can distinguish between the Christian absurd and nonsense, but that even if such criteria were available they would be irrelevant to the "subjective thinker."

4

We have attempted to find within the *Postscript* a relatively straightforward albeit bizarre argument for the "subjective truth" and uniqueness of the Christian faith, and we have come to the conclusion that viewed as such it is a colossal failure. Yet this conclusion raises more problems than it solves. The argument appears to be so bad that we can question whether it could have been seriously meant. Thus, we find ourselves confronted with a decision, which Kierkegaard would no doubt have found amusing: either we must dismiss him as an extremely muddleheaded thinker, who in opting for a subjectivist position, tried and failed to posit criteria in terms of which we can distinguish between Christianity and nonsense, or we shall have to make a new and more strenuous effort to come to grips with that enigma called Kierkegaard.

Now even apart from a consideration of Kierkegaard's frequent but not overly consistent treatment of the question of the precise status of the Christian absurd in his other writings, it is apparent from the structure of the work, its pseudonymous character, and the *First and Last Declaration* which Kierkegaard appended to it in his own name, that such a straightforward, undialectical reading of the *Postscript* involves a serious misunderstanding. As is well known, Kierkegaard proclaims in this "Declaration" that none of the teachings of the pseudonymous are to be regarded as his.

> So in the pseudonymous works there is not a single word which is mine, I have no opinion about these

> works except as a third person, no knowledge of their
> meaning except as a reader, not the remotest pri-
> vate relation to them, since such a thing is impossible
> in the case of a doubly reflected communication.

This is no doubt somewhat of an overstatement,
and is to some extent contradicted by his analysis of
his authorship in *The Point of View,* but it does provide us with an important clue for understanding the
Postscript. Let us begin then with a consideration of
the character of the pseudonymous author. The name,
Johannes Climacus, is that of a sixth century monk
of the monastery at Sinai, and the surname was derived from the title of his work: *Scala Paradisi.* Thus,
Kierkegaard's use of the pseudonym clearly suggests
the notion of climax, or ascent from purely human to
specifically Christian categories. It has been suggested
that the pseudonym represents Kierkegaard's own attitude during his student days at the University.[7] But
within the context of the *Postscript* he repeatedly describes himself as a non-Christian humorist who is
concerned with the subjective problem of how to become a Christian. This raises the question: to what
extent are Climacus' external, i.e., non-Christian perspective and humoristic orientation reflected in the
structure of the work?

Climacus defines humor as a boundary stage between the ethical and religious modes of existence,
corresponding on a higher level to irony, which is the
boundary between the aesthetic and the ethical. The
essential quality of the humorist is his ability to recognize contradiction, and specifically the contradiction
between the inwardness of the religious life and all its
outward manifestations. The humorist, Climacus
contends,

[7] T. H. Croxall, *Assessment,* prefaced to his translation of
Johannes Climacus, or *De Omnibus Dubitandum Est* (Stanford, California, 1958), pp. 18–19.

. . . sets the God-idea into conjunction with other things and evokes the contradiction—but he does not maintain a relationship to God in terms of religious passion *stricte sic dictus,* he transforms himself instead into a jesting and yet profound exchange-center for all these transactions, but he does not himself stand related to God. (p. 451)

Thus, the humorist knows something about the existential difficulties of the God-relationship. He is able to recognize objectivistic or superstitious perversions of this relationship, but he comprehends in an intellectual, i.e., objective, sort of way, what the believer appropriates existentially. Since the God-relationship lies in subjectivity, his very awareness of the difficulties of such a relationship requires a certain degree of inwardness, but since he does not himself make the "leap," but rather withdraws into the realm of jest, he is obviously lacking the decisiveness of the truly committed person. Now given Climacus' own description of the stance of the humorist *vis-à-vis* Christianity, one would expect to find this reflected in his own analysis of faith, i.e., one would expect this analysis to be in its very essence humorous, and therefore to some extent objective.

The humorous aspect of the argument is suggested by the curious parallelism to Hegel, and this suggestion is further strengthened by a Journal entry wherein Kierkegaard writes: "Hegel is a Johannes Climacus, who did not, like the giants, storm the heavens by setting mountain upon mountain, but entered by means of his syllogisms."[8] Thus, both Hegel and Climacus are stormers of the heavens, searchers for the Absolute, and the main difference between them lies in their respective routes to this exalted goal. The one proceeds by way of speculative philosophy, the other by

[8] *Papirer,* II A 335, Thulstrup's Commentary, *Philosophical Fragments,* 2nd ed. (Princeton, 1962), p. 148.

means of "the principle of subjectivity." Yet both attempts are equally futile, for despite the difference of their approaches, they both end up at the same place, viz., the identification of Christianity and nonsense. This follows for Hegel because the attempt to mediate between philosophy and Christianity destroys the decisiveness which is the very essence of the Christian faith, and it follows for Climacus because the attempt to locate the paradox on a scale of subjectivity, undercuts any possible means of determining the uniqueness of the Christian absurd.

In light of these considerations is it outlandish to view the whole "argument" of Climacus as a kind of perverse parody of Hegel? The dialectical structure of the analysis, and the "objective" concern for the ultimate reconciliation of the "how" and the "what" in Christian faith, which parallels the culmination of the *Phenomenology of Mind* in Spirit's consciousness of itself as Spirit, the reconciliation of subject and object in Absolute knowledge, certainly suggests such an interpretation. Moreover, this reading enables us to view the "argument" of the humorous Climacus as a jest, and thus, to overlook the philosophical absurdity of his position. But it naturally gives rise to the question: what is the point of the jest? Why should Kierkegaard's critique of Hegel take the form of a parody? Is he simply playing with us, or is he perhaps asking us to reconsider the possibility raised by the failure of Jacobi and Lavater to understand Lessing's earnestness: "unless it should happen to be the case that one cannot understand earnestness without understanding jest" (p. 66)?

The answer, if it is to be found, may very well lie in Kierkegaard's conception of the problem of existential communication, and the recognition of the need for such communication to employ indirection and "double reflection." This possibility becomes very appealing when we recall that in his "Declaration" Kierkegaard characterized his pseudonymous works as examples of "doubly reflected communication," and that within the *Postscript* itself, Climacus begins his account of the "subjective problem" with an analysis of that very concept.

For Climacus, the problem of communication is grounded in the recognition of the different goals of objective and subjective reflection. Objective reflection, as we have seen, is concerned only with results, i.e., with the attainment of a body of authenticated truths. As results they can be directly communicated in a series of propositions. The subjective thinker, on the other hand, is not concerned with the acquisition of a given body of truths, with "finding something out," but with "existing in 'the truth'," appropriating it existentially. This different goal demands a different type of reflection, "the reflection of inwardness or possession, by virtue of which it belongs to the thinking subject and no one else" (pp. 167–68). This uniquely personal quality of subjective reflection brings with it two consequences which determine the problem of existential communication. First, since the subjective thinker is concerned with the task of living in the truth he is constantly in the process of becoming. "Subjective truth," e.g., religion, faith, is not the sort of thing which one can simply acquire once and for all, but rather it requires a continual effort at re-appropriation. Thus, "subjective truth" can never be a permanent acquisition in the form of a result: "Subjective thought puts everything in process and omits the results." Second, the reflection of inwardness demands a "double reflection," both an intellectual reflection which leads to recognition, and an existential reflection which leads to appropriation. "In thinking," Climacus writes of the subjective thinker, "he thinks the universal; but as existing in his thought and as assimilating it in his inwardness, he becomes more and more subjectively isolated" (p. 68).

Thus, it is the very essence of subjective thought or existential reflection that it cannot be directly communicated, for to do so is to translate it into a result, and thus to contradict its "existential" character. Climacus offers several examples to illustrate this point, the most interesting of which is the analysis of the attempt to express the by now familiar conviction: "Truth is inwardness, there is no objective truth, but the truth consists in personal appropriation" (p. 71). How then is this "doctrine" to be proclaimed? An enthusiast, Climacus suggests, may expend great zeal in the propagation of this truth. He may make a special point of proclaiming it on every possible occasion. He may publish it in a learned treatise, and as a result gain many new adherents to his "doctrine," who in turn would strive to win others to the cause. However, as a consequence of such an endeavor, the champion of subjectivity succeeds only in rendering himself comical. In propagating the doctrine in this manner he has turned it into a result—an objective truth, a theory *about* the significance of subjectivity, and thus contradicted himself.

But how is this situation to be avoided? How is it possible for the subjective thinker, for one who really believes that the existential appropriation of the truth is the essential factor, to communicate this conviction without contradicting himself, without turning his conviction into a theory about subjectivity? According to Climacus the first requirement of such a communication is that it be expressed in such a way so as not to induce an immediate intellectual assent. Its goal is not the coercion of the recipient to a point of view, but his emancipation so that he may come to understand it inwardly, and as Climacus tells us: "The inwardness of understanding consists in each individual coming to understand it for himself" (p. 71). Such a goal, however, precisely because it is formulated in recognition of the freedom of the other cannot be achieved directly. Here Climacus is in thorough agreement with the Socratic contention that the only authentic relationship between individuals is the maieutic one, and it is because of this that he holds that any communication of a "personal" truth must be indirect, and that this indirection requires both artistry and self-control.[9]

The artistry is expressed in the form of the communication, and it consists in the elusiveness which forces the individual to reflect back upon himself. This elusiveness is the negative element in the process of communication, and it is decisive, for operating as a repellent factor, it prevents one from regarding such communication as a straightforward objective presentation of a doctrine. It is in terms of these considerations that we must understand "the subtle principle" of subjective thought: ". . . that the personalities must be held devoutly apart from one another, and not permitted to fuse or coagulate into objectivity. It is at this point that objectivity and subjectivity part from one another" (p. 73).

If this conception of the nature of existential communication is applied to the content of the *Postscript*, some interesting results follow. The book, as we have seen, points to the difficulties of becoming a Christian. It contends that in the ethical and religious spheres "truth is subjectivity," that subjectivity or passion stands in a direct correlation with objective uncertainty, and finally, that as an objective absurdity, Christianity is the objective correlate of the maximum degree of inwardness, and thus, can be regarded as the "true" or ultimate form of religiousness. We further saw that despite Climacus' protestations to the contrary, this view led to a consistent misologism, which ends with the identification of Christianity and nonsense. In proceeding in this way, however, it would seem that like

[9] In this connection it is interesting to note that in the very year of the publication of the *Postscript* we find Kierkegaard commenting in his Journal: "The reason why several of Plato's dialogues end without results is more profound than I used to think. It is an expression of Socrates' maieutic art, which makes the reader or the hearer himself active, and so does not end in a result, but in a sting." *The Journals*, no. 528.

the vast body of Kierkegaard's commentators, and "existential philosophers" in general, we have become "town criers of inwardness." We have attempted to treat as a philosophical proposition ("truth is subjectivity") what by its very nature cannot be regarded as such without contradiction. Is it any wonder then that qua philosophical proposition it reduces itself to an absurdity? The absurd consequences of this consistently misologistic position can now be seen to provide the repellent factor, the elusiveness necessary to indirection, which the author has artistically devised in order to avoid achieving a "result," and to throw his readers back upon themselves.

In light of these considerations let us return to Climacus' argument. The starting point of his trouble, the decisive passage which gives rise to the misologistic consequences is the assertion: "When subjectivity is the truth, the *conceptual determination* of the truth must include an expression of the antithesis to objectivity." The key words here are "conceptual determination" for they make clear that Climacus' misologism is a direct consequence of the conceptualization of the "principle of subjectivity"! But to conceptualize is to objectify, and, as we have seen, to speak objectively about inwardness (and Christianity, it will be remembered, is the highest form of inwardness) is stupidity. Thus, unless we are to view Kierkegaard as guilty of the very stupidity which he went to such great lengths to condemn, we must view the whole "argument" as a jest, as an expression of the author's artistry, the intent of which is not to "prove" the superiority of Christianity or even to show us in a theoretical way that the absolute paradox makes a kind of sense as *supra rationem* which is lacking in garden variety nonsense, but rather to help us realize existentially what it means to become a Christian, and to see that the only valid concept which we can form about Christianity is that it defies conceptualization. Moreover, it is only in light of these considerations that we can appreciate the significance of Kierkegaard's reflection: "Dialectically it is easy to see that Johannes Climacus' defense of Christianity is the most extreme that can be made and only a hair's breadth from an attack."[10] It is the most extreme that can be made because it consists essentially in pointing to its utter incommensurability with all human categories, and the "hair's breadth" which distinguishes this from an attack is nothing more than the double reflection of the subjective thinker. If this be omitted, and the *Postscript* viewed as an essay in existential apologetics, then it is indeed an attack for it leads to the ultimate identification of Christianity and nonsense.

Thus, as a genuine subjective thinker, for whom "everything is dialectical," and whose main work contains "not only a conclusion but a revocation" (p. 547), Kierkegaard remains perpetually elusive. Like Socrates, of whom he was a life long admirer, he believed that his task was not to expound but to sting, and hence any attempt to pin him down, to look for results in the form of an existential philosophy or Christian apologetic in his writings is, to use Climacus' analogy, "like trying to paint Mars in the armor that made him invisible," the supreme irony being, as Climacus points out and the whole history of Kierkegaard scholarship verifies, that such efforts seem to have "a partial success" (p. 73).

[10] *The Journals*, no. 994.

KANT AND KIERKEGAARD
ON DUTY AND INCLINATION

George Schrader

Discussions of Kierkegaard's ethical views have tended
to focus on the highly dramatic "teleological suspension of the ethical" in *Fear and Trembling* to the neglect of his sustained discussion of the ethical life in
Either/Or and other of his writings. In *Fear and
Trembling* Kierkegaard makes the trenchant point that
the ethical justification of action presupposes the validity of the ethical as such and, hence, can provide
only a qualified and limited warrant. Essentially this
same point has been made by a number of moralists
who would not be caught with a book of Kierkegaard
in their hands. But it is the other side of this point
which Kierkegaard chose to emphasize, namely that,
insofar as a person is ever called upon to act as an
individual, he stands outside the ethical sphere and,
thus, can find no ethical justification for his action. If
ethical justification is equated with rational justification,
then the action of the individual qua individual must
presumably go without any justification whatever. It
is this equation, suggested if not explicitly espoused
by Kierkegaard, that has aroused the ire of rational
moralists. Or, perhaps I should say of the defenders
of rational ethics, since their passion not infrequently
belies their profession of rationality.

The representation of the ethical in *Fear and
Trembling* is transparently Kantian. Kierkegaard takes

This essay was originally published in *The Journal of Philosophy*, November 7, 1968, Vol. LXV, No. 21. It is reprinted
with the kind permission of the author and the editor of *The
Journal of Philosophy*.

the Kantian conception of morality as its highest possible expression in order to show that ethics cannot incorporate the individual. The religious imperative, addressed to the solitary individual, supersedes the moral imperative which speaks to man in his capacity as universally human. Kant had, of course, considered the possibility of such a conflict of imperatives, but opted decisively for the primacy of the moral. But Kant's argument begs the question by assuming the ultimate validity of the rational/universal. If man is ever called upon to act in his capacity as a unique and irreplaceable individual, he must act without the guidance of Kant's moral principles.

Kierkegaard's critique of Kantian ethics is, then, a critique of ethics as such. Accepting Kant's formulation of ethics, Kierkegaard attempts to delineate the "scope and limits" of the ethical—a task which Kant had neglected to perform. The issue raised here is not limited to the potential conflict between moral and religious imperatives. More fundamentally it concerns the nature and function of reason and its relevance or irrelevance to the decisions and behavior of the individual. In effect, Kant and Kierkegaard agree that the individual per se is beyond the ethical and, hence, exempt from the dictates of reason. The difference between them is that, whereas Kant suppresses this aspect of human decision virtually to the point of denying its possibility, Kierkegaard accords it supreme importance. Understandably enough, existentialist writers have been particularly concerned about the sphere of action that lies beyond the limits of the Kantian and, perhaps, all rationally formulated ethics. Can duty be applicable to men save with respect to that which is demanded of all men? Can reason apply to situations that are intrinsically unrepeatable? Both existentialist thinkers and their critics have, I think, been too ready to reply in the negative. In thus relegating individual decision and action to the province of the irrational, they have sold reason short. It can be argued, I believe, that in addressing himself to the situation of the individual Kierkegaard was only exploring territory clearly demarcated by Kant. He can surely be forgiven for ignoring the "no trespass" signs.

The situation in *Either/Or* is radically different. Kierkegaard's objective in this work is not to set forth the limitations of the ethical, but to defend it. The first volume is devoted to an elaborate analysis of what might be termed the "aesthetic of practical reason" and the second volume to a defense of the ethical life in a modified Kantian form. It is unfortunate that the preoccupation with *Fear and Trembling* has obscured the fact that Kierkegaard's constructive ethical theory is intimately and directly related to Kant's and constitutes one of the most interesting and important revisions of Kant's ethical theory. It will be the burden of this paper to show that Kierkegaard offered an alternative conception of the ethical a priori and, in particular, a more satisfactory view of the relationship between duty and inclination.

Before turning to Kierkegaard's ethics, it may be useful to take note of a few salient and highly controversial features of the Kantian theory. The abstract character of the moral law and the formalism it engenders have caused endless and seemingly incurable difficulty for Kant's readers. Pure practical reason appears to be so pure in its a priori domicile, that putting it to work with the material contents of volition is a frightfully difficult undertaking. In spite of countertendencies, Kant never finally overcame a predilection for a Platonic duality between reason and inclination (appetite) and, hence, viewed reason as performing a controlling and repressive function with respect to inclination. This Platonic bias may well account for the fact that Kant saw no need for an Aesthetic of practical reason and neglected almost entirely to analyze inclination and empirical desire in the Second Critique. An aesthetic of practical reason would concern itself with those concrete empirical processes for which reason is legislative. Moreover, it would provide a foundation for a transcendental deduction of the principles of practical reason. It can be argued that such an aesthetic is just as important for ethics as the aesthetic of theoretical reason is for empirical cognition. Indeed, many of the difficulties with respect to Kant's formalism can be traced to the absence of a detailed analysis of moral sensibility. In attempting to offer such an aesthetic, as I believe he did in the first volume of *Either/Or,* Kierkegaard filled in a crucially important hiatus in Kant's theory.

Another important feature of Kant's ethics is the impersonality that seems to be required for the sake of objectivity and universality. We are enjoined to treat ourselves and others as ends and not as means merely; yet, no account is given of the way in which we are involved with or come to know other persons. Moreover, for the harmonious ordering of the social community, Kant relies on the highly indirect device of commitment to identical rational principles. Integration of persons into a common world is achieved by the constraining force of external forms rather than the mutual accommodation of competing human interests. If successful, Kant's program offers a rather neat way of avoiding personal involvement. So long as we follow the same score, we don't need to hear one another to be in tune. Kant's pessimism about the material component of human action and interaction accounts for his exaggerated stress on the role of reason in morality. Only if one despairs of the possibility of achieving a community of persons through the intercourse of everyday life need one rely so exclusively on the harmony of volition at the abstract level.

Kant's theory of duty and inclination is sufficiently familiar that I need not delineate it in this paper. I wish to argue that Kierkegaard's analysis of the aesthetic life can be used for the interpretation and, perhaps, revision of Kant's ethics. Even to approach Kierkegaard one needs Kant's ethical theory as background material for understanding such concepts as desire, duty, apriority, etc. But it is with Kierkegaard's use of these concepts that I will be primarily concerned.

The most interesting and for our purposes the most important thesis of Kierkegaard's exposition in *Either/Or* is that the ethical life presupposes the aesthetic mode and represents a transformation of it. Although there is, in one sense, a radical discontinuity between the aesthetic and the ethical, the discontinuity of the either/or disjunction is superseded by the transition to the ethical. The argument of the second volume is that the ethical life *relativizes* and thereby transcends the aesthetic while losing nothing of its concreteness. Indeed, the argument is even stronger, namely that the ethical is necessary for the preservation of the aesthetic which might otherwise succumb to despair. The development of aesthetic sensibility is necessary for the ethical life even though the ethical represents a leap beyond it. Unlike Kant, who seems to have regarded inclination as a necessary though somewhat regrettable feature of human existence, Kierkegaard views it as an essential and praiseworthy aspect of human life. The more developed is one's aesthetic sensibility, the richer the content of one's existence and the more significant the individual. Elsewhere Kierkegaard asserts that: "the more consciousness the more self." Thus the more his wants, needs, and desires are developed, the more self he possesses. The reason is that man's sensibility is an integral aspect of his consciousness and an essential manifestation of his existence. Whereas Kant's view of the moral sensibility was more or less Platonic and repressive, Kierkegaard's is Hegelian and ringingly affirmative.

In his *Aesthetic of Pure Reason* Kant had excluded feeling and volition. This move precluded the possibility of a unitary sensibility by dichotomizing the cognitive and affective faculties. For Kierkegaard, on the other hand, sensibility is unitary and inclusive. It represents the sentiency of the total person rather than any special perceptual faculty or apparatus. The basic phenomenon to be analyzed in the aesthetic mode is what Kierkegaard termed the "sensuous erotic." Thus the stages in the development of the sensuous erotic are stages in the development of the individual human being. As sensuous, man is concretely and materially alive to himself and his world; as erotic he seeks for ends and objects that lie beyond him. Kierkegaard adopted the then current notion of *Geist,* or spirit, to designate the individual person. As for Hegel, all categories are thus categories of spirit, though for Kierkegaard they apply only to finite human subjects.

In referring to man as spirit, Kierkegaard was only making the point that man is essentially a self or person and to be understood by the use of categories appropriate to his existence. As undeveloped, man is only an immediate self—but a self nonetheless. In calling attention to his sensuous erotic nature, Kierkegaard sought to emphasize that this is the immediate form of existence. The term "immediacy" is, of course, another Hegelian category, but a singularly useful one. It enabled Kierkegaard to preserve the unity of the self while attempting to account for its development. Moreover, it avoids the philosophically fatal identification of the self with one of its presumed "higher" faculties. Although the language used here is rather highflown, the concept is quite simple. It is the whole self that is concrete and sensible and, thus, the whole self that develops in, with, and through the development of the sensuously concrete. Other philosophers, such as Merleau-Ponty, have made a similar point by emphasizing the centrality of the body. So long as it is a conscious and sentient body and the body of a person about which we are talking, it makes little difference whether we use the more Hegelian language of Kierkegaard or the language of Merleau-Ponty.

One further point about the sensuous erotic must be noted. As has been observed, it is immediate in the sense that it is undeveloped and capable of development. But in another sense the sensuous erotic is immediate however fully it may be developed. Kierkegaard's handling of these concepts is somewhat confusing in that he uses immediacy both as a category ranging over the entire sensible/concrete aspect of existence and as a stage within immediacy. He talks about immediate stages of immediacy, and this is confusing unless one keeps clearly in mind that immediacy in the more general sense means the sensuous as such and in the specific sense refers to an undeveloped phase of the former. He could have used different terms, but then it would have been more difficult for him to make the rather subtle dialectical point that any internal development of the immediate is just that, namely a blown-up immediacy. Kierkegaard was enough of a Hegelian to regard mediation as requiring negation. Thus we are not beyond the immediate until it has been radically questioned and transcended. Aesthetic immediacy is preserved within the ethical mode but with a change of signature, as it were.

The sensuous erotic is immediate in that it is the given concrete empirical aspect of existence. There is, of course, nothing particularly novel about this aspect of Kierkegaard's anthropology. Virtually all moralists from Plato on have included an irreducible empirical component in their conception of human existence. It is not, therefore, the fact that Kierkegaard stresses the sensuous erotic as foundational for ethics that is most significant. It is rather the way in which he relates aesthetic immediacy to other components in existence that makes it philosophically interesting.

As was noted earlier, Kant regarded empirical desire as radically contingent and more or less external to the rational will. He could not view it as altogether beyond the scope of practical reason, else he would not have been able to demonstrate that reason can be effective in controlling action. Reason can impose an order on man's empirically given nature even though it cannot transform it from within. Over and over Kant gives us examples to show that, no matter what our impulses may be, we can follow the dictates of reason. Morally viewed, our affective life is required to conform to rational canons which it does not supply from itself and which it may on occasion find harshly constraining. Whatever the ends of inclination may be, they are never to be viewed as moral ends. Nor can they be transformed into moral ends by an internal focusing. This does not mean, as some of Kant's interpreters have concluded, that moral virtue *requires* an opposition between inclination and duty. It does mean that, however closely the ends of inclination and the requirements of duty converge, they can never be fused or share a common end.

The relationship between Kant and Kierkegaard is highly complex since they agree on certain fundamental points while differing sharply on others. Kierkegaard agrees fully with Kant that the sensuous erotic can never generate moral duties. Moreover, Kierkegaard agrees with Kant that we simply desire what we desire, and though our desires posit ends for action they never establish ends with the force of moral constraint. But here the agreement ends. Unlike Kant, Kierkegaard views the sensuous erotic as developed through the agency of reason and imagination and as an expression of the total person rather than merely of the "natural" component of his nature.

Still, the contrast between them should not be exaggerated, for Kant did assign to practical reason an instrumental role in the definition of happiness as an end. Since all inclinations are, on Kant's view, conscious and involve a representation of an end, they share common features with rational volition. It is true, also, that happiness as the natural end of human striving is included within the highest good. The fact remains, however, that the moral good is the supreme end of human volition and a condition for the realization of happiness. Only a virtuous man is worthy of happiness, but virtue does not guarantee and may not facilitate the achievement of happiness. Nor does the attainment of happiness witness to the attainment of a virtuous life. The harmony between these two components of the complete good for man depends upon a subordination of the natural to the moral component rather than to an integration of the two. Kant's conception of duty requires that we maintain the distinction between natural and moral ends even where happiness and virtue coincide in a human life. Kant might well have developed his ethical theory along different lines to provide for a stronger unity of the natural and moral good for man; but to do so he would have had to make some basic revisions in his anthropology.

The chief difference between Kant and Kierkegaard is, then, that Kierkegaard makes much of the role of consciousness in the development of inclination whereas Kant virtually ignored it. Had Kant devoted to it anything like the attention he paid to the relation between sensible intuition and understanding, he might well have given us something like Kierkegaard's analysis of aesthetic immediacy. I am convinced that an adequate interpretation of Kant's ethics requires a careful formulation of the aesthetic on which it is based. And that can be done by looking to his lectures on anthropology and the many scattered references he makes to what might be termed "moral sensibility" throughout his writings. It is not our objective to undertake that important and much neglected task in this paper. Suffice it to say that a "deduction of the categories of practical reason" might well have assigned to imagination, understanding, and reason the same sort of role in the development of empirical desire that Kant had assigned them in the case of sensible intuition.

In his analysis of the sensuous erotic Kierkegaard attempts to preserve both the empirically determinate and the plastic character of inclination. As was noted earlier, he regards desire as concrete and contingent but, yet, as in need of articulation and development.

He thus rejects a familiar tenet of empiricism that what is contingently given must be completely determinate. The issue here is precisely the same as the problem that has plagued sense-datum theories. There are some advantages in treating the distinction between the empirically determinate and the conceptually indeterminate as substantive. But it is by no means necessary and creates more problems than it solves. Precisely the same phenomenon may be empirically given as this or that while still subject to further determination. Such determination might take the form, as in many epistemological theories, of construing what is given by subsuming it under higher-order forms. An alternative and altogether plausible theory is to view the process of determination as the development of themes intrinsic to the empirical datum itself. It is the latter alternative for which Kierkegaard opts. This means in effect that the empirical process must supply the categories necessary for its own development and interpretation. And it entails that to understand, evaluate, and criticize an empirical process we must adopt a position within rather than outside the process itself. We cannot hope, in other words, to be a successful *observer* to our own desires any more than we can observe our sensations. As I hope to point out, this way of viewing sensibility has interesting implications for the formulation of ethical norms.

Sartre adopts a basically Kierkegaardian point of view in his analysis of the "pour soi." *Facticity* and *transcendence* are regarded as polar categories which apply to one and the same phenomenon. It follows from this conception of existence that no segment of human life is ever devoid of concreteness such that it cannot be characterized and described in detail. But neither can it be exhaustively described within an objective frame. It is what it is but, also, what it may yet become. The situation is somewhat like the writing of a novel where at any point the language is quite definite and the action determinate. Yet, at no point could the novel be written in one and only one way—nor in just any way whatever. We must wait to see how the initial themes will be developed before we can finally assess the meaning of the characters and the action. The novel succeeds or fails as judged by what it attempts to do with the materials it has selected.

As Kierkegaard views it, every empirical desire has an intrinsic theme. The theme constitutes what might be termed the rational or intentional form of the desire. It may be prereflective or highly reflective. From the outset it represents the consciousness of a self and is thus an element of self-consciousness. The full awareness of the theme depends, therefore, upon the eruption of self-consciousness from a more immediate stage in which it is embryonically present. Kierkegaard alludes to bashfulness as a paradigm of the transitional consciousness which hovers between childish innocence and the explicit awareness of sexuality. For every theme, however, there is an indefinite range of variations for its expression. Sexual desire, for example, is sexual desire no matter how varied the forms in which it is made manifest. Empirical determinacy is thus in nowise incompatible with human freedom. The theme and the materials are given, but how they are to be combined and expressed is left to our ingenuity.

Choice, too, plays a significant role in the development of the sensuous erotic. Both the end and the means must be selected from the range of available possibilities. The basic motivation, however, is always provided by the desire itself. We must focus our wants and take the necessary steps to satisfy them, though nothing more than hypothetical imperatives or conditional choices are involved. If a desire loses its urgency or dries up altogether, there is no further point in the activity it has previously supported. Here again we encounter an exceedingly subtle point on which Kierkegaard places great stress. All empirical desires are ours in a quite obvious sense no matter how we view them. But there are two quite different senses in which they may be our desires. They may be ours in that we just happen to have them as those appetites or inclinations which constitute our empirically given nature. The desires themselves have not been freely chosen nor have we assumed responsibility for the fact that we have them. In so far as we live exclusively in the mode of aesthetic immediacy, our contingent desires constitute the foundation for our existence. In its lustier and more simple forms, desire exhibits a powerful elan and affords appropriately zestful satisfactions. But all desire is subject to such hazards as boredom and apathy. Activities, including one's life work, may suddenly lose their point as interest wanes. Fortunate is the man for whom other lively appetites take over to supplant the faded appetites. Unhappy is the man who cares about nothing at all. Even a complexly ordered life that is structured by elegant taste rests on a contingent foundation and may be swept away by an alteration in or disappearance of the desire that supports it. Lacking apriority, the aesthetic life has no final defense against despair.

What happens, then, when aesthetic content is subsumed under ethical forms? Is the differentiation between the ethical and the aesthetic a distinction without a difference? The difference must be clearly exhibited if we are to avoid the conclusion that it is only a verbal distinction. It is easy to see how eating, for example, may have ethical significance if one believes that one has a duty to nourish the body, to afford oneself pleasure, etc. We might then eat even when we feel no hunger or, in the extreme case, prefer not to exist. Kant regarded the will as capable of supporting and governing our impulsive life so as to master the inevitable contingencies involved. But Kant's answer to the problem is not Kierkegaard's, and it is Kierkegaard's solution that needs clarification. Stated formally, the difference between their respective answers is that for Kant the rational will performs the task of *directing* and *controlling* our empirical desires, whereas for Kierkegaard the will *identifies* itself with these desires as its own essential expression. In the first instance, I do not view my body or my appetites as so integral a part of my existence or so essential an aspect of my freedom as my rational will. In the second instance, I view it as *the* essential expression of my volition—indeed as my way of existing in the world. On Kierkegaard's analysis, I cannot properly regard my sensuous erotic nature as in any way accidental, a mere instrumentality that I must make use of in order to exist. Ethically speaking, I am my own concrete immediacy; in affirming my inclinations as essentially mine I am only choosing myself.

But, you might say—as Kierkegaard anticipated—this is rather silly, since I cannot, after all, be anything other than myself. Isn't this typical of the high-sounding and presumably edifying slogans which pass for ethical precepts among existentialist writers? Admittedly if it means only: be what you are; and, if everyone is necessarily what he is, Kierkegaard offers us a palpably empty injunction. But the matter is not quite so simple as that. In the first place, there are conspicuous ways in which we may deny our sensuous nature. It is precisely man's ability to alienate himself from himself through such devices as repression that makes psychotherapy so important an institution in contemporary life. The fact that many philosophers deplore the exaggerated stress on human alienation hardly suffices to eliminate it as a human possibility. It would be ridiculous to maintain that all or most human beings are self-alienated. In fact, numbers are of no significance whatever. The number of alienated persons has no more bearing on the question of alienation as a human possibility than the number of liars has with respect to the possibility of distorting truth. If one is uneasy in talking about alienation—as some people are —it is quite easy to change the terminology for characterizing the same phenomenon. In the case of Kant's ethics, for example, it is impossible to talk about moral volition without presupposing the transcendence of the rational will with respect to empirical desire. Is the morally developed man to be viewed, then, as self-alienated? I would say that, in a perfectly straight-forward sense of the term, he is, and, for that reason, the moral consciousness is, in the language of Hegel, an irremediably "unhappy consciousness." But if one doesn't like those terms, one can use the familiar language of the "empirical" and the "transcendental", and continue to speak of duty as the necessity of bringing the empirical into conformity with the demands of the transcendental.

The transition from Kant to Kierkegaard is an easy one, since both require the development of a reflective consciousness and a will capable of making decisive choices. The important issue between them concerns the manner in which the will operates. Both of them recognize that one must be somehow distanced from one's own inclinations if one is to view them ethically. The difference between them is, as I interpret it, that for Kant a permanent distancing is essential to the moral life whereas for Kierkegaard the distance must be surmounted through an act of will which unifies the self.

The distinction does, I believe, represent a difference with regard to both the way in which one interprets the relation between moral volition and inclination, and the manner of action that follows from the interpretation. If practical reason is externally related to inclination, it can only control and direct it. But if, on the other hand, reason can operate immanently as a formative principle in the shaping of inclination, reason and the moral will can receive *expression* through the agency of empirical desire. To return to our example, I will certainly view hunger and eating differently in the two instances. If, following Kierkegaard, I regard my eating as an essential rather than an accidental feature of my existence, the manner of my eating and the meaning I give to it will be as important for me as any other activity in which I engage. Aesthetically viewed, according to Kierkegaard's representation, everything is contingent and accidental. Ethically viewed, however, everything becomes an essential expression of the individual. This does not mean that by virtue of the transition to the ethical the individual creates himself. It does mean that he assumes complete responsibility for himself, including without qualification his full sensuous nature.

The ethical consciousness thus requires as a condition not only reflective transcendence of the initial aesthetic immediacy, but an act of resignation through which the individual chooses himself in his concrete determinacy. Resignation is not enough, however, to constitute ethical volition, which requires, also, the positive affirmation of oneself. And it is just here that the determinacy/plasticity polarity to which we alluded earlier becomes important. The sensuous erotic has its own intrinsic ends but not in so determinate a fashion that no further choice of meaning is possible. On the contrary, it is the necessity for a further definition of meaning that makes ethical volition possible. Kierkegaard placed very great stress on the *how,* that is, on the manner of willing. The very same activity may be aesthetically based or the expression of ethical resolve. The difference in manner is that in the latter case the choice involves *apriority.* The ethically determined individual commits himself to pursue whatever end he seeks regardless of consequences. And it is, of course, this posture toward consequences which inevitably alarms the advocates of utilitarian ethics. The situation is, however, not really so bad as it seems, for consequences are not so much to be ignored as discounted in advance. But even a utilitarian is, I suppose, committed to the attempt to promote happiness even though the attempt fails and, forbid the thought, actually increases unhappiness.

Unfortunately, it will be necessary to terminate this discussion just where we have reached the point of greatest ethical interest. What difference does it make with respect to the choice of ends or of norms in pursuit of ends to view inclination and desire as an essential expression of the existing subject? The outline of an answer can be sketched as follows: (1) The individual thereby assumes responsibility for his entire affective life. It is the internal rather than the external form and meaning of his empirical desires with which he is concerned. This represents a far more stringent demand upon the moral subject than Kant thought could be reasonably defended. This point is worthy of emphasis in view of the invitation to license which is not infrequently attributed to Kierkegaard and others who hold a similar view of man's responsibility for himself. (2) The projects of the individual become a priori necessary in so far as they reflect a commitment of will. This consequence involves a number of difficulties which need to be sorted out. It is fairly easy to see how friendship, marriage, or a career can be the result of a decision for which the individual assumes moral responsibility. Unless he is abstracted from himself, these commitments reflect his inclinations and serve to focus and unify them. As commitments they represent material obligations for which he is responsible.

If we were to formulate the supreme principle governing such obligations it might be stated as: one should assume complete responsibility for whatever one chooses. Or, conversely: one should choose only that for which one is prepared to assume full responsibility. Such an imperative obviously makes personal responsibility the supreme condition of morality. In this respect the emphasis is shifted from Kant's stress on rational volition to an even stronger demand on the moral subject, namely that he be responsible for the material as well as the formal/rational features of his volition. Kierkegaard's imperative does not lay down material rules for conduct any more than does the Kantian imperative. Although more demanding, it has the advantage of including the content of sensibility within volition and, hence, avoids the Kantian problem of schematization.

One factor, however, is conspicuously missing from the Kierkegaardian ethics, namely one's responsibility toward other persons. But there is no particular difficulty in supplying this dimension along Kantian lines. Here again Kierkegaard has a potential advantage in being able to start from the concrete involvement of individuals with one another. Marriage, which Kierkegaard takes as the paradigm of the ethical in *Either/Or*, is after all an interpersonal relationship. If only the ethically developed individual can possess himself, only he can appropriate the ethical reality of another person. Other persons must be accorded the same freedom and capacity for autonomous volition that one accepts for oneself. The ethical dimension of human relationships thus constitutes a modification of the spontaneously developed interplay among persons.

There are serious problems here which Kierkegaard never faced directly, namely that our ethical projects require the consent and cooperation of other persons whose freedom always transcends our own. Sartre, Camus, and others have dealt directly with this question with varying success. As Sartre has recognized, Marxism with its stress on the role of sociohistorical conditions in stamping the moral life of individuals constitutes an important and inescapable challenge to existentialist ethics. The Kantian doctrine of individual freedom is radicalized and exaggerated by Kierkegaard and his followers. Although subjectivity is possible only through an inward turn out of one's social involvement, the individual is expected to achieve mastery over his world through an exercise of will. It is by no means clear, however, that the individual can achieve an authentic existence or fulfillment as a person regardless of the social conditions under which he lives. Individual responsibility represents an essential and, perhaps, the most fundamental aspect of the moral life; but it stands in polar relationship to the material-social world which can neither be created nor transformed by the action of a single individual. An adequate theory of ethics must take account of both factors if it is to understand the human condition and prescribe valid principles for criticizing and transforming it. No synthesis of the polar factors may be possible; still, we must discover how we can most adequately credit each with its proper validity without losing the tension between them. We need a theory of responsibility that accords to the individual full scope for his freedom while recognizing that moral obligation shades off into the social and is shared with others.

KIERKEGAARD AND SCEPTICISM

Richard H. Popkin

It may seem odd to discuss Kierkegaard and Scepticism, or the Scepticism of Kierkegaard. Kierkegaard
is considered nowadays as one of the foremost religious teachers of modern times. He himself proclaimed
that his mission was to introduce Christianity into
Christendom. Hence, he hardly seems to have been
a man with doubts about religious matters. A man who
devoted his whole agonized life to a crusade to awaken
mankind to the cosmic importance of the truth that
Jesus is God does not appear to have much to do
with scepticism. When we speak of scepticism, we
usually have in mind someone like Voltaire or Ber-
trand Russell, someone who devotes himself to expressing doubts about the tenets of various religions.

However, over a half-century before Kierkegaard,
the extremely irreligious sceptic, David Hume, who
was often called the Great Infidel, concluded his most
irreligious work, the *Dialogues Concerning Natural Religion,* with the strange claim, "To be a philosophical
sceptic is, in a man of letters, the first and most essential step towards being a sound, believing Christian."[1] Although Hume may not have proceeded from

This essay contains two lectures given by the author in November 1957 as Visiting Professor at the State University of
Utrecht. It was originally published in *Algemeen Nederlands
Tijdschrift Voor Wijsbegeerte En Psychologie,* 1958/59, Vol.
LI. It is reprinted with the kind permission of the author and
the editor of *Algemeen Nederlands Tijdschrift Voor Wijsbegeerte En Psychologie*. It has been revised by the author especially for this volume.

[1] David Hume, *Dialogues Concerning Natural Religion,* ed.
by Norman Kemp Smith, 2nd ed. (London 1947), p. 228.

scepticism towards religious belief, Kierkegaard, I think, saw the intimate and basic relation between philosophical scepticism and acceptance of religious belief, and saw that scepticism was not necessarily the enemy of religion, but could be, rather, its truest friend and ally.

In the strange collection of works that make up the writings of Kierkegaard, attributed to various pseudonyms—the short stories, the psychological studies, the attacks on Christian practices, the religious rhapsodies, etc.—one finds a small group of philosophical works that form the crucial bridge in the march from the ordinary world of human life to the religious world that Kierkegaard was advocating. And, as I shall try to show subsequently, these transitional works, the short *Philosophical Fragments,* the lengthy continuation, *Concluding Unscientific Postscript,* the unfinished fragment, *De Omnibus Dubitandum Est,* plus *Fear and Trembling,* and the magnificent *Training in Christianity,* all develop a most far reaching philosophical scepticism as the basis of true faith, and show that faith without complete doubt regarding the possibility of rational knowledge is always inadequate, and ultimately disastrous. Thus, the rational doubts that the sceptics have raised against scientific, mathematical, philosophical, and moral knowledge lead not, for Kierkegaard, to the irreligious or humanistic conclusion of a Voltaire or a Hume, but rather to a new advocacy of Christianity. The evidence that can be offered that we have no adequate proof for any proposition whatsoever becomes, for Kierkegaard, not a reason for disbelief, but the only basis for belief. In order to understand this transformation, or transmutation, of doubt into the basis for belief, I should like first to look backward into some of the previous history of the relationship of sceptical and religious thought. In terms of this survey, I think we shall be better able to see what Kierkegaard was trying to accomplish, and the extent to which he avoided some of the difficulties of his predecessors.

1

In the sixteenth century one finds the beginning of new intellectual movement, a revival of ancient sceptical thought, only with a crucial difference. It was a scepticism purporting to furnish a new defense of religion, especially Catholicism. The original sceptics of ancient Greece were concerned to show that objections could be raised about the truth of any proposition whatsoever, objections that could not be satisfactorily answered. As a result, the ancient sceptics held, one should suspend judgment as to whether any proposition was true or false. Instead, they claimed one should follow nature, accept the conventions and beliefs of one's society, without ever committing oneself as to whether these views were true. The sceptics of the sixteenth century adapted the kinds of doubts that had just been rediscovered to certain problems in the Christian world. One finds first a use of the arguments of the Greek Sceptics to undermine the confidence of the Reformers. If nothing can be known, then Calvinism cannot be known.[2]

But, besides employing these doubts as what one Jesuit of the time called, "the new machine of war" to devastate the Reformers,[3] a more important sceptical movement emerged, principally through the efforts

[2] Gentian Hervet, preface to Sextus Empiricus, *Adversus Mathematicos* (Paris and Antwerp 1569). Cf. R. H. Popkin, "Scepticism and the Counter-Reformation in France," *Archiv für Reformationsgeschichte,* "Jahrgang" 51 (1960), pp. 58–61. This essay has been reprinted in the Bobbs-Merrill Reprint Series in European History, E-172. See also R. H. Popkin, *The History of Scepticism* (revised edition) (New York 1968), Chapters II and IV.

[3] On Veron and his method for attacking the Protestants, see Popkin, "Skepticism and the Counter-Reformation," pp. 63–69; and *History of Scepticism*, pp. 57–63.

of Michel de Montaigne and his disciples. The "philosophy" of Montaigne is a picture of the age in which he lived, an age in which all the accepted beliefs were being challenged. The intellectual and religious systems that had been constructed in the Middle Ages were crumbling, and it was becoming more and more difficult to tell what to believe. Just as Montaigne's world was falling apart, he happened to read the main surviving ancient sceptical work, the writings of Sextus Empiricus. Montaigne's private sceptical crisis was portrayed in his longest essay, the rambling *Apologie de Raimond Sebond*. Purporting to defend an earlier rational theologian, Sebond, Montaigne presented the crisis of modern man, who could no longer find any basis for believing anything. Any belief could be challenged. Our faculties for discovering the truth were unreliable. Our senses were untrustworthy, our reason based on principles which we could never tell were true. All we possess is a maze of conflicting opinions. In this sad situation, God has fortunately chosen to reveal the truth to us. And Montaigne insisted the only truths we could have come from God. The rest of what we think we know is only smoke, wind and dreams. Scepticism aids us in the search for truth by destroying our illusions, our confidence in our rational abilities. When we have gone through a sceptical crisis, when we have seen that we have no assurance for any of our opinions, and no guarantees of the truth of any of the things we know, then we have made the first step. The second step is, according to Montaigne, to empty one's mind of all that is doubtful, thus leaving one's mind blank, awaiting God's message. And finally, if God so wills, the truth will be revealed to us, and we will accept it on faith alone, since our rational capabilities will not help us. This union of scepticism and faith, which is one of the ever-recurring themes of Montaigne's *Apologie de Raimond Sebond,* was, the author claimed, the message of St. Paul in his first letter to the Corinthians where the Apostle proclaimed, "For

Christ sent me not to baptize, but to preach the gospel: not with the wisdom of words, lest the cross of Christ should be made of no effect. For the preaching of the cross is to them that perish foolishness; but unto us which are saved it is the power of God. For it is written, I will destroy the Wisdom of the wise, and will bring to nothing the understanding of the prudent. Where is the wise? Where is the scribe, where is the disputer of this world? hath not God made foolish the wisdom of this world? For after that in the wisdom of God the world by wisdom knew not God, it pleased God by the foolishness of preaching to save them that believe. For the Jews require a sign, and the Greeks seek after wisdom: But we preach Christ crucified, unto the Jews a stumbling block, and unto the Greeks foolishness."[4] As Montaigne interpreted this passage from Scripture, the weaknesses of the human intellect, its inability to discover anything that it could be certain was true, by the use of its own capacities, the maze of contradictions that human reasoning came to, were all part of a Divine plan, a plan to humiliate us. If we could only recognize our own total inadequacies to discover the truth, then we would accept without question whatever God chose to reveal to us. And, as St. Paul had said, God had deliberately chosen to make true what seemed foolish to our so-called wisdom, and false what seemed wise to us. Thus, by rejecting our own rational standards and methods we could become believers. Hence, Montaigne declared,

> The participation we have in the knowledge of truth, such as it is, is not acquired by our own force: God has sufficiently given us to understand that by the testimony He has chosen out of the common people, simple and ignorant men, whom he has been pleased to employ to instruct us in His admirable secrets. Our faith is not of our own acquiring, 'tis

[4] I Corinthians 1: 17–23.

purely the gift of another's bounty; 'tis not by meditation or by virtue of our own understanding that
we have acquired our religion, but by foreign authority and command; the weakness of our judgment more
assists us than force, and our blindness more than
our clearness of sight; 'tis rather by the mediation
of our ignorance than of our knowledge that we know
anything of the divine Wisdom. 'Tis no wonder if our
natural and earthly means cannot conceive that supernatural and heavenly knowledge; let us bring nothing
of our own, but obedience and subjection.[5]

And, it is through scepticism, Montaigne tells us, that
we can reach the proper state to receive faith.

The disciples of Montaigne developed this view
which they called "Sceptical Christianity." First Montaigne's adopted son, the priest Father Pierre Charron
expounded the union of scepticism and faith as the
view of the Christian mystics, and as the proper answer
to the Reformers. We come to know God only by realizing our ignorance, and by rejecting all the false or
dubious opinions that clutter up our minds. By means
of this wholesale rejection of all the alleged fruits of
man's intellectual activities, one comes to true wisdom,
the realization that we know nothing. We are thereby
prepared for God. Our mind is blank, ready to receive
God's message. In this state, Charron proudly proclaimed one can never be a heretic, since one asserts
nothing unless God reveals some truths to us.[6] The
Reformers, on Charron's account, make the dreadful,

[5] Michel Montaigne, "Apologie de Raimond Sebond," in *Les
Essais de Michel de Montaigne,* ed. by Pierre Villey, Tome II
(Paris 1922), p. 230. The translation is that of Charles Cotton.
[6] Pierre Charron, *Les trois veritez* (Paris 1595), pp. 17–20
and 26: *De la Sagesse,* Livre II, chap. ii, in *Toutes les Oeuvres
de Pierre Charron Parisien, Docteur es Droicts, Chantre et
Chanoine* (Paris 1635); *Petit Traticé de Sagesse* (Paris 1635),
chap. IV, pp. 223–26, and Popkin, "Skepticism and the Counter-
Reformation," pp. 73–76; and *History of Scepticism,* pp. 57–63.

dogmatic error of trying to measure religious truths according to their own lights, of making their own feeble minds the standard for determining which religion is true. The sceptic makes no judgment of his own, but is always ready to receive God's judgment. Since the sceptic doesn't judge, he cannot decide to join the Reformation, and hence remains on the Catholic side.[7]

Another disciple of Montaigne, François de la Mothe Le Vayer, the teacher of the Dauphin of France, carried the theme of Christian scepticism or sceptical Christianity still further. Any intellectual activity which attempted to gain knowledge about God or what He had created was impious. Science, for example, was an attempt to measure the creation of an Infinite Creator by the miserable, weak, unreliable faculties of finite man. Science was an attempt to limit God's achievements to what man could understand. By doubting everything, one gave up the vain presumption of so-called learned men of trying to understand. When one could achieve the state of suspense of judgment on all matters, one was both truly wise, and close to religious truth. One was wise in not pretending to know what one could not know or did not know.[8] And,

> The soul of a Christian Sceptic is like a field cleared and cleansed of bad plants, such as the dangerous axioms of an infinity of learned persons, which then receives the dew drops of divine grace much more happily than it would do if it were still occupied and

[7] Charron, *Trois veritez*, Livre III, esp. chaps., i–iii and xii; and *Sagesse*, Livre II, chap. ii, p. 22.

[8] Cf. François de la Mothe Le Vayer, "Opuscule ou petit traitté sceptique sur cette façon de parler, n'avoir pas le sens commun," in *Oeuvres de François de la Mothe Le Vayer* (Paris 1669) vol. IX; "Prose chagrine," *Oeuvres*, IX, and "Discours pour montrer que les doutes de la philosophie sceptique sont de grand usage dans les sciences," *Oeuvres*, XV. On La Mothe Le Vayer, see Popkin, *History of Scepticism*, pp. 92–99.

filled with the vain presumption of knowing everything with certainty and doubting nothing.[9]

The Christian sceptic leaves his doubts at the foot
of the altar, and accepts what God obliges him to believe by faith alone.[10]

The theory of Montaigne and his followers has been
interpreted in two opposite ways. And these two interpretations have represented the two directions in which
modern scepticism has developed, one to the libertin-
ism, and free thought of Voltaire and Hume, the
other to the irrational and anti-rational defense of faith
of Kierkegaard. Most commentators from Pascal down
to the twentieth century have assumed that the aim of
Montaigne's scepticism was not to defend Christianity,
but to destroy it. By showing that all is in doubt, and
that human reason is incapable of discovering any natural or religious truths by its own devices, does it
follow that one ought to believe Christianity by faith
alone, or does it follow that one ought to believe nothing? Actually, the sceptical position of Montaigne in
itself implies no conclusion as to what one ought, or
can do, about it. The avowed position of Montaigne,
Charron, La Mothe Le Vayer, and others is the non-
sequitur, all is in doubt, therefore one ought to believe
in Christianity. But if all is doubt, why believe anything? Some thinkers in the seventeenth century, and
many since have decided that, in fact, Montaigne and
his followers were not believers, but actually were secret atheists making fun of religion, by showing that
belief in Christianity is irrational and unreasonable.
The cynical attitude towards belief of Voltaire's article
on "Faith"[11] has been assumed to be Montaigne's

[9] La Mothe Le Vayer, "Prose chagrine," p. 362.

[10] Ibid., p. 361.

[11] Voltaire, *Dictionnaire philosophique*, ed. Julien Benda,
texte établi par Raymond Naves (Paris 1954), art. "Foi", I,
pp. 202–3. Here Voltaire tells the story of a discussion between
Pico della Mirandola and Pope Alexander VI concerning who

view. The "reasonable" scepticism of Hume, if fundamentally all is doubt, one ought to believe only what a reasonable, sophisticated worldly gentleman finds psychologically plausible, has been taken as the message of Montaigne's *Apology*.

On the other hand, some, though few indeed, have interpreted Montaigne's position as a sincere fideism, a theory that religious knowledge rests on faith alone, and that without faith man is left in doubt about everything. There has been a recent revival of considering Montaigne as a religious thinker rather than as one of the foremost enemies of Christian belief. But, as far as I know, I am the only one who has seriously argued that not only Montaigne, but also his disciples from Charron through the various so-called *libertins érudits* of the seventeenth century *could* have been sincere advocates of Christianity and theoreticians of a type of sceptical Counter-Reformation.[12] The question of the actual degree of belief or disbelief of the early Christian sceptics may be difficult or impossible to determine, and it raises a problem that we shall meet with again in examining the views of Bayle and Kierkegaard. But for our purposes what is significant is

might be the father of a child of the Pope's daughter. Pico declares he believes it to be the husband, though the husband is impotent. Pico insists he believes this on faith, and faith consists in believing things *because* they are impossible. Finally Voltaire's Pope asks Pico, "Tell me what merit can there be in telling God that one is convinced of things which actually one cannot be convinced of? What pleasure can this give to God? Between ourselves, to say that one believes what it is impossible to believe, is to lie. . . ." "Pico della Mirandola made a great sign of the cross. Eh! God the Father, he exclaimed, may your Holiness forgive me, you are not a Christian —No, on my faith, said the Pope.—I did not think so, said Pico della Mirandola."

[12] Cf. Popkin, "Skepticism and the Counter-Reformation," *History of Scepticism*, Chapters III and V; see also "Theological and Religious Scepticism," *Christian Scholar*, XXXIX (1956), pp. 150–52 and seq.

not the intentions of Montaigne and his followers, but the two lines of development that resulted in the seventeenth and eighteenth centuries, the advocacy of a purer and purer fideism by Pascal, Bayle and Huet, and the sceptical attack on religion of Hume and Voltaire.

Pascal regarded Montaigne as a complete unbeliever, and saw the state of the sceptic who doubted everything as the misery of man without God. Unfortunately, for Pascal, in the natural state in which we find ourselves the only conclusion we can come to is that scepticism is the truth.[13] But rather than accepting this calmly, as Montaigne and his followers appeared to do, for Pascal this is the most miserable situation imaginable. Why? Because we have an innate compulsion to believe and to seek for truth. Our sad state is that by rational activity we are forced into complete scepticism, and by our natural instincts we are forced into beliefs. We struggle incessantly for a resolution, and for a knowledge of truth, which we can only have through God. The sceptical problem is not so much a matter of enlightened theory, and humorous anecdotes, as it was for Montaigne and his followers, but it is a life and death struggle for peace and salvation. In a lengthy and poignant passage, Pascal summed up man's plight.

> The chief arguments of the sceptics—I pass over the lesser ones—are that we have no certainty of the truth of these principles apart from faith and revelation, except in so far as we naturally perceive them in ourselves. Now this natural intuition is not a convincing proof of their truth; since, having no certainty, apart from faith, whether man was created by a good God, or by a wicked demon, or by chance, it is doubtful whether these principles given to us are true, or false, or uncertain, according to our origin. Again,

[13] Blaise Pascal, *Pensées,* texte de Brunschvicg, ed. Ch. - Marc des Granges (Paris 1951), No. 432, p. 182.

no person is certain, apart from faith, whether he is awake or sleeps, seeing that during sleep we believe that we are awake as firmly as we do when we *are* awake; . . .

whether the other half of our life, in which we think we are awake, is not another sleep a little different from the former, from which we awake when we suppose ourselves asleep? . . .

I notice the only strong point of the dogmatists, namely, that, speaking in good faith and sincerely, we cannot doubt natural principles. Against this the sceptics set up in one word the uncertainty of our origin, which includes that of our nature. . . .

So there is open war among men, in which each must take a part, and side either with dogmatism or scepticism. For he who thinks to remain neutral is above all a sceptic. . . . he who is not against them is essentially for them. . . .

What then shall man do in this state? Shall he doubt everything? Shall he doubt whether he is awake, whether he is being pinched, or whether he is being burned? Shall he doubt whether he doubts? Shall he doubt whether he exists? We cannot go so far as that; and I lay it down as a fact that there never has been a real complete sceptic. Nature sustains our feeble reason, and prevents it raving to this extent.

Shall he then say, on the contrary, that he certainly possesses truth—he who, when pressed ever so little, can show no title to it, and is forced to let go his hold?

What a chimera then is man! What a novelty! What a monster, what a chaos, what a contradiction, what a prodigy! Judge of all things, imbecile worm of the earth; depositary of truth, a sink of uncertainty and error; the pride and refuse of the universe!

Who will unravel this tangle? Nature confutes the sceptics, and reason confutes the dogmatists. What

then will you become, O men! who try to find out by
your natural reason what is your true condition? You
cannot avoid one of these sects, nor adhere to one
of them.

Know then, proud man, what a paradox you are
to yourself. Humble yourself, weak reason; be silent,
foolish nature; learn that man infinitely transcends
man, and learn from your Master your true condition, of which you are ignorant. Hear God.[14]

Thus, for Pascal, reason leads us to scepticism, nature keeps us from scepticism, and herein is our
hopeless conflict and misery. Only by the Grace of
God can we be saved from this morass. The saving
faith is not founded on reason, since only after we have
faith can we have any certainty. Scepticism is not
the road to faith, but a stage before faith that is transcended by faith.

The crisis of man led by reason to complete doubt,
and by nature to dogmatic belief, was developed more
casually by the remaining sceptics we shall consider
before Kierkegaard. The Bishop Huet, teacher of the
Dauphin of France, and later Bishop of Avranches at
the end of the seventeenth century, presented, a calm
enlightened fideism in his notorious *Traité philosophique de la foiblesse de l'esprit humain.* In Huet's
account, in one sense everything is in doubt, in the
sense that we discover no complete guarantee of the
truth of anything by the use of our own faculties alone.
Neither in mathematics, nor in science, nor in religion
can we, by employing our reason and our senses,
achieve an indubitable certitude. But this type of doubt
is only theoretical. In fact, we have a sufficient degree
of assurance to live and act.

> . . . it is one Thing to live, another to philosophize.
> When therefore the Question is about the Conduct
> of our Lives, and the Performance of our Duty, we

[14] Ibid., No. 434, pp. 183–84. The translation is that of
W. F. Trotter.

cease to be Philosophers, to be Opponents, doubtful or uncertain; and become poor, simple, credulous Idiots; we call Things by their Names, and re-assume our Understanding and Manners; we conform our Manners to those of other Men, and to their Laws and Customs. I who, a while ago, doubted whether I did exist, or whether there were any more Men, do now banish all those Thoughts, and as if I was sure both of my own and other Men's Existence: I eat and drink, I visit my Friends, I show my Respects to them, and entertain them: I affirm and deny that this is true, or that is false.[15]

We live with our doubts because the doubts only occur, for Huet, with regard to the foundations of what we believe, not the actual beliefs. God, fortunately, through both a natural and a revealed way shows us what to believe. Thus, we can doubt the reasons for all beliefs, but we end up with the beliefs because we are led both super-naturally and naturally to accept them. So, fundamentally everything we know comes from God, and it comes without anguish or tears. If we just live naturally and religiously, we are shown what to believe, even though we know that everything is in one sense doubtful.

Huet's separation of theoretical doubt and practical belief is in sharp contrast to the far-reaching scepticism of Pierre Bayle. In the formulation of Bayle's fideism most of the ingredients of Kierkegaard's irrationalism make their clearest appearance. Before speaking of Bayle's views I should like to say a little about the author, and the setting of his theory. Bayle was one of the large group of French Protestants who fled to the Netherlands in the last quarter of the seventeenth century. From his new home in Rotterdam he set forth

---

[15] Pierre - Daniel Huet, *Traité philosophique de la foiblesse de l'esprit humain* (Londres 1741), pp. 242–43. This work was written in the 1690's and first published after the author's death in 1723. The translation is from the 1725 English edition.

a most unusual type of fideism that was to have far-reaching consequences in paving the way for the scepticism of the Age of Reason. Bayle's scepticism seems to have grown out of the controversies within the Walloon Church between the liberal, rational faction which held that the articles of religion should be based upon reasonable evidence and should be acceptable to a reasonable man, and the orthodox faction which held that the articles of religion were based upon faith, and were to be accepted whether they made sense to a rational man, or not. Bayle took the orthodox view and turned it into a super-scepticism, and a basis for a totally irrational, incomprehensible, immoral blind faith. This finished product looked so ridiculous and unreasonable that subsequent generations found in Bayle the arsenal of the Enlightenment, a battery of weapons that would destroy any religious faith man might still have. The extreme-anti-rationalism of Bayle, possibly equalled and surpassed only by Kierkegaard, was to become the opening wedge to an Age of Reason.

Bayle's view is, perhaps, best set forth in the footnotes to his article on the Greek sceptic, Pyrrho, in his *Dictionnaire historique et critique*. In note B Bayle reported a conversation between two abbés on whether there is any reason to be a sceptic any more, now that the truth has been revealed. One abbé says there is more reason than ever. First of all, modern science and modern philosophy lead one to complete scepticism, since they lead us to doubt that the qualities we see, the colors, tastes, smells, etc. are really in physical things. Instead we are taught that material objects are actually just extended parts in motion, and the rest is only appearances in our minds. But, Bayle points out, for all we know, the extension and motion we see are also only ideas in our minds, and we have no evidence that anything exists outside of our minds. This argument which was to plague philosophers down to the twentieth century was followed by a more remarkable contention—that we could not even be sure that what was self-evident or what was demonstrable, was true. In fact, if one accepted Christianity, Bayle claimed, one could not also believe that what was self-evident or demonstrable was necessarily true, or that self-evidence is the mark of truth. If the doctrines of the Trinity, the Fall, and Transubstantiation were accepted as true, then the most basic axioms of logic and philosophy could not also be true even though they are self-evident. The revealed truths are in direct conflict with the truths of reason, and the standards of reason. Hence, if we accept Christianity we must reject the standards and the maxims of rationality.[16] At times Bayle insisted that this was the essence of faith, namely that it was complete and absolute opposition to reason. If one believed, it was not because of any evidence, but in spite of the fact that reason could furnish evidence against the article of belief.[17]

The theory Bayle usually advanced (though he was sometimes sufficiently sceptical to reject even his own theory)[18] was that the attempt to discover truth in any area whatsoever always leads to complete doubt. Hence, the rational world always ends up in complete scepticism. Because of this, one must turn from reason to faith, and accept the faith blindly since there is not and cannot be any evidence for it. One of Bayle's fa-

[16] Pierre Bayle, *Dictionnaire historique et critique*, 5 ed. (Amsterdam, etc. 1740), art. "Pyrrhon", Rem. B. pp. 732–33. This part of Bayle's views appears in Pierre Bayle, *Historical and Critical Dictionary* (Indianapolis 1965), trans. R. H. Popkin, pp. 194–204.

[17] See, for example, Bayle's "II. Eclaircissement. Quelle est la maniere dont il faut considérer ce que j'ai dit concernant les Objections des Manichéens," and "III. Eclaircissement. Que ce qui a été dit du Pyrrhonisme, dans ce Dictionnaire, ne peut point préjudicier à la Religion," in *Dictionnaire*, T. IV, pp. 630–47 and in *Historical and Critical Dictionary*, pp. 409–35.

[18] Cf. Popkin, "Pierre Bayle's Place in 17th Century Scepticism," in *Pierre Bayle, Philosophe de Rotterdam* ed. Paul Dibon (Amsterdam 1959) and Popkin, introduction to *Historical and Critical Dictionary*.

vorite quotations is the conversation of the Mareschal
d'Hoquincourt and le Père Canaye by the irreligious
writer, St. Evremond,

> "The devil take me if I believed anything, but
> since that time I could bear to be crucified for re-
> ligion. It is not that I see more reason in it than
> I did before; on the contrary, I see less than ever.
> But I know not what to say to you, for I would
> submit to be crucified without knowing why or where-
> fore." "So much the better, my Lord," replied the
> father, twanging it very devoutly through the nose,
> "so much the better; these are not human impulses
> but are inspired by heaven. Away with reason: this
> is the true religion, away with reason. What an extraor-
> dinary grace, my Lord, has heaven bestowed upon
> you!"[19]

Bayle made religion a totally irrational matter, as we
shall see Kierkegaard also did, but Bayle also seems
to have believed that one could offer rational evidence
for irrationalism. In spite of his complete scepticism
about reason, one finds Bayle saying over and over
again that one can prove the bankruptcy of reason,
and one can prove that one must turn from the rational
world to the irrational world of blind faith.[20] In this
respect we shall find Kierkegaard's irrationalism still
more far-reaching.

If one asks in view of Bayle's irrationalism why he
should believe in Christianity, if he really did, the only
answer seems to have been that of Bayle's erstwhile
friend, and later long-time enemy, Pierre Jurieu, the

[19] Bayle, *Dictionnaire*, "Eclair. III," T. IV, p. 645.

[20] See, for example, Bayle, *Dictionnaire*, "Eclair. III", T. IV,
pp. 641–42; *Réponse aux questions d'un provincial*, in *Oeuvres diverses* (La Haye 1727), T. III, pp. 832 and 836; and
Entretiens de Maxine et de Themiste, *Oeuvres diverses*, T. IV,
pp. 44 and 47; and Popkin, "Bayle's Place in 17th Century
Scepticism."

leader of the orthodox French Calvinists. Jurieu (1637–1713) had been professor of theology at the last Calvinist school in France, and had gotten Bayle a post there. They both fled to Rotterdam after the Revocation of the Edict of Nantes, and were very close for a few years. Jurieu was carrying on polemical warfare against Catholics, liberal Protestants and Socinians. He soon decided that Bayle was one of the greatest enemies of religion, a secret atheist. Bayle, however, kept claiming that his own theology was just that of his former sponsor and friend. Jurieu insisted that the basis of his faith was "I believe it, because I want to believe it."[21] One could only discern that Scripture was Divine if God gave the reader Grace. No scientific or rational evidence could give decisive certainty, in view of the sceptical problems.[22] The sole basis for belief for Jurieu, and perhaps for Bayle, was personal subjective desire. The belief was sound if it were forced upon one by the action of God's Grace. Jurieu, in spite of this, insisted on the punishment or excommunication of all who did not share what he regarded as the true beliefs. Bayle, however, saw a problem that was to plague Kierkegaard, that if belief was really irrational and blind, and based on no evidence whatsoever, there was also no way of being completely sure of what constituted the true faith, or when one had it.[23] And hence, in Bayle's hands, Chris-

[21] Pierre Jurieu, *Seconde Apologie pour M. Jurieu, ou response à un libelle sans nom presenté aux Synodes de Leyden & de Naerden . . . le 2de Mai 1691* (Rotterdam 1692), pp. 8–10; and *Traité de la nature et de la grace* (Utrecht 1688), pp. 225ff.

[22] Jurieu, *Seconde Apologie*, pp. 13–15; and *Traité de la nature et de la grace*, pp. 243ff. on Jurieu's theology, see R. H. Popkin, "Hume and Jurieu: Possible Calvinist Origins of Hume's Theory of Belief," *Rivista Critica di Storia della Filosofia*, Anno 1967, pp. 400–11.

[23] Bayle, *Commentaire philosophique sur ces paroles de Jesus-Christ.* Contrain-les d'entrer, Part II, chap. x, in *Oeuvres diverses*, T. II, p. 437.

tianity seemed to have been shorn of any foundation whatsoever, and if one happened to be a Christian it was only a personal idiosyncracy.

The last part of this survey of scepticism and religion that I wish to deal with is the scepticism of David Hume, since it is this non-religious form that actually brought Kierkegaard to his own religious scepticism. Hume like most of his contemporaries in the eighteenth century, took Bayle to be ridiculing religious belief, and to be showing in all possible ways that everything was in doubt. If so, what should one believe? One could not be, in practice, a complete sceptic, a doubter about everything, because no one was so constituted. Hence, one must, like Huet, separate the theoretical doubts that can be raised, from the practical certainties, that are forced upon one. Bayle's arguments, Hume found, "admit of no answer, but produce no conviction."[24] Hume followed Bayle in raising doubts about every possible belief, but Hume also found that human nature is such that in spite of the doubts, one is forced to believe. This state of affairs he attributed not to the revelations of some deity, as Huet did, but to some original animal habits in the human beast. What we call a reasonable outlook is only one set of habits forced upon us by nature. An unreasonable outlook is another set of habits. The ones Hume preferred, which he naturally called the reasonable ones, were those of the so-called enlightened reasonable Scotchman of the eighteenth century. In these terms, Hume found when he examined religious belief, the vulgar, superstitious people were unreasonable, and

---

[24] This is what Hume said about Berkeley in likening him to Bayle, cf. David Hume, *An Enquiry Concerning Human Understanding*, Selby-Bigge ed. (Oxford 1951), p. 155n. On Hume on the incredibility of scepticism, see Popkin, "David Hume and the Pyrrhonian Controversy," *Review of Metaphysics*, VI (1952–53), pp. 65–81; and "The Skeptical Precursors of David Hume," *Philosophy and Phenomenological Research*, XVI (1955–56), pp. 61–71.

believed in Christianity. The reasonable man would see
that there was no evidence that there was a God, but
he would find that he had to believe in some sort of
Designer or Architect of the universe, and that this
belief entailed no creed, no religious practices, and in
fact no religion.[25] Both atheism and theism Hume regarded as extravagances of unreasonable people. Of
Christianity, Hume could only say,

> So that, upon the whole, we may conclude, that
> the *Christian Religion* not only was at first attended
> with miracles, but even at this day cannot be be-
> lieved by any reasonable person without one. Mere
> reason is insufficient to convince us of its veracity;
> And whoever is moved by *Faith* to assent to it, is
> conscious of a continued miracle in his own person,
> which subverts all the principles of his understanding,
> and gives him a determination to believe what is
> most contrary to custom and experience.[26]

It was of this passage that Hamann, one of those
whom Kierkegaard admired most, said "This is ortho-
doxy and a testimony to the truth from the mouth of
an enemy and persecutor."[27] In the wave of anti-
Christianity, of deism, pantheism, atheism, and ag-
nosticism that emerged from the Age of Reason Kierkegaard saw that in the very scepticism that had
undermined belief lay the basis for belief. The unreasonableness of Christianity was not the reason for rejecting it, but for affirming it. Surrounded by "rea-

[25] Hume, *Dialogues Concerning Natural Religion,* p. 227.
[26] Hume, *Enquiry Concerning Human Understanding,* p.
131.
[27] Johann G. Hamann, *Schriften,* Theil I (Berlin 1821), p.
406, "so ist diess allemal Orthodoxie, und ein Zeugniss der
Wahrheit in dem Munde eines Feindes und Verfolgers dersel-
ben." On the impact of this interpretation of Hume by Hamann
on Kierkegaard, see Walter Lowrie, *Kierkegaard* (London
1938), pp. 165–67.

sonable" men, who were proceeding to build a new and better world by the proper use of reason, shorn of that unfortunate superstitious vestige, Faith, Kierkegaard offered a new challenge. The Enlightenment had destroyed religious faith, by misunderstanding the lessons of scepticism. The Christian scepticism developed from Montaigne to Bayle had been transformed into an anti-religious scepticism by the Age of Reason. Kierkegaard was to offer a new and stronger advocacy of Christian scepticism, of faith without reason, on the sceptical foundations of the Enlightenment. He was to strike out as the voice crying in the wilderness against the irreligious scepticism and the new rationalism of his age. The latter he would destroy through a revitalized scepticism, the former he would reject through reassertion of the fideistic conclusion of the Christian sceptics.

2

The previous survey of the relationship of scepticism and religion from Montaigne up to the Enlightenment has indicated how sceptical argumentation and theory was used by some thinkers as a defense of religious belief, and how, in the Age of Reason, scepticism became a basis for disbelief in religion. The eighteenth century emphasis on the unreasonableness of religion ushered in an era of considering religion as an unfortunate legacy from a previous, unintelligent age. The fact that earlier sceptics had stressed, that the central tenets of Christianity cannot be established by rational or scientific means, became not a reason for believing, but rather a reason for disbelieving.

In the late eighteenth century, there was a strange figure, J. G. Hamann, in Germany, who was the lonely voice crying in the wilderness. He saw that the sceptical arguments of Hume could well provide the rationale for a renewed faith in Christianity instead of its rejection. Hamann translated Hume's most irreligious work, the *Dialogues Concerning Natural Re-*

ligion, and commented on it, in the hopes of making rational men like Immanuel Kant see the light, and turn from reason to faith. Hamann's crusade met with little success at the time, but it was his insight that was to flower in the work of Søren Kierkegaard.[28] It was Kierkegaard who was to develop so dramatically a new rendition of the relationship of philosophical scepticism and religious belief, and to develop a new sceptical onslaught against the outlook of his age, so that a new Age of Faith might begin.

Kierkegaard was born in Copenhagen in 1813, and lived a relatively unexciting life. He left his home town only a few times; he had one romance; he studied philosophy and theology, and he wrote a large body of cryptic works, carrying on a crusade of monumental proportions, a crusade to conquer the Christian world by introducing it to what he considered the real meaning and message of Christianity. His journals reveal the quest for faith, his conversion and inspiration, and this enormous, grandiose campaign to awaken them that sleep, the human race.

The strategy of Kierkegaard's crusade was to present his theme on a series of different fronts, through publishing a weird series of works, each of which had its place in a master plan, known to its author, but not the reader. The works are weird, first of all, in that they are alleged to have been written by an assortment of authors, by strange people with names like Johannes Climacus, Anti-Climacus, Virgilius Hofniensis, Johannes de Silentio, and Søren Kierkegaard. Each alleged author has his point of view, his attitudes, and his purpose. Some of the authors disagree. In one work they get together and discuss their views. This strange world looks at first glance like madness, but there is also method in this madness. The Kierke-

28 Cf. Philip Merlan, "Hamann et les Dialogues de Hume," *Revue de Metaphysique et de Morale,* LIX (1954), pp. 285–89; and "Hume and Hamann," *Personalist,* XXXII (1951), pp. 11–18.

gaardian literature has a unity, and the various invented authors unfold, at a series of levels, the central message. The lowest group are the so-called aesthetic authors, whose function it is to awaken interest in man's plight, in the emptiness and sordidness of ordinary human existence. On this level, Kierkegaard's authors are masters of human psychology. And his story from *Either/Or,* "The Diary of a Seducer" is a magnificent presentation of a human tragedy, of a life lived on the surface, solely for the pursuit of pleasure. No message is advanced. Just a picture painted of how the world ordinarily goes on.

The second level of authors are the philosophical ones, those who explore the possibility of understanding the human world, and of developing a theory of knowledge, and a system of values. And philosophically, their achievement turns out to be almost entirely negative. They attack and decimate the dogmatic philosophers, those who claim that we can have any guaranteed rational knowledge about ourselves, our world, or our values. The philosophical authors develop the bankruptcy of intellectual endeavour, and point out the irrationality of the solution Kierkegaard will propose—a religious solution.

Finally the last group of authors are the religious ones, some who are fanatical, and some who are groping. And on this level Kierkegaard himself emerges as one of the principal writers, signing many of the works in his own name. He rhapsodizes on religious themes, he preaches, he prophesies. He rants and raves against philosophers and philosophy. And finally, in his last work, he unleashes a tirade against the Christian world, in his *Attack on Christendom,* one of the most virulent denunciations of accepted religious practices ever written.

The message of Kierkegaard can, I believe, best be grasped by starting with his scepticism, since Kierkegaard accepts and develops Hume's claim that to be a philosophical sceptic is the first and most essential step towards becoming a true and believing Christian. In *Philosophical Fragments, Concluding Unscientific Postscript, De Omnibus Dubitandum Est, Fear and Trembling,* and *Training in Christianity* a powerful and devastating scepticism is developed as well as a most sceptical interpretation of Christianity to be accepted on faith alone.

Kierkegaard's philosophical pseudonym, Johannes Climacus, presents a series of sceptical problems which show why we cannot obtain necessary knowledge about the world, that is, knowledge that cannot possibly be false. The sorts of information that might constitute true knowledge are either historical data, that is information about events that occur in time, or they are eternal truths. The former possibility is ruled out because all historical statements are only probable and could be false. No necessary demonstration can be given of them (no logical contradiction is involved in denying their supposed truth). Also, the very fact that they are historical shows that at some time they were not true (for if they were always true, they would constitute eternal truths and not historical statements.)[29]

On the other hand, Climacus argued, eternal knowledge is only about concepts and how they are related, and tells us nothing about what occurs in the world. Eternal knowledge deals with essences, not existences, and hence eternal knowledge is vacuous as regards what is necessarily true about this world, since it tells us nothing about what must be in this world. All it tells us is that *if* certain objects exist, then they must have certain properties and relations. But whether or not these objects exist is a historical and not an eternal matter.[30] Therefore, we can develop a System, à la

[29] Søren Kierkegaard, *Philosophical Fragments* (Princeton 1946), "Interlude," esp. pp. 60–66.

[30] Søren Kierkegaard, *Philosophical Fragments* (Princeton 1946), "The Absolute Paradox," pp. 31–33, esp. n. 2, pp. 32–33.

Hegel, of necessary truths about the logical relations of concepts, but not about existential affairs.[31]

And, still further, all of our alleged knowledge is ultimately historical information, even if it is an attempt to deal only with concepts. Anything which we consider as knowledge is somebody's thoughts, and as such constitutes part of somebody's intellectual life. Our thinking and our attempt at knowing always starts in a historical situation in our lives, and whatever we think and believe we know, even mathematical truths, are part of our intellectual biographies. We cannot achieve an absolute standpoint, outside of historical events, and therefore our conceptualizing still remains within the temporal, historical sphere. So, we remain unable to attain true knowledge.[32]

According to Climacus, our attempt to bridge the gap between our historical existence and the unchanging world of eternal truth represents "the comedy of the higher lunacy."[33] The quest for necessary knowledge only results in finding a Hegelian cookbook, a list of all the recipes, but no food. It does not satisfy our hunger for knowledge, and the Hegelian cookbook, in the final analysis, is only a historical product in the life of a Hegelian, and hence is only historical information, too, and not genuine knowledge. What we can learn historically is only gossip, news about what has happened or is happening—news that can never be necessary.

The beginning and the end of the scepticism of Kierkegaard, as portrayed in the quest for knowledge of Johannes Climacus, is the contention that in order for a human being to achieve any true knowledge, two miracles would have to take place. First it would be a miracle if there were necessary truth about the world,

[31] Kierkegaard, *Concluding Unscientific Postscript* (Princeton 1944), pp. 99–113.

[32] Kierkegaard, *Concluding Unscientific Postscript* (Princeton 1944), *loc. cit.*

[33] Kierkegaard, *Philosophical Fragments,* p. 34, n. 3.

a historical proposition that was incapable of being false, or a necessary truth that dealt with an existential reality. And, secondly, there would have to be a miracle for us to be able to recognize it as a necessary truth about the world, and not as just historical information about ourselves. If we pursue the truth without the aid of miracles, we end up in complete scepticism. We only discover the impossibility, in a rational sense, of there being the kind of truth we seek, and the futility of our seeking it. From a historical point of departure, aided solely by our rational capacities, we end only in despair when we seek for necessary truth.[34]

When one reaches this state of sceptical despair, what does one do about it? Climacus suggests that there are two alternative courses of action, both of which involve acts of the will and not reason. These courses are that one can either *will* to doubt everything, or *will* to believe something. Both of these are resolutions to do something in view of the rationally insoluble sceptical crisis. The resolution to doubt leaves one a sceptic both in theory and practice. The resolution to believe does not overcome the theoretical grounds for sceptical doubt, but enables one to affirm on the practical level.[35]

If one resolves or chooses to be a believer, what should one believe? This question admits of no rational solution, since the decision to believe is made in spite of the insoluble sceptical difficulties that exist in determining the truth or falsity of any given proposition. If one believes, it is not because of the existence of any rational evidence, but in spite of the absence of all rational evidence. In fact, Climacus insists, to believe and to know are two separate and opposite acts. If adequate evidence existed for a proposition, one would know it, and hence have no need to believe it.

[34] Kierkegaard, *Philosophical Fragments,* pp. 6–12, 36–38 and 93.

[35] Kierkegaard, *Philosophical Fragments,* pp. 67–69.

The need for the act of belief is inversely proportional to the evidence at hand. And pure belief occurs when there is no evidence and there can be no evidence for what is believed. The absence of any evidence for a proposition eliminates any claims that the proposition is known to be true. The impossibility of any evidence excludes any rational acceptance of the proposition, and leaves it as something that could only be believed, not known. Hence Kierkegaard accepted Tertullian's dictum, "credo quia absurdum est" almost as a definition of belief.[36]

Put in another way, this theory of belief is summed up on another of Kierkegaard's favorite citations, that of J. G. Hamann regarding Hume's essay "On Miracles." "Lies and novels must needs be probable; hypotheses and fables too; but not the truth and foundation of our faith."[37] This amounts to a rejection of the "reasonable" scepticism of Hume or Voltaire in favor of the "unreasonable" scepticism of Bayle and Jurieu. Since fundamentally all is in doubt, one believes not on a basis of probabilities, customs or experience, but in spite of them all. One believes because one wants to, not because the reasonable man of common sense would.

What belief does one have? What is the absurdity or impossibility that one accepts? For Kierkegaard it is a belief in that which could not possibly occur (according to our rational lights), a belief that God has existed or does exist in the temporal, historical order. Since it follows from the definition of God as an eternal Being, that He cannot have been or be a temporal one, the proposition "God has existed, or does exist in time" asserts a genuine logical impossibility. Therefore, since the event is impossible, there can be no evidence that it has occurred or does occur, and there can be no

[36] Kierkegaard, *Philosophical Fragments*, pp. 40–41; and *Postscript*, pp. 182ff.

[37] Hamann, *Schriften*, I, P. 425; and Kierkegaard, *Fragments*, p. 42–43.

knowledge of the event. There can only be belief. And, if one resolves to believe this, and if the belief is "true" (that is if it corresponds to what is actually the case in the world), one believes something that can only be supernaturally true, that is true by a miracle, since it is contrary to our natural lights.[38]

To connect this analysis of belief with Christianity, Kierkegaard's philosophical spokesman, Johannes Climacus, tries to show that from our point of view and from God's, this blind belief in the absurd or impossible is all that we can expect. When we search for true knowledge, we end up in complete scepticism. We realize that, for various theoretical reasons, we cannot ascertain that any proposition about the world is necessarily true. Having made this discovery, we can, if we so desire, will to believe. Since to believe a proposition is to accept it without evidence, the purest belief is one in something that is impossible, for then no evidence could ever exist. If one believes that God existed in time, one has such a pure belief. Such a belief can only be known to be true if two miracles occur, one that makes the impossible actual, the other that makes us capable of recognizing it. We can only be subjectively certain, that is completely assured, and free from the presence of doubts in our minds. But, at the same time we are always objectively uncertain, since we can never tell if our belief that God has existed, or does exist, in time corresponds with the "real" facts of the case. The believer believes, and believes without hesitation that what he believes is true, but he will never know, if there is a God, and if it is His decision and action that determines whether what is believed is also true.[39]

The person who accepts this theory of scepticism and belief, and who believes in Christianity, that is who believes that Jesus is God and that He has existed

[38] Kierkegaard, Fragments, pp. 49–51; and Postscript, pp. 290–91 and 339–40.

[39] Kierkegaard, Postscript, Part II, esp. chaps. 2 and 3.

in human history, is led to a radical reinterpretation of Christianity. God has chosen to make His Own Incarnation a matter that we can believe in, but never know. Therefore, He must have chosen to offer us *no* evidence of the fact that the Incarnation has occurred, and left it a matter that we can only accept on faith. Hence there can be no historical or rational information regarding the occurrence of the Incarnation of Jesus that could constitute a basis for knowing that it had happened. On this basis, Johannes Climacus argues that historical records of events in Palestine in the first century, Biblical information about the character, moral teachings, and miracles of Jesus, and rational analysis of His doctrines would all be irrelevant to establishing the only crucial belief of Christianity, that the historical Jesus is God. Historical records could only tell us about probable historical facts. The Bible only tells us the facts about an individual, but provides no indication or assurance that He is God. A logical or rational analysis only yields hypothetical necessary knowledge of the form "if God has appeared in history, then . . . ," but does not tell us if the antecedent is true. The central tenet of Christianity remains only an item for faith, since nothing we could know, or accept as probable, is or could be, evidence for it.[40]

This picture of Christianity devoid of all rational or historical foundations is buttressed by Climacus by suggesting this is what one would expect of a deity. He compares the situation to that of the king who wants to marry a poor maiden, but only wants to do so if she really loves him for himself, and not his power, position or wealth. So, he approaches her incognito, completely incognito. Only this way can he avoid either forcing her or seducing her into a decision, and only this way can he be sure she has chosen because she wants to. God vis-à-vis man may be doing the

---

[40] Kierkegaard, *Fragments,* chaps. 4 and 5; and *Training in Christianity* (London 1941), pp. 28–39.

same. If we could see or figure out that an Incarnation had occurred, we might be forced by God's power, or seduced by the possibility of His rewards into acknowledging God's presence. If we can in no way discern it, and yet we believe it, then our belief in it is only because we want to believe in it.[41]

This picture of a purely fideistic Christianity, devoid of all possible evidence of its truth, is very similar to the interpretation of the Christian religion offered earlier by the theoretician of irrationalism among the French refugees in the Netherlands, Pierre Jurieu. For Jurieu the Bible contains no religious information except for a believer, the reported miracles are open to natural interpretations unless one is a believer. Faith must precede any alleged evidence, and *"I believe it, because I want to believe it"* and this is the only possible "justification" of the faith.[42]

Thus Kierkegaard, like Jurieu, tries to eliminate all questions of evidence for probability from matters of faith, and tries to base his acceptance of Christianity on its Paradox, its absurdity, that God has existed in time. The supreme merit of Christianity, Climacus tells us, is that it expresses the total absurdity, going beyond all other previous religions in asserting that the impossible has occurred.[43] But is the central assertion of Christianity, that Jesus is God, *the* sole claimant to the title of being *the* Total Absurdity. It seems to me that what is absurd, on Kierkegaard's rendition, is the paradox of *an* Incarnation, and not of *the* Incarnation. An unlimited number of similarly absurd beliefs to Christianity would seem to be easy to construct, such as the alleged belief that Kierkegaard was God, that Johannes Climacus was God, that the Domtoren of Utrecht is God, etc., etc. If there are no rational or probable criteria for evaluating beliefs, there does not seem to be

[41] Kierkegaard, *Fragments*, chap. 2.

[42] Jurieu, *Seconde Apologie*, pp. 8–15; and *Traité de la nature et de la grace, Seconde traité*, chap. 2.

[43] Kierkegaard, *Fragments*, chap. 5, esp. p. 92.

any reason for choosing one of these paradoxes or absurdities rather than another. All one can do is reiterate Jurieu's maxim as one's "reason" for one's belief, *"I believe it, because I want to believe it."*

And, one can ask further, on the basis of Kierkegaard's sceptical theory, can one tell when one has found the right or true belief? Ultimately, it would seem that one is compelled to say no. Kierkegaard's theory appears to lead to a conclusion and a climax as sceptical as that of Pierre Bayle's. Even after "the leap into Faith," one can have no assurance that what one believes is what is true, what God has done, and not merely what one thinks, believes, or hopes is true. In the final analysis, there is no way of distinguishing the true revelation from a personal, idiosyncratic belief.[44] All standards have been discarded, and all that is left is one's faith, and one's faith that it is the true faith.

And, still further, as Kierkegaard admits in *Fear and Trembling,* one cannot tell who has the faith. The outsider who looks for the man of faith can never tell a true Abraham from anyone else, since he cannot judge the sincerity of what is said, or the reason for the actions performed.[45] A man may claim to have faith, as the Christian sceptics of the sixteenth and seventeenth century did, but may actually have had none.[46] A man without faith can act externally the same way as the believer.[47] And even the man himself cannot be sure whether or not he is a man of faith. Kierkegaard admits that even Abraham may be a demon, believing in himself, and not in God. So that one can never be certain

[44] Bayle, *Commentaire philosophique,* Part II, chap. x, in *Oeuvres diverses,* T. II, esp. pp. 437–38.

[45] Kierkegaard, *Fear and Trembling* (Princeton 1945), "Preliminary Expectoration," pp. 33–78, and 114–16.

[46] Cf. Popkin, "Theological and Religious Scepticism", *Christian Scholar,* XXXIX (1956), pp. 150–58.

[47] Kierkegaard, *Fear and Trembling,* "Problem III," esp. pp. 164ff.

whether one has the right faith, or even if one has faith.[48]

To conclude, the sceptical Christianity of Kierkegaard accepts the full consequences of Hume's irreligious scepticism, and admits that Christianity is opposed to all reason and experience. But in accepting these consequences, it is possible that Kierkegaard has made religion so irrational that it becomes both unintelligible and unrecognizable, that it becomes a faith so blind that it cannot see. And, when all standards of beliefs have been rejected except pure faith, one may wonder whether this leads to *a* religion, or instead to an anarchy of private individual faiths, that cannot be discussed or communicated. Kierkegaard, in following out the implications of a faith that comes after or from a total scepticism about man's rational abilities, has developed a most forceful reassertion of religion. But in rejecting all rational standards, he has made religion a totally subjective matter of which one can be sure only by one's subjective feelings. And each believer has been cut off from all others. Each stands isolated on what he personally believes to be the Rock of Faith. And each has no way of telling whether it is madness or Divine Grace that provides the miracle of his faith.

[48] Kierkegaard, *Fear and Trembling*, discussion on demonism, pp. 144ff.

KIERKEGAARD'S *ON AUTHORITY AND REVELATION*

Stanley Cavell

"I myself perceive only too well," Kierkegaard says in beginning a second Preface to his Cycle of Ethico-Religious Essays, "how obvious is the objection and how much there is in it, against writing such a big book dealing in a certain sense with Magister Adler." His first answer to this objection is just that the book is "about" Adler only in a certain sense, the sense, namely, in which he is a Phenomenon, a transparence through which the age is caught. But that is scarcely a serious answer, because what the objection must mean is: Why use the man Adler in this way? And Kierkegaard has an answer to this as well: it enabled him to accomplish something which "perhaps it was important for our age that [I] should accomplish and which could be accomplished in no other way." This is not a moral defense for his treatment; it does not, for example, undertake to show that an action which on the surface, or viewed one way, appears callous or wanton, is never-

This essay was originally prepared for a colloquium at the University of Minnesota sponsored by its philosophy department in January 1966. "Kierkegaard's *On Authority and Revelation*" by Stanley Cavell is reprinted by permission of Charles Scribner's Sons from *Must We Mean What We Say?* edited by Stanley Cavell. Copyright © 1969 Stanley Cavell. The book mentioned in the title, *On Authority and Revelation: The Book on Adler, or a Cycle of Ethico-Religious Essays,* was translated, with an Introduction and Notes, by Walter Lowrie (Princeton: Princeton University Press, 1955). All references are to this edition. Although never published as a book in Danish, the text may be found in Kierkegaard's *Papirer.*

theless justified or anyway excusable. Kierkegaard goes
on to offer what looks like an aesthetic defense of his
treatment of Adler—"without him [I] could not have
given my presentation the liveliness and the ironical
tension it now has." This moral shock is succeeded by
another as we realize that the presentation in question
is not offered for its literary merit, but for its value as
a case study; it is the justification of a surgeon, whose
right to cut into people is based on his skill and credentials and whose right to present his cases to others
is based on his office and on the obligation to transmit
his knowledge to his peers.

Why, on this ground, is the Adler case of profit? Of
what is he a typical, and until now undiagnosed, case?
He is a case of a particular and prevalent and virulent
confusion, and an initial diagnosis is broached: "Disobedience is the secret of the religious confusion of
our age" (xviii). But what is the secret? Isn't this just
what the case was widely known to be all about? Adler's claim to have had a revelation was certainly a
case for the Church, and in particular a case of confusion; he was suspended on the ground that his mind
was deranged (Lowrie's Preface, p. ix) and finally de-
posed after replying evasively to the ecclesiastical in-
terrogatories. This seems patently a case of trying
unsuccessfully to evade the Church's authority. But it
seems Kierkegaard's view of the case is different:
". . . the whole book is essentially . . . about the
confusion from which the concept of revelation suffers
in our confused age. Or . . . about the confusion involved in the fact that the concept of authority has
been entirely forgotten in our confused age" (p. xvi).
The concept is *entirely forgotten*. This suggests not
merely that Adler, for instance, was disobedient in
this particular case; it suggests that Adler would not
have known what obedience consisted in. And it implies that no one else would have known either, in
particular not the Church. The concept of revelation,
on the other hand, is not forgotten; it is confused.
Adler suffers from this, but so do all men in our age,

in particular men of the Church. When Bishop Mynster appealed to Adler's mental derangement as the ground for suspending him, he was evading the same thing Adler would come to evade, the claim to a revelation; and in this evasion the Church is disobedient to its divine command to preach and clarify, to hold open, the word of God.

So the case deepens. For it is not merely that the situations of the extraordinary preacher and the ecclesiastical authority are morally analogous, each suffering his own confusion and each falling into his own disobedience. The third Preface Kierkegaard composed seems to me to go farther, almost saying that they suffer identical consequences, the same confusion of mind, that they are both, as the age is, spiritually deranged. The political events of 1848, which called out this final Preface, are interpreted by Kierkegaard as an attempt to solve a religious problem in political terms, an attempt which will go on, and with increasing confusion and fury, until men turn back to themselves:

> Though all travel in Europe must stop because one must wade in blood, and though all ministers were to remain sleepless for ruminating [about constitutional amendments, votes, equality, etc.] and though every day ten ministers were to lose their reason, and every next day ten new ministers were to begin where the others left off, only to lose their reason in turn—with all this not one step forward is made, an obstacle to it is sternly fixed, and the bounds set by eternity deride all human efforts. . . . Ah, but to get the conflagration quenched, the spontaneous combustion brought about by the friction of worldliness, i.e., to get eternity again—bloodshed may be needed and bombardments, *item* that many ministers shall lose their reason (p. xxi).

The book on Adler is about a minister who has lost his reason, and the flat ambiguity of Kierkegaard's "many ministers" registers exactly the ambiguity of

concepts, the confusion of realms, which he finds the
cause, and the content, of our sickness. Both political
and religious ministers madly try to solve religious
problems with political means, the one by "levelling"
worldly differences into a horrible parody of what is,
Christianly, already a fact; the other by trying to approach by reason what is always grasped by faith, or
by trying to make a shift of emotion do what only a
change of heart can do. This points to a second ambiguity in Kierkegaard's prediction, recorded in the
phrase "shall lose their reason." To lose their reason,
religiously understood as "[letting] the understanding
go" (p. xxii) is precisely what the ministers, what we
all, should do; it is precisely because we are incapable
of that "leap into the religious" (but equally incapable
of letting go of religious categories, of "Christianity
of a sort") that we are confused. This is one way Adler
is seen by Kierkegaard as a Satire upon the Present
Age, and one prompting, throughout the book, for
Kierkegaard's recourse to his categories of the comic
and ironic. Adler performed the one saving act, he
lost his reason; only he did it the way he does everything else, the way things normally are done in our
reflective age: he did it literally, not religiously. He
went crazy. But just in this lies the real defense of
Adler, the *moral* answer to the question "Why expose
Adler?" The derangement of this minister is shared by
all ministers. Of course in his case the derangement
may have got out of hand, he went too far; but this,
as Kierkegaard says in the concluding sections of his
book, is to his "advantage" as a Christian, because
it came from a real spiritual movement toward inner
self-concern. Religiously considered, other ministers
are in the same, or in a worse, state; so it is unjust that
Adler should be singled out for deposition on the
ground of derangement. And the Bishop should have
considered it religiously. For the Church, Adler is not
a transparent medium, but an opaque glass, a mirror.
Perhaps this is a way of seeing why, while Kierkegaard

calls Adler a satire on the present *age,* he calls him an epigram on the Christendom of our age—a terse and ingenious expression of it.

Of course this does not mean that there are no valid religious grounds on which to question and perhaps depose Adler. What it means is that providing these religious grounds, in our age, for our age, will require *overcoming the specific confusion* which has deprived us of religious ground altogether; hence the form of activity will be one of *regaining clarity.* (In this book, Kierkegaard characterizes our age in a few, very specific, and often repeated, ways; his task is to provide correctives specific to them. For example, he finds that we are absent-minded, so his task is to provide presence of mind; he finds us lightminded (lightheaded?), so his task is to inject seriousness and balance; he finds us *distrait,* so his task is to attract our attention.) In his first Preface Kierkegaard says he uses the Adler case "to defend dogmatic concepts," and in the second Preface he claims that from the book one will "get a clarity about certain dogmatic concepts and an ability to use them" (p. xv). By "defend dogmatic concepts" he does not mean "provide a dogmatic backing for them," but rather something like "defend them as themselves dogmatic"; as, so to speak, carrying their own specific religious weight—something, it is implied, theology now fails to do—and this is a matter of coming to see clearly what they mean. So his task is one of providing, or re-providing, their meaning; in a certain sense, giving each its definition. This definition is not to provide some new sense to be attached to a word, with the purpose of better classifying information or outfitting a new theory; it is to clarify what the word does mean, as we use it in our lives—what it means, that is, to anyone with the ability to use it. Now an activity which has the form of taking us from confusion to clarity by means of defining concepts in such a way has, from Socrates to Wittgenstein, signalled philosophical activity.

As I do not insist that philosophy is exhausted in this activity, so I do not insist that Kierkegaard is, in this book, exclusively philosophical. The question I want to turn to is, rather: How far is the book on Adler to be considered a book of philosophy? There are several reasons for pressing this question:

1. It recognizes that the *kind* of writing before us is problematic, and so keeps faith with Kierkegaard's own efforts, as an author and as a Christian, to write distinct kinds of works.

2. This book is itself about writing, about the differences between real and fake authors: our amnesia of the concept of authority is expressed by an amnesia of genuine writing and reading: speech, never easy, has now fully become talk. Adler's confused disobedience to religious authority is not merely analogous to, but is instanced by his disobedience, as an author, to the requirements of art. Adler's books are not only fake religion, they are fake books—and the one because of the other.

3. The emphasis on philosophy distinguishes Kierkegaard's effort here from other efforts with which it may be confused:

a) If one says he writes to defend Christianity and to reform Christendom, then one must know his differences from (say) Luther. "[Luther's] . . . day is over," Kierkegaard said in a work composed during the period in which he was reading and writing about Adler; "No longer can the individual . . . turn to the great for help when he grows confused."[1] Luther saw the Church in bondage, Kierkegaard sees it in a position of false mastery and false freedom; Luther's problem was to combat a foreign institution motivated politically and economically, but Kierkegaard's problem is that the mind itself has become political and economic; Luther's success was to break the hold of an

---

[1] Søren Kierkegaard, *The Present Age* (New York: Harper & Row, 1962, Torchbook), pp. 58, 81.

external authority and put it back into the individual soul, but what happens when *that* authority is broken? Luther's problem was to combat false definitions of religious categories, but Kierkegaard has to provide definition for them from the beginning; Luther could say, "The mass is not a sacrifice, but a promise," and now Kierkegaard's problem is that no one remembers what a promise is, nor has the authority to accept one.

b) The emphasis on philosophy serves as a corrective to calling it psychology. Kierkegaard is often praised in our age as a "profound psychologist," and while I do not wish to deny him that, it seems to me attractively misleading praise, especially about such efforts as the present book; because what is profound psychology in Kierkegaard's work is Christianity itself, or the way in which Kierkegaard is able to activate its concepts; and because the way he activates them, wherever else it is, is through philosophy, through attention to the distinct applicability of concepts—perhaps one could say, attention to the a priori possibility of applying the concepts in general: it is what Kant called Transcendental Logic, what Hegel called Logic, why Oxford philosophers are moved to speak of their attention to words as a question of logic; Wittgenstein called it "grammar." Take the originating concern of the book on Adler: "How far a man in our age may be justified in asserting that he had a revelation" (p. 91). This is the question the Church ought to have confronted—in order to confront itself, as it stands, with the fact that it cannot answer it. Because this question of being "justified in asserting" is not a matter of determining how likely it is, given a certain man's psychological make-up and given a particular historical condition, that he had or will have a revelation (it is always unlikely); nor a matter of determining whether one is religiously prepared to receive a revelation (for, religiously speaking, there is no human preparation possible); nor a matter of determining psychological variation and nuance in different instances of the ex-

perience of a revelation and tracing its antecedents
and consequences in a particular man's worldly existence. The question is whether, no matter *what* occurs
in a man's life, we are conceptually prepared to call
it a revelation, whether we have the power any longer
to recognize an occurrence as a revelation, whether
anything any longer could conceivably count for us as
a revelation—could, so to speak, *force us to assert* that
what has taken place is a revelation. Of course, anyone can, and occasionally will, *use the word* "revelation," to refer perhaps to a striking or unexpected
experience—this, as emerged in the interrogation of
Adler, is what happened in his case. And quite generally: ". . . every Christian term, which remaining
in its own sphere is a qualitative category, now, in
reduced circumstances, can do service as a clever expression which may signify pretty much everything"
(p. 103). The serious issue, which is simultaneously
the logico-philosophical and the Christian issue, remains: for a Christian church to be in a position in
which it has to say that God is hidden or distant or
silent, is one thing; for it to be in a position in which
it would not find it conceivable that God should speak
to us, is something else. In the latter case, the implication is, one should stop referring to such a thing as
Christianity altogether.

Let me, then, call attention to two procedures characteristic of Kierkegaard's writing which I think of as
philosophical, and philosophically correct:

1. He frequently wishes to show that a question
which appears to need settling by empirical means or
through presenting a formal argument is really a conceptual question, a question of grammar. (This is one
way of putting the whole effort of the book on Adler.)
Take the question John Stuart Mill raises in his essay
on Revelation (Part IV of *Theism*): "Can any evidence suffice to prove a divine revelation?" Mill's answer, after careful consideration and reasoning is that
"miracles have no claim whatever to the character of

historical facts and are wholly invalid as evidences of
any revelation"; but he adds to this the concession that
if a certain sort of man ". . . openly proclaimed that
[a precious gift we have from him] did not come from
him but from God through him, then we are entitled to
say that there is nothing so inherently impossible or
absolutely incredible in this supposition as to preclude
anyone from hoping that it may perhaps be true. I say
from hoping; I go no further. . . ." From a Kierkegaardian perspective, Mill has gone nowhere at all, and
indeed there is nowhere to go along those lines. For
the answer to his question is just, No. The statement
"A revelation cannot be proven by evidence" is not an
empirical discovery, nor a sensible topic for an argument; it is a grammatical remark. (Religiously speaking, such a thing *is* "absolutely incredible.") One factor of Mill's hope is that there is a God through whom
the gift can have come; and he regards someone as
"entitled" to this hope because there is some evidence
for his existence. For Kierkegaard, to hope for such a
thing on such a ground is not an act of piety and intellectual caution; it is a hope for nothing: *hoping it*
is as incoherent as *believing it firmly*. Other grammatical remarks in, or to be elicited from, the book
on Adler are, for example, "Religion only conquers
without force"; "One must *become* a Christian";
"Christianity is not plausible."

2. The other philosophical procedure to be mentioned is what Kierkegaard calls "qualitative dialectic."
Very generally, a dialectical examination of a concept
will show how the meaning of that concept changes,
and how the subject of which it is the concept changes,
as the context in which it is used changes: the dialectical meaning is the history or confrontation of these
differences. For example, an examination of the concept of *silence* will show that the word means different things—that silence is different things—depending
on whether the context is the silence of nature, the
silence of shyness, the silence of the liar or hypocrite,

the short silence of the man who cannot hold his
tongue, the long silence of the hero or the apostle,
or the eternal silence of the Knight of Faith. And the
specific meaning of the word in each of those contexts is determined by tracing its specific contrasts with
the others—the way its use in one context "negates"
its use in another, so to speak.

There is one dialectical shift which is of critical importance for Kierkegaard, that which moves from "immanent" to "transcendent" contexts. It is, I believe,
when he is speaking of this shift that he characteristically speaks of a *qualitative* (sometimes he adds, decisive) difference in meaning. (This is the point at
which his insistence on God as "wholly other" finds its
methodological expression.) The procedure is this: he
will begin with an immanent context, appealing to
ordinary contexts in which a concept is used, for example, ordinary cases of silence, or of authority, or of
coming to oneself, or of being shaken, or of living in
the present, or of offense . . . ; and then abruptly
and sternly he will say that these concepts are decisively
or qualitatively different when used in a transcendental
sense, when used, that is, to characterize our relationship to God. ("The situation is quite otherwise . . .";
"It is quite another matter with . . .") Sometimes he
is *merely* abrupt and stern, and offers us no further
help in understanding; as if to say, You know perfectly
well what I mean; as if to rebuke us for having forgotten, or for refusing to acknowledge, something of
the clearest importance. Sometimes, of course, he does
go further; then he will describe what the life of a
man will look like which calls for description, which
can only be understood in terms of—which (he sometimes puts it) *is lived in*—Christian categories. A man's
life; not a striking experience here and there, or a
pervasive mood or a particular feeling or set of feelings. As if to say: in that life, and for that life, the
Christian categories have their full, mutually implicat-
ing meaning, and apart from it they may have any or

none (pp. 103, 104, 115, 165). And contrariwise, a life which does not invite, require description in terms of (is not lived within) the mutual implications of these categories—no matter how religious it is in some sense, and however full it may be of sublime and intricate emotion—is not a Christian life.

When I said that I thought this procedure was philosophically correct, I did not mean to suggest that I found it philosophically clear. As an *account* of "qualitative differences of meaning" (in terms of "immanence," "transcendence," "qualitative," etc.), I find it all but useless. But it begins and ends in the right place, with the description of a human existence; and each difference in each existence makes what seems intuitively the right kind of difference. And it seems to me right that Kierkegaard should suggest that we *do* or could know, without explanation, what it means to say that a man "stands before God" or that "This night shall thy soul be required of thee"; know what they mean not just in *some* sense, but know what they mean in a sense which we may wish to call *heightened*. That we may not know this all the time is no proof against our knowing; this may only indicate what kind of knowledge it is—the kind of knowledge which can go dead, or become inaccessible. Nor would the fact that we cannot *explain* the (heightened) meaning of such utterances prove that we do not understand them, both because it is not clear what an explanation would consist in, and because knowing where and when to use an utterance seems proof that one knows what it means, and knowing where and when to use it is not the same as being able to give an explanation of it. It is true that in the religious case an explanation seems *called for;* but this may only mean, one might say, that we are perplexed about *how* we know its meaning, not whether we do; and even that not all the time. And, again, this particular situation may be characteristic of a particular kind of meaning rather than a situation in which meaning is absent. There might even be an explanation for the sense, as I wish to put it, that we are balancing on the edge of a meaning. And Kierkegaard's explanations, however obscure, are not obviously wrong. He does not, for example, say that religious utterances are metaphorical.

While Kierkegaard's account sometimes refuses explanations of meaning, sometimes seems to rebuke us for being confused about a meaning which should be clear with a qualitatively decisive clarity, sometimes seems to suggest a mode of explanation for that sense of "balancing on the edge of a meaning," he would nevertheless not be surprised at Positivism's claim, or perception, that religious utterances have *no* cognitive meaning. Indeed, he might welcome this fact. It indicates that the crisis of our age has deepened, that we are no longer *confused,* and that we have a chance, at last, to learn what our lives really depend upon. Utterances we have shared about our infinite interests no longer carry any cognitive meaning. Well and good; we have now completely forgotten it. Then it is up to each man to find his own.

"To imagine a language," says Wittgenstein in one of his best mottoes, "is to imagine a form of life." When a form of life can no longer be imagined, its language can no longer be understood. "Speaking metaphorically" is a matter of speaking in certain ways using a definite form of language for some purpose; "speaking religiously" is not accomplished by using a given form, or set of forms, of words, and is not done for any further purpose: it is to speak from a particular perspective, as it were to mean anything you say in a special way. To understand a metaphor you must be able to interpret it; to understand an utterance religiously you have to be able to share its perspective. (In these ways, speaking religiously is like telling a dream.) The religious is a Kierkegaardian Stage of life; and I suggest it should be thought of as a Wittgensteinian form of life. There seems no reason not to believe that, as a given person may never occupy this stage, so a given age, and all future ages, may as a whole not occupy it—that the form will be lost from men's lives altogether. (It would be a phenomenon like everyone stopping having dreams.)

It is Kierkegaard's view that this has happened to the lives of the present age. Wittgenstein, late in the *Investigations,* remarks that "One human being can be a complete enigma to another. We learn this when we come into a strange country with entirely strange traditions; and, what is more, even given a mastery of the country's language. We do not *understand* the people. (And not because of not knowing what they are saying to themselves.) We cannot find our feet with them." Toward the end of the book on Adler, Kierkegaard has this:

> Most men live in relation to their own self as if they were constantly out, never at home. . . . The admirable quality in Magister A. consists in the fact that in a serious and strict sense one may say that he was fetched home by a higher power; for before that he was certainly in a great sense "out" or in a foreign land . . . spiritually and religiously understood, perdition consists in journeying into a foreign land, in being "out" . . . (pp. 154–55).

One may want to say: A human being can be a complete enigma to himself; he cannot find his feet with himself. Not because a particular thing he does puzzles him—his problem may be that many of the puzzling things he does do *not* puzzle him—but because he does not know why he lives as he does, what the point of his activity is; he understands his words, but he is foreign to his life.

Other major writers of the 19th century share the sense of foreignness, of alienation, Kierkegaard describes; and not merely their own alienation from their societies, but of self-alienation as characteristic of the lives common to their time; which is perhaps the same

as seeing their time as alienated from its past. They
can be understood as posing the underlying concern
of Kierkegaard's book: ". . . how it comes about that
a new point of departure is created in relation to the
established order" (p. 192; cf. p. xxi). Kierkegaard's
answer is that it comes "from ABOVE, from God,"
but the test of this answer depends on confronting it
with the major answers given it by (say) Marx, and
Freud, and Nietzsche (both the Nietzsche of the *Birth
of Tragedy* and the Nietzsche of *Zarathustra*). This
should forcibly remind one how little of the complexity
of Kierkegaard's book I have brought out; for politics,
psychology, art, and the final break with God are all
themes of the dialectical situation within which *The
Book on Adler,* like Adler himself, is produced. I began by indicating some lines through which the religious plane intersects the psychological; let me end
with a word or two about its intersection in this book
with the political and with the aesthetic.

The Introduction, written one year before the *Com-
munist Manifesto,* starts the imagery of the newspaper
which recurs throughout the book—the image of its
gossip, of its volatilization of concepts, the universal
(no-man's) intelligence it wishes to be, the fourth
estate which undermines the idea of *estates* altogether
with their recognized authority and responsibilities,
pulverizes them into a gritty mixture called the public,
from whom nothing but violence and distraction can
be expected. Four years earlier Marx had written some
articles for his newspaper[2] against a rival editor who
had raised the question: "Should philosophy discuss
religious matters in newspaper articles?" Marx despises
the mind which could frame this question as passionately as Kierkegaard would, and Marx responds to it
by criticizing it, as Kierkegaard would; that is to say,

---

[2] These pieces are collected under the title "The Leading
Article of No. 179 of *Kölnische Zeitung,*" in a volume of selected writings of Marx and Engels entitled *On Religion* (Mos-
cow: Foreign Languages Publishing House, n.d.).

he responds dialectically. The point of application of his criticism is evidently different, not to say opposite from Kierkegaard's, but it clarifies for me a particular lack in Kierkegaard's "ethico-religious investigation" of his age and of the way that determines its possibilities for a new departure. He was deeply responsive with the "criticism of religion" which Marx said is now (in 1844) complete in Germany (*Critique of Hegel's Philosophy of Right*). Kierkegaard can be seen as attempting to carry its completion to the North, while at the same time one of his dominating motives would be to criticize religion's criticizers. Nothing an outsider can say about religion has the rooted violence of things the religious have themselves had it at heart to say: no brilliant attack by an outsider against (say) obscurantism will seem to go far enough to a brilliant insider faced with the real obscurity of God; and attacks against religious institutions in the name of reason will not go far enough in a man who is attacking them in the name of faith. The criticism of religion, like the criticism of politics which Marx invented, is inescapably dialectical (which is, I take it, a reason Marx said it provided the origin for his criticism), because everything said on both sides is conditioned by the position (e.g., inside or outside) from which it is said. (This emerges in so differently conceived a work as Hume's *Dialogues,* in its outbreaks of irony.) Kierkegaard is fully dialectical where religious questions are concerned, as is displayed not merely in his long attention to different Stages of life, but in the many particular examples in which the same sentence is imagined to be said by men in different positions and thereby to mean differently. (On the recognition that they mean differently depends salvation, for the Gospel saves not because of what it says but because of who it is who has said it.) But his dialectical grasp is loosened when he comes to politics, where his violence does not see its own position and where the object he attacks is left uncriticized. He attacks newspapers and gossip and the public, as no doubt they deserve (on religious and on every other ground); but he does not consider, as it is Marx's business to consider, that what is wrong with them is itself a function of the age (not the other way around), and that a press which really belonged to the public (a public which belonged to itself) would reflect its audience otherwise than in gossip, and that its information would become, thereby, personal—existential in the relevant sense. We now know that this has not happened, but we should not therefore know that it is inevitable that it has not happened. I do not suggest that if it did happen Kierkegaard's problems would become solved, or irrelevant. But to the extent such a question is neglected, Kierkegaard's damning of society to perdition and his recourse to the individual, is suspect—it may be that a fear of the public is only the other side of a fearful privacy, which on his own ground would create the wrong silence and the wrong communication and provide no point for a new departure.

In our age, as yet an unknown distance from that of Kierkegaard, we are likely to read his books as aesthetic works, thus apparently denying his fervent claims that they are religious (even, with the present book, ignoring his claim that it can be understood essentially only by theologians—a remark I choose to interpret ironically or aesthetically, as a rebuke to theologians for not attending to their job of defending the faith, in the categories of the faith, but instead help deliver it bound and gagged into the hands of philosophy). We read him running the risk, and feeling the pinch, of his damning outbursts against the merely curious, who translate the real terrors of the religious life into sublime spectacles of suffering with which to beguile their hours of spiritual leisure (cf. pp. 158–59).

I take heart from the realization that both his and our concepts of aesthetics are historically conditioned; that the concepts of beauty and sublimity which he had in mind (in deploring the confusion between art and religion) are ones which our art either repudiates or is determined to win in new ways; that, in particular, our serious art is produced under conditions which Kierkegaard announces as those of apostleship, not those of genius. I do not insist that for us art has become religion (which may or may not describe the situation, and which as it stands describes phenomena other than those I have in mind) but that the activity of modern art, both in production and reception, is to be understood in categories which are, or were, religious.

The remarkable Introduction is, in effect, an essay in aesthetics—or is something I wish aesthetics would become. Its distinction between "premise-authors" and "genuine authors" is drawn in a vital place—the place at which one must criticize a given work, perhaps the work of a given period, not as deficient in this or that respect, but dismiss it as art altogether. This kind of occasion is characteristic of the modern in the field of art. It does not arise as a problem until some point in the 19th century. I might call the problem "the threat of fraudulence," something I take to be endemic to modern art. One cannot imagine an audience of new music before Beethoven, or viewers of the paintings or spectators of the theater of that period, as wondering, or having the occasion to wonder, whether the thing in front of them was a piece of genuine art or not. But sometime thereafter audiences did begin to wonder, until by now we grow up learning and cherishing stories of the outrage and rioting which accompanied the appearance of new works, works *we* know to be masterpieces. At the same time, the advanced critics of the period in which this is becoming manifest (e.g., Matthew Arnold, Tolstoy, Nietzsche) were finding that it was precisely the work acceptable to the public which was the real source of fraudulence. It is characteristic of our artistic confusion today that we no longer know, and cannot find or trust ourselves to find occasion to know, which is which, whether it is the art or its audience which is on trial. Kierkegaard, who knew one when he saw one, defines the genuine author in terms of his moral relation to his work and to his audience: having a position of his own, the real author can give to the age what the age needs, not what it demands, whereas the fraudulent artist will "make use of the sickness of our age" (p. 5) by satisfying its demands; the genuine author "needs to communicate himself" (p. 8) whereas the false author is simply in need (of praise, of being in demand, of being told whether he means anything or not); the genuine is a physician who provides remedies, the false is a sick man, and contagious (p. 11). Kierkegaard has other ways of capturing the experience of this difference (which he calls a qualitative difference), and when we find him saying that

> . . . it is a suspicious circumstance when a man, instead of getting out of a tension by resolution and action, becomes literarily productive about his situation in the tension. Then no work is done to get out of the situation, but the reflection fixes the situation before the eyes of reflection, and thereby fixes (in a different sense of the word) the man . . . (p. 173)

we recognize that writers in our time, such as Georg Lukacs and Sartre, have not deepened this definition of the problem of modernism. Adler is, of course, a premise-author, and Kierkegaard goes on in the body of his book to use the out-throw of imagery and contrasts which emerge in this Introduction to mark the features by which one knows that Adler is no better an apostle than he is an author; in both fields he lacks, in a word, the authority. I do not suppose Kierkegaard meant to suggest that a genuine author has to have, or claim, God's authority for his work, but his description of the apostle's position characterizes in detail the position I take the genuine modern artist to find himself in: he is pulled out of the ranks by a message which he must, on pain of loss of self, communicate; he is silent for a long period, until he finds his way to saying what it is he has to say (artistically speaking, this could be expressed by saying that while he may, as artists in former times have, begin and for a long time continue imitating the work of others, he knows that this is merely time-marking—if it is preparation, it is not artistic preparation—for he knows that there are no techniques at anyone's disposal for saying what he has to say); he has no proof of his authority, or genuineness, other than his own work (cf. p. 117) (artistically speaking, this is expressed by the absence of conventions within which to compose); he makes his work repulsive, not, as in the case of the apostle, because of the danger he is to others (p. 46) but because mere attraction is not what he wants (artistically, this has to do with the various ways in which art has today withdrawn from, or is required to defeat, its audience); he must deny his personal or worldly authority in accomplishing what he has to do (artistically, this means that he cannot rely on his past achievements as securing the relevance of his new impulse; each work requires, spiritually speaking, a new step); art is no longer a profession to which, for example, a man can become apprenticed (religiously speaking, it is a "call," but there is no recognized calling in which it can be exercised); finally, the burden of being called to produce it is matched by the risk of accepting it (religiously speaking, in accepting or rejecting it, the heart is revealed). Art produced under such spiritual conditions will be expected to have a strange, unheard of *appearance*. Kierkegaard puts it this way:

> That a man in our age might receive a revelation cannot be absolutely denied [i.e., I take it, denying it

would suffer the same confusion as affirming it], but
the whole phenomenal demeanor of such an elect
individual will be essentially different from that of
all earlier examples . . . (p. 46).

All this does not mean (it is not summarized by saying) that the artist *is* an apostle; because the concept
of an apostle is, as (because) the concept of revelation is, forgotten, inapplicable. So, almost, is the concept of art.

To the extent that one finds such considerations an
accurate expression of one's convictions about the
modern enjambment of the impulse to art and to religion, one will want to re-examine the whole question of Kierkegaard's own authorship—a task which
could take a form related to Kierkegaard's book on
Adler: for Kierkegaard is a "case" with the same dimensions, and no less a phenomenon than Adler, if
harder to see through. In particular, in the light of our
un-aestheticizing of aesthetics, what shall we make of
Kierkegaard's famous claim for himself that he was,
from the beginning, a *religious* author, that the pseudonymous works were part of a larger design which,
at the appropriate moment, emerged in directness?[3]
Since, presumably, he denied being an apostle, his
claim says nothing about any special spiritual position
he occupies as a Christian; he, like many others—like
Adler—is a writer about religious matters. What the
claim means, to our position, is that he is a *genuine*
author, that he shares *that* fate. One fate of the genuine
modern author is exactly his indirectness; his inability,
somehow just because of his genuineness, to *confront*
his audience directly with what he must say. Kierkegaard's claim to religious authorship sounds too much
as though the pseudonymous works were a strategy
he employed for the benefit of others; whereas those

---

[3] See Søren Kierkegaard, *The Point of View for My Work
as an Author* (New York: Harper & Row, 1962, Torchbook).

works ought to be seen as a function of his inner strategy, as a genuine writer, to find ways of saying what he has it at heart to say. For it is very peculiar to us—in an age of Rilke, Kafka, Joyce, Mann, Beckett, non-objective painting, twelve-tone music—to hear an artist *praising* the strategy of indirectness, thinking to encompass its significance by acknowledging its usefulness as a medium of communication. What else have we had, in major art of the past hundred years, but indirectness: irony, theatricality, yearning, broken forms, denials of art, anti-heroes, withdrawals from nature, from men, from the future, from the past. . . . What is admirable in a work like *Fear and Trembling* is not its indirectness (which, so far as this is secured by the pseudonym, is a more or less external device) nor its rather pat theory about why Abraham must be silent. What is admirable, exemplary, is its continuous awareness of the pain, and the danger, of that silence —of the fear of the false word, and the deep wish that the right word be found for doing what one must: what, to my mind, Kierkegaard's portrait of Abraham shows is not the inevitability of his silence, but the completeness of his wish for directness, his refusal of anything less. Exemplary, because while we are stripped of Abraham's faith and of his clarity, it is still his position we find ourselves in. For certainly we cannot see ourselves in Kierkegaard's alternative, we are not Tragic Heroes: our sacrifices will not save the State. Yet we are sacrificed, and we sacrifice. Exemplary, because in our age, which not only does not know what it needs, but which no longer even demands anything, but takes what it gets, and so perhaps deserves it; where every indirectness is dime-a-dozen, and any weirdness can be assembled and imitated on demand—the thing we must look for, in each case, is the man who, contrary to appearance, and in spite of all, speaks.

THE VIEW FROM PISGAH:
A READING OF *FEAR AND TREMBLING*

Louis Mackey

Fear and Trembling, by Johannes de Silentio, is an attempt to understand the story of Abraham and Isaac recounted in Genesis 22. Of course it may be assumed that the author is familiar with the whole saga of Abraham; the faithfulness of God to Abraham from the time he first left his home in Ur of the Chaldees to sojourn in a strange land until the day of the miraculous birth of Isaac in the senescence of his parents, and the faithfulness of Abraham to God throughout all the trials and disappointments of his long pilgrimage. It is only against this background of promise, delay, frustration, and eventual fulfillment that the scene on Mount Moriah exhibits the bitterness and poignance that it held for Abraham himself and still holds for Johannes de Silentio.[1] It also goes without saying that Johannes had read St. Paul's interpretation of the faith of Father Abraham in Romans 4 and the roll of the heroes and types of faith in Hebrews 11.

His interest, however, is not exegetical but existential. After a short Preface (of which more later) the book opens with a "Prelude" or *stemning*. The

This essay has not appeared before in print. A briefer discussion of *Fear and Trembling* along these lines may be found in Chapter 5 of the author's book *Kierkegaard: A Kind of Poet* (Philadelphia: University of Pennsylvania Press, 1971).
[1] For the story of Abraham, see Genesis 12 through 25. For an illuminating literary treatment of the story, see Erich Auerbach, *Mimesis* (Garden City, New York, 1957), Chapter 1. Cf. also my essay, "Kierkegaard's Lyric of Faith: A Look at *Fear and Trembling*," *The Rice Institute Pamphlet,* July 1960.

literal meaning of *stemning* is "tuning" or "tone," so
that a better translation might be "mood" or "atmosphere." For it introduces the book by establishing the
mode and the tonality of the considerations to follow.
In the manner of a fairy tale it begins, "Once upon a
time . . ." there was a child who heard, revered, and
in his simplicity comprehended the story of Abraham
and Isaac, how God tempted Abraham, how he kept
the faith, and how he received his son again by a miracle. But the increase of years brings about a dissociation of sensibilities. Maturity separates the passion and
the reflection that are united in the pious immediacy
of the child, and the man finds that the greater his enthusiasm, the less his understanding. In his disenchant-
ment he desires to achieve an imaginative contemporaneity with Abraham in the moment of his ordeal.
If I could only be with him on Mount Moriah, he
thinks, I might understand how he felt and why he
did the things that made him the father of faith! He
does not wish for a philosophical comprehension that
"goes beyond" faith by fitting it into a system of metaphysics; he simply wants to know the feeling of the
reality of faith. He is not a "learned exegete," for he
cannot even read Hebrew, though he is willing to assume that those who do experience no difficulty at all
understanding Abraham.

The irony of this last suggests irresistibly that the
perplexed young man of the Prelude is none other
than the author, John of Silence. Johannes de Silentio:
if we read "de" as the aristocratic particle it seems to
be, then he is John of the realm or kingdom of silence.
In another reading the title page of his book says "Fear
and Trembling, a dialectical lyric, by John, *about* silence." Either or both will serve: for silence is his
domain, and silence the burden of his dialectical lyric.
Johannes' character, which is part and parcel of his
literary method, is presaged by the motto he has
picked for his book: *"Was Tarquinius Superbus in
seinem Garten mit den Mohnköpfen sprach, verstand*

der Sohn, aber nicht der Bote."[2] If there is any message about faith in *Fear and Trembling,* it will be an
enigmatic message. Only the sons, those who are already members of the spiritual household of Abraham, will understand it; but not the messengers,
those—perhaps philosophers and theologians—who like
Abraham's servants witness the mystery from a distance and even convey information about it, but do
not comprehend their own witness and their own message. Johannes de Silentio seeks an understanding of
faith. But he is saying nothing about it that can be
understood by those who do not already understand.
True to his name, he is keeping silent.

Perhaps he is silent because there is something that
men need to listen for, a still small voice that cannot
be heard amid the clamor of the intellectual market
place. Something of the sort is indicated by his respect-
ful Preface. In these days, he complains (the allusions
are topical and local, but the complaint itself is timely
enough), faith is being sold, or sold out, at bargain
prices. In fact the price is so low it is doubtful if anyone will care to buy. The intelligentsia have doubted
everything, transcended faith, and understood all truth.
At least they say they have, and it would be bad taste
to doubt their veracity. But it is strange that they
should appeal to Descartes as their patron. For Descartes was "a quiet and solitary thinker"—a man

---

2 Søren Kierkegaard, *Fear and Trembling* and *The Sickness
unto Death* (Garden City, New York, 1954), p. 21. "What
Tarquinius Superbus spoke in the garden by means of the poppies, the son understood, but not the messenger." Tarquin, king
of Rome, was bent on the destruction of Gabii. His son, having
worked his way into the confidence of its people, sent to his
father asking what to do next. Tarquin, distrustful of the
messenger, took him into the garden, where he proceeded to
cut off the heads of the tallest poppies with his sword. This
was reported to the son, who understood thereby that he was to
cause the death of the leading citizens of Gabii, and went
straight to the task.

of silence—"not a bellowing night-watchman,"[3] who never doubted *de fide*. Strange, too, that every philosophy professor has got beyond faith. For how many and how great are the saints and martyrs who had all they could do just to *keep* the faith until death. Nowadays, Johannes sighs, we all start where the saints and martyrs left off, and faith has gone begging for takers. As for himself:

> The present writer is nothing of a philosopher; he is, *poetice et eleganter,* an amateur writer who . . . writes because for him it is a luxury which becomes the more agreeable and more evident, the fewer there are who buy and read what he writes. He can easily foresee his fate in an age when passion has been obliterated in favor of learning, in an age when an author who wants to have readers must take care to write in such a way that the book can easily be perused during the afternoon nap. . . . He foresees his fate—that he will be entirely ignored.[4]

There is the dissociation of sensibilities again, in the demeaning of passion by learning. There, too, is an "afternoon nap" that will make its major appearance later in more solemn and dreadful surroundings. And there is Johannes, an idler who writes for himself because he enjoys it and can afford it, retreating once more into his characteristic silence.

The words *"poetice et eleganter"* are reminiscent of the subtitle of *Fear and Trembling,* "Dialectical Lyric." A suitable translation might be "philosophical poem" or "poetic philosophy." The former is recommended by the fact that Johannes' lyric is substantive and his dialectic adjectival, though there is plenty of lyric in his dialectic (the Problemata) and an abundance of dialectic in his lyric (the Prelude and the

---

[3] Kierkegaard, op. cit., p. 22.
[4] Ibid., p. 24.

Panegyric). With the "profoundest deference"[5] to the philosophers, before whom he prostrates himself at the close of his Preface, Johannes de Silentio will attempt to write the poetry of faith.

The attempt fails. In the remainder of the Prelude Johannes offers a series of four dramatic scenes, each of which imagines one way Abraham might respond to the divine command: "Take Isaac, thine only son, whom thou lovest . . . , and offer him . . . for a burnt offering. . . ."[6] He may, in preparing the sacrifice, prefer to let Isaac think that his father is an idolatrous and bloodthirsty monster, rather than jeopardize the boy's faith in God by insisting upon the truth. The command may destroy Abraham's own faith and deprive him of that joy in God and in Isaac that was the substance of his life. Having obeyed the command, he may still suspect that it was not God's will but his own sinfulness that made him willing to kill his son; he becomes a perpetual penitent, his confidence in God and in himself is weakened, and he has lost Isaac forever by doubting his paternal love. Or perhaps, at the moment Abraham draws the knife, he reveals to Isaac a hand clenched in anguish and a body shuddering with terror; the ram appears and Isaac lives, but he lives in despair ever after, having lost faith in God and in his father.

> Thus and in many like ways that man of whom we are speaking thought concerning this event. Every time he returned home after wandering to Mt. Moriah, he sank down with weariness, he folded his hands and said, "No one is so great as Abraham! Who is capable of understanding him?"[7]

Nothing the imagination puts together can contain all the data of the biblical account: that Abraham loved

[5] Ibid., p. 24.
[6] Ibid., p. 27 (Genesis 22: 2).
[7] Ibid., p. 29.

Isaac and yet was willing to sacrifice him, that having
given him up he could yet receive Isaac again with
rejoicing and without remorse, that through it all Abraham kept faith with the God of the covenant while yet
obedient to the God of the command. These are contradictions that exceed the poet's capacity for representation and stop the mouth of lyric fancy. So John
of Silence is brought to silence.

Almost. For Johannes is not a pettifogging philosopher who measures enthusiasm and passion by the
finite yardstick of the understanding. What he cannot understand he may yet admire. From his aborted
essay in religious drama Johannes turns to compose a
hymn of praise to Father Abraham and the power of
faith which passes the power of poesy. His Panegyric
opens with a meditation on heroism and poetry. Life
were desperate, he writes, if there were no eternal consciousness in man, if the greatest of human achievements were but the by-product of an aimless and chaotic play of natural forces. Empty and comfortless
were life, if transcience were its essence and oblivion
its end. But it is not so. As God created both man and
woman to assure the continuance of the race, so He
created the hero, that there might be no dearth of
magnificence, and the poet, that the hero's renown
might remain forever in the remembrance of mankind. Abraham is the hero of faith, and John of Silence
the poet who will jealously guard the entrusted treas-
ure against the assaults of time.

But how shall the poet measure the magnitude of
his hero? Every man is great in proportion to that
which he loves: Abraham loved God. Every man is
great in proportion to his expectation: Abraham,
trusting the promises of God, expects the impossible.
Every man is great in proportion to that with which
he strives: Abraham strives with God. So

Abraham was greater than all, great by reason of
his power whose strength is impotence, great by rea-

son of his wisdom whose secret is foolishness, great
by reason of his hope whose form is madness, great
by reason of the love which is hatred of oneself.[8]

Greater than the greatness of Jeremiah lamenting
in exile is the greatness of the father of faith rejoicing in his son and seed. For it is human to weep and
to grieve, greatly human to give up one's life and
one's hope. But it is greater than human to believe
against understanding, to hope against expectation, and
to hold onto one's life with joy.

Abraham's struggle to hold fast to the promises of
God in the face of His demands is a struggle against
time:

> . . . Abraham believed, and believed for this life.
> Yea, if his faith had been only for a future life, he
> surely would have cast everything away in order to
> hasten out of this world to which he did not belong.
> But Abraham's faith was not of this sort, if there be
> such a faith; for really this is not faith but the fur-
> thest possibility of faith which has a presentiment of
> its object as the extremest limit of the horizon, yet
> is separated from it by a yawning abyss within which
> despair carries on its game. But Abraham believed
> precisely for this life, that he was to grow old in the
> land, honored by the people, blessed in his genera-
> tion, remembered forever in Isaac. . . .[9]

Had Abraham doubted, he would have driven the
sacrificial knife into his own heart and forfeited the
world for the sake of his "eternal consciousness." The
heroism of doubt is easy to understand and a pleasure
to admire. But Abraham believed and by believing became "the guiding star which saves the anguished."[10]
Had he in irresolution discovered the ram before he

8 Ibid., p. 31.
9 Ibid., pp. 34–35.
10 Ibid., p. 35.

drew the knife, he would have been remembered forever not as the father of faith but as the author of consternation. But he did not doubt and he did not waver: he believed, and he drew the knife, and still he believed.

The encomiast is forced to conclude that his hero is no ordinary human hero; Abraham's constancy is beyond man's capacity as it is beyond man's understanding. It was God who required of an old man his only son, the son of promise. But it was God also who gave strength to his arm to draw the knife and strength to his soul to hold onto his faith. The God of the covenant does not fail to keep His promises; the God of the trial provides that which He demands. The God of promise and the God of temptation are one God. By God's election Abraham became the father of Isaac and the father of faith, but God himself is the author and finisher of faith as He is the father of all paternity in heaven and in earth. Johannes' title is from a Pauline text, and his lyric a rhapsody on its theme: "Work out your own salvation with fear and trembling. For it is God which worketh in you both to will and to do of his good pleasure" (Phil. 2: 12–13).

The panegyric cannot continue. John of Silence is reduced to dumb apostrophe: "Venerable Father Abraham! . . . thou hadst no need of a panegyric. . . ."[11] Abraham does not need the eulogy of a poet to protect him from forgetfulness and the acids of time. In the power of faith he has already conquered time and won the temporal. "Thousands of years have run their course since those days, but thou hadst need of no tardy lover to snatch the memorial of thee from the power of oblivion, for every language calls thee to remembrance. . . ."[12] The poet has chosen a hero who wants and will suffer no poet. Not

[11] Ibid., p. 37.
[12] Ibid., p. 37.

even the most reverent lover can praise a power which is impotence, a wisdom which is foolishness, a hope which is madness, and a love which is hatred of self. These are contradictions that disarm even admiration. A man can give up the temporal for the eternal, but only God can restore the temporal. It is the power of God that returns Isaac to Abraham's faith after Abraham's obedience has given him up. And no man can fitly praise God.

Once again Johannes de Silentio sinks in awe before a heroism that his rhetoric cannot duly celebrate nor his fancy adorn. He who would praise the father of faith ends by begging indulgence for the insufficiency of his decorum:

> . . . Forgive him who would speak in praise of thee, if he does not do it fittingly. He spoke humbly, as if it were the desire of his own heart, he spoke briefly, as it becomes him to do, but he will never forget that thou hadst need of a hundred years to obtain a son of old age against expectation, that thou didst have to draw the knife before retaining Isaac; he will never forget that in a hundred and thirty years thou didst not get further than to faith.[13]

The lyricist is through, his powers broken against the paradox of faith. And so the dialectician, whose business it is to deal with contradictions, takes the field.

Johannes the dialectician wants to examine some problems that are posed by the story of Abraham and Isaac. But there is something he must first spit out of his system before he gets to the problems themselves. Hence his Preliminary Expectoration, which is methodological preparation for the Problemata just as the Prelude provided an atmospheric setting for the Panegyric. At the beginning and end of his expectoration

13 Ibid., p. 37.

Johannes contrasts the function of the dialectician with the role usually assumed by the preachers when they are moved to uplift their congregations with the story of Abraham and Isaac. The dialectician ideally is an honest and honorable thinker who does not "lack the courage to think a thought whole."[14] So honest is he that, should he run across a thought that terrified him, he will refuse to think it at all rather than tenderize it for his delicate palate. If worst comes to worst—for example, if a dialectical inquiry should disclose that Abraham is simply and solely a murderer—then the dialectician is honorable enough to keep it to himself rather than initiate others into such dreadful torments of the spirit. Not the least of the talents required in a dialectician is the ability to keep his mouth shut.

The parson, however, prates merrily away to all and sundry about the greatness of Abraham, who was willing to offer to God the best he had. Of course he takes care to keep this "best" quite vague, so that no one is troubled by the consideration that in Abraham's case the best happened to be his only son, to whom he owed the duty of solicitous paternal love and whom in fact he proposed to kill. Fortunately most of the congregation sleep through the sermon (there's that afternoon nap again), and no one is misled by his reverence's prattle. But should there be a chance insomniac in the pews who hears the sermon and goes home resolved to emulate the heroism of Abraham on his own family: in that case the parson is on the spot bright and early Monday morning to confront, accuse, convict, and convert the wretched sinner—who only wanted to murder his son in obedience to the pastor's counsel. So thoughtless that he can, without noting the discrepancy, contradict on Monday what he said on Sunday, the parson is the very opposite of the honest dialectician, who thinks a thought whole or not at all. So insensitive that he can with his ranting pro and

14 Ibid., p. 41.

con breed chaos in the souls of his parishioners, without observing in himself any more than a tendency to
excessive perspiration and a swelling vein in the fore-
head, the parson is the opposite of the honorable
dialectician, who turns the chaos inward and keeps his
suffering to himself. It's a good thing, Johannes observes in a footnote, that there is more sense in
the world than you would expect from the average
sermon.[15]

Or perhaps the parson explains that Abraham's experience is only a test of his faith. Fair enough. But
the preacher depicts the trial in foreshortened perspective, with the outcome deceptively assured in advance.
Should a sufferer from insomnia happen to hear the
sermon, he may feed on the false hope that all his own
troubles are but temporary. If only I wait a moment,
he thinks, I shall surely see the ram and hear the voice
of the angel, just as the parson says. The parson, finding his charge in this state on Monday, might denounce
his indolent optimism with the admonition that "all
of life is a trial." This is so true that it may be the main
point of Johannes' book. But it happens to contradict
the impression that the same preacher so carefully con-
trived to produce on Sunday in his capacity as pulpit
poet.

Alas, complains the honest dialectician. Who speaks
in honor of faith? Love still has its priests in the poets.
But who in these days glorifies faith? What Johannes
says at this point was said in 1843, but it might have
been said yesterday. Philosophy does not revere the
Paradox; philosophy goes beyond faith to resolve (or
dissolve) all mysteries. Theology sits painted and
rouged at the window like a tawdry whore offering
her favors to philosophy. What is it but whoredom
when the custodians of the Paradox undertake to make
the scandal of faith respectable to the scientific world-
view, or tailor it to match the latest fad in German
philosophy?

[15] Ibid., p. 40n.

Johannes will have no part of these cheap editions of Abraham. If I were to preach on Abraham, he says (in a passage that describes exactly what he has done, is doing, and will continue to do throughout his book), I would first of all take my time at it. I would drag out that three-day journey to Mount Moriah for at least a month of Sundays. I would distill every drop of manly and paternal feeling out of Abraham's sufferings. My auditors would smell the smoke of the sacrificial wood, feel the edge of the knife, see it glint in the morning sun, hear the weeping of Isaac begging for his life on behalf of the youthful promise still hidden in his loins. In short I would do everything in my power to prevent my hearers from lightly undertaking an imitation of the dread deed of Abraham. I would go out of my way to give them the opportunity to avoid Abraham's problem altogether. For if a dialectician is to speak about Abraham, then he is duty-bound to be painfully clear about the incomprehensible difficulty of Abraham's case, not covering over the contradictions with a verbal bouquet, but letting them stand out in all their starkness and horror. The job of the dialectician is to keep silence in the presence of the paradox, which speaks louder and more forcefully than all the flowered oratory of the preachers.

That the story of Abraham contains paradoxes there can be no question, in view, first of all, of the ambiguity of his motives. He proposes to offer his *son* to *God*. Ethically speaking Abraham wanted to murder Isaac; religiously speaking he was prepared to sacrifice him. It is this contradiction between murder and sacrifice, between the ethical and the religious interpretations of his action, that generates the "dread and distress, the fear and trembling" of Abraham's situation. Within the religious dimension alone there are further agonies. The God who—presumably, for Abraham has no surety that the voice he hears is the voice of God—asks for the sacrifice of Isaac is the same God who miraculously gave Isaac in the first place. Or again: it is possible that God—if it is God and not a demon who speaks—demands the death of Isaac only to discover if Abraham has the moral courage and the paternal devotion to refuse. If Abraham is any kind of dialectician, i.e., if he is at all an honest man, he will not be able to sidestep the thought, and the prodigious dread of the thought, that he may be tempting God when he draws the knife on his son.

These and a multitude of like contradictions make up "the dialectical conflict of faith and its gigantic passion."[16] John of Silence has encountered the cul-de-sac of dialectic:

> . . . When I have to think of Abraham, I am as though annihilated. I catch sight every moment of that enormous paradox which is the substance of Abraham's life, every moment I am repelled, and my thought in spite of all its passion cannot get a hairs-breadth further.[17]

He cannot "think himself into"[18] Abraham because Abraham is the paradox that repels thought. Before the paradox every honest thinker is mute.

But this side of Abraham there is plenty to be understood. Though he cannot comprehend faith, Johannes can at least manage the preliminary expectoration. The movement preparatory for faith he calls "infinite resignation." Infinite resignation means, algebraically, the renunciation of the finite and the temporal for the infinite and the eternal. Faith means, after having renounced the finite and the temporal, the confidence that one will receive them again. Abraham's willingness to sacrifice Isaac in obedience to God's command was his infinite resignation. His certainty that God would nevertheless not take Isaac was his faith.

16 Ibid., p. 43.
17 Ibid., p. 44.
18 Ibid., p. 44.

The "knight of resignation" believes that God transcends the world incommensurably. If need be he will evacuate his worldly life for the sake of an ideal relationship to God. If I were in Abraham's shoes, says Johannes, I would sacrifice Isaac and continue to believe that God is love. But it would be all over between God and me as far as this world is concerned. My act of renunciation would be noble and poetic, like the magnificence of a tragic hero. But it would also show that I did not love Isaac as Abraham did. And if God were to restore him to me, I would be nonplused, as a young man who has taken monastic vows because he cannot have the girl he loves would be embarrassed to find her in his arms after the cowl is already about his ears. Abraham on the contrary receives Isaac with joy and thanksgiving. Not because he did not really give him up, for he cut the wood, bound Isaac, and drew the knife. But even while he gave him up, Abraham believed that God would not require Isaac or that, requiring him, He would yet give him back. By resignation Abraham gave up the finite, by faith he got it back again "every inch."[19] This movement of faith, Johannes confesses, I cannot understand and certainly not execute. Abraham's faith is a faith "by virtue of the absurd." By faith he receives the world—symbolized by Isaac—after he has let it go. His whole life after faith is a new creation in which he does not the least thing but "by virtue of the absurd."

"Virtue" is "power" (*kraft*). The power by which a man makes the movement of faith is not a power indigenous or intelligible to himself. It is a power "from beyond" and therefore from the human point of view absurd and paradoxical. A man believes "by the power . . . of the absurd, by the power of the fact that with God all things are possible."[20] The only power that can save a man in Abraham's situation, a man who has drained all his own potencies in the act of resig-

[19] Ibid., p. 48.
[20] Ibid., p. 57.

nation, is the paradoxical power of God. And this is the impossible possibility that can only be grasped by faith. "He who loves God without faith reflects upon himself; he who loves God believingly reflects upon God."[21] On his own Abraham does nothing but give up Isaac; he gets him back by virtue of God.

It would be a terrible error, of the sort to which parsons are prone, to hurry on to faith without making the preliminary expectoration by which one spits out the world. Abraham is great by reason of his strength which is weakness, for it is only in the weakness of man that the power of God is efficacious. God cannot be deceived out of the necessary condition of resignation, and no man can acquire faith by a too previous assurance of the "result." Only he that loses his life saves it; only the man who draws the knife gets Isaac. When a man has compressed the whole meaning of his life in a single object, as Abraham poured himself wholly into Isaac, and when that object is unattainable, as the continued possession of Isaac was made impossible by God's command, then he relinquishes his claim to the object and with it his whole claim on life itself. In so doing he becomes a "knight of infinite resignation," and his resignation is the extreme limit of human possibility.[22] For a man's "eternal validity" —the acme of his dignity as a spiritual creature—is his ability to transform his love for the world into a love for God, the power to renounce the world without hope of recompense. At this farthest outpost of his manhood, where the finite and the temporal have become dust and ashes, the knight is at one with God "in the infinite," and his love for the creator so consumes his entire passion that he retains the creation in spirit by giving it up in fact. In the pain of renunciation he is reconciled to existence by the "eternal consciousness" which he gains by cleaving to God alone and letting all else go. To do great things in the world is magnifi-

[21] Ibid., p. 47.
[22] Cf. Ibid., p. 52n.

cent; even more magnificent, the summit of human greatness, as the case of every tragic hero shows, is to relinquish the world altogether.

This, Johannes adds, I can do. And I do not hesitate to call him a coward who wants to believe that he cannot make the movement of infinite resignation. He who will not draw the knife is no knight; he who anxiously looks back over his shoulder for the ram when it is time for the resolute step forward to the altar is a "cowardly and effeminate" nature, a cithara player and not a man.[23]

Johannes is aware that his view of man and human dignity is not a reasonable view. So he says, "To this end"—that is, the end of infinite resignation—"passion is necessary. Every movement of infinity comes about by passion, and no reflection can bring a movement about."[24] Reason never produces a decisive and resolute action of any sort, for reason is "the broker of the finite."[25] Its domain is the market place of probabilities and comparisons, wherein a man calculates shrewdly how he may meet the demand of the age, how he may satisfy his friends and neighbors, how much he may gain on X by giving up a little on Y, and the like. No man ever vowed his love to a maiden as the result of such rational deliberation. And no man ever truly married a wife because of reflection, though indeed many men have *taken* wives as they take shares in a corporation. Reason says that the rich brewer's widow is quite a respectable match, but the knight— the man of passion—would rather recollect his unattainable love for the princess in the solitude of his monastery cell than stretch his legs in the privileged marriage bed with the wealthy and quite respectable, but unloved, brewer's widow.

The conclusions of passion, Johannes says, are the

23 Cf. Ibid., pp. 38, 59.
24 Ibid., p. 53n.
25 Ibid., p. 47.

only reliable and convincing conclusions.[26] Passion
produces action, while reason continues to shuffle the
counters of probability in defense of an inhumane and
Philistine self-interest. Passion, not reason, defines the
human, or as Lessing observed, the passions make all
men equal.[27] For all men experience passion, and
each man learns its meaning from scratch. Reason is a
"differential attribute," a talent which some men have
and some do not, a resource that some possess in
abundance and others in short supply. Fortunately, the
results of rational investigation can be inherited: as the
result of our fathers' ingenuity this generation may go
to the stars or blow itself up. But every man must learn
the joy of love, the bitterness of hatred, the bliss of
union, and the pain of separation for himself; and every
man learns them in the same way: from experience,
or as passion literally says, from suffering.[28]

Passion defines man; and the extreme passion,
which is therefore the extremest human possibility, is
the passion of infinite resignation. More than this no
man can do by and for himself. By resignation he
acquires his "eternal consciousness," but not a thing
more. If a man is not just to let go the temporal in
order to gain the eternal, but beyond that to regain the
temporal, then more than human power is needed.
For this the power of faith is needed, and faith, as
Johannes has already noted, is not of man but—paradoxically—of God. Yet for all its absurdity, faith is a
far more blessed thing than resignation, a consummation devoutly to be wished if indeed it may even be
hoped for. It is better to get the princess than to recollect her in the cell, better to go home rejoicing with
Isaac than to return a tragic hero. "The knight of faith
is the only happy one, the heir apparent to the finite,
whereas the knight of resignation is a stranger and a

26 Ibid., p. 109.
27 Ibid., p. 77n.
28 Ibid., p. 130.

foreigner."[29] So when Johannes asks, Why did Abraham do what he did? he answers himself: he did it for God's sake, because God required it, and for his own sake, because he would do what God required. Likewise, what Abraham receives from God's hand is simply his own life. In action and in passion Abraham and God are happily one: such is the paradoxical union of finite and infinite that is realized in faith.

So paradoxical is faith that Johannes the dialectician can no more talk sense about it than Johannes the poet can imagine it or praise it. Faith is something which "no thought can master, because faith begins precisely there where thinking leaves off."[30] And indeed no one should talk about faith at all if talking means the thoughtless babble of the preachers or the philosophers' wordy pretension to total comprehension. But a dialectician may still talk, if he can by his talking make clear that faith is "a tremendous paradox—which is capable of transforming a murder into a holy act well-pleasing to God, a paradox which gives Isaac back to Abraham. . . ."[31] If he defines the absurdity of faith with precision, the dialectician does service in the forecourt of the temple to protect the paradox against the ineffectual assaults of enemies who know not what they attack, and against the impotent and meretricious embraces of these philosophers and theologians who foolishly believe that they have understood and surpassed faith. Johannes' Problemata embody his attempt at rigorous dialectical definition of the paradox of Abraham.

Each of Johannes' three problems begins with a paragraph describing something he calls "the ethical," and the second paragraph of each problem begins with a statement that "if this is the way it is, then Hegel is right," etc. Everything that is said about the ethical in this division of the book is qualified by the "if," for it

29 Ibid., p. 61.
30 Ibid., p. 64.
31 Ibid., p. 64.

is Johannes' intent to demonstrate that there may be something which escapes an ethical interpretation of human life: faith. The "ethical" in this context does not refer to any particular system of ethics, but simply to the attitude that reads all of human life in ethical terms and measures every human action by a moral yardstick.

Problem I asks, Is there a teleological suspension of the ethical? The answer is, from an ethical point of view, no. If man achieves his highest destiny in the fulfillment of moral obligation, and if this obligation applies without qualification to all men at all times and places, then there is no way a man may justifiably assert his individuality in opposition to the universal norm of ethics. The man who acts so as to set himself outside the universal is simply evil. And since, on this supposition, the moral universal is the highest court of appeal, there is no possible redemption and no conceivable pardon for such an "exception."

But the story of Abraham suggests that in the situation of faith the individual does find a justified standpoint outside the universal:

> For faith is this paradox, that the particular is higher than the universal—yet in such a way, be it observed, that the movement repeats itself, and that consequently the individual, after having been in the universal, now as the particular isolates himself as higher than the universal.[32]

Abraham (the particular) was faithful to the universal (his duty to his son) until it broke against the command of God. Through his fidelity to the universal he entered into that "absolute relationship to the absolute" by which he became "the individual who as the particular is superior to the universal."

> Faith is precisely this paradox, that the individual as the particular is higher than the universal, is jus-

[32] Ibid., p. 65.

tified over against it, is not subordinate but superior—yet in such a way, be it observed, that it is the particular individual who, after he has been subordinated as the particular to the universal, now through the universal becomes the individual who as the particular is superior to the universal, for the fact that the individual as the particular stands in an absolute relation to the absolute.[33]

It should not surprise anyone that Johannes' description of faith is full of contradiction, for faith is a "teleological suspension of the ethical," a suspension of the ethical imperative for the sake of a higher *telos*. In Abraham's case the father's duty to his son is lifted for the sake of his obedience to God. From the ethical point of view that is absolutely paradoxical. Johannes, here as everywhere a man of silence, has nothing to say about this claim of faith. He only wants to clarify the absolute disjunction: *either* there is such a suspension of the ethical, in which case the ethical is not the norm and goal of human striving; *or* "If this be not faith, then Abraham is lost, then faith has never existed in the world . . . because it has always existed."[34] If there is no teleological suspension of the ethical, then the position of supremacy claimed by faith is in fact occupied by ethics, and there is no faith because faith—i.e., the highest *telos*—has always existed in the form of ethical action.

Abraham is not, like Agamemnon, Jephtha, and Brutus, a tragic hero who sacrifices a private good to a more universal good. The power in tragedy is the ethical power of infinite resignation, but the religious power of faith is the *vis comica,* the spirit of comedy. The tragic hero stays well within the ambience of ethics. What Abraham does is strictly between himself and God, and whatever value it has it has for Abraham—and God—alone. Johannes repeatedly argues that Abraham cannot be mediated; his action cannot be

[33] Ibid., p. 66.
[34] Ibid., p. 65.

reconciled with the universal it violates. He remains forever alone with God in the dread and distress of his trial. Significantly the only figures Johannes can find to compare with Abraham are the Mother of God who, although she was highly favored among women, was also Our Lady of Incomparable Sorrows, her soul pierced by the sword, and those disciples of the Lord who, in spite of the scandal and the offense, sat at meat with Him, believed in Him, followed Him to Golgotha, and became the Apostles of the Crucified. Like Abraham these cannot be mediated; they too are beyond human understanding, and their faith a miracle beyond human working.

The silence which Johannes keeps in the presence of Abraham is a silence he recommends to his contemporaries and his readers, lest by much talking and weak thinking they blather themselves out of the miracle and into the universal mutual admiration society of fools.

Problem I suggests Problem II: Is there an absolute duty toward God? Johannes' solution is again simple: if a man's ethical obligations define his whole duty, then these are the only divinity there is. The ethical norm is the supreme power to which man owes his allegiance, and compliance with it the last end toward which he strives. But the claim of faith is that the individual—as an individual and not as an instance of the universal—has an absolute duty toward God—the Absolute Individual and not the ethical universal—which reduces his moral duties to relativities. Thus Abraham's duty to God supersedes his duty to his son.

This is a paradoxical kind of duty. Duty by definition is universal, but the particularity of the bond between God and Abraham defies reduction to universality and mocks the ethical understanding of obligation. Yet if this paradox does not hold, there is no such thing as faith. Worse: the inclination to faith is a temptation that every man is morally bound to avoid.

But the alternatives are clear: *either* faith, *or* Abraham is a murderer and there's an end of it.

In this connection Johannes quotes a parallel from the New Testament, Luke 14: 26. The verse, following directly upon the parable of the great supper and the little excuses, introduces its own interpretation:

> 26. If any man come to me, and hate not his father, and mother, and wife, and children, and brethren, and sisters, yea, and his own life also, he cannot be my disciple.

> 27. And whosoever doth not bear his cross, and come after me, cannot be my disciple.

> 28. For which of you, intending to build a tower, sitteth not down first, and counteth the cost, whether he have sufficient to finish it?

> 29. Lest haply, after he hath laid the foundation and is not able to finish it, all that behold it begin to mock him,

> 30. Saying, This man began to build, and was not able to finish.

> 31. Or what king, going to make war against another king, sitteth not down first, and consulteth whether he be able with ten thousand to meet him that cometh against him with twenty thousand?

> 32. Or else, while the other is yet a great way off, he sendeth an ambassage, and desireth conditions of peace.

> 33. So likewise, whosoever he be of you that forsaketh not all that he hath, he cannot be my disciple.

Johannes argues, against a euphemistic exegesis, that in this context the word "hate" is meant in a strong sense. If "hate" is softened to *"minus diligo, post-*

habeo, non colo, nihil facio,[35] one arrives at the curious notion that an absolute devotion to God enjoins pallid halfheartedness toward self, kindred, and fellows. That love for God should demand the renunciation of all other affections is credible and a "worthy conception of the Deity."[36] But no man would be so stupid or so conceited as to regard defective filial devotion in his wife as a proof of her connubial passion. Shall the sign of religious commitment be a lukewarm fellow feeling? Johannes' own exegesis is more rigorous:

> The absolute duty may cause one to do what ethics would forbid, but by no means can it cause the knight of faith to cease to love. This is shown by Abraham. The instant he is ready to sacrifice Isaac the ethical expression for what he does is this: he hates Isaac. But if he really hates Isaac, he can be sure that God does not require this, for Cain and Abraham are not identical. Isaac he must love with his whole soul; when God requires Isaac he must love him if possible even more dearly, and only on this condition can he *sacrifice* him; for in fact it is this love for Isaac which, by its paradoxical opposition to his love for God, makes his act a sacrifice. . . . Only at the moment when his act is in absolute contradiction to his feeling is his act a sacrifice, but the reality of his act is the factor by which he belongs to the universal, and in that aspect he is and remains a murderer.[37]

The man who recognizes an absolute duty toward God does not cease to love what is other than God. He does not cease, for example, to acknowledge his moral obligations. Otherwise his infinite resignation is a sham. But by his duty to God he is bound to be pre-

35 Ibid., p. 82.
36 Ibid., p. 84.
37 Ibid., p. 84.

pared to do things which, objectively and in reality, have the moral character of evil.

Johannes does not explain the intrusion of this bit of gospel commentary into his discussion of Abraham. Its significance becomes clear in the larger view, but for the moment Johannes might admonish his reader in the words of the same gospel: "He that hath ears to hear, let him hear" (Luke 14: 35).

Back to the problem at hand. Most men think in terms of two categories of practical reason: the ethical (the universal) and the selfish (the particular). Faith claims, and the proper understanding of Abraham requires, that there is a third category: that of the individual who does not by self-interest sink beneath the universal, but through the universal rises to a particularity superior to the universal. At the subethical level there is Cain, who killed Abel out of self-interest and hatred. At the ethical level there is the tragic hero, who, whatever sacrifices he may have to make, reposes securely in the universal. And at the level of faith: Abraham. Such at least is the claim of faith. Whether the claim is true no one can say. But unless it is true, Abraham is condemned, and "faith" is a terrible temptation to be resisted with all possible vigor.

Of course, Johannes adds, there is a mark whereby one can distinguish the genuine knight of faith from the counterfeit. To wit, the true knight is always incommunicado. He keeps to himself, whereas the false knights are great sectarians, always clubbing together for mutual encouragement and plotting holy wars against the infidel. Johannes sports with the Rotarian temper of the pseudo-knights of faith, but a sober reader may wonder who is really the butt of this joke. The sole criterion by which to tell a knight of faith is his silence and his secrecy. Is this not the most futile of all criteria, that a knight of faith can be recognized only by the fact that he cannot be recognized? So it is, and this becomes the subject of Johannes' Problem III.

The problem is, Was Abraham justified in keeping silent about his purpose before Sarah, Eleazar, and Isaac? The moral imperative demands revelation. Every man shall be prepared to declare to his fellows the purpose and intent of his actions. Only thieves, murderers, and adulterers need the cover of night to obscure their deeds. The honest man acts openly in the light of day. Readiness for community is part of the universal good commanded by ethics.

But Abraham keeps silent. He has to keep silent, for there is no way he can explain to anyone else what he intends to do with Isaac on Mount Moriah. His only recorded utterances are instinct with the most terrible irony. To his servants at the foot of the mount he says: "I and the lad will go yonder and worship, and come again to you." (Gen. 22: 5) The remark is true, but it says nothing about his real intentions. More terrible still is the dialogue with Isaac at the place of sacrifice:

> And Isaac spake unto Abraham his father, and said, My father: and he said, Here am I, my son. And he said, Behold the fire and the wood: but where is the lamb for a burnt offering? And Abraham said, My son, God will provide himself a lamb for a burnt offering. . . . (Gen. 22: 7–8)

Jehovah-jireh: the Lord will provide.[38] That, of course, is the whole import of the story of Abraham and Isaac. The irony of Abraham is a holy irony, but it is no less ironical for all that. *Jehovah-jireh* tells Isaac precisely nothing; for all practical and moral purposes Abraham is silent.

An overingenious reader may wonder if the silence of Abraham has anything to do with the silence of Johannes de Silentio. Is the lyric-dialectical persona only a satyr mask hiding the countenance of a knight

[38] Genesis 22: 7–8, 14.

of faith? Since he cannot be recognized as such, he might be another Abraham. But these are surely vain speculations, for we have Johannes' own word for it that he is only an ironist.

Be that as it may. Faith paradoxically asserts that there is a silence and a concealment superior to ethical community and revelation. Either this paradox, or else faith is a demonic temptation. That there are many kinds of silence is the theme of Johannes' protracted digression on aesthetics. There is an innocent silence that seeks to spare the feelings of others: for example, *de mortuis nil nisi bonum*. There is the frivolous secrecy beloved by comic playwrights: the mistaken identity, for example, without which very few comedies could be written. And there is demonic silence: the enforced secrecy of a man committed to evil. Kierkegaard's Seducer is bound to silence by his nefarious purpose; his way of life includes a commitment to that silence without which he cannot carry through his program of betrayal.

The ethical verdict on all such forms of silence is easily arrived at. Of the innocent silence ethics says that it is the product of a misconceived and misdirected sympathy; better to have the matter out than to presume to shield another from the truth. The secrecy employed by the comedian is a nugatory fiction unworthy of ethical consideration. The silence of the demon is unqualified evil. He must be compelled to speak, even as Christ caused the dumb man to speak by casting out the devil that possessed him. For if the demoniac is made to reveal himself in public utterance his demonia will be annulled by the community of the good.

If the ethical is coterminous with the human, Abraham's silence is the involuntary silence of the demon. And yet faith sees his reserve as the sign of his complicity not with the devil but with God. Either there is a silence that is justified over against ethical revelation, or Abraham is lost and the incommunicado of faith is but the horrible and vacuous isolation of the demoniac. Johannes once again gets no further than to faith. Not even that far, for he always ends short of faith with his monotonous either/or: either there is a teleological suspension of the ethical, an absolute duty toward God, and a justified silence, or—. Either faith, or— the rest *is* silence.

It might be supposed, from his constant reference to "the ethical," that the terms of Johannes' disjunction are faith and ethics. Either faith or ethics provides the guide for human life and the norm for human achievement. *Fear and Trembling* has often been read as a comment on the discrepancy between ethics and religion. But there is that mighty "if" that qualifies everything John of Silence says about "the ethical." His conviction—which he holds with exceptional vigor and tenacity—that infinite resignation is the supreme act of a man shows that his book has nothing to do with those questions about the propriety of waiving ethical rules which his commentators have so often foisted upon him. Equally irrelevant are all attempts to parallel the case of Abraham with made-up instances of unmotivated evil or real examples of supererogatory sanctity. John of Silence is not concerned at all with sanctions, human or divine, and the paradox he poses is not religion versus ethics. A man on trial, an Abraham, could never parcel out his dilemma in these tidy compartments. The real alternative is: either faith or despair. His analysis of Abraham ironically dissembles Johannes' belief that a faith which passes understanding and exceeds human agency is the only alternative to a resignation that heroically expires in an ecstasy of impotence.

In plainer terms: Christianity is the only power that can extricate a man from the predicament of suffering and guilt into which he precipitates himself by his own efforts to secure his relationship to God. It is not without reason that John of Silence has introduced New Testament allusions into his discussion at several criti-

cal points. His reference to the Blessed Virgin and
the disciples of the Lord, as well as his analysis of
Luke 14: 26 and his citations of the dumb demoniac,
not only illumine the situation of Abraham; they also
suggest the use Johannes wants to make of his
patriarch-hero. These, plus the text from which the
title of his book is lifted (*"Work out your own salvation* with fear and trembling, for *it is God which worketh* in you . . ."), show clearly enough that whatever
Johannes says about Abraham is to be understood
obliquely of the Christian believer.

There are two other passages in the New Testament
that are decisive in this connection. Although he does
not wish to be classed as a "learned exegete," Johannes has betrayed no slight expertise *in sacra pagina,*
and it may be supposed that he knows the verses in
question. First from the Epistle to the Hebrews:

> By faith Abraham, when he was tried, offered up
> Isaac: and he that had received the promises offered
> up his only begotten son, of whom it was said,
> that in Isaac shall thy seed be called: accounting
> that God was able to raise him up, even from the
> dead; from whence also he received him in a figure.
> (Hebrews 11: 17–19)

The second is from St. Paul's explanation of Abraham, "our father, as pertaining to the flesh," in his
letter to the Jewish Christians at Rome:

> He staggered not at the promise of God through
> unbelief; but was strong in faith, giving glory to God;
> and being fully persuaded that, what he had prom-
> ised, he was able also to perform. And therefore it
> was imputed to him for righteousness. Now it was
> not written for his sake alone, that it was imputed
> to him; but for us also, to whom it shall be imputed,
> if we believe on him that raised up Jesus our Lord

from the dead; who was delivered for our offences, and was raised again for our justification. (Romans 4: 20–25)

The words that stand out in the passage from Hebrews are the words "in a figure." It is reasonable to suppose that *Fear and Trembling,* in its own lyric and dialectical way, is an essay in the figural reading of the Old Testament. Abraham is the "father of faith" because he is a type or figure of faith, foreshadowing the faith of the New Covenant. The typology is reduplicated in *Fear and Trembling* itself: whatever John of Silence says about Abraham is also to be understood as "in a figure." To be sure the figure is presented by understatement and dissemblance. But the clues are there, and for all its irony this problematic book demands typological resolution.

Along with this general observation it is necessary to look more closely at the kind of figural interpretation found in *Fear and Trembling.* According to the predominant medieval tradition, a scriptural text, besides its literal meaning, may carry three modes of spiritual significance: the allegorical, the moral, and the anagogical. At the literal level, the story of Abraham and Isaac probably has something to do with the elimination of human sacrifice as a cultic element in primitive Semitic religion. Johannes de Silentio may or may not have known about this, but in any case it is clear that he is not interested in that dimension of the biblical record. In the allegorical reading favored by the author of the Epistle to the Hebrews, the sacrifice and restitution of Isaac prefigures the redemption of the world by the Passion and Resurrection of Our Lord Jesus Christ. But neither is Johannes concerned to read the story at this level. His reading is guided by the words of the Pauline text: "Now it was not written for his sake alone . . . But *for us also . . . if we believe . . .*" (Romans 4: 23–24; my emphasis). It is the moral sense alone that interests John of Silence. Abraham's faith is the pattern after which the Christian must model his own belief. Or as Johannes says, Abraham is the *paradigm* of faith. As *femina* is the paradigm for all first-declension nouns, so Abraham is the paradigm according to which all instances of faith are to be declined in all cases. Not for his sake alone, but for us also if we believe, God is able to perform what He has promised.

A "learned exegete" in the Middle Ages, expounding the faith of Abraham tropologically, would have viewed it from within as a confirmed believer examining the sources and prophecies of his own salvation. His lyric-dialectic character, his profession of unfaith, and his running polemic against the parsons and theologians besotted with philosophy exclude Johannes from the promised land of churchly theology. Like Moses, he can see but he may not enter. But from his standpoint on Mount Pisgah he casts down a few hints as to the Christian-moral significance he glimpses in the saga of Abraham and Isaac. In the course of Problem III, after sifting through a handful of literary parallels, Johannes notes that none of these is strictly analogous to Abraham's case. He continues:

> If there might be any analogy, this must be found in the paradox of sin, but this again lies in another sphere and cannot explain Abraham and is itself far easier to explain than Abraham.[39]

This is a typical twist of irony, better suited to unsettle than to satisfy the understanding. For the condition of the sinner who needs forgiveness and can only have it by virtue of the absurd is, *mutatis mutandis,* exactly the analogy Johannes is trying to draw. Earlier in Problem III he says as much, though again in an offhand way as an ironist might. In the course

[39] Kierkegaard, op. cit., p. 121.

of reviewing the legend of Agnes and the merman[40] he speculates that the merman (a demonic figure) might be saved for marriage with Agnes, but only by

> recourse to the paradox. For when the individual by his guilt has gone outside the universal he can return to it only by virtue of having come as the individual into an absolute relationship with the absolute.[41]

If the reader's attention has dozed off during this lengthy and somewhat pedantic literary exercise, the sentence immediately following should awaken him and put him on his guard: "Here I will make an observation by which I say more than was said at any point in the foregoing discussion."[42] A footnote explains:

> In the foregoing discussion I have intentionally refrained from any consideration of sin and its reality. The whole discussion points to Abraham, and him I can still approach by immediate categories—in so far, that is to say, as I am able to understand him. As soon as sin makes its appearance ethics comes to grief precisely upon repentance; for repentance is the highest ethical expression, but precisely as such it is the deepest ethical self-contradiction.[43]

From other pseudonyms and from the *Edifying Discourses:* repentance (or the eternal recollection of guilt) is the "highest expression" of that religion which itself is only a tensing of ethical passion to the uttermost. But the uttermost is the breaking point. Re-

[40] The legend of Agnes and the merman is enshrined in the ballad "Agnete hun stander på højelandsbro," which may be found in *Danske Sange* (Copenhagen: Politikens Forlag, 1954), pp. 6–7. See also Matthew Arnold's poem, "The Forsaken Merman," which is based on this legend.

[41] Kierkegaard, op. cit., p. 108.

[42] Ibid., p. 108.

[43] Ibid., p. 108n.

pentance not only sums up all that a man can do to bind himself to God; it also reveals that his God-relationship is consummated negatively in self-denial, and is therefore the "deepest ethical self-contradiction."

> Sin is not the first immediacy, sin is a later immediacy. By sin the individual is already higher (in the direction of the demoniacal paradox) than the universal, because it is a contradiction on the part of the universal to impose itself upon a man who lacks the *conditio sine qua non.* . . . An ethics which disregards sin is a perfectly idle science; but if it asserts sin, it is *eo ipso* well beyond itself.[44]

Sin is the paradoxical Christian obverse, the transcendent dialectical reversal, of the immanent and pathetic consciousness of guilt. It is not the "first immediacy" of creation, to which Abraham belongs. That immediacy is exhausted in the strenuous exercises of Kierkegaard's Religion A, but Abraham has not yet reached the *terminus ad quem* of total guilt. His trial is, so to speak, a special case. Sin is the prologue to the "later immediacy," the new dispensation of grace by which a man is returned in virtue of the absurd to the unity and simplicity of childhood wistfully recalled in Johannes' Prelude. The man originally flawed by sin is beyond the end of his ethical rope and beyond the reach of the universal imperative. He is already higher—demonically—than the universal and may through faith be reconciled to the universal by his "absolute relationship with the absolute." But

> what is said here does not by any means explain Abraham; for it was not by sin Abraham became the individual, on the contrary, he was a righteous man, he is God's elect. So the analogy to Abraham will not appear until after the individual has been brought

[44] *Ibid.,* p. 108.

to the point of being able to accomplish the universal, and then the paradox repeats itself.[45]

More irony. Of course sin does not explain Abraham. But Abraham, with his lesser problem and his
patriarchal promise, does explain, as a figure explains
that of which it is a figure, the predicament of the man
for whom the ethical is permanently suspended by sin
and to whom is given, by virtue of the absurd, the
promise of the grace of forgiveness. And in such a
knight of faith—the Christian believer—the paradox of
Abraham will repeat itself when he attempts to live
the new life that is given to him beyond the extremity
of guilt and condemnation.

It would be unseemly for a messenger to expound
too confidently—and to other messengers at that!—the
meaning of that enigma which can only be understood
by the son. In an Epilogue that harks back to the "clearance sale" of his Preface, Johannes tells of a trick
once hit upon by the merchants of Holland to improve
the market in spices.

> One time in Holland when the market was rather
> dull for spices the merchants had several cargoes
> dumped into the sea to peg up prices. This was a
> pardonable, perhaps a necessary device for deluding
> people. Is it something like that we need now in the
> world of spirit? Are we so thoroughly convinced that
> we have attained the highest point that there is noth-
> ing left for us but to make ourselves believe piously
> that we have not got so far—just for the sake of hav-
> ing something left to occupy our time? Is it such a
> self-deception the present generation has need of, does
> it need to be trained to virtuosity in self-deception,
> or is it not rather sufficiently perfected already in the
> art of deceiving itself? Or rather is not the thing most
> needed an honest seriousness which dauntlessly and

[45] Ibid., p. 108.

incorruptibly points to the tasks, an honest seriousness which lovingly watches over the tasks, which
does not frighten men into being over hasty in getting the highest tasks accomplished, but keeps the tasks
young and beautiful and charming to look upon and
yet difficult withal and appealing to noble minds.[46]

Is *Fear and Trembling* an exercise in pious self-
deception or an honest and serious call to the task of
believing? Johannes' irony suggests the former, but his
lyric and dialectical intensity belies the latter. Perhaps
the case is Socratic. For if the suspicion is correct that
our age, which has gone far beyond faith, is already
sufficiently self-deceived, then to deceive this generation out of its self-deception is the best service an
honest seriousness can render to the times. In a figure
and for us also, deception and seriousness may be the
same thing. In a world where all men stand on their
heads an upright man is bound to look queer. One
thing is sure in any case:

> Faith is the highest passion in a man. There are
> perhaps many in every generation who do not even
> reach it, but no one gets further. Whether there be
> many in our age who do not discover it, I will not
> decide, I dare only appeal to myself as a witness who
> makes no secret that the prospects for him are not
> the best, without for all that wanting to delude him-
> self and to betray the great thing which is faith by
> reducing it to an insignificance, to an ailment of child-
> hood which one must wish to get over as soon as
> possible. But for the man also who does not so much
> as reach faith life has tasks enough, and if one
> loves them sincerely, life will by no means be wasted,
> even though it never is comparable to the life of those
> who sensed and grasped the highest.[47]

[46] Ibid., pp. 129–30.
[47] Ibid., p. 131.

The person spoke more truly than he knew: all of life is a trial. Those who finish with life before life has had its way with them are like children who finish playing before their holiday is over: as these are wretched and deficient children, so those are miserable and unprofitable servants. Even the man who does not get as far as faith will find occupation enough for a lifetime. But the high passion of faith is like the speed of light: the only absolute in a world of relativities. And the man who is too eager to exceed it may find himself moving steadily backward.

So John of Silence ends, without the understanding of faith that he sought. His prospects, he confesses, are "not the best."[48] He catches a glimpse of the possibility of faith, imminent just over the edge of his imaginative and intellectual horizons, but he cannot testify to its reality. Denied the joy of possession, he must rest content with the promise and the vision.

[48] Ibid., p. 131.

A
Bibliography
of
Books and Articles
about
Søren Kierkegaard
in
English for the years
1956–70

A Supplement
to
Himmelstrup, Jens (ed.). *Søren Kierkegaard:*
International Bibliografi. Copenhagen:
Nyt Nordisk Forlag, 1962.

My hope is that the following bibliography may prove to be of use both to the casual reader and to the serious scholar. The essential bibliographical tool for Kierkegaard studies is Jens Himmelstrup's outstanding work, *Søren Kierkegaard: International Bibliografi* (Copenhagen: Nyt Nordisk Forlag, 1962). Himmelstrup compiled his multi-language bibliography in Copenhagen, where access to English and American periodicals was somewhat limited. Accordingly, his treatment of English-language books and periodicals is incomplete. This bibliography is intended to supplement Himmelstrup's listings for the years prior to 1956, as well as to bring it up to date for the most recent period. Equipped with Himmelstrup and this supplement, the reader should be in a position to survey the secondary literature in English on Søren Kierkegaard.

I should point out that Aage Jørgensen published in November 1971 a multi-language supplement to Himmelstrup entitled *Søren Kierkegaard-litteratur 1961–1970: En foreløbig bibliografi* (Aarhus: Akademisk Boghandel, 1971). Jørgensen's excellent work has been of great use to me in compiling the present list. I have also benefited from the bibliography appended to Lewis Lawson's *Kierkegaard's Presence in Contemporary American Life: Essays from Various Disciplines* (Metuchen, N.J.: The Scarecrow Press, Inc., 1970).

The following bibliographic sources have been consulted in the compiling of this supplement:

Bibliography of Philosophy: A Quarterly Bulletin. Paris: Librarie Philosophique J. Vrin. Years 1956–68.

Cumulative Book Index: World List of Books in the English Language. Edited by Nina R. Thompson. New York: H. W. Wilson Co. Years 1957–November 1970.

Essay and General Literature Index. Edited by Estelle A. Fidell. New York: H. W. Wilson Co. Years 1956–June 1970.

Index to Religious Periodical Literature. Edited by Lucy W.

Markley. New York: American Theological Library Association. Years 1957–62.

International Index: A Guide to Periodical Literature in the Social Sciences and Humanities. New York: H. W. Wilson Co. Years 1956–December 1970.

PMLA Annual Bibliography. Compiled by Paul A. Brown. New York: PMLA. Years 1956–69.

Reader's Guide to Periodical Literature. New York: H. W. Wilson Co. Years 1956–70.

Répertoire Bibliographique de la Philosophie. Publié sous les auspices de L'Institut International de Philosophie avec le patronage de L'UNESCO. Louvain: Éditions de L'Institut Supérieur de Philosophie. Years 1956–69.

The Subject Index to Periodicals. London: The Library Association. Years 1956–June 1970.

Jørgensen, Aage. Søren Kierkegaard-litteratur 1961–1970: En foreløbig bibliografi. Aarhus: Akademisk Boghandel, 1971.

Lawson, Lewis. Kierkegaard's Presence in Contemporary American Life: Essays from Various Disciplines. Metuchen, N.J.: The Scarecrow Press, Inc., 1970.

Books

Arbaugh, George B. and George E. Kierkegaard's Authorship: A Guide to the Writings of Kierkegaard. Rock Island, Ill.: Augustana College Library, 1967.

Brandt, Frithiof. Søren Kierkegaard 1813–1855: His Life—His Works. Tr. by Ann R. Born. Copenhagen: Det Danske Selskab, 1963.

Brown, James. Kierkegaard, Heidegger, Buber and Barth: Subject and Object in Modern Theology. New York: Collier Books, 1962.

Carnell, E. J. The Burden of Søren Kierkegaard. Grand Rapids: Wm. B. Eerdmans Publishing Co., 1965.

Cochrane, Arthur L. Existentialists and God: Being and the Being of God in the Thought of Søren Kierkegaard. Philadelphia: Westminster Press, 1956.

Crites, Stephen. *In the Twilight of Christendom: Hegel vs. Kierkegaard on Faith and History*. Chambersburg, Pa.: American Academy of Religion, Studies in Religion, Number Two, 1971.

Croxall, Thomas H. *Glimpses and Impressions of Kierkegaard*. Welwyn: J. Nisbet, 1959.

——. *Kierkegaard Commentary*. London: J. Nisbet, 1956.

Dewey, Bradley R. *The New Obedience*. Washington: Corpus Instrumentorium, Inc., 1968.

Diem, Hermann. *Kierkegaard: An Introduction*. Tr. by David Green. Richmond: John Knox Press, 1966.

——. *Kierkegaard's Dialectic of Existence*. Tr. from German by H. Knight. London: Oliver & Boyd, 1959.

Dupré, L. K. *Kierkegaard as Theologian*. London: Sheed & Ward, 1963.

Eller, Vernard. *Kierkegaard and Radical Discipleship: A New Perspective*. Princeton: Princeton University Press, 1967.

Garelick, H. M. *The Anti-Christianity of Kierkegaard*. New York: Humanities Press, 1966.

Gates, J. A. *The Life and Thought of Kierkegaard for Everyman*. London: Westminster Press, 1960.

George, A. G. *The First Sphere*. Bombay: Asia Publishing House, 1966.

Gill, J. H. (ed.). *Essays on Kierkegaard*. Minneapolis: Burgess Publishing Co., 1969.

Grimsley, Ronald. *Søren Kierkegaard and French Literature: Eight Comparative Studies*. Cardiff: University of Wales Press, 1966.

Hamilton, Kenneth. *The Promise of Kierkegaard*. Philadelphia: J. B. Lippincott Company, 1969.

Hanna, Thomas. *The Lyrical Existentialists*. New York: Atheneum, 1962.

Harper, Ralph. *The Seventh Solitude: Man's Isolation in Kierke-

gaard, Dostoevsky, and Nietzsche. Baltimore: Johns Hopkins Press, 1965.

Heinecken, Martin. *The Moment Before God*. Philadelphia: Muhlenberg Press, 1956.

Hubben, W. *Dostoevski, Kierkegaard, Nietzsche, and Kafka*. New York: Collier Books, 1962.

Johnson, H. A., and Thulstrup, Niels (eds.). *A Kierkegaard Critique*. New York: Harper & Bros., 1962.

Lawson, Lewis. *Kierkegaard's Presence in Contemporary American Life: Essays from Various Disciplines*. Metuchen, N.J.: The Scarecrow Press, Inc., 1970.

Lefevre, Perry (ed.). *The Prayers of Kierkegaard*. Chicago: University of Chicago Press, 1956.

Mackey, Louis. *Kierkegaard: A Kind of Poet*. Philadelphia: University of Pennsylvania Press, 1971.

Malantschuk, Gregor. *Kierkegaard's Thought*. Edited and Translated by Howard V. and Edna H. Hong. Princeton: Princeton University Press, 1971.

———. *Kierkegaard's Way to the Truth*. Minneapolis: Augsburg Publishing House, 1963.

Meyer, Henrietta Hilda. *Reflections upon the Life and Thought of Søren Kierkegaard*. London: Guild of Pastoral Theology, 1966.

Miller, L. L. *In Search of the Self*. Philadelphia: Muhlenberg Press, 1962.

Naesev, Vincent. *The Sampler: The Danish Existentialist on the Morals of the Press*. Privately printed, 1952.

Pelikan, Jaroslav. *Human Culture and the Holy. Essays on the True, the Good, and the Beautiful. Kierkegaard, Paul, Dostoyevski, Luther, Nietzsche, and Bach*. London: Student Christian Movement Press, 1959.

Perkins, Robert L. *Søren Kierkegaard*. Richmond: John Knox Press, 1969.

Price, G. *The Narrow Pass*. London: Hutchinson & Co., 1963.

Rohde, H. P. (ed.). *The Auctioneer's Sales Record of the Library of Søren Kierkegaard.* Copenhagen: The Royal Library, 1967.

Rohde, Peter P. *Søren Aabye Kierkegaard 1813–1855.* London: George Allen & Unwin, 1963.

——. *Søren Kierkegaard: The Father of Existentialism.* Tr. by Reginald Spink. Copenhagen: Udenrigministeriets Pressebureau, 1963.

Shestov, Lev. *Kierkegaard and the Existential Philosophy.* Tr. by Elinor Hewitt. Athens, Ohio: Ohio University Press, 1969.

Shmuëli, Adi. *Kierkegaard and Consciousness.* Tr. by Naomi Handelman. Princeton: Princeton University Press, 1971.

Sikes, Walter W. *On Becoming the Truth: An Introduction to the Life and Thought of Søren Kierkegaard.* St. Louis: Bethany Press, 1967.

Smit, Harvey Albert. *Kierkegaard's Pilgrimage of Man: The Road of Self-Positing and Self-Abdication.* Delft: W. D. Meinema, 1965.

Sponheim, Paul R. *Kierkegaard on Christ and Christian Coherence.* New York: Harper & Row, 1967.

Thomas, J. H. *Subjectivity and Paradox.* Oxford: Blackwell's, 1957.

Thompson, Josiah. *Kierkegaard: A Biographical Essay.* New York: Alfred A. Knopf, Inc., 1973.

——. *The Lonely Labyrinth: Kierkegaard's Pseudonymous Works.* Carbondale: Southern Illinois University Press, 1967.

Thomte, R. *Kierkegaard's Philosophy of Religion.* New York: Greenwood Press, 1969.

Wolf, H. C. *Kierkegaard and Bultmann: The Quest of the Historical Jesus.* Minneapolis: Augsburg Publishing House, 1965.

Zuidema, S. U. *Kierkegaard.* Philadelphia: Presbyterian & Reformed Publishing Co., 1960.

Articles

Adorno, T. W. "On Kierkegaard's Doctrine of Love," *Studies in Philosophy and Social Science*, VIII (1940) 413–29.

Ahlstrom, Sidney E. "The Continental Influence on American Christian Thought Since World War I," *Church History*, XXVIII (September 1958), 256–72.

Allen, E. L. "Introduction to Kierkegaard," *Durham University Journal*, XXXVI (December 1943), 9–14.

——. "Kierkegaard and Karl Marx," *Theology*, XL (February 1940), 117–21.

——. "Pascal and Kierkegaard," *London Quarterly and Holborn Review*, CLXII (April 1937), 150–64.

Allison, Henry E. "Christianity and Nonsense," *Review of Metaphysics*, XX (March 1967), 432–60.

——. "Kierkegaard's Dialectic of the Religious Consciousness," *Union Seminary Quarterly Review*, XX (March 1965), 225–33.

Anderson, Betty C. "The Melville-Kierkegaard Syndrome," *Rendezvous*, III (1968), 41–53.

Anderson, Raymond E. "Kierkegaard's Theory of Communication," *Speech Monographs*, XXX, 1–14.

Angoff, Charles. "Letters and the Arts," *Living Age*, CCCLVIII (March 1940), 89.

Ansbro, John J. "Kierkegaard's Gospel of Suffering," *Philosophical Studies*, XVI (1967), 182–92.

Auden, W. H. "Knight of Doleful Countenance," *The New Yorker*, XLIV (May 25, 1968), 141–42, 146–48, 151–54, 157–58.

Babbage, S. Barton. "Søren Kierkegaard," *Evangelical Quarterly*, (January 1943), 56–72.

Barrett, Cyril. "Søren Kierkegaard: An Exception," *Studies* (Dublin), XLV (1956), 77–83.

Barth, Karl. "Kierkegaard and the Theologians," tr. by H. M. Rumscheidt, *Canadian Journal of Theology*, XIII (January 1967), 64–65.

———. "Thank You and a Bow: Kierkegaard's Reveille," tr. by H. M. Rumscheidt, *Canadian Journal of Theology*, XI (January 1965), 3–7.

Bedell, George C. "Kierkegaard's Conception of Time," *Journal of the American Academy of Religion*, XXXVII (1969), 266–69.

Bernstein, Richard J. "Consciousness, Existence, and Action: Kierkegaard and Sartre," in his book, *Praxis and Action: Contemporary Philosophies of Human Activity*. Philadelphia: The University of Pennsylvania Press, 1971, 84–164.

Billeskov-Jansen, F. J. "The Universality of Kierkegaard," *American-Scandinavian Review*, LI, 145–49.

Bixler, J. S. "On Being Absurd!" *The Massachusetts Review*, X (1969), 407–12.

Blackham, H. J. "The Comparison of Herzen with Kierkegaard: A Comment," *Slavic Review*, XXV (June 1966), 215–17.

Blanshard, Brand. "Kierkegaard on Faith," *The Personalist*, XLIX (1968), 5–23.

Bogen, James. "Kierkegaard and the 'teleological suspension of the ethical,'" *Inquiry*, V (1962), 305–17.

———. "Remark on the Kierkegaard-Hegel Controversy," *Synthese*, XIII (1961), 372–89.

Bolman, Frederick de W., Jr. "Kierkegaard in Limbo," *Journal of Philosophy*, XLI (December 21, 1944), 711–21.

———. "Reply to Mrs. Hess," *Journal of Philosophy*, XLII (April 13, 1945), 219–20.

Bowen, James K. "'Crazy Arab' and Kierkegaard's 'Melancholy Fantastic,'" *Research Studies*, XXXVII, 60–64.

Brookfield, C. M. "What Was Kierkegaard's Task? A Frontier to Be Explored," *Union Seminary Quarterly Review*, XVIII, 23–35.

Broudy, H. S. "Kierkegaard's Doctrine of Indirect Communication," *Journal of Philosophy*, LVIII (April 27, 1961), 225–33.

Buch, Jorgen. "Kierkegaard Anniversary," *Hibbert Journal*, LXII (October 1963), 24–26.

——. "A Kierkegaard Museum," *American Book Collector*, XII (1961), 5–7.

Callan, Edward. "Auden and Kierkegaard: The Artistic Framework of *For the Time Being*," *Christian Scholar*, XLVIII (Fall 1965), 211–23.

——. "Auden's *New Year Letter*: A New Style of Architecture," *Renascence*, XVI (Fall 1963), 13–19.

Campbell, R. "Lessing's Problem and Kierkegaard's Answer," *Scottish Journal of Theology*, XIX (March 1966), 35–54.

Cardinal, Clive H. "Rilke and Kierkegaard: Some Relationships Between Poet and Theologian," *Bulletin of the Rocky Mountain Modern Language Association*, XXIII (1969), 34–39.

Celestin, George. "Kierkegaard and Christian Renewal," *Dominicana*, XLIX (Summer 1964), 149–57.

Chari, C. T. K. "On the Dialectic of Swami Vivekenanda and Søren Kierkegaard: an 'Existential' Approach to Indian Philosophy," *Revue Internationale de Philosophie*, X, No. 37 (1956), 315–31.

——. "Søren Kierkegaard and Swami Vivekenanda: A Study in Religious Dialectics," *Vedanda Kesari*, XXXIX (June 1952), 107–10.

Charlesworth, James H. "Kierkegaard and Optical Linguistics," *Kierkegaardiana*, *VII*. Copenhagen: Munksgaard, 1966, 131–34.

Anonymous. "Choose, Leap, and Be Free," *Times Literary Supplement*, XLV (March 9, 1946), 109–11.

Christensen, M. G. "Gruntvig and Kierkegaard," *Lutheran Quarterly*, II (November 1950), 441–46.

Clive, Geoffrey. "Demonic in Mozart," *Music and Letters,* XXXVII (January 1956), 1–13.

———. "Seven Types of Offense," *Lutheran Quarterly,* X (February 1958), 11–25.

———. "The Sickness unto Death in the Underworld: A Study of Nihilism," *Harvard Theological Review,* LI (1958), 133–67.

Closs, August. "Goethe and Kierkegaard," *Modern Language Quarterly,* X (September 1949), 264–80.

Cochrane, A. C. "On the Anniversaries of Mozart, Kierkegaard, and Barth," *Scottish Journal of Theology,* IX (September 1956), 251–63.

Cole, J. D. "Kierkegaard's Doctrine of the Atonement," *Religion in Life,* XXXIII (Autumn 1964), 592–601.

Cole, J. Preston. "The Existential Reality of God: A Kierkegaardian Study," *Christian Scholar,* XLVIII (Fall 1965), 224–35.

———. "The Function of Choice in Human Existence," *Journal of Religion,* XLV (July 1965), 196–210.

Collins, J. "Faith and Reflection in Kierkegaard," *Journal of Religion,* XXXVII (January 1957), 10–19.

Comstock, W. R. "Aspects of Aesthetic Existence: Kierkegaard and Santayana," *International Philosophical Quarterly,* VI (June 1966), 189–213.

Cook, E. J. Raymond. "Kierkegaard's Literary Art," *The Listener,* LXXII (November 5, 1964), 713–14.

Copleston, Frederick C. "Existence and Religion," *Dublin Review,* CCXX (Spring 1947), 50–63.

Crites, Stephen. "The Author and the Authorship: Recent Kierkegaard Literature," *Journal of the American Academy of Religion,* XXXVIII (March 1970), 37–54.

———. "Pseudonymous Authorship as Art and as Act," in Josiah Thompson (ed.), *Kierkegaard: A Collection of Critical*

Essays. Garden City, New York: Doubleday & Company, Inc., 1972, pp. 189–236.

Croxall, T. H. "The Death of Kierkegaard," *The Church Quarterly Review,* CLVII (1956), 271–86.

———. "A Strange but Stimulating Essay on Music," *Musical Times,* XC (February 1949), 46–48.

Dallen, James. "Existentialism and the Catholic Thinker," *Catholic World,* CC (February 1965), 294–99.

Davison, R. M. "Herzen and Kierkegaard," *Slavic Review,* XXV (June 1966), 191–221.

———. "Reply," *Slavic Review,* XXV (June 1966), 218–21.

Demson, D. "Kierkegaard's Sociology with Notes on Its Relevance to the Church," *Religion in Life,* XXVII (Spring 1958), 257–65.

De Rosa, Peter. "Some Reflections on Kierkegaard and Christian Love," *The Clergy Review* (London), XLIV (1959), 616–22.

Dewey, Bradley R. "The Erotic-Demonic in Kierkegaard's 'Diary of the Seducer,' " *Scandinavica,* X (1971), 1–24.

———. "Kierkegaard and the New Testament," *Harvard Theological Review,* LX (October 1967), 391–409.

Diamond, Malcolm L. "Faith and Its Tensions: A Criticism of Religious Existentialism," *Judaism,* XIII (Summer 1964), 317–27.

———. "Kierkegaard and Apologetics," *Journal of Religion,* IV (April 1964), 122–32.

Dietrichson, Paul. "Kierkegaard's Concept of Self," *Inquiry,* VIII (Spring 1965), 1–32.

Dru, Alexander. "Kierkegaard: A Great Christian Thinker," *Listener,* LIV (November 17, 1955), 841–42.

———. "Reply with Rejoinder," *Dublin Review,* CCXXI (Spring 1948), 183–88.

Duncan, Elmer H. "Kierkegaard's Teleological Suspension of

the Ethical: A Study of Exception-Cases," *Southern Journal of Philosophy*, I (Winter 1963), 9–18.

———. "Kierkegaard's Uses of Paradox—Yet Once More," *Journal of Existentialism*, VII (Spring 1967), 319–28.

Dupré, Louis K. "The Constitution of the Self in Kierkegaard's Philosophy," *International Philosophical Quarterly*, III (December 1963), 506–26.

Durfee, Harold A. "The Second Stage of Kierkegaardian Scholarship in America," *International Philosophical Quarterly*, III (1963), 121–39.

Earle, William. "Hegel and Some Contemporary Philosophies," *Philosophy and Phenomenological Research*, XX (March 1960), 352–64.

———. "The Paradox and Death of God: Kierkegaard and Nietzsche," in C. W. Christian and Glenn R. Wittig (eds.), *Radical Theology: Phase Two.* Philadelphia: J. B. Lippincott Company, 1967, 27–42.

———. "Phenomenology and Existentialism," *Journal of Philosophy*, LVII (January 21, 1960), 75–84.

Edwards, Brian F. M. "Kafka and Kierkegaard: A Reassessment," *German Life and Letters*, XX (April 1967), 218–25.

Edwards, C. N. "Guilt in the Thought of Søren Kierkegaard," *Encounter*, XXVII (Spring 1966), 141–57.

Eller, Vernard. "Existentialism and the Brethren," *Brethren Life and Thought*, V (Summer 1960), 31–38.

———. "Fact, Faith, and Foolishness: Kierkegaard and the New Quest," *Journal of Religion*, XLVIII (January 1968), 54–68.

———. "Kierkegaard Knew the Brethren! Sort of," *Brethren Life and Thought*, VIII (Winter 1963), 57–60.

Evans, Robert O. "Existentialism in Greene's 'The Quiet American,'" *Modern Fiction Studies*, III (Autumn 1957), 241–48.

Fabro, Cornelio. "The Problem of Desperation and Christian

Spirituality in Kierkegaard," *Kierkegaardiana, IV*. Copenhagen: Søren Kierkegaard Selskabet, 1962, 62–69.

——. "The 'Subjectivity of Truth' and the Interpretation of Kierkegaard," *Kierkegaard-Studiet*, I (1964), 35–43.

——. "Why Did Kierkegaard Break Up with Regina?" *Orbis Litterarum*, XXII, 387–92.

Fairhurst, Stanley J. "Søren Kierkegaard [a Bibliography]," *Modern Schoolman*, XXI (November 1953), 19–22.

Farber, Marjorie. "Subjectivity in Modern Fiction," *Kenyon Review*, VII (Autumn 1945), 645–52.

Fasel, Oscar A. "Observations on Unamuno and Kierkegaard," *Hispania*, XXXVIII (December 1955), 443–50.

Fenger, Henning. "Kierkegaard—A Literary Approach," *Scandinavica*, III (May 1964), 1–16.

Ferm, Deane W. "Two Conflicting Trends in Protestant Theological Thinking," *Religion in Life*, XXV (Autumn 1956), 582–94.

Fitzpatrick, M., Jr. "Current Kierkegaard Study: Whence-Whither?" *Journal of Religion*, L (January 1970), 79–90.

Fleisner, E. M. "Legacy of Kierkegaard," *New Republic*, CXXXIII (December 26, 1955), 16–18. *Reply:* CXXXIV (January 9, 1956), 22–23. *Rejoinder:* CXXXIV (January 23, 1956), 23.

Ford, Richard S. "Existentialism: Philosophy or Theology?" *Religion in Life*, XXVIII (Summer 1959), 433–42.

Forshey, Gerald. "Pharaoh, Kierkegaard, and Black Power," *Christian Advocate*, XII (May 30, 1968), 7–8.

Anonymous. "Four Articles on Kierkegaard," *Anglican Theological Review*, XXXVIII (1956), 1–41.

Freehof, Solomon B. "Aspects of Existentialism," *Carnegie Magazine*, XXII (April 1949), 292–94.

Friedrich, Gerhard. "Reply to Llewellyn Jones," *Christian Century*, LXIX (June 4, 1952), 674–75.

Fromm, H. "Emerson and Kierkegaard: The Problem of Historical Christianity," *Massachusetts Review*, IX (Autumn 1968), 741–52.

Gallagher, Michael P. "Wittgenstein's Admiration for Kierkegaard," *Month*, XXIX (January 1968), 43–49.

Gallagher, T. "Søren Kierkegaard," in Frederick Patka (ed.), *Existentialist Thinkers and Thought*. New York: Philosophical Library, 1962, 75–92.

Gardiner, Patrick. "Kierkegaard's Two Ways," *British Academy Proceedings*, LIV (1968), 207–29.

Garelick, Herbert. "The Irrationality and Supra-rationality of Kierkegaard's Paradox," *Southern Journal of Philosophy*, II (Summer 1964), 75–86.

Genêt. "Letter from Paris," *The New Yorker*, XL (May 16, 1964), 170.

Gerber, R. J. "Kierkegaard, Reason, and Faith," *Thought*, XLIV (Spring 1969), 29–52.

Gill, Jerry H. "Kant, Kierkegaard and Religious Knowledge," *Philosophy and Phenomenological Research*, XXVIII (1967–68), 188–204.

Gimblett, Charles. "SK: A Strange Saint," *London Quarterly and Holborn Review*, CLXXX (October 1955), 280–82.

Glicksberg, C. I. "Aesthetics of Nihilism," *University of Kansas City Review*, XXVII (December 1960), 127–30.

Anonymous. "Gloomy Dane: The Sesquicentennial of Kierkegaard's Birth," *Tablet*, CCXVII (May 4, 1963), 482.

Goulet, Denis A. "Kierkegaard, Aquinas, and the Dilemma of Abraham," *Thought*, XXXII (1957), 165–88.

Graef, H. C. "Prophets of Gloom," *Catholic World*, CLXXXIII (June 1956), 202–6.

Green, Allan. "Søren Kierkegaard in Berlin," *Finsk Tidskrift*, VI (1957), 261–68.

Grene, Marjorie. "Kierkegaard: The Philosophy," *Kenyon Review*, IX (Winter 1947), 48–69.

Griffith, Richard M. "Repetition: Constantine (S.) Constantius," *Journal of Existential Psychiatry*, II (Summer 1962), 437–48.

Grimsley, Ronald. "Hugo, Kierkegaard, and the Character of Nero," *Revue de Littérature Comparée*, XXXII, 230–36.

———. "Kierkegaard and Descartes," *Journal of the History of Philosophy*, IV (January 1966), 31–41.

———. "Kierkegaard and Leibniz," *Journal of the History of Ideas*, XXVI (July 1965), 383–96.

———. "Kierkegaard and Scribe," *Revue de Littérature Comparée*, XXXVIII (1964), 512–30.

———. "Kierkegaard, Vigny and 'the Poet,'" *Revue de Littérature Comparée* (1960), 52–80.

———. "Modern Conception of the Demonic," *Church Quarterly Review*, CLVIII (April–June 1957), 185–94.

———. "Romantic Melancholy in Chateaubriand and Kierkegaard," *Comparative Literature*, VIII (Summer 1956), 227–44.

———. "Rousseau and Kierkegaard," *Cambridge Journal*, VII (July 1954), 615–26.

———. "Some Implication of the Use of Irony in Voltaire and Kierkegaard," in François Jost (ed.), *Actes du IVe Congrès de l'Association Internationale de Littérature Comparée, Fribourg 1964 (I–II)*, The Hague/Paris: Mouton & Co., 1966, 1018–24.

Halevi, Jacob L. "Kierkegaard and the Midrash," *Judaism*, IV, 13–28.

———. "Kierkegaard's Teleological Suspension of the Ethical: Is It Jewish?" *Judaism*, VIII (Fall 1959), 292–302.

Hamburger, Michael. "Under the Volcano: *The Last Years: Journals 1853–55*," *Spectator* (February 5, 1965), 174–75.

Hamilton, Kenneth M. "Created Soul—Eternal Spirit: A Continuing Theological Thorn," *Scottish Journal of Theology*, XIX (March 1966), 23–34.

———. "Kierkegaard on Sin," *Scottish Journal of Theology*, XVII (September 1964), 289–302.

———. "Man: Anxious or Guilty? A Second Look at Kierkegaard's *The Concept of Dread*," *Christian Scholar*, XLVI (Winter 1963), 293–99.

Hamilton, William. "Daring to be the Enemy of God: Some Reflections on the Life and Death of Mozart's Don Giovanni," *Christian Scholar*, XLVI (Spring 1963), 40–54.

Hanzo, Thomas. "Eliot and Kierkegaard: 'The Meaning of Happening' in *The Cocktail Party*," *Modern Drama*, III, 52–59.

Hare, Peter H. "Is There an Existential Theory of Truth?" *Journal of Existentialism*, VII (Summer 1967), 417–24.

Haroutunian, Joseph. "Protest to the Lord," *Theology Today*, XII (October 1955), 295–96.

Hartman, Robert S. "The Self in Kierkegaard," *Journal of Existential Psychiatry*, II (Spring 1962), 409–36.

Hartt, J. N. "Christian Freedom Reconsidered: The Case of Kierkegaard," *Harvard Theological Review*, LX (April 1964), 133–44.

Heinecken, M. J. "Kierkegaard as Christian," *Journal of Religion*, XXXVII (January 1957), 20–30.

Held, M. "Historical Kierkegaard: Faith of Gnosis," *Journal of Religion*, XXXVII (October 1957), 260–66.

Hems, John M. "Abraham and Brand," *Philosophy*, XXXIX (April 1964), 137–44.

Hendry, George S. "The Gospel in an Age of Anxiety," *Theology Today*, XII (October 1955), 283–89.

Herbert, Robert. "Two of Kierkegaard's Uses of 'Paradox,'" *Philosophical Review*, LXX (1961), 41–56.

Hess, M. W. "Browning: an English Kierkegaard," *Christian Century*, LXXIX (May 2, 1962), 569–71.

———. "Browning and Kierkegaard as Heirs of Luther," *Christian Century*, LXXX (June 19, 1963), 799–801.

——. "The Dilemma in Kierkegaard's 'Either/Or,'" *Journal of Philosophy*, XLII (April 13, 1945), 216–19.

——. "Kierkegaard and Socrates," *Christian Century*, LXXXII (1965), 736–38.

——. "Three Christians in Literature: Browning, Kierkegaard, Heine," *Christianity Today*, VIII (April 24, 1964), 13–15.

——. "What Luther Meant by Faith Alone," *Catholic World*, CXCIX (May 1964), 96–101.

Hill, Brian V. "Søren Kierkegaard and Educational Theory," *Educational Theory*, XVI (October 1966), 344–53.

Hill, E. F. F. "Kierkegaard: The Man and His Thought," *World Review* (December 1948), 58–62.

Holmer, Paul. "James Collins and Kierkegaard," *Meddelelser fra Søren Kierkegaard Selskabet*, IV (1954), 1–8.

——. "Kierkegaard and Logic," *Kierkegaardiana*, II (1957), 25–42.

——. "Kierkegaard and the Sermon," *Journal of Religion*, XXXVII (January 1957), 1–9.

——. "Kierkegaard and Theology," *Union Seminary Quarterly Review*, XII (March 1957), 23–31.

Holmes, Roger W. "The Problems of Philosophy in the Twentieth Century," *Antioch Review*, XXII (Fall 1962), 287–96.

Hong, Howard. "The Kierkegaard Papers," *TriQuarterly*, No. 16 (Fall 1969), 100–23.

Hook, S. "Two Types of Existentialist Religion and Ethics," *Partisan Review*, XXVI (Winter 1959), 58–63.

Horgby, Ingvar. "Immediacy–Subjectivity–Revelation," *Inquiry*, VIII (Spring 1965), 84–117.

Horn, Robert L. "On Understanding Kierkegaard Understanding . . . ," *Union Seminary Quarterly Review*, XXI (March 1966), 341–45.

Hubben, William. "Kierkegaard and the Friends," *Friends Intelligencer* (October 1953), 230–34.

Hyman, Frieda Clark. "Kierkegaard and the Hebraic Mind," *Journal of Ecumenical Studies,* IV (Summer 1967), 554–56.

Irving, John A. "Thoughts on Existentialism," *Queen's Quarterly,* LVII (Autumn 1950), 298–303.

James, Ingli. "The Autonomy of the Work of Art: Modern Criticism and the Christian Tradition," *Sewanee Review,* LXX (Spring 1962), 296–318.

Jansen, F. J. B. "Universality of Kierkegaard," *American Scandinavian Review,* LI (June 1963), 145–49.

Jørgensen, Carl. "The Ethics of Søren Kierkegaard," *Atti XII Congr. intern. Filos.,* 243–50.

Johannesson, E. O. "Isak Dinesen, Søren Kierkegaard, and the Present Age," *Books Abroad,* XXXVI (Winter 1962), 20–24.

Johnson, Howard. "The Deity in Time: An Introduction to Kierkegaard," *Theology Today,* I (January 1945), 517–36.

——. "Review of Gemenskapsproblemet hos Søren Kierkegaard (P. Wagndal)," *Review of Religion,* XXI (November 1956), 77–79.

Johnson, William A. "The Anthropology of Søren Kierkegaard," *Hartford Quarterly,* IV (Summer 1964), 43–52.

Jones, W. Glyn. "Søren Kierkegaard and Paul Martin Møller," *Modern Language Review,* LX (January 1965), 73–82.

Kainz, Howard P. "Ambiguities and Paradoxes in Kierkegaard's Existential Categories," *Philosophy Today,* XII (1969), 138–45.

——. "The Relationship of Dread to Spirit in Man and Woman, According to Kierkegaard," *The Modern Schoolman,* XLVII (1969), 1–13.

Kaufmann, R. J. "A Poetry for Sisyphus," *Prairie Schooner,* XL (Spring 1966), 23–43.

Kaufmann, Walter. "A Hundred Years After Kierkegaard," *Kenyon Review,* XVIII, 182–211.

Anonymous. "Kierkegaard and the Bible," *Theology Today*, X (July 1953), 247–48.

Anonymous. "Kierkegaard in France," *Times Literary Supplement*, XXXIV (May 23, 1935), 324.

Killinger, John. "Existentialism and Human Freedom," *English Journal*, L (May 1961), 303–13.

King, Joe M. "Kierkegaard as an Existentialist," *Furman Studies*, XV, 35–44.

King, W. L. "Negation as a Religious Category," *Journal of Religion*, XXXVII (April 1957), 109.

Klemke, E. D. "Insights to Ethical Theory from Kierkegaard," *Philosophical Quarterly* (St. Andrews), X, No. 41, 322–30.

———. "Logicality vs. Alogicality in the Christian Faith," *Journal of Religion*, XXXVIII (April 1958), 107–15.

———. "Some Misinterpretations of Kierkegaard," *Hibbert Journal*, LVII (1958–59), 259–70.

Koenker, Ernest B. "Søren Kierkegaard on Luther," in Jaroslav Pelikan (ed.), *Interpreters of Luther: Essays in Honor of Wilhelm Pauck*. Philadelphia: Fortress Press, 1968, 231–52.

Kraft, Julius. "The Philosophy of Existence," *Philosophy and Phenomenological Research*, I (March 1941), 339–58.

Kreyche, G. "A Glance at Existentialism," *Ave*, CII (October 9, 1965), 10–13.

Kritzeek, J. "Philosophers of Anxiety," *Commonweal*, LXIII (March 2, 1956), 572–74.

Kroner, Richard J. "Existentialism and Christianity," *Encounter*, XVII (Summer 1956), 219–44.

———. "Kierkegaard's Understanding of Hegel," *Union Seminary Quarterly Review*, XXI (January 1966), 233–44.

Kurtz, P. W. "Kierkegaard, Existentialism, and the Contemporary Scene," *Antioch Review*, XXI (Winter 1961–62), 471–89.

Lal, Basant Kumar, "Kierkegaard's Approach to Ethics," *The Philosophical Quarterly* (Amalner, India), XXXVIII (1965–66), 181–90.

Lampert, E. "Herzen or Kierkegaard," *Slavic Review*, XXV (June 1966), 210–14.

Langan, T. "The Original Existentialist Revolt: Søren Kierkegaard," in Etienne Gilson (ed.), *Recent Philosophy: Hegel to the Present*. New York: Random House, 1966, 69–78 (notes 684–86).

Larsen, Robert E. "Kierkegaard's Absolute Paradox," *Journal of Religion*, XLII, 34–43.

Lawson, Lewis A. "Cass Kinsolving: Kierkegaardian Man of Despair," *Wisconsin Studies in Contemporary Literature*, III (Fall 1962), 54–66.

——. "Kierkegaard and the Modern American Novel," in Jean Jacquot (ed.), *Le théâtre moderne, II: Depuis la deuxième guerre mondiale*. Paris: Éditions du Centre Nationale de la Recherche Scientifique, 1967, 113–25.

——. "Walker Percy's Indirect Communications," *Texas Studies in Literature and Language*, XI (Spring 1969), 867–900.

Lee, R. F. "Emerson Through Kierkegaard: Toward a Definition of Emerson's Theory of Communication," *A Journal of English Literary History*, XXIV (September 1957), 229–48.

Lefevre, Perry. "Hong Translation of Kierkegaard's *Papirer*," *Journal of Religion*, L (January 1970), 69–78.

——. "Snare of Truth," *Pastoral Psychology*, XIX (October 1968), 33–44.

Lessing, Arthur. "Hegel and Existentialism: On Unhappiness," *Personalist*, XLIX (Winter 1968), 67–77.

Levi, A. W. "A Hundred Years After Kierkegaard," *Kenyon Review*, XVIII (Spring 1956), 169–81.

——. "Socrates in the Nineteenth Century," *Journal of the History of Ideas*, XVII (January 1956), 104–6.

Livingston, G. H. "Kierkegaard and Jeremiah," *Asbury Seminarium*, XI (Summer 1957), 46–61.

Lowrie, Walter. "Existence as Understood by Kierkegaard and/or Sartre," *Sewanee Review*, LVIII (1950), 379–401.

——. "Qualified Retraction and an Unqualified Apology," *Theology Today*, XVI (July 1959), 267.

Lund, Margaret. "The Single Ones [Kierkegaard and Nietzsche]," *Personalist*, XLI (1960), 15–24.

Lund, Mary Graham. "The Existentialism of Ibsen," *Personalist*, XLI (Summer 1960), 310–17.

Lønning, Per. "The Dilemma of 'Grace Alone,'" *Dialog*, VI (Spring 1967), 108–14.

Löwith, Karl. "Nature, History, and Existentialism," *Social Research*, XIX (March 1952), 79–94.

Macfadden, R. "Nuclear Dilemma, with a Nod to Kierkegaard," *Theology Today*, XVII (January 1961), 508–18.

MacIntyre, Alasdair. "Søren Aabye Kierkegaard," in Paul Edwards (ed.), *The Encyclopedia of Philosophy, IV*. New York: The Macmillan Co., 1967, 336–40.

Mackey, Louis. "The Analysis of the Good in Kierkegaard's 'Purity of Heart,'" in Irwin C. Lieb (ed.), *Experience, Existence, and the Good: Essays in Honor of Paul Weiss*. Carbondale: Southern Illinois University Press, 1961, 260–74.

——. "Kierkegaard and the Problem of Existential Philosophy," *Review of Metaphysics*, IX (March, June 1956), 404–19, 569–88.

——. "Kierkegaard's Lyric of Faith: A Look at *Fear and Trembling*," *Rice Institute Pamphlets*, XLVII (1960), 30–47.

——. "Loss of the World in Kierkegaard's Ethics," *Review of Metaphysics*, LX (June 1962), 602–20.

——. "Philosophy and Poetry in Kierkegaard," *Review of Metaphysics*, XXIII (December 1969), 316–32.

——. "The Poetry of Inwardness," in George A. Schrader (ed.), *Existential Philosophers: Kierkegaard to Merleau-Ponty*. New York: McGraw-Hill, 1967, 45–107.

——. "Some Versions of the Aesthetic: Kierkegaard's *Either/Or*," *Rice University Studies*, L (Winter 1964), 39–54.

——. "The View from Pisgah: A Reading of *Fear and Trembling*," in Josiah Thompson (ed.), *Kierkegaard: A Collection of Critical Essays*. Garden City, New York: Doubleday & Company, Inc., 1972, pp. 407–442.

Madden, M. C. "Kierkegaard on Self-Acceptance," *Review and Expositor*, XLVIII (July 1951), 302–9.

Magel, Charles R. "Kierkegaard's Logically Contradictory Christianity," *Graduate Review of Philosophy*, III (Winter 1960).

Mairet, Philip. "Delayed Action," *New Statesman*, LXXII (July–December 1966), 234–35.

Malmquist, C. P. "A Comparison of Orthodox and Existential Psychoanalytic Concepts of Anxiety," *Journal of the Nervous and Mental Diseases*, CXXXI (1960), 371–82.

Manger, Philip. "Kierkegaard in Max Frisch's Novel *Stiller*," *German Life and Letters*, XX (January 1967), 119–31.

Marcel, Gabriel. "Some Reflections on Existentialism," *Philosophy Today*, VIII (Winter 1964), 248–57.

McInerny, Ralph. "The Ambiguity of Existential Metaphysics," *Laval Théologique et Philosophique*, XII (No. 1, 1956), 120–24.

——. "Connection Seen in Ethics of Kierkegaard and Aquinas," *Christian Messenger*, LXXXII (March 5, 1964), 4.

——. "Ethics and Persuasion: Kierkegaard's Existential Dialectic," *Modern Schoolman*, XXXIII (May 1956), 219–39.

——. "Kierkegaard and Speculative Thought," *New Scholasticism*, XL (January 1966), 23–25.

——. "The Teleological Suspension of the Ethical," *Thomist*, XX (1957), 295–310.

McKinnon, Alastair. "Barth's Relation to Kierkegaard: Some Further Light," *Canadian Journal of Theology*, XIII (January 1967), 31–41.

——. "Believing the Paradox: A Contradiction in Kierkegaard?" *Harvard Theological Review*, LXI (October 1968), 633–36.

——. "Kierkegaard and his Pseudonyms: A Preliminary Report," *Kierkegaardiana*, *VII*. Copenhagen: Munksgaard, 1966, 64–76.

——. "Kierkegaard: 'Paradox' and Irrationalism," *Journal of Philosophy*, LXII (November 4, 1965), 651–52.

——. "Kierkegaard: 'Paradox' and Irrationalism," *Journal of Existentialism*, VII (Spring 1967), 401–16.

——. "Kierkegaard's Irrationalism Revisited," *International Philosophical Quarterly*, IX (June 1969), 165–76.

——. "Kierkegaard's Pseudonyms: A New Hierarchy," *American Philosophical Quarterly*, VI (1969), 116–26.

McKinnon, A., and Roger Webster. "A Method of 'Author' Indentification," *Computer Studies in the Humanities and Verbal Behavior*, II (1969), 19–23.

McMinn, J. B. "Value and Subjectivity in Kierkegaard," *Review and Expositor*, LIII (October 1956), 477–88.

McPherson, T. "Second Great Commandment: Religion and Morality," *Congregational Quarterly* (London), XXXV (July 1957), 212–22.

Anonymous. "Meant for Mankind: Kierkegaard and Christianity as the Regulating Weight," *Times Literary Supplement*, LXVIII (March 20, 1969), 281–83.

Mesnard, Pierre. "The Character of Kierkegaard's Philosophy," *Philosophy Today*, I (June 1957), 84–89.

Michaelson, C. "Kierkegaard's Theology of Faith," *Religion in Life*, XXXII (Spring 1963), 225–37.

Minear, Paul S. "Kierkegaard Centennial," *Theology Today*, XII (July 1955), 244–46.

————. "Thanksgiving as a Synthesis of the Temporal and the Eternal," *Anglican Theological Review*, XXXVIII, 4–14.

Mitchell, Charles. "*The Lord of the Flies* and the Escape from Freedom," *Arizona Quarterly*, XXII (Spring 1966), 27–40.

Moore, S. "Religion as the True Humanism—Reflections on Kierkegaard's Social Philosophy," *Journal of the American Academy of Religion* (March 1969), 15.

Mourant, John A. "The Limitations of Religious Existentialism," *International Philosophical Quarterly*, I (1961), 437–52.

Muggeridge, Malcolm. "Books," *Esquire*, LXX (September 1968), 30.

Murphy, Arthur E. "On Kierkegaard's Claim That 'Truth is Subjectivity,'" in his book, *Reason and the Common Good: Selected Essays*. Englewood Cliffs, N.J.: Prentice-Hall, 1963, 173–79.

Murphy, J. L. "Faith and Reason in the Teaching of Kierkegaard," *American Ecclesiastical Review*, 145 (1961), 233–65.

Naess, Arne. "Kierkegaard and Values of Education," *Journal of Value Inquiry*, II (Fall 1968), 196–200.

Nagley, Winfield E. "Kierkegaard on Liberation," *Ethics*, LXX (October 1959), 47–58.

————. "Kierkegaard's Irony in the 'Diapsalmata,'" *Kierkegaardiana*, *VI*. Copenhagen: Munksgaard, 1966, 51–75.

Nakamura, Kohei. "On the Relation of Human Being and Science by Kierkegaard," *Kierkegaard-Studiet*, I (1964), 69–73.

Neumann, Harry. "Kierkegaard and Socrates on the Dignity of Man," *Personalist*, XLIII (1967), 453–60.

Nicholson, G. E. "A Dramatic Approach to Christianity," *Christendom*, IX (Autumn 1944), 462–75.

Noxon, James. "Kierkegaard's Stages and *A Burnt-Out Case*," *Review of English Literature*, III (January 1962), 90–101.

Noyce, Gaylord B. "Wounded by Christ's Sword," *Interpretation,* VIII (October 1954), 433–43.

O'Donnell, William G. "Kierkegaard: The Literary Manner," *Kenyon Review,* IX (Winter 1947), 35–47.

Anonymous. "The 'Offense' of the God-Man: Kierkegaard's Way of Faith," *Times Literary Supplement,* XXXVI (March 27, 1937), 229–30.

Ofstad, Harald. "Morality, Choice, and Inwardness," *Inquiry,* VIII (Spring 1965), 33–72.

O'Mara, Joseph. "Kierkegaard Revealed," *Studies,* XXXVIII (December 1949), 447–56.

Otani, Hidehito. "The Concept of a Christian in Kierkegaard," *Inquiry,* VIII (Spring 1965), 74–83.

Otani, Masaru. "The Past and Present State of Kierkegaard Studies in Japan," *Orbis Litterarum,* XVIII (1963), 54–59.

———. "Self-manifestation of Freedom in 'Anxiety' by Kierkegaard," *Orbis Litterarum,* XXII, 393–98.

Owen, P. O. "Existentialism and Ascetical Theology," *Church Quarterly Review,* CLX (April–June 1959), 226–31.

Pait, James A. "Kierkegaard and the Problem of Choice," *Emory University Quarterly,* II (December 1946), 237–45.

Palmer, Donald D. "Unamuno's Don Quixote and Kierkegaard's Abraham," *Revista de Estudios Hispánicos,* III (1969), 295–312.

Paul, W. W. "Faith and Reason in Kierkegaard and Modern Existentialism," *Review of Religion,* XX (March 1956), 149–63.

Percy, Walker. "The Message in the Bottle," *Thought,* XXXIV (Fall 1959), 405–33.

Perkins, Robert L. "Persistent Criticisms: Misinterpretations of Søren Kierkegaard's Ethical Thoughts," in *Memorias del XIII Congreso Internacional di Filosofía, VII.* México: Universidad Nacional Autónoma de México, 1964, 377–88.

———. "Søren Kierkegaard's Library," *American Book Collector,* XII (1961), 9–16.

———. "Two Nineteenth Century Interpretations of Socrates: Hegel and Kierkegaard," *Kierkegaard-Studiet, International Edition* [Osaka, Japan], IV (1967), 9–14.

Perry, E. "Was Kierkegaard a Biblical Existentialist?" *Journal of Religion,* XXXVI (January 1956), 17–23.

Petras, John W. "God, Man and Society, the Perspectives of Buber and Kierkegaard," *Journal of Religious Thought,* XXIII (1966–67), 119–28.

Pittenger, W. Norman. "Søren Kierkegaard," *Anglican Theological Review* (Evanston), XXXVIII (1956), 1–3.

Pondrom, Cyrena Norman. "Two Demonic Figures: Kierkegaard's Merman and Dostoevsky's Underground Man," *Orbis Litterarum,* XXIII (1968), 161–77.

Poole, Roger C. "Hegel, Kierkegaard and Sartre," *New Blackfriar's,* XLVII (July 1966), 532–41.

———. "Kierkegaard on Irony," *New Blackfriar's,* XLVIII (February 1967), 245–49.

Popkin, R. H. "Kierkegaard and Scepticism," *Algemeen Nederlands tijdschrift voor Wijsbegeerte en psychologie,* LI (1958–59), 123–41.

———. "Theological and Religious Scepticism," *Christian Scholar,* XXXIX (June 1956), 150–58.

Anonymous. "Prayer," *Theology Today,* XIII (January 1957), 447–48.

Prenter, R. "The Concept of Freedom in Sartre Against a Kierkegaardian Background," tr. by H. Kaasa, *Dialog,* VII (Spring 1968), 132–37.

Reck, Donald W. "The Christianity of Søren Kierkegaard," *Canadian Journal of Theology,* XII (1966), 85–97.

Reichmann, Ernani. "Kierkegaard in Brazil," *Kierkegaardiana,* V. Copenhagen: Munksgaard, 1964, 78–79.

Replogle, Justin. "Auden's Religious Leap," *Wisconsin Studies in Contemporary Literature,* VII (Winter 1966), 47–75.

Rhodes, Donald W. "The Christianity of Søren Kierkegaard," *Canadian Journal of Theology,* XII (April 1966), 85–97.

Roberts, David Everett. "A Review of Kierkegaard's Writings," *Review of Religion*, VII (March 1943), 300–17.

Roberts, J. D. "Kierkegaard on Truth and Subjectivity," *Journal of Religious Thought*, XVIII (1961), 41–56.

Roubiczek, Paul. "Søren Kierkegaard," *The Times* [London] (April 27, 1968), 10.

de Rougemont, Denis. "Kierkegaard and Hamlet: Two Danish Princes," *The Anchor Review* I (1955), 109–27.

Ruoff, J. E. "Kierkegaard and Shakespeare," *Comparative Literature*, XX (Fall 1968), 343–54.

Ruotolo, L. "Keats and Kierkegaard: The Tragedy of Two Worlds," *Renascence*, XVI (Summer 1964), 175–90.

Schmitt, R. "Kierkegaard's Ethics and Its Teleological Suspension," *Journal of Philosophy*, LVIII (October 26, 1961), 701–2.

———. "The Paradox in Kierkegaard's Religiousness A," *Inquiry*, VIII (Spring 1965), 118–35.

Schrader, George A. "Kant and Kierkegaard on Duty and Inclination," *Journal of Philosophy*, LXV (November 7, 1968), 688–701.

———. "Norman Mailer and the Despair of Defiance," *Yale Review*, LI (December 1961), 267–80.

Schrag, Calvin. "Kierkegaard's Existential Reflections on Time," *Personalist*, XLII (1961), 149–64.

———. "Note on Kierkegaard's Teleological Suspension of the Ethical," *Ethics*, LXX, No. 1 (1959–60), 66–68.

Schrag, Oswald O. "Existential Ethics and Axiology," *Southern Journal of Philosophy*, I (Summer 1963), 39–47.

Schutz, A. "Mozart and the Philosophers," *Social Research*, XXIII (Summer 1956), 219–42.

Scudder, J. R., Jr. "Kierkegaard and the Responsible Enjoyment of Children," *Educational Forum*, XXX (May 1966), 497–503.

Sechi, Vanina. "Art, Language, Creativity and Kierkegaard," *Humanitas,* V (1969–70), 81–97.

Seidel, George J. "Monasticism as a Ploy in Kierkegaard's Theology," *American Benedictine Review,* XX (1969), 281–305.

Sen, Krishna. "Kierkegaard and St. Thomas," *Philosophical Quarterly* (Amalner, India) (1956–57), 69–74.

Sharper, P. J. "Review of *Journey Through Dread* by A. Ussher," *Commonweal,* LXIII (October 28, 1955), 96–98.

Sjursen, Harold P. "Method and Perspective When Reading Kierkegaard," *Kierkegaardiana, VIII.* Copenhagen: Munksgaard, 1971, 199–211.

Skinner, J. E. "Philosophical Megalomania," *Theology and Life,* IX (Summer 1966), 146–59.

Slatte, H. A. "Kierkegaard's Introduction to American Methodists," *Drew Gateway,* XXX (Spring 1960), 161–67.

Smith, J. W. "Religion A/ Religion B: A Kierkegaard Study," *Scottish Journal of Theology,* XV (1962), 245–65.

Smith, Joyce Carol Oates. "The Existential Comedy of Conrad's Youth," *Renascence,* XVI (Fall 1963), 22–28.

———. "Ritual and Violence in Flannery O'Connor," *Thought,* XLI (Winter 1966), 545–60.

Smith, Ronald Gregor. "Hamann and Kierkegaard," *Kierkegaardiana, V.* Copenhagen: Munksgaard, 1964, 52–67.

———. "Hamann Renaissance; Excerpt from Introduction to J. G. Hamann," *Christian Century,* LXXVII (June 29, 1960), 768–69.

Sokel, W. H. "Kleist's Marquise of O, Kierkegaard's Abraham, and Musil's Tonko: Three Stages of the Absurd or the Touchstone of Faith," *Wisconsin Studies in Contemporary Literature,* VIII (Autumn 1967), 505–16.

Sontag, Frederick. "Kierkegaard and the Search for a Self," *Journal of Existentialism,* VII (Summer 1967), 443–57.

Spiegelberg, Herbert. "Husserl's Phenomenology and Existentialism," *Journal of Philosophy*, LVII (January 21, 1960), 62–74.

Spinka, Matthew. "Søren Kierkegaard and the Existential Theology," in his book, *Christian Thought: From Erasmus to Berdyaev*. Englewood Cliffs, N.J.: Prentice-Hall, 1962, 146–55.

Sponheim, Paul. "Christian Coherence and Human Wholeness," in Bernard E. Meland (ed.), *The Future of Empirical Theology*. Chicago: The University of Chicago Press, 1969, 195–220.

——. "Kierkegaard and the Suffering of the Christian Man," *Dialog*, III (Summer 1964), 199–206.

Stack, George J. "Aristotle and Kierkegaard's Concept of Choice," *The Modern Schoolman*, XLVI (1968–69), 11–23.

——. "Concern in Kierkegaard and Heidegger," *Philosophy Today*, XII (1969), 26–35.

——. "Kierkegaard and the Phenomenology of Repetition," *Journal of Existentialism*, VII (Winter 1966–67), 111–28.

Stanley, Rupert. "Søren Kierkegaard," *New-Church Magazine* (April–June 1947), 23–27.

Starkloff, C. "The Election: Choice of Faith," *Review for Religious*, XXIV (1965), 444–54.

Steinberg, Milton. "Kierkegaard and Judaism," *Menorah Journal*, XXXVII (Spring 1949), 163–80.

Strickland, Ben. "Kierkegaard and Counseling for Individuality," *Personnel and Guidance Journal*, XLIV (January 1966), 470–74.

Sulzbach, Marian Fuerth. "Time, Eschatology, and the Human Problem," *Theology Today*, VII (October 1950), 321–30.

Swenson, David F. "Søren Kierkegaard," *Scandinavian Studies and Notes*, VI (1920–21), 1–41.

Anonymous. "Søren Kierkegaard," *The American Book Collector*, XIII (January 1963), 6–8.

Anonymous. "Søren Kierkegaard: The Attack upon Christendom," *Together* (January 1967), 58.

Anonymous. "Søren Kierkegaard: Danish Moralist and Author," *Review of Reviews,* IX (February 1894), 236.

Anonymous. "Søren Kierkegaard: Prophet with Honor," *Christian Century,* LXXX (July 24, 1963), 943.

Tavard, George H. "Christianity and the Philosophy of Existence," *Theological Studies,* XVIII (March 1957), 1–16.

Anonymous. "That Blessed Word, Existential," *Christian Century,* LXXII (November 30, 1955), 1390–92.

Thielicke, H. "Nihilism and Anxiety," *Theology Today,* XII (October 1955), 342–45.

Thomas, J. H. "The Relevance of Kierkegaard to the Demythologizing Controversy," *Scottish Journal of Theology,* X (1957), 239–52.

Thompson, Josiah. "The Master of Irony," in Josiah Thompson (ed.), *Kierkegaard: A Collection of Critical Essays.* Garden City, New York: Doubleday & Company, Inc., 1972, pp. 105–67.

———. "Søren Kierkegaard and his Sister-in-Law Henriette Kierkegaard," *Fund og Forskning,* XII (1965), 101–20.

Thomte, Reidar. "Kierkegaard in American Religious Thought," *Lutheran World,* II (Summer 1955), 137–46.

———. "New Reflections on the Great Dane," *Discourse,* VI (Spring 1963), 144–55.

Tracy, David. "Kierkegaard's Concept of the Act of Faith: Its Structure and Significance," *Dunwoodie Review* (1963), 194–215.

———. "Kierkegaard's Concept of the Act of Faith: Its Structure and Significance," *Dunwoodie Review,* IV (1964), 133–76.

Updike, John. "The Fork," *The New Yorker* (February 26, 1966), 115–34.

Wadia, A. R. "Søren Kierkegaard," *Aryan Path,* XXXV (October 1964), 446–50.

Wahl, Jean. "Existentialism: A Preface," *New Republic*, CXIII (October 1, 1945), 442–44.

Walker, Jeremy. "The Idea of Reward in Morality," *Kierkegaardiana, VIII*. Copenhagen: Munksgaard, 1971, 30–52.

———. "Kierkegaard's Concept of Truthfulness," *Inquiry*, XII (Summer 1969), 209–24.

Webber, R. H. "Kierkegaard and the Elaboration of Unamuno's *Niebla*," *Hispanic Review*, XXXII (April 1964), 118–34.

Weiss, Robert O. "The Levelling Process as a Function of the Masses in the View of Kierkegaard and Ortega y Gasset," *Kentucky Foreign Language Quarterly*, VII, 27–36.

Whittemore, Robert C. "Pro Hegel, Contra Kierkegaard," *Journal of Religious Thought*, XIII (Spring–Summer 1956), 131–44.

Widenman, Robert. "Kierkegaard's Terminology—and English," *Kierkegaardiana, VII*. Copenhagen: Munksgaard, 1966, 113–30.

———. "Some Aspects of Time in Aristotle and Kierkegaard," *Kierkegaardiana, VIII*. Copenhagen: Munksgaard, 1971, 7–22.

Wiegand, William. "Salinger and Kierkegaard," *Minnesota Review*, V (May–July 1965), 137–56.

Wilburn, Ralph G. "The Philosophy of Existence and the Faith-Relation," *Religion in Life*, XXX (Autumn 1961), 497–517.

Wild, John. "Existentialism: A New View of Man," *University of Toronto Quarterly*, XXVII (October 1957), 79–95.

———. "Kierkegaard and Contemporary Existentialist Philosophy," *Anglican Theological Review*, XXXVIII (1956), 15–32.

Will, Frederic. "A Confrontation of Kierkegaard and Keats," *Personalist*, XLIII (1962), 338–51.

Wilshire, Bruce W. "Kierkegaard's Theory of Knowledge and New Directions in Psychology and Psychoanalysis," *Re-*

view of Existential Psychology and Psychiatry, III (1963), 249–61.

Wolf, H. C. "Kierkegaard and the Quest of the Historical Jesus," *Lutheran Quarterly,* XVI (February 1964), 3–40.

Woodbridge, Hensley Charles. "A Bibliography of Dissertations Concerning Kierkegaard Written in the U.S., Canada, and Great Britain," *American Book Collector,* XII (1961), 21–22.

———. "Søren Kierkegaard: A Bibliography of His Works in English Translation," *American Book Collector,* XII (1961), 17–20.

Wrighton, B. "Thoughts on Kierkegaard," *Arena,* I (1933), 317.

Yanitelli, Victor. "Types of Existentialism," *Thought,* XXIV (September 1954), 495–508.

Zeigler, Leslie. "Personal Existence: A Study of Buber and Kierkegaard," *Journal of Religion,* XL (1960), 80–94.

Zuurdeeg, Willem F. "Some Aspects of Kierkegaard's Language Philosophy," *Atti XII Congr. Intern. Filos.,* 493–99.

Zweig, P. "Genius for Unsavoriness," *The Nation* (September 23, 1968), 283–84.

Øksenholt, Sven. "Kierkegaard's Lichtenberg: A Reconsideration," *Proceedings of the Pacific Northwest Conference on Foreign Languages,* XVI, 50–56.

INDEX LOCORUM

Kierkegaard's works are listed below in order of their publication. When a work has been translated into English under a title other than the original, the alternate English title is given in parentheses. If no English translation of a work exists, this too is noted in parentheses. The letter "n" after a page number indicates that reference to the work in question is made only in a footnote.

J.T.

xiv.